WOMEN, MEN, AND SPIRITUAL POWER

WOMEN, MEN, AND SPIRITUAL POWER

Female Saints and Their Male Collaborators

John W. Coakley

COLUMBIA UNIVERSITY PRESS   NEW YORK

COLUMBIA UNIVERSITY PRESS

Publishers Since 1893

New York   Chichester, West Sussex

Library of Congress Cataloging-in-Publication Data

Coakley, John Wayland.

Women, men, and spiritual power : female saints and

their male collaborators / John W. Coakley.

p.   cm.

Includes bibliographical references and index.

ISBN 0–231–13400–2 (cloth : alk. paper) —

ISBN 0–50861–1 (e-book)

1. Women mystics. 2. Authority—Religious aspects—

Catholic Church. 3. Power (Christian theology) 4. Church

history—Middle Ages, 600–1500 5. Monasticism and reli-

gious orders. I. Title. II. Series.

BV5083.C55   2006

270.4'082—dc22

2005053783

Columbia University Press books are printed on permanent

and durable acid-free paper.

Printed in the United States of America

c 10 9 8 7 6 5 4 3 2 1

In memory of my parents

CONTENTS

ACKNOWLEDGMENTS

I AM PLEASED TO express my thanks for the help and support I have received in writing this book. An associate fellowship at the Center for Historical Analysis at Rutgers University from 1995 through 1997 gave me a chance to discuss my work with a lively, diverse, and insightful group of scholars. A fellowship from the National Endowment for the Humanities made possible a productive year of research in 1997 and 1998. I am especially grateful to Caroline Bynum for encouragement over many years and for generous aid and advice at several crucial points in the project. I am also grateful for the counsel of Carole Slade, Jo Ann McNamara, David Waanders, Carmela Franklin, Bernard McGinn, Paul Fries, E. Ann Matter, Giles Constable, Karl Morrison, Renée House, and the late Ernest McDonnell. Scholars who have read and commented on the manuscript in whole or part include Maura Spiegel, the late Richard Tristman, Anne Clark, Jodi Bilinkoff, Paul Lachance, Molly Morrison, Carole Slade, Caroline Bynum, and the anonymous readers for Columbia University Press. I am greatly indebted to them all. I am also indebted to my students at New Brunswick Theological Seminary, who have influenced the book in many ways. Librarians at New Brunswick Theological Seminary, General Theological Seminary, and Rutgers University have been of invaluable service. I thank the University of Pennsylania Press for permission to include, in chapter 5, some portions of my essay "A Marriage and Its Observer" from the volume *Gendered Voices*, edited by Catherine Mooney (1999). This project has taken shape during the years in which the lives of Mary Coakley and Philip Coakley have also been taking shape, and I cherish our wide-ranging conversations. My greatest debt, to Margaret Coakley, I will not try to put into words.

Note on Translations

A list of published English translations of several of the medieval texts I will be discussing will be found in the bibliography, pages 325–26. But when I quote from any text, the translation is my own unless otherwise noted.

WOMEN, MEN, AND SPIRITUAL POWER

"You Draw Us After You"

When you come out from the cells of contemplation where the eternal king has so often brought you as his bride, your fruitfulness for us is something better than wine or the fragrance of the finest perfumes. For it is then that, through your writings, you make us partakers of the visions of holy things that you saw with unveiled face when you were in the embrace of your bridegroom. Running along quickly amid the fragrance of your perfumes, you draw us after you.[1]

—GUIBERT OF GEMBLOUX TO HILDEGARD OF BINGEN, 1175

I N THE WEST, the period from the late twelfth century through the end of the Middle Ages witnessed a new kind of female saint or holy woman, known for a combination of asceticism and interiorized devotion typically accompanied by visions, revelations, and mystical states.[2] The names of some of these women are familiar to the general reader today—Catherine of Siena and Julian of Norwich, for example—but there were also many others who had their own small or large groups of admirers in the period.[3] Contemporaries wrote vitae (saints' lives) about such women. Some of the women also produced writings of their own, usually in the form of spiritual autobiographies and collections of revelations. These account for much of what Peter Dronke has called the "astounding proliferation" of literary works by women from the twelfth century on, against the mere handful of such works that survive from earlier periods.[4] Well into the twentieth century, modern scholars tended to treat these holy women, with a few exceptions, as examples of what was excessive or even pathological in medieval piety. But in the past few decades attitudes have changed, and scholars now recognize the importance of the sources about these women, not least for what they tell us about major aspects of medieval religious life and thought, for instance, eucharistic devotion, beliefs about purgatory, and the cult of the humanity of Christ.[5]

One conspicuous factor in the lives of late-medieval holy women is the place occupied by men. It had a double aspect. On the one hand, men exercised authority over the women. Religious women were under supervision of male clerics. So also were the women of the new "semireligious" movements, that is, Beguines and other lay penitents, many of whom came eventually under the supervision of the mendicant friars.[6] Also in almost every case it was men, usually clerics, who wrote the vitae of women and thus had the power to determine how they would be remembered, placing themselves as interested mediators between the women and their public. Even when a woman wrote in her own voice, a man very often stood between her and her readers, as editor or at least as scribe. In these ways clerics functioned as figures of power and control.[7] But on the other hand, the men—often the very same men—also typically cast themselves as the women's admiring followers, pupils, or friends.[8] In the late twelfth century the monk Guibert of Gembloux, writing to Hildegard of Bingen, pictured her as the bride of the opening verses of the Song of Songs, now coming out of the bridegroom's chamber to meet himself and her other admirers and bring them into her experience by conveying the visions and revelations she had received in the bridegroom's embrace. "You draw us after you," he told her, paraphrasing the Song.[9] Many more men after Guibert would express this feeling of being drawn to holy women. They expressed it in terms of an intense fascination rooted in the conviction that the women possessed some essential spiritual quality or gift lacking in themselves, and not infrequently they professed a subservience to these admired women that could seem to undermine their own authority over them.

If these two aspects of the relations of clerics with female saints—authority and control on one hand, fascination and often subservience on the other—appear to be in tension with each other, it is a tension that masks a deeper connection between them. For here authority and subservience do not stand unambiguously in a relationship of "either/or." The Gregorian Reform of the eleventh and twelfth centuries had worked to bring all precincts of the church firmly under the authority of a clergy clearly defined as not only male but also celibate, and thus without obligation to wives.[10] Yet the very exclusion of women from the realm of priestly authority ironically endowed them with a new significance outside it. For there were desirable aspects of Christian experience that the institutional authority could not guarantee to clerics and indeed often seemed to block them from: the deeply affective elements of faith, the Spirit that blows where it will, the immediate presence of God. These became the particular province of holy women. Precisely as the clerics claimed ecclesiastical authority over the women who by definition lacked it themselves, they tended to invest those women with the potential to symbolize, and to provide for them, even if only vicariously, what remained beyond that authority—what the men themselves wanted but found to lie beyond their grasp. And so it was authority itself that engendered subservience, as clerics put themselves willingly under the sway of those who seemed to be able to show them the pearl of great price that their authority could not obtain for them. In this sense the encounters between clerics and holy women touched upon fundamental and perennial issues of spiritual life in social context. These included not only the nature and limits of religious authority itself but also the proper conditions for access to the divine and the factors at work in the delicate interplay between human relations and mystical presence.

In this book I explore some encounters between holy women and the clerics who associated with them. I examine closely a series of such cases—specifically nine pairs of men and women—in which the sources make possible a sustained look at what was at stake for those involved, especially for the men. In each of these instances the woman had a reputation for extraordinary supernatural experiences and powers, and each of the men was a monk or cleric who not only knew the woman well but also wrote some substantial piece of hagiography about her. In each instance, moreover—and this is what makes these nine pairs distinctive—the man wrote about the woman in such a way as to include himself extensively. In other words, he wrote not just about her in her own right but also about his interactions with her and his responses to her and in general about himself in relation to her. In his account of the woman we can observe him in his own right as a man, with a gender-specific perspective on both her and himself.[11] The texts that constitute these nine cases span the period from about 1150, when the new ideals of female sanctity were just beginning to take shape,[12] until about 1400, when increased clerical nervousness about the charismatic powers of such women was making their male collaborators more cautious about what they wrote.

My choice of the nine cases has important implications for the nature and scope of this study, and I want to be sure that from the outset these are as clear to the reader as I can make them. Many, perhaps even most, hagiographical texts about women in this period make some mention of male figures, whether monks or clerics (in some cases, but not always, their confessors) who collaborated with the women in making their revelations known or otherwise aided or defended them. But I have not attempted to take account of all such texts nor to sift the evidence necessary to come to comprehensive conclusions about the relations that actually existed between saintly women and their male collaborators or about the full range of variables that may have affected these. I also have not attempted to examine all the texts about holy women that we know to have been written by such men, and therefore I cannot generalize definitively about why and how female saints' collaborators wrote about them. But limiting this study to collaborator-hagiographers who explicitly placed themselves in their narratives, though it restricts the breadth of cases to be examined, allows an in-depth look at certain men's perspectives on their own lives and the significance that saintly women held for them: those perspectives and that significance are my proper subject here.

What emerges from the men's writings when we follow them over the course of the period in question is a story of a wide-ranging experiment in the matter of human access to God. Through their eyes, we watch them and the women trying out one set of roles or another, either thinking of themselves as undertaking a joint enterprise seeking God or else picturing God as initiating the encounter with them, to use each in various ways as a medium for the benefit of the other and those around them. In these accounts, unsurprisingly, the man's official authority remains largely unchallenged, but in spite of, or else because of, that ostensible security, we find him exploring the possibilities of the woman's *un*-official authority with steady interest and carefully registering the balances that were struck between them. Overall these writings suggest a period in which it was thoroughly imaginable for both sorts of authority, in their distinctly gendered forms, to coexist and even to build upon one another.

The book proceeds chronologically. After the first chapter, which introduces the issues of religious authority that will be addressed throughout the book, the remaining chapters consider the nine cases individually. The second and third chapters introduce the notion of the woman's sphere of authority as something discrete from the man's as it began to emerge in the writings of the two Rhineland nuns who were the most famous female visionaries of the twelfth century, and their collaborators: Elisabeth of Schönau (1129–1164) and her brother Ekbert (ca. 1120–1184); and Hildegard of Bingen (1098–1179) and the monk Guibert of Gembloux (ca. 1125–1213), who corresponded with Hildegard and then wrote about her in the last years of her life. Both Elisabeth and Hildegard lived in cloistered communities, but most of the women to be discussed in the subsequent chapters lived in the midst of lay society, as was particularly characteristic

of thirteenth-century female saints, and it was within lay society that they interacted with clerics. The fourth chapter considers the earliest and most influential
instance of a cleric writing about such a woman: the vita of the Beguine Mary
of Oignies (1177–1213), by the famous preacher James of Vitry (1160/70–1240),
who drew the distinction between spheres of authority particularly starkly and
played with the conceit of role reversal as he idealized Mary. The fifth through
the eighth chapters then treat of a series of other clerics of the thirteenth and
early fourteenth centuries who display these same tendencies, though each has
his own distinctive version of the experimental balance between the women's
powers and their own: the learned Dominican Peter of Dacia (1230/40–1289)
who saw the supernatural experiences of the Beguine Christine of Stommeln
(1242–1312) as a foil for his own longings; the anonymous Franciscan friar who
combined his sense of his own stark difference from the Italian mystic Angela
of Foligno (d. 1309) with a commitment nonetheless to share her theological
explorations; the Franciscan Giunta Bevegnati (d. after 1311) who reflected in
explicit and even systematic terms on the relation of his own clerical powers to
the charisms of the penitent Margaret of Cortona (1247–97); and the south German priest Henry of Nördlingen (d. after 1351), whose letters to the Dominican
nun Margaret Ebner (1291–1351) incorporated a notion of separate spheres of
authority within a notion of friendship. Then in the ninth and tenth chapters,
the two final cases suggest the imminent end of this experiment in the balanc-
ing of gendered authorities: the vita of the great Dominican penitent Catherine
of Siena (1347–80) by her confessor Raymond of Capua (ca. 1330–1399), and
the several writings about the Prussian recluse Dorothy of Montau (1397–1394)
by the canon John Marienwerder (1343–1417). Both authors, though still interested in setting off the women's sphere of authority from their own, displayed
nonetheless a certain calculated detachment as well as a polemical concern to
demonstrate the saints' genuineness, which bespeak a new atmosphere of caution toward charismatic women at the turn of the fifteenth century.

I add a final word about my approach to the sources. I will be examining the
men's understanding of the women and themselves specifically as they gave it
expression in particular texts that they wrote in particular circumstances. The
nature of the texts and the circumstances is in every case important to the
conclusions that can be drawn. I am not principally concerned to use these
texts as clues to the actual events in the lives of the saints or in their interactions with those around them as, for instance, Aviad Kleinberg has done in
his study of hagiographical texts about several late-medieval saints.[13] In Jean-
Claude Poulin's terms, I am concerned not with "lived" sanctity but rather with

"imagined" sanctity,[14] in the sense that even to the extent that the author can be demonstrated to be a reliable source concerning the acts of the saint herself and those around her, I am reading him not to establish those acts themselves but to observe the way he decides to present her, and his relationship with her, in the hagiographical text at hand. His way of presenting her will reflect, in particular, the demands of the genre of hagiography to instruct and edify the reader—demands that could cause him to construe truth about a saint's life in a way very different from the way a modern historian working from empirical evidence would understand it, as some recent scholars have strongly argued.[15] On the other hand, my study does not focus primarily, as many literary studies have done, on the genre of hagiography itself or its typical themes, motifs, or structures, though the implications of the hagiographical nature of the texts remains an important consideration throughout.[16] Rather, I am primarily interested in the text as an expression of the historical person of the writer, hagiographical intentions and all. My focus is on his act of shaping the text, his choices and decisions in doing so. About these, the text itself provides a wealth of revealing evidence, often with the support of other sources. In that sense, this book is indeed about something lived and not only imagined—not the acts of saints however, but rather the acts of hagiographers, the making of hagiography.

CHAPTER 1

The Powers of Holy Women

THE SUBSEQUENT CHAPTERS OF this book will discuss certain female saints who were thought in their time to possess certain supernatural powers. The particular powers of these women were typical of late-medieval female saints as they appear in a large body of works of hagiography that extends well beyond the relatively small group of texts that will constitute our nine cases. The present chapter examines the powers of women as presented in some of that broader literature in order to suggest the terms of a question or problem that will be basic to all of our cases, namely, the relationship between the women's powers and the powers of ecclesiastical men.

Late-medieval works of hagiography about women are indeed full of stories about their powers: the women prophesy, they warn, they advise, and sometimes they expound upon ideas, all from a direct knowledge or consciousness of things divine. The authors of those hagiographical works were, for the most part, clerics. When we read their writing, we find ourselves thinking not only about the women's powers but also about the powers of the clerics themselves, namely, to preach and teach, to administer sacraments, and in general to rule the church: for they see the women's lives in the light of their own concerns, which are shaped by their own calling. The two sets of powers are based on putatively different authorities: an authority derived from outside the structures of the church in the first instance, and one derived from within those structures in the second. The question of the relation between these two authorities is a basic question that has been raised perennially in Christian tradition, a function of Christian attempts at an understanding not only of the church but of the work of the Holy Spirit.[1] In the later Middle Ages the question was an especially pressing one, and for clerics it gave the powers of female saints a special significance.

FEMALE SANCTITY IN THE LATER MIDDLE AGES

A few comments are in order first about sanctity in general, and female sanctity in particular, in the period from the twelfth century through the end of the Middle Ages. By "sanctity" here I mean not only the "ideal" of virtue embodied by given saints—in Hippolyte Delehaye's phrase, "the harmonious ensemble of Christian virtues practiced to a degree that a rare elite is in a position to attain"—but also more broadly the terms in which they were perceived by their audiences, that is, by those who considered them saints.[2] Sanctity in this sense was not limited to people officially canonized. This was indeed the period in which the papacy took control of canonization processes and, in effect, strictly limited the number new people who could officially be called "saint."[3] But this development did not limit the number of those *venerated* as saints, which on the contrary grew at a faster rate than before; this was indicative of what André Vauchez has called a "modernizing" of sanctity, a new interest in contemporary saints. The saints of the ancient church, though their cults certainly continued, no longer dominated either clerical or lay devotion as they had in the earlier medieval centuries.[4] The majority of the newly venerated were never canonized and therefore were technically not "saints" but rather "blessed (*beati*)." But in practical terms, veneration was veneration, and in this sense there was little real distinction between them.[5]

Another characteristic of sanctity in the high and later Middle Ages was a greater variety in the religious roles and social backgrounds of the saints. In the Mediterranean areas (but not in the north until the fifteenth century) an increasing proportion of saints came from the bourgeoisie (though generally among the well-to-do in any case) rather than the ruling classes.[6] There were also saints from the new orders of the mendicant friars, as distinct from the older monastic orders, and more saints from the ranks of the laity.[7] From the middle of the thirteenth century, it was the friars in particular who made a specialty of the promotion of new saints, both from their own ranks and from among the lay penitent movements of the time, with which they had close ties.[8] The new importance of mendicant and lay saints reflects the religious revival of the twelfth and thirteenth centuries that broadened the base of religious concern in society, characterized by what Herbert Grundmann called a "new consciousness" of the Christian faith as something personally compelling and directly accessible, which "sought to realize Christianity as a religious way of life immediately binding upon every individual Christian, a commitment more essential to the salvation of his soul than his position in the hierarchical *ordo* of the Church or his belief in the doctrines of the Fathers of the Church and its theologians."[9]

This broadening of the base of sanctity had special significance for female sanctity. Among earlier medieval female saints in the West, who had had a great vogue especially in Merovingian Gaul and Anglo-Saxon England, queens and abbesses had dominated.[10] In the later Middle Ages, female saints—who appear to have accounted for a larger proportion of new saints in the thirteenth, fourteenth, and fifteenth centuries than in the centuries just before and after[11]— were no longer so exclusively from convents or royal families. The idea of a Christian perfection available beyond the restricted world of the cloister had wide appeal among women, and many embraced voluntary poverty and the *vita apostolica*. These women often formed communities without rules, which then had entered complex relationships with the male religious orders, in some cases becoming cloistered, in other cases not, but eventually coming under the supervision of the male religious orders.[12] Among lay saints, such women were prominent. In the early thirteenth century in the Low Countries, for example, certain Beguines, as well as certain Cistercian nuns influenced by Beguine spirituality, acquired saintly reputations and, even though their cults of devotion do not seem to have been large, inspired a remarkable body of hagiography.[13] In the Italian cities, beginning later in the thirteenth century, many cults arose around lay penitent women with substantial local support, enjoying the formidable promotion of the mendicant orders.[14] The mendicants were indeed more likely to promote lay women than lay men, and in their hagiography they showed more interest in women's interior life of devotion than in that of men.[15] And it was women who become the most famous lay saints of the period.[16] Dozens of contemporary vitae of thirteenth- and fourteenth-century Italian penitent women survive, most of which were composed by mendicant friars.[17]

The trends in sanctity in the period also implied changing notions of what should be remembered about the lives of saints and thus new fashions in hagiography. In the earlier medieval centuries, saints appeared to their admirers preeminently as the loci or media of a divine power that was expressed in miracles and great deeds of charity or asceticism. Newer saints still functioned in this way in hagiographical accounts, but they also appeared increasingly as people with a privileged subjective experience of the divine.[18] An illustration may be helpful. The fourth-century hermit and bishop Martin of Tours, one of the most famous saints of the early Middle Ages, and the thirteenth-century friar Francis of Assisi, the most famous of the new saints of the later Middle Ages, were both commemorated in influential works of hagiography written shortly after their deaths: the vita of Martin by Sulpicius Severus, and several vitae of Francis, the earliest of which was by the friar Thomas of Celano. Setting aside the obvious differences of the particulars and contexts of the saints' lives, we cannot but see a strong similarity in the saintly ideals in these works: in each saint, an active life of great public consequence is deeply rooted in ascetic monastic virtues.[19] But there is a crucial difference in the hagiographers' approach to this ideal: whereas Sulpicius presents Martin from the outset as for all intents and purposes someone fully formed and concentrates on his marvelous deeds, Thomas instead traces the process of Francis's dawning awareness of his faith and calling, in the context of a saintly career that only gradually found its shape. In this sense Thomas shows a new interest in the saint's humanity and subjectivity.[20] It is not that the newer saints lacked supernatural powers; Thomas duly reported his saint's healings and exorcisms just as earlier medieval hagiographers would have done. But these acquired a different cast in context of a more careful charting of the saint's embrace of the gospel.[21] Not incidentally the preeminent miracle of Francis's life was the appearance of Christ's wounds on his body, an index of his own spirituality in its supposed conformity to Christ's poverty and sufferings. External bodily signs of a saint's inner life were to be, if anything, even more conspicuous when the saints were women.[22]

In the case of female saints of the later Middle Ages, as compared to men this hagiographical representation of subjective experience displayed distinctive themes. Descriptions of the physical aspects of women's devotional practice are particularly striking. Apparently to a greater extent than male saints, they tended to practice an extreme asceticism that sometimes included a complete abstinence from food, and they were much more likely both to acquire the stigmata on their bodies as evidence of their identification with Christ and his Passion and, especially in the context of receiving the Eucharist, to experience "raptures" or trances that alienated them from their own senses and rendered their bodies stiff and numb.[23] This emphasis on the body in the women's religious expression, as Caroline Bynum has shown, was full of theological significance. Texts about female saints in this period present their physical identification with Christ's humanity and Passion as a function not just of their own humanity but also, and more specifically, of their femaleness, which was assumed to predispose their bodies to be, like his, loci of nurture and suffering.[24] Such identification gave women, in comparison to men, a privileged position as intimates of Christ, beneficiaries of his mystical presence and recipients of divine revelations, even as it in turn presupposed women as inferior, as the weaker sex, whose bodies were soft, porous, and vulnerable and thus, ominously, more susceptible to demonic influence as well.[25] We see the Christ-centeredness and its physical manifestation most clearly in texts from the thirteenth century on-ward;[26] in the texts about two twelfth-century figures to be discussed in chapters 2 and 3 below, Elisabeth of Schönau and Hildegard of Bingen, ecstasies and Passion-centered devotion do not yet figure strongly. But the association of women with visions is nonetheless evident in those texts. So is the association of humility with divine favor and accordingly of weakness with exaltation—an old Christian paradox with roots in the New Testament which takes, in all of our texts, a gendered form.

THE POWERS OF WOMEN

What exactly were the powers of these women—the powers associated with female sanctity? For many of the hagiographers, it was precisely the women's closeness to Christ, paradoxically linked with their supposed physical weakness and inferiority to men, that generated these powers. In any event, the powers appear mostly as a function of the women's internal personal contact with the divine or the other world. Stories of their miracles in the world external to themselves, such as exorcisms, physical healings, and other interventions into nature, are not entirely lacking in this literature, but these are relatively few in number, especially by earlier medieval hagiographical standards.[27] It is also true that the women typically displayed external signs of sanctity on their bodies, such as the stigmata, and that typically for them the personal experience of God was something "embodied," inseparable from its physical manifestations, and thus never purely internal. But it was now mainly by the fruit of their private prayers and extraordinary consciousness of the divine that women performed their services for other people. For such purposes, the most significant and extraordinary events of their lives occurred within themselves rather than in the world outside them.

An example will illustrate the powers of such a woman and how they might figure in a work of hagiography: the vita of the Cistercian nun Lutgard of Ay-wières by the Dominican friar Thomas of Cantimpré (1200/01–ca. 1270), one of the major works of the mid-thirteenth-century flowering of hagiography in the southern Low Countries. Lutgard was a woman from the town of Tongres, and in her youth she escaped an attempted rape by an aspiring suitor and became a Benedictine nun in a convent at St. Trond. In Thomas's telling, the external events and circumstances of her life were not particularly remarkable either before or after her transfer at the age of twenty-four to the Cistercian convent of Aywières, where she was satisfied to be isolated from her convent sisters by her inability to speak French and, during her last eleven years, by blindness. But miracles all the while witnessed to her remarkable inner life. Already in her years at St. Trond, as Thomas reports, signs began to attend her: her body levitated, light appeared around her while she prayed, oil dripped miraculously from her fingers, and at her consecration someone had a vision of her being crowned with a "golden crown."[28] Then in the Aywières years, as the signs continued to appear regularly, she began also making contacts with God on behalf of others, and these become Thomas's chief interest as his work progresses. He tells stories of her prayers and vicarious sufferings for persons in purgatory who appeared to her in visions to ask her help, including Pope Innocent III, and many stories of her effective prayers for the living, including both other nuns and lay people whom she liberated from temptations.[29] She takes on the task of interceding for a disgraced knight who eventually becomes a monk; and other men come to contrition for their sins just at the sight of her.[30] She obtains the grace of consolation for a layman who has confessed his sins but without a sense of relief, and she gives an abbot assurance of his own salvation.[31] Her private prayers also exorcise demons from people known to her.[32] And she receives a variety of revelations apart from intercessions per se: for instance, a revelation of an interpretation of a Psalm, later found to be also in the Glossa Ordinaria of Scripture and thus consistent with learned opinion, and another regarding the identity of a set of saint's relics.[33] Or again, she receives a revelation that a Franciscan apostate, the brother of a certain nun, would return to his order, another that the duchess of Brabant would die soon and had better prepare herself, another telling her the sins of a recluse who had been too embarrassed to confess them, another that a feared Tartar invasion would not take place.[34] She appears here above all as figure of access to the divine and a point of contact with the other world.

Though the women's power as exercised for others was not always a matter of words—Lutgard and many other holy women were said to have effected conversion in others simply by being looked at, and similar effects were attributed to the sight of women's stigmata and raptures—language was their usual medium.[35] And in many, even most, of the stories that show them helping others through speech, they articulate *revelations*, that is, messages from God or Christ or from saints or from souls in the other world; these messages have come to them in the form of visions, dreams, or supernatural locutions, or even what to a modern eye may look like simple intuitions. The *principle* that it was possible for women to exercise such powers legitimately (without reference for the moment to the particular content of a given revelation), even though otherwise they were prohibited from preaching or teaching in public, appears to have been widely accepted. Thomas Aquinas, for example, affirmed that prophecy, as a "gift," was not restricted to men as was the sacrament of priestly ordination.[36] The vitae of women, in giving attention to these powers, stand in a long Christian literary history of revelation, which stretches back far beyond the period, via the otherworld-journey literature of the early Middle Ages, to the prophecies and apocalyptic visions of Scripture; now revelation becomes, if not uniquely the province of women, nonetheless their particular specialty.[37] Sometimes in these vitae, the disclosure of a revelation itself constitutes the woman's act of service, as in Lutgard's prophecies about a Tartar invasion or about the death of the duchess; at other times the revelation may serve to solicit the woman's prayers or confirm their results, as when Lutgard learns of the state of particular souls in purgatory or heaven. In either case the revelation, imparting otherwise inaccessible knowledge, is essential to the story at hand.

In anticipation of the texts to be discussed later in this study, it will be useful here to distinguish broadly between three kinds of subject matter in the revelations of holy women in the hagiography of this period, which imply, respectively, within the action reported in the texts, potentially different audiences: first, revelations on the state of souls, which helped the woman herself or clerics associated her to minister to individuals; second, revelations on matters of ecclesiastical, geopolitical, or broadly historical import, usually implying a public audience beyond the woman's immediate circumstances, as in the case of Lutgard's Tartar prophecy; and third, revelations about matters of Christian doctrine or Scripture or obscurities of God's dispensations, such as the revelation of a Psalter interpretation to Lutgard, which, in some cases anyway, could claim a hearing from monks or clerics in discussion of theology or religious practice.

The first of these subject matters, concerning the state of souls, is by far the most plentiful in the sources about women. It appears in a variety of ways and with a variety of responses on the part of the saints but with the same thrust, namely, to aid in the salvation of others or in their pastoral care. Often, as in several instances in the vita of Lutgard, these are associated with a saint's intercessory prayers. Sometimes such intercessions were at the request of the person being helped, as when the Franciscan hagiographer Vito of Cortona (d. ca. 1250) reports that the saintly penitent Humiliana dei Cerchi of Florence (d. 1246) interceded on behalf of another friar who wanted to become more devout and that sometime later she alerted him when, according to her knowledge, his desire was about to be fulfilled.[38] The saint could also more proactively seek out persons to help, as in another vita by Thomas of Cantimpré, that of the Beguine Christine of St. Trond: he writes that after dying and visiting hell, purgatory, and heaven, Christine came back to life with a great zeal for souls and received daily revelations from God concerning the spiritual peril of persons who were about to die, whom she would then visit and exhort.[39] This sensitivity to the spiritual condition of others could also appear as a state of awareness apart from specific acts of prayer, as in vitae of Bridget of Sweden (ca. 1303–1373) and Catherine of Siena (1346–1380), which describe them both as able to smell the sinfulness of people they met.[40] Often this sort of revelation identified a particular unconfessed sin, as for instance when the hagiographer of the Vallombrosian abbess Humility of Faienza (d. 1310) describes her receiving a revelation both of a certain nun's sin and of the same nun's impending death and so urging her to confess immediately.[41] Or, as was often the case, the revelations could involve persons who had already died. According to the vita of Bridget of Sweden by her confessors, for instance, Bridget would solicit revelations about the state of deceased persons in response to requests from their loved ones.[42] In communicating such revelations the dead themselves often played a part, as when Innocent III appeared from purgatory to Lutgard or when the Dominican nun Benevenuta Boiani of Cividale (1255–1292) saw her deceased father, who in life had been a lawyer tainted with "worldly business," appear to her in great distress from purgatory asking her prayers and later appeared to her from heaven thanking her for her help.[43] Examples of such revelations that tell of the state of souls and invite some pastoral response could be easily multiplied; scarcely a single vita of a female saint in this period lacks some instance.[44]

It is not incidental to the popularity of these pastoral revelations for clerical hagiographers that they tended not to pose a challenge to ecclesiastical authority. Not only do they not supplant priests' functions, but they also specifically support their powers: often in these texts, as will be seen, a woman's revelations send a penitent to the confessional or cause devout persons to have masses said for the souls of departed loved ones or bolster a priest's own devotion or the power of his preaching. Even when a woman declared on the basis of revelation that a given priest was tainted with unconfessed sins or had left the Host unconsecrated—revelations that for instance were reported of the fifteenth-century Franciscan reformer Colette of Corbie (1381–1447)—the effect was to take priesthood seriously, that is, to hold priesthood to account for itself rather than to undermine or attempt to supplant it.[45] The theme of coordination between male priestly functions and female prophetic functions is a very important one in this literature, as will become clear in the chapters to follow.

Such revelations of pastoral import were therefore wide-ranging, amply described, and a prominent feature of the hagiography about women. The second subject matter, the kind that concerns future events and the great affairs of church or state, is not so ubiquitous in the hagiographical texts and had the potential to be more controversial. Here the major examples are certain figures who appeared on the scene in the late fourteenth century, around the time of the Great Schism (1378–1415), and who inaugurate the tradition of female prophecy in which Joan of Arc would later stand: most notably Bridget of Sweden and Catherine of Siena, whose famous revelations urged, among other things, the return of the papacy from Avignon to Rome. But there were also several lesser-known prophetesses who stood on one side or another of the controversies, including Marie Robine (d. 1399), Constance of Rabastens (fl. ca. 1385), and Jane Mary of Maillé (1331–1414).[46] It is true that politically significant revelations are not lacking in women's hagiography in the two preceding centuries; indeed, passing references to revelations of this sort, such as Thomas of Cantimpré's mention of Christine of St. Trond's clairvoyant warning to her patron Count Louis of Looz of a plot against his life, are not even uncommon.[47] But with the exception of Hildegard, whose apocalyptic critiques of clerics and princes were no small part of her legacy,[48] the figure of the politically focused female prophet of the late fourteenth century was without major antecedents. The potential offense of such persons to the established powers they criticized no doubt helps explain their rarity; the crisis and weakened condition of the church's divided hierarchy at the time of the schism gave such women's prophecies a legitimacy that a more secure ecclesiastical establishment would not have allowed. Indeed, this legitimacy was lost again once the schism was mended.[49]

The third type of women's revelations, which has to do with doctrine or Scripture or the obscurities of God's dispensation, had its high vogue early in the period, although it never entirely disappeared from the hagiography about women. The great twelfth-century female recipients of such revelations were the Benedictine nuns Hildegard of Bingen and Elisabeth of Schönau. Hildegard, for instance, received revelations on the philosophical question of universals and on a number of questions of biblical interpretation—for instance, how Adam and Eve could see things before the Fall opened their eyes (Gen. 3:6; cf. 3:7) and what is to be understood by the "tongues of angels" (1 Cor. 13:1)—that were posed to her by the Cistercian monks of Villers.[50] Elisabeth, as will be seen, received detailed revelations about the lives and deaths of St. Ursula and her fellow martyrs, whose relics had supposedly been discovered at Cologne, and consulted her heavenly sources for answers to questions that were debated in the schools; Elisabeth's texts show that like Hildegard, she had a learned audience for such revelations, both at her own monastery of Schönau and in other monastic communities.[51]

Though hagiographers of thirteenth- and fourteenth-century women would continue to report such revelations of divine obscurities, these tend to concern nondoctrinal matters; they are much more cautious than the male collaborators of Hildegard and Elisabeth about reporting revelations that touch on matters of doctrine. Scholastic theologians were firm in their denial that women had the right to preach or teach publicly, perhaps all the firmer because both the activities of women in the heretical groups and the persistent implications of hagiographical images of women in teaching roles (most famously Catherine of Alexandria and Mary Magdalene) kept the question from being merely speculative.[52] The thirteenth- and fourteenth-century hagiographers' reticence about ascribing doctrinal revelations to female saints, moreover, is consistent with what will be seen to be the firm distinction between their own sphere of authority and that of the women. Nonetheless the figure of Angela of Foligno in the account of her life written by an anonymous friar at the turn of the fourteenth century, also to be discussed later, stands as a notable exception: here the woman's revelations do address patently doctrinal matters such as the question of the nature of God (though not incidentally, the identity of her audience remains obscure).

CLERICS AND THE POWERS OF WOMEN

If the contemporary hagiography therefore provides a view of the powers of holy women as they appeared to the clerics who wrote about them, it also presents a picture of interactions between such women and clerics. The extent of those interactions appears, in one sense at least, natural enough: church office itself had become an unambiguously masculine preserve, clerical marriage being rejected in the strongest terms and women explicitly excluded from the priesthood and positions of monastic authority except over other women; and the fact that only priests could exercise pastoral care, including the sacrament of penance, meant that female saints, like all devout people, came into close contact with them.[53] Descriptions of clerics' encounters with such women naturally find their way into hagiography; accordingly, hagiographical texts offer some clues to not only what clerics thought about the women but also, in effect, how they thought about themselves—or anyway, men like themselves—in relation to them. (I omit reference for the present to hagiographers who wrote directly about themselves, for these will be the proper subject of the chapters to follow.) Here the clerical response to the women's charismatic powers is two-sided: not only do clerics typically appear displaying a sense of responsibility for close supervision of the women, but many also show a deep attraction toward the women's holiness itself. We also find attempts to conceive of the women's authority as in some sort of balance or interaction with their own and thus not just to describe but also to conceptualize their encounters with them.

As for the responsibility to supervise, it is important to remember that the features of female sanctity that made it distinctive put female saints not only in a position of influence and service, as the accounts of their revelations suggest, but also in a position of danger. For occupying no office in the church and yet receiving recognition on the basis of their direct line to God, the women had obvious potential to subvert the authority of the men who did possess office; and there is plenty of evidence in this period of a strong mistrust of putatively charismatic women.[54] The mistrust is already evident in clerical response to the early Beguines, whose very existence fell outside the established structures of the religious life and therefore—such was the worry—outside of established authority. So it was that the thirteenth-century French poet Rutebeuf (not himself a cleric but allied with the antimendicant Paris master William of St.-Amour) pilloried the purported powers of such women: "[The Beguine's] word is prophecy. If she laughs, it is good manners; if she weeps, it is devotion; if she sleeps, she is in ecstasy; if she dreams, it is a vision; if she lies, think nothing of it."[55] The tone is ironic, but suspicion of this sort made women's claims to knowledge of God anything but frivolous in their consequences: the Beguine mystic Marguerite Porète was executed in 1310 for writings that continued afterward to circulate innocuously under the names of male authors.[56] Hagiographical accounts of women's raptures routinely describe skeptical observers inflicting pain on them to test if they are really beyond their senses.[57] Skepticism about holy women's powers, moreover, deepened considerably in the early fifteenth century, in the aftermath of the Great Schism, its attendant crisis of ecclesiastical authority, and the allegations by prominent churchmen such as John Gerson and Henry of Langenstein that female prophets had precipitated the crisis. By that point, as the late chapters of this book will illustrate, the question of the genuineness of women's charisms became more pressing and central in hagiography, and the number of women identified as witches—who were distinguished by supernatural experiences and powers that in formal terms were strikingly similar to those of the charismatic female saint—was soon to go steeply on the rise.[58] In the hagiographical works about women throughout the period in question, that is, even before the ominous developments of the early fifteenth century, this clerical concern to discipline and test saintly women is frequently evident in some measure. Given the hagiographical assumption of the woman's sanctity, the concern is rarely in the foreground. But thorough obedience to confessors is routinely reported of these female saints,[59] and in the case of one saint in particular, the ascetic queen Elizabeth of Thuringia (1207–1231), that obedience—to her confessor Conrad of Marburg—became the chief theme of the various works of hagiography that she inspired.[60]

Though clerics' sense of responsibility to the supervision of these women finds expression in the hagiography, what generally occupies the foreground is their fascination with the women's powers and the benefit these bestowed on the clerics themselves. There was indeed a certain safety inherent in their encounters with holy women, in the sense that the women's ostensible subordination to themselves minimized the potential of threat to their authority as priests, which in fact, in the men's telling, such women typically supported with enthusiasm. When it came to reflecting on questions of authority, that apparent safety made it possible for the male observers to make the most of the differences between the women's powers and their own, to heighten those differences and focus their attention on the very distinctiveness of the women and their powers. What could be at stake for a cleric in being attracted to a female saint is apparent in many of the mendicant accounts of lay women; the vita of the Florentine Humiliana dei Cerchi (d. 1246) by the Franciscan friar Vito of Cortona (d. ca. 1250) may serve as an example. Humiliana was a young woman who, after being widowed, returned to her father's house. There she resisted her family's attempts to marry her off again and lived as a recluse with a growing reputation for her devotion and asceticism.[61] She took the habit of a Franciscan tertiary and thus came into close association with friars. The friars supervised her, hearing her confessions and giving her the Eucharist. But Vito pictures them also coming to her for help of a personal sort, asking her to use her revelatory powers to advise them in matters concerning their own spiritual lives and calling. Thus she receives a revelation for one unnamed friar that he will persevere in chastity and intercedes for another to give him relief from temptations.[62] A Friar Buonacorso of Todi "frequently commended himself to her, asking that through her he might obtain from God a gift of devotion," and she eventually announces to him that his request would be granted. One day soon afterward he "was so infused with grace, that, tasting divine sweetness abundantly, he was made drunk, full of the wine of divinity."[63] And a friar named Michael, her "teacher in the way of devotion" who is mentioned several times in the vita, comes to her for similar help:

> Friar Michael, praying on a certain day in her presence, and not having devotion, said to her as though inwardly moved, "my daughter, pray for me, because I am all dry." The obedient daughter obediently lifted her eyes to heaven and prayed to the Lord. And he was immediately infused with such grace, that it appeared very obvious that he could not receive the fullness of the grace that was infused.[64]

Here the saint performs a personal service, which suggests a lack on the part of the friars themselves and a perception of the woman's powers as providing an emotional content to the friar's calling, which he otherwise would not have. There is more here than the complementarity of women's powers and men's powers: there is also a sense that the woman will somehow have the power to give the man something he otherwise does not have, a sense of supplementing the man's own experience. The saint represented a point of access to the divine, with many benefits that, so it seemed, were not to be had otherwise.

Finally, in addition to this sense of clerical dependence on the women's powers, and sometimes intertwined with it, hagiographers of women also sometimes described clerics' relationships with women in a way that explored the differences between the women's powers and their own. A twelfth-century work provides a good example: the vita of the recluse Christina of Markyate (1096/8–1155/66), written sometime after 1142 by an anonymous monk from the English abbey of St. Albans in Hertfordshire.[65] We learn from the vita that Christina was a noblewoman and that after an adventurous early life during which she managed to foil her parents' considerable efforts to marry her to a certain nobleman, she lived chastely with a male recluse, Roger of Markyate. After Roger's death she entered into a close relationship with a man of considerable influence, the abbot Geoffrey of St. Albans (d. 1147). The hagiographer formally presents her relationship with Geoffrey as a quid pro quo arrangement. Geoffrey, for his part, appears to have provided her material aid: she "was being afflicted in the furnace of poverty," and even though such poverty bred virtue, still God "reckoned that it was the right time to help her even in these matters" through Geoffrey.[66] As for her side of the bargain, she was to provide Geoffrey with her prayers. These he badly needed.

Their love was mutual, though according to the measure of holiness of each. He sustained her in external things, and she commended him attentively to God by her holy prayers. Nor was she any less solicitous about him than about herself. Indeed, she was more so. With such zeal did she attend to his salvation that, marvelous to say, whether he was close by or far away he could hardly offend against God in deed or word without her knowing it immediately through the spirit. Nor did she neglect to reprove him frightfully in his presence whenever she had perceived him sinning gravely in his absence— thinking injury from a friend better than flattery from an enemy.[67]

Although the emphasis here is on Christina's contribution rather than Geoffrey's, still the formal complementarity is clear enough: Geoffrey supplies "external," presumably material support; Christina provides the prayers—and through the prayers, the benefit of her charismatic ability to discern sins.

Christina's powers therefore—in this case in the form of revelations that emerge from her virtuous intercessions—supply services for Geoffrey that he could not supply for himself. In fact, this and her other charismatic assistance to Geoffrey loom much larger in the vita than anything that he does for her, for all the formal balance of services between them. Their roles often appear not so much balanced as reversed: the figure with evident power becomes dependent on the one without it. Little is said about what Christina received from Geoffrey, but there are several stories of her intercessions on his behalf, each of them involving some extraordinary demonstration of power based on her own favor in the sight of God. The incident that first brought them together is a case in point: it was on the request of a deceased member of the St. Albans community who had come to Christina in an apparition that she sent a message to Geoffrey to divert him from some unnamed headstrong action that he was undertaking without consulting the chapter of the monastery. Geoffrey scorned the message first, but he received a visit from the same deceased figure who attacked him for not having acted on it. From that point on he solicited her advice and was careful to follow it.[68] In another incident, Christina is described as having a vision while praying for Geoffrey in which she sees herself in a room with two white-robed personages (the first two persons of the Trinity?), with a dove, apparently the Holy Spirit, on their shoulders, whereas she sees Geoffrey outside the room, trying unsuccessfully to get in. As she prays she sees the dove beginning to fly, apparently with the possibility of reaching Geoffrey; she, "strengthened by this vision, did not cease her prayers until she could see that the aforementioned man [Geoffrey] either possessed the dove or was possessed by it."[69] Earlier, when Geoffrey had become extremely ill and sent a message to ask her help, she received a revelation that her prayers would be answered and that he would be well enough to visit her in five days' time, and she intimated as much to the incredulous waiting messenger, who later confirmed the prophecy when it came true.[70] Her prayers also kept Geoffrey from undertaking several dangerous journeys in his official capacity.[71]

The powers that Christina exercised for Geoffrey's benefit were rooted precisely in a holiness that he did not possess: and that fact, one soon sees, is crucial to the narrative. The significance of the relationship between them finally rests in Christina's superiority because of her higher status with Christ. The hagiographer makes this point, subtly but clearly, toward the end of the work when he reports a vision in which Christina saw herself, Christ, and Geoffrey together at the altar:

> When she looked at the altar she saw the kindly Jesus standing there, showing in his expression and bearing his mercy for sinners. And turning her eyes she saw her friend for whom she had labored [i.e., Geoffrey] standing to her right, which was to the left of the Lord. And when they knelt to pray, since the virgin's left was to the Lord's right(for they faced opposite ways), she feared lest he [Geoffrey] be on the Lord's left, and began to burn to know how he might be transferred to the right. She thought it unbearable to be nearer than her beloved to the Lord's right hand, for she saw that the right side of God was the place of greater honor. But rather than be raised up while her beloved was kneeling down in prayer, she wanted to be moved over in some other way; yet in that desire she realized quickly that the right hand of mercy, which she was grasping, was what she sought above all things. And so, among the other edifying things that they often said to each other, she used to repeat to her friend that the love of God was the one thing in which it is not right to put anyone else before oneself.[72]

The hagiographer uses the scene to picture Christina's humble regard and affection for Geoffrey, an affection that Christ is shown to override, but with the gentle but unmistakable implication that it is to be valued, and finds expression, precisely in the context of her own favored position with Christ. Geoffrey, for his part, approves of, even revels in, her superiority to himself in this sense, in part anyway because it is the condition of her ability to do what she does for him. Concerning Christina's habit of going into a rapture when receiving the Eucharist from him, Geoffrey would say to her, "it is much to my glory if, though unaware of my presence, you present me to Him, whose own presence is so sweet to you that you are unable to perceive mine."[73]

As the case of Christina and Geoffrey illustrates, the men who turned their attention to holy women could have a strong interest in stressing the women's differences from themselves. The hagiographer assumes behind the evident contrast between the powers of the respective figures an identity of origin in the blessing of God and consequently a fundamental harmony, but oddly the assumption of that harmony seems to have had precisely the effect of strengthening the clerics' sense of oppositeness from women they regarded as genuine in their gifts. For if such a woman had, by definition, something valid to supply to the church and themselves, then the very contrast between their powers provided a sense of the desirability of what she had to offer. The more definite the distinction between clerics' powers and the powers of such a woman, and the stronger the apparent difference between the two, then the greater was the charismatic woman's importance for the cleric in the sense that it was all the clearer that she had what he needed, that is, *what he did not already have access to*. In such a context of the simultaneous assumption of safe connection between the two types of authority, on the one hand, and a stark contrast between them, on the other, the encounter between holy women and clerics could take on a certain air of urgency and fascination—as an exploration of the deeper aspects of access to God now tantalizingly offered, and, in a more objective sense, as an appropriation of the women's services for very desirable ends.[74]

INFORMAL AND INSTITUTIONAL POWERS

In hagiographical narrative about holy women, this question of the relation between authorities is typically posed in the highly specific and often homely context of an individual woman's life. But this was no mere incidental issue in the Christianity of the time. For in the late-medieval centuries, the hierarchy of the church, following in the path of the Gregorian reform, claimed preeminence over the whole of society, asserting its authority with unprecedented clarity and ostensible confidence; at the same time, the religious fervor of the time produced many people of reputed holiness and supernatural power outside the offices of the church, including not only women, who were in any case excluded from clerical office, but some male prophets and visionaries as well, all of whom in effect claimed a personal authority to act.[75] Thus the question: What ought to be the stance of the church, holy in itself, toward the possibility of holiness expressed beyond its own structures and offices?

In André Vauchez's useful terminology, the extraordinary powers exercised by people outside those structures and offices are "informal" powers, that is, powers that "do not proceed from the exercise of a function of hierarchic type or from the appearance of a privileged *status*, but from a particular charism claimed and utilized as such." The distinction between such informal powers and "institutional powers"—that is, powers of a "hierarchic type" as exercised by clerics—is of fundamental importance in the present context, and it is fairly easily drawn. Such informal powers include, among other things, personal advice or direction based upon clairvoyance about people and events; and teachings based upon grand revelations of the whole shape of history or upon claims of extraordinary personal contact with the divine essence or visions of Christ.[76] These powers based themselves on the authority of an individual charism, that is, of a gift bestowed by the Spirit on those individuals directly. This supposed provenance distinguishes these informal powers from the properly institutional powers that priests and bishops possessed on the basis of their offices, that is, powers that "proceed from the exercise of a function of a hierarchic type." Thus the prophet and the mystic discerned hidden truths on the basis of an extraordinary divine presence or inspiration working in them directly, independent of any office they might otherwise have held, whereas the priest and the bishop performed the sacraments and ruled the church on the basis of the authority given to them by the institution.

What complicates this otherwise straightforward distinction between informal and institutional powers, however, is the fact that the offices of the church, and indeed the church itself, were also considered to be charisms, gifts of the Spirit. In this sense Max Weber's concept of "charisma" as a quality of extraordinary leaders that arises from their own attributes and emphatically not from the routine authority of "everyday" institutions, though clearly relevant to any discussion of informal powers as understood here, imposes a somewhat more inflexible line between the charismatic and the institutional than the late-medieval situation would suggest.[77] For even though the powers of the priest were indeed institutional in the sense of being derived from his office in the church, the priest himself, with the authority of tradition behind him, would have construed his powers as ultimately no less charismatic, in the sense of manifesting a spiritual gift, than the informal powers of prophets or visionaries. St. Paul spoke in the same breath of spiritual gifts and of the incipient offices (1 Cor. 12); in the early-medieval centuries it had been bishops who, with a full array of thaumaturgic and prophetic powers, dominated the field of sainthood; and in the present the priest regularly effected the miracle of the sacrament of the altar and possessed the power to exorcise.[78]

Why then did clerics tolerate informal powers at all, if the Spirit already worked through the church, that is, through themselves? Indeed, their tolerance was often reluctant; in the late-medieval centuries the church took especially seriously its responsibility to "prove" the genuineness of those who claimed these informal powers.[79] In this sense, clerics had the upper hand, serving as the judges and in some sense even appearing as the natural antagonists of such people. But that was not the whole of their response. Here we are faced with a source of profound ambiguity in Christian conceptions of authority. Precisely the belief that the Spirit and not the office was the final authority, even though the Spirit spoke through the office, implied that the church, whatever its claims for itself, could never wholly substitute itself for the Spirit. In every age of the church's history one can point to prominent instances when, as Yves Congar put it, "a purely spiritual influence was brought to bear, apart from all hierarchical authority," however strongly that authority was being asserted at the time.[80] In this sense a deep affinity had to be assumed between informal powers—if judged valid, that is—and institutional powers, for all their potential to interfere with each other. Even when the two appear out of harmony, we should not think of them as absolute opposites or adversaries so much as, in Vauchez's apt characterization, "two poles between which is established a permanent dialectical tension, more or less strong according to place and time."[81] Clerics, moreover, did not simply attach themselves to their proper pole of this dialectic but also felt the magnetic force of the other pole, that is, the power of perceived holiness in its direct noninstitutional expression—a force that could seem irresistible. And clerics brought a variety of interests and needs of their own to their experience of that other holiness. In this way the encounter of those who possessed institutional powers with those who possessed informal ones could be complex. It certainly was two-sided, expressing both the impulse to test and control informal powers and, at the same time, another impulse, one of attraction to the personal charisms of those who exercised those powers, which brought clerics sometimes paradoxically under the sway of people who were otherwise subordinate to them. We will see evidence of all of this in the chapters to follow.

CHAPTER 2

Revelation and Authority in Ekbert and Elisabeth of Schönau

I N 1152, AT THE AGE of twenty-three, the nun Elisabeth of the Benedictine monastery of Schönau in the diocese of Trier began to receive revelations in the form of visions.[1] At some point shortly afterward, or anyway before the spring of 1155, her brother Ekbert, then a canon at Bonn but soon to become a monk at Schönau, began what would become a large body of writings that described those visions.[2] As recent scholarship has made abundantly clear, Elisabeth appears in these writings as a person of considerable interest in her own right.[3] The visions themselves are clearly her own, and not Ekbert's creations. But throughout the writings Ekbert also makes much reference to himself and to his interactions with Elisabeth, and he does not hesitate to show the reader how much he had to do with this extraordinary woman and her visions. The writings thus present themselves, in part, as an insider's picture—the first such picture we have—of what happened between a visionary woman and a close male associate and of the meaning she held for him.

Although Ekbert causes the reader to see much of himself, self-disclosure is not itself the point. For although he presents himself as a person thoroughly devoted to, even fascinated by, Elisabeth, as well as deeply curious about the substance of her revelations, he actually says little, directly anyway, about his own desires or the state of his own soul, even insofar as his encounter with Elisabeth had a bearing on these. In the course of two centuries after Ekbert, as we shall see in subsequent chapters, some male associates of holy women would indeed say much about the state of their own souls in their writings about those women, as they experimented with the idea of their own subservience to the women, whom they saw as addressing those needs and in some sense becoming their own directors. But here in the visionary records of Elisabeth, Ekbert puts himself rarely, if at all, in the position of receiving direction. He is not out to expose particulars of his own life in relation to hers but rather to establish that he has exercised proper authority in the matter of her visions. His self-inclusion serves to show that he has asserted his *own* direction over Elisabeth unambiguously, making clear his right to test the visions and to determine which ones would and would not be communicated to a broader audience, and he shows himself influencing the topics of certain visions, if not their actual substance. Ekbert's accounts of the visions attempt therefore to demonstrate how Elisabeth depended upon him but not how he might have depended upon her. His own visibility here serves to certify the safe harnessing and proper channeling of Elisabeth's powers.

ELISABETH, EKBERT, AND THE VISIONS

Elisabeth was born in 1128 or 1129, entered the double (i.e., male and female) Benedictine monastery of Schönau when she was twelve, and made her profession as a nun there at some point later in her adolescence.[4] She was eventually to become the superior or *magistra* of the sisters at Schönau.[5] But unlike the older visionary *magistra* Hildegard of Bingen, with whom she exchanged letters, Elisabeth would not be remembered for the exercise of her office but for her visions alone. From their outset in 1152, the visions continued until just before her death in 1165.[6] As Peter Dinzelbacher has suggested, they reflect a moment of change in the history of medieval visionary literature: there are still elements here of the spatially defined "otherworld journeys" typical of earlier medieval writings, mostly by men, but they also sometimes display the engagement with personal figures (in her case especially a guiding angel and various saints), diminished spatial orientation, and greater emotional involvement that would characterize the mainly female visionaries of the high and later Middle Ages, who, however, would typically encounter Christ himself in their visions, as Elisabeth does not.[7]

As for Ekbert, he was born no later than 1132, but it is unknown if he was older or younger than Elisabeth.[8] Before becoming a monk at Schönau in 1155, he had been a canon in Bonn and before that, for some length of time in the 1140s, a student at Paris.[9] He was himself to become abbot of Schönau in 1165 or 1166. Ekbert's friendship with Rainald of Daissel, who was his fellow student at Paris and later archbishop of Cologne and Frederick Barbarossa's chancellor, suggests that he moved in influential circles.[10] He was also a person of considerable intellectual and literary accomplishment. In addition to the records of Elisabeth's visions, he also wrote a series of discourses against the Cathars and several devotional works, of which mention will be made below.[11]

Ekbert began collaborating with Elisabeth on the records of her visions while he was still at Bonn, and continued to do so for the rest of her life. Over time, these visionary writings took the form of several distinct literary works that were circulated widely in monastic circles in the twelfth and thirteenth centuries, especially in northern France, the Low Countries, and England, both individually and in a collection that exists in various redactions.[12] The last and fullest redaction, which Ekbert compiled sometime between Elisabeth's death in 1164 and his own in 1184,[13] includes: three books (*Libri visionum*) that relate her ongoing visions in chronological sequence so as to constitute a sort of "diary";[14] a work called *Liber viarum dei* (Book of the ways of God), which relates a series of revelations in the form of sermons by her attendant angel about the various paths of the Christian life;[15] a vision affirming the corporeal resurrection of the Virgin, which circulated both by itself and as a part of the second *Liber visionum*;[16] an extended set of visions about St. Ursula and her companion martyrs whose relics had been, it was thought, discovered recently at Cologne;[17] several letters by Elisabeth, with more or less visionary content;[18] and an account of Elisabeth's death in the form of a letter from Ekbert to some of their female relatives (*Epistola Eckeberti ad cognatas suas de obitu domine Elisabeth*).[19]

Ekbert makes his appearance in these texts in a variety of ways. He sometimes addresses the reader directly about the terms of his relationship to Elisabeth, as in the prologue to the first visionary book, in which he describes the circumstances and process of their collaboration, and in *De obitu*, in which he speaks more personally of her influence upon him and casts himself as eyewitness to her death.[20] Once, at her putative invitation, he includes his own allegorical explanation of a vision.[21] As Anne Clark has shown, some of the evidence of Ekbert's presence in the texts suggests that he widened Elisabeth's horizons, expanding her subject matter beyond herself and her community toward other, broader concerns—especially following his ordination to the priesthood at Rome in 1155, when he gave up his career at Bonn for good and joined the Schönau community.[22] Even in the texts produced before that moment, the voice of Elisabeth sometimes addresses him directly, as at the beginning of the first *Liber visionum* when she explains at length her expectations of their collaboration, and when she occasionally speaks to him by name in the course of the visionary narratives, reminding the reader that he was their immediate recipient,[23] but after his arrival there is an unmistakable change in the style and content of the visions, beginning at the nineteenth chapter of the second *Liber visionum*. From here on the visions, now undated and longer than the previous ones, contain revelations about their kinfolk and about associates of Ekbert's and, most significantly, exhibit a new visionary modus operandi whereby Ekbert often, on his own or others' behalf, supplies Elisabeth with the questions that she then poses to an angel who by that point habitually appears in the visions as her guide—questions that touch on, among other things, matters of theological controversy.[24] Through this visible role as prompter Ekbert not only displays his influence on her but also preserves evidence of the genuine discreteness of Elisabeth's voice, as in his report of her savvy refusal to obtain a direct reply to Ekbert's question whether the church father Origen, whose teachings had been condemned, would be finally damned—a refusal that, as Clark has suggested, is unlikely to have been Ekbert's invention.[25] Some of the visions also contain revelations addressed to him, as when she reports John the Baptist explaining an allegorical vision she has had of the heavenly city, with instructions to convey the explanation to Ekbert; indeed, the angel appears quite conscious of Ekbert, to whom he refers several times.[26] Thus Ekbert appears explicitly throughout these texts. Let us now look a little more closely at the themes and motives of these appearances.

EKBERT'S CONCERNS

What does Ekbert reveal about his own mind in his reports of his interactions with his sister? He appears most interested in rather erudite matters: he raises various questions about doctrine and ecclesiastical practice, enlisting Elisabeth as a kind of a research assistant to help him find answers. We can also glimpse some other concerns in Eckbert, concerns that arise from his own devotion and spiritual longings: he was certainly a man conscious of, and articulate about, his own spirituality, and he knew his encounters with Elisabeth to be relevant to it. But he appears reticent to say much about such concerns, and in fact we might miss the traces of that side of Ekbert, were there not some evidence from outside the visionary corpus itself that hints, as we shall see, at a kind of self-revelation that future male associates of holy women will do much more than hint at. The reticence appears to be no accident; Ekbert had strong reasons to restrict the reader's view of the intersections between his inner life and hers.

Ekbert's erudition is most conspicuous at the end of the third *Liber visionum*, where he gives his own lengthy explanation of one of her visions. This was a vision of a moving wheel upon which a bird perched with difficulty; extending from the wheel was a stone-posted ladder extending to heaven, and next to it, a shining male figure, his members made of various substances, standing cruciform. She had an accompanying vision of Gregory the Great, who informed her, "you cannot understand what these things mean, but talk to the doctors, who read the scriptures: they will know."[27] And so she appealed to Ekbert himself, as he reports, clearly implying that he met the qualifications: "now therefore, most beloved brother, I ask you to take up the task of searching the divine scriptures to try to find an interpretation that suits this vision."[28] So the invitation, ostensibly anyway, calls forth his explication of the vision. He begins it by exclaiming that he is in fact "not a doctor, not a steward of the mysteries of God, but rather an insignificant man of small understanding, and even less when it comes to discerning the secrets of God."[29] But notwithstanding this topos of humility, scriptural allusions appear by the dozens in the pages that follow: the wheel signifies the changeable world, which is deceptively beautiful in the manner of the harlot of the book of Revelation (Rev. 17:4); the bird signifies the righteous person who falls and recovers seven times (Prov. 24:16, Vlg.); the stone posts of the ladder signify the Father and the Son, recalling Jesus' recommendation to build on stone (Matt. 7:24) and the Psalmist's description of a "rock of refuge" (Psalm 103:18); the Christ-figure's head signifies his divinity (1 Cor. 11:3); and so forth.[30] For all intents and purposes it *is* as a "doctor, a steward of the mysteries of God," that he presents himself here, with the blessing of Elisabeth and, indirectly, her heavenly friends.

Ekbert also appears as a learned man when he shows himself influencing the questions Elisabeth brings to her visionary world. This influence appears in its most concentrated form in a series of passages in the third *Liber visionum* that have to do with angels. Here Elisabeth poses several questions of her heavenly informant that had been widely discussed by twelfth-century theologians, for instance by Peter Lombard in his *Sentences*. How can it be, she asked, that angels, if incorporeal, can sometimes be seen?[31] Did Lucifer's whole order of angels apostatize with him, and did any angel from any other order fall as well?[32] Did Lucifer apostatize all at once or only gradually? (This she asked "as directed by a more learned person.")[33] Who is the chief of the angels?[34] Does each person have a guardian angel, and is that angel reassigned after the person's death?[35] She also asked for an interpretation of Deuteronomy 32:8—"when the most high divided the peoples, when he separated the sons of Adam, he established limits for the people according to the number of the sons of Israel, the angels of God"—a passage that was assumed to state a relation between the number of the fallen angels and the number of the elect souls. The explicit reference to Ekbert comes at the end of the angel's answer to the last of these questions: he says that the number of blessed souls who will eventually join the persevering angels will equal the number of angels who had fallen, and adds, "say these things to your brother, and if he wants to ask anything more, tell me."[36] This suggests that Ekbert had been the source of the question, and when Elisabeth immediately adds, "I asked *therefore* another time about the above verse" and receives a further explanation that it also refers to the fixing of the number of the elect after the fall of Adam and the crime of Cain, the follow-up question appears to have been Ekbert's also. In light of the angel's comment, the "more learned" prompter of the prior question about Lucifer's fall was likely also he.[37]

Ekbert's report of the angel's invitation, at any rate, stakes out a pivotal place for himself in a lively discussion between the angel, Elisabeth, and various people with access to her—a discussion in which the angel was not simply the source of oracles but a schoolman in his own right, prepared to defend and explain his positions. When, as Ekbert subsequently reports, "a certain brother" objects to the angel's teaching that a single order of angels had fallen, on the grounds of the apparent distinction between the "principalities and powers" defeated by Christ (Col. 2:15), the angel counters that the phrase "principalities and powers" refers to the potentials of particular angels rather than to orders, and he presents an argument in support: if angels had fallen from various orders, then the elect souls who replace them would have to be separated from one another, which cannot be the case since the elect souls have their own place together in heaven.[38]

Not all of Ekbert's prompting has to do with angels. He also appears proposing questions about other matters of doctrine and of ecclesiastical practice; similar questions are attributed to unnamed prompters who, if they were not in fact Ekbert, must have been people who took part in that same broad discussion with Elisabeth in which he had a key role. In a passage in the third visionary book, Elisabeth asks the Virgin Mary, "as advised beforehand (*premonita*) by my brother, who at that moment was celebrating the divine office for us," whether Origen, who praised the Virgin highly but some of whose views the church has found heretical, would be ultimately saved (the answer was inconclusive).[39] Similarly it was as she had been "*premonita*"—by whom is not said, but the word is used with express reference to Ekbert twice, including the case just cited—that she asks St. Paul on his feast day whether the Greeks, whom he originally converted, would be damned for not now including the *filioque* in the Creed (the answer was yes).[40] And it was when *premonita* by "a certain brother" that she asks John the Evangelist about the discrepancy between traditions as to the day of his death.[41] This was also true in the case of her famous revelation on the corporeal assumption of the Virgin, though it was "one of our elders," not necessarily Ekbert, who directed her to ask the angel whether the Virgin had been assumed into heaven corporeally or only spiritually; the stated reason for asking was that the writings of the fathers left the matter unclear.[42] Ekbert also drew on his own learning to call attention to possible errors in Elisabeth's revelations and so to put them to the test. Thus he challenged the angel's technical vocabulary: in Sermon 4 of *Liber viarum dei* "my brother asked me to ask the angel" why married people are told to abstain from "fornication," a term which does not apply to the married—to which the angel responded that since married people learn their concupiscence before marriage, adultery is in fact rooted in fornication.[43] Similarly, in the third book of visions, after Elisabeth sees a vision of the sun with a crowned virgin sitting on it, whom the angel identifies as a figure of the humanity of Christ, she asks John the Evangelist, "as I had been *premonita*," why a figure that represented Christ's humanity had a female and not a male form, and she was told that Christ presented himself this way "so that the vision can fit more suitably the representation of his blessed mother as well"—a reinterpretation that, one suspects, reflects the influence of the person prompting her.[44]

Ekbert thus openly displays his erudition and his theological interests within the visionary corpus. What, then, of that other, more personal, side of the literary Ekbert that I have mentioned—the Ekbert who is attuned to his own longings and the condition of his soul? Here it is worth noting that his interventions in Elisabeth's visionary world do occasionally reflect his own circumstances beyond his theological interests per se: as a canon at Bonn he wrote her a letter asking her to attempt a visionary glimpse of that town's patron saints Cassius and Florentius on their feast day, and in the second visionary book Elisabeth discerns, apparently on Ekbert's behalf, the state of two deceased associates of his—one Gerard, whom Elisabeth identifies as a "colleague of my brother at Bonn," and "Master Adam," presumably the Paris master whom Ekbert otherwise mentions in a letter to his onetime Paris schoolmate the archbishop Rainald of Dassel.[45] It is also worth noting that, outside the realm of these visionary writings, Ekbert produced some highly affective works of devotion in which he showed himself articulate about the experience of the soul. These include a *salutatio* to the Virgin, which contains the earliest known instance of a prayer addressed to the Virgin's heart, and other works in which he describes and cultivates an emotional response to the Incarnation, as for instance in his *Stimulus dilectionis,* or *Stimulus amoris,* a work that was to have an important place in the late-medieval tradition of meditations on the life of Christ, circulating widely among the meditations attributed to Anselm of Canterbury and as such partially incorporated by Bonaventure into the classic Franciscan treatise of this genre, the *Lignum vitae.*[46] In the *Stimulus* Ekbert calls forth affective responses to the ironies of the Incarnation—he scorns, for instance, his reader's attachment to a comfortable bed in contrast to the squalor of the Nativity—and, when he comes to an extended treatment of the Passion, he shifts to the first-person singular addressing Christ ("I, lost man, was the cause of all your sadness, all your difficulty"), eventually adopting the vivid conceit of being affixed to the cross by various "nails" corresponding to the virtues that he will acquire by his devotion.[47] The visionary corpus is, of course, of a different genre altogether from such a devotional work, and one would not expect Ekbert to be writing in the same voice there as in the *Stimulus dilectionis.* But keeping that voice in mind, there is at least some trace of this spiritual self-expressiveness in the visionary corpus.

The clearest such trace is to be found in the letter *De obitu,* Ekbert's account of Elisabeth's death. Here he writes directly of her effect upon him. Clark has pointed out that this is the text in which Ekbert shows most interest in the details of Elisabeth's own devotional practice, including her habits of prayer, diet, and corporeal penance, such that she appears here not simply as visionary but as also in a fuller sense as "holy woman";[48] accordingly, he presents himself here as her devotee and not simply her collaborator in the visions. Early in the letter he writes that Elisabeth "bore me into a light that was new beyond what I had known, she drew me to the familiar ministry of Jesus my Lord, she often brought me, in a mellifluous voice, consolations and instructions of God from heaven, she made my heart to taste the first-fruits of a sweetness hidden with the saints in God."[49] Whatever "consolations and instructions" these were, Ekbert clearly acknowledges a strong personal influence and appears to confirm other evidence (to be considered presently) that Elisabeth affected his decision to become a priest. Further on in *De obitu* Ekbert pictures himself at Elisabeth's deathbed as a scaled-down Elisha to her Elijah, declaring his wish to have visions of his own, apparently of the magnitude of hers, after her death: "I do not presume to say like the prophet: 'pray that there be your double spirit in me' [2 Kings 2.9] but if the Lord wishes to give me your spirit alone, it will suffice."[50] The wish suggests that he wanted not just to be devoted to her, but also to be *like* her—not just to receive benefits from her, that is, but to be graced as she was graced. That Ekbert did claim anyway the gift of revelations, appears from a passing remark in one of the Ursuline texts, that a certain martyr's identity revealed to Elisabeth had also been revealed to "the brother by whom the bodies were brought," namely himself.[51] But here in *De obitu* he shows himself desiring the greater gift that he observed in her.

That Elisabeth had a strong personal influence upon Ekbert is clear enough therefore from the visionary collection. It would be surprising if his close connection with Elisabeth had not affected him, and his biblically erudite *Sermones contra Catharos*, written around 1164, suggest one way in particular in which it may have done so. As Raoul Manselli has pointed out, in those sermons Ekbert testifies to his own extensive contact with Cathars in his years at Bonn, yet he apparently had not written against them earlier. It seems no accident that by this time Elisabeth had issued the antiheretical prophecy preserved in the third *Liber visionum* (and apparently influenced, in turn, by Hildegard's anti-Cathar revelations of 1163) that contains an exhortation to "*litterati*" to make use of the New Testament against the heretics.[52]

Surely, then, Elisabeth influenced Ekbert. But the fact remains that for all his visibility in the visionary corpus he is remarkably restrained about saying so. The matter of his ordination as priest illustrates the point. In the first *Liber visionum*, Elisabeth reports herself praying to the Virgin for

> a certain man familiar to me. He was in deacon's orders and I had frequently exhorted him not to delay to ascend to the priesthood. But he, giving various reasons for his fear, admitted that he did not yet dare to undertake a thing so lofty. Therefore in my prayer, when I made mention of this thing before my lady, she responded in these words: "tell my servant, do not fear, but do what you are to do, and give as your reason that this is your service to me, which you ought to have done but have not."[53]

That the man in question was Ekbert a reader might suspect; Emecho of Schönau, who was Ekbert's successor as abbot as well as his biographer, relates the same episode with explicit reference to him, quoting the revelation in question as it appeared in the visionary collection and adding—with the implication of cause leading to effect—that Ekbert subsequently went to Rome and received ordination there from the pope.[54] But in Ekbert's own account he does not name himself. Citing the precedent of that account, Clark has speculated that an unnamed priest mentioned in the second visionary book may also be Ekbert:

a priest who was practically inconsolable with remorse for having spilled consecrated wine on the corporal during mass, and whom Elisabeth tried unsuccessfully to comfort with a consoling message from her angel, before bringing him
assurance of aid from the Virgin with the direction to place the stained corporal
among the monastery's relics, and finally, a year later, receiving visions of the
gradual disappearance of the stain and an assurance that his "sin of negligence"
had been purged.[55] Whether or not this priest was Ekbert, such anxiety and
tearful scrupulosity would certainly be believable in the author of the *Stimulus
dilectionis*, and—as indeed in the matter of the ordination—the special favor of
the Virgin would be appropriate for an author who was otherwise so obviously
her devotee. But again he does not name himself.

Why is Ekbert reticent to speak about his own life in the context of his relations with Elisabeth? Here a concern about Elisabeth's detractors appears
important: he is at pains to avoid any appearance of self-interest that might
compromise his claims for Elisabeth and her visions. This is most evident in
the matter of his own monastic profession, which he discussed in a letter to the
abbot of Reinhausen, in the course of defending Elisabeth's visions against the
charge of detractors that they are only "a woman's invention [quasi figmenta
mulierum]." If the charge were true, he says, then he himself would surely know
it and therefore would be lying about her, presumably for glory or gain—but
this cannot be, he explains:

> When I was a canon of the church in Bonn, the glory of the world smiled
> upon me quite enough, and from his full hand the Heavenly Provider
> poured quite enough temporal abundance on me. If now—having attached
> myself fully to the bosom of the Lord, and having nine years ago embraced
> the monastic life, solely from love of him, by no necessity, and obliged by
> no weakness—if now I weave a tissue of lies in order to gain a whisper of
> silly glory or vile temporal profit for my sister or for me, I would be like the
> salt that has lost its savor [Mt. 5.13].[56]

Here Ekbert asserts that he entered the monastery not from "necessity" or
"weakness" but only from love of God, and in context he strongly implies
that the event was therefore none of Elisabeth's doing. But we know from
Emecho a different version of the story, in which Elisabeth plays a dominant,
if slightly reluctant, role as catalyst to Ekbert's decision—of which, given the
concerns Ekbert expresses to the abbot of Reinhausen, it is not surprising
that he gives no clue in the visionary corpus. According to Emecho, when

Ekbert was at Rome being ordained to the priesthood, Elisabeth had a vision in which she saw him defeat the devil in combat only after St. Benedict had brought him a monastic habit and a pastoral staff. Later, at Ascension that year (1155) when he was celebrating mass at Schönau, she heard a heavenly voice calling him, and at Pentecost was told by the angel that her vision of a tree growing from the monks' great altar represented Ekbert, whom she must exhort to "renounce the world." She hesitated to do this "because she knew that he was brought up delicately from childhood," presumably, that is, because the rigors of the monastic life would be beyond him, but, after being chided by the angel for hesitating, she did exhort him to become a monk, at the same moment seeing the angel "attending near him and exhorting him to this same renunciation"—at which point Ekbert immediately acquiesced, stated his intention to make his monastic profession, and never wavered until he had done so, nor afterward regretted it.[57] This is what Emecho says, but Ekbert nowhere reports these events, nor are the visions in Emecho's account included in the visionary corpus. And Emecho's report of Elisabeth's vision of his combat with the devil, with its implication that he would not have persevered in virtue had he not received the monastic habit, stands perhaps not in outright contradiction to, but at least in some tension with, Ekbert's interested assertion to the abbot of Reinhausen that no weakness impelled him into Elisabeth's monastery.

If Ekbert's reticence about exposing his spiritual affections here is linked to his concern for Elisabeth's reputation, that concern merits a closer look. In fact, the whole of Ekbert's presentation of himself in the visionary corpus, as we shall see, witnesses to his careful attention to the interactions between the visionary and her audience—interactions that he wants to be seen supervising.

Ekbert as Director

Ekbert's role in Elisabeth's life, to the extent that he allowed it to appear in these works, had to do almost exclusively with her visions. He does not appear as her confessor—a role that their abbot, Hildelin, filled both before and after Ekbert's entry into Schönau—nor otherwise as her spiritual adviser in the sense of attending to her ascetic practices or the state of her soul.[58] But in the matter of her visions, his role is large: he represents himself not only deciding how the visions were to be communicated to a broader audience but also influencing their subject matter and testing their veracity. He shows himself taking charge of communication between Elisabeth and her audience, in such a way that Elisabeth herself appears as in a certain sense his subordinate.

Although Ekbert says nothing about the actual process of receiving the visionary reports from Elisabeth and then editing and collecting them, he presents the overall task as his alone, and we have a few clues about what was in his mind as editor. In the preface to the first of the *Libri visionum* he explains that he was in the position to compile the visionary accounts because Abbot Hildelin had commanded her to reveal them to him:

> Since therefore all the things that happened around her, are seen to be to the glory of God and to the edification of the faithful, in this book, for the most part, are written according to her narration, which she revealed individually to one of her brothers of the order of clerics, to whom she was closer than to anyone else. For since she hid much from those inquiring, because she was very fearful and humble of spirit, by command of the abbot she was obliged to tell everything intimately to the one [i.e., Ekbert] who, by virtue of his kinship and love, diligently investigated everything and was eager to hand it on to posterity.[59]

The abbot made his command apparently while Ekbert, "of the order of clerics," was still at Bonn; he had begun not only to listen but to write even before his permanent arrival at Schönau.[60] Much later, in a prologue that he prefixed to the first of the *Libri visionum* in his final redaction of the collection, Ekbert claims that in writing the visions he had not *added* anything to them, although he did translate portions from the German:

> I Ekbert, brother of the handmaid of God, having been drawn to the monastery of Schönau from Bonn, and at first a monk, and thence by the grace of God called to be abbot—I wrote all these things, and others that are read of her revelations, in such a way that where the words of the angel were Latin I have left them, and where they were German I have translated them as clearly as I could, adding nothing out of my own presumption, seeking nothing of human favor, nothing of earthly advantage, as God is my witness, to whom all things are uncovered and open.[61]

But if he did not add to the visions, he did omit some things. As he put it in a letter to the abbot Reinhard of Reinhausen:

I acknowledge that many great and marvellous things—things that would usefully serve to instruct many people—I negligently allowed to pass by, either because of the malice of her detractors, which wearied me and made me stop altogether, or because of preoccupation with the business of the monastery, or because of a lack of parchment.[62]

Though Ekbert here attributes the omissions to his own negligence as aggravated by various factors, still his own calculation may have also played a role. According to Emecho, Ekbert "wrote down those things which he saw to be useful for the faithful, but about those which would be of no profit for readers, he remained quiet."[63] And although we cannot know what he omitted altogether from the outset, there is evidence of his removal of material from the visionary corpus in the redaction process. In an early redaction, for example, Ekbert included the minatory prophecy of which Eisabeth had written to Hildegard as bringing her mockery—but he later removed it, perhaps because "the malice of her detractors" was still generating such mockery.[64] Or again: probably out of deference to the Premonstratensian cloister of Ilbenstadt, which possessed the head of the Ursuline martyr Verena, Ekbert removed from the Ursuline revelations the putative wish of Verena herself that her head be brought to Schönau where her body lay.[65]

If Ekbert thus had Elisabeth's audience in mind as he edited a given portion of the visionary texts, he seems also to have had them in mind at a much earlier phase of the process: at several points in the visionary corpus we see him prompting visions from Elisabeth on behalf of persons outside Schönau. In a letter to the abbot Gerlach of Deutz, Elisabeth mentions that it was Ekbert who, apparently at Gerlach's request, directed her to ask her angel what had happened to a piece of the consecrated Host that a boy at Deutz had sneezed out of his mouth and that had then been trampled by bystanders. (It had been miraculously preserved, she said.)[66] In another letter, to the abbess of Dietkirchen, we learn from Elisabeth that when the abbess's representatives had come to visit her, Ekbert had accompanied them and was the one to remind her of the abbess's long-standing desire for "admonition and consolation" from her. After Elisabeth had received from her angel a revelation that included the prophecy that the abbess would "always rejoice…where there is the sweetest odor of cinnamon and balsam," Ekbert obliged Elisabeth to return to the angel to find out what "cinnamon and balsam" signified.[67]

The texts also show Ekbert exercising direction over her. One notable instance concerns Elisabeth's revelation about a St. Potentinus. It is in a letter to the abbot and monks of the monastery of Steinfeld, appended to her revelations about the Ursuline martyrs, that Ekbert discusses her revelations about this Potentinus. His body was buried, along with other relics, at Steinfeld, but the abbot and monks knew nothing about him and, like the abbot Gerlach of Deutz whose questions launched Elisabeth into her Ursuline visions, they asked her for information.[68] Ekbert writes that he intervened strongly with her on their behalf: "I asked her, I say, or rather—since she resisted greatly and for a long time because of the tongues of detractors—I *obliged* her with great zeal, and the One who is the knower of hidden things opened up to me, through her, what I sought."[69] In other words Ekbert's insistence produced the results, and the angel had now finally informed Elisabeth about this Potentinus. The story, like that of Ursula and her companions, concerns martyrs from the high nobility: Potentinus, the Christian son of a pagan king in Gaul, was martyred along with several associates including his brother Castor and sister Castrina, while traveling to Westphalia to be consecrated a bishop. The relics were buried in their present location because it was there that, in the process of being returned to Gaul by the faithful, they became miraculously heavy and therefore unmoveable.[70]

We observe Ekbert's direction of Elisabeth when he then describes the aftermath of this vision, in which he apparently overruled a negative response from her angel to his questioning. Upon hearing her report of the vision, he asked her to find out from the angel whether Potentinus had been a contemporary of Maximinus, bishop of Trier; he asked this, he tells the Steinfeld monks, because of "a certain song which you had shown me some days before, when I was with you," which identified him as such.[71] But when Elisabeth was in her visionary mode again and was about to pass this question along, the angel "stood as though with indignation averting his face from her," and she, mortified to have offended him, asked St. Stephen the protomartyr who appeared to her at the same time (it being his feast day) to intervene, and afterward the angel turned to her and criticized Ekbert:

"Your brother offends me and my brothers [i.e., the angels]. For he knew from histories, that there was a Theban legion before the time of St. Maximinus, and when he enjoined you to ask that question, he did it as though to try me, in case I was going to say anything contrary to the speech I had made concerning the time of the aforementioned martyrs." And he added: "you will not have placated me unless first you make satisfaction to each of the orders of my brothers singly."[72]

What we see here is a trace of a conflict, perhaps even a confrontation, between Ekbert and Elisabeth. The conflict is between two claims: the angel's claim—implicitly her own claim—of the veracity of her visions, and Ekbert's claim to be the judge of that veracity. Elisabeth's angel is challenging Ekbert here. For his question has had the effect of testing Elisabeth's vision for inner consistency—Ekbert does not deny it—and the angel has not only tried to resist the test but has demanded "satisfaction" for the outrage of it. Elisabeth had had previous success in a similar, and likewise subdued, confrontation with her abbot, as will be seen. But this time the angel backs down, or at least that is the impression Ekbert wants to give his readers. For Ekbert takes no note of the angel's response but goes ahead to report what other questions he asked Elisabeth to address to the angel: whether Castor was in holy orders, whether Castrina was a virgin, how they could accompany their brother without parental permission, and whether the site of their martyrdom had a name. Ekbert offers no apology—and gives the angels no "satisfaction"—for his questions.

The passage in the visionary corpus that most directly describes Ekbert's role in Elisabeth's visionary enterprise similarly, if subtly, asserts Ekbert's authority over her. That passage is Elisabeth's own introduction to the visions, expressed in her voice, addressed to Ekbert and contained in his preface to the first of the *Libri visionum*. Here the voice of Elisabeth articulates a complex dilemma about her public role as a visionary. On the one hand, she worries about what people will think of her if her visions are publicized. She is afraid that whether or not people find "holiness" in her and by implication accept her visions, she will be judged negatively. For even those who accept her visions will accuse her of a lack of humility about her gifts. Having embraced a life of separation from the world, she considers that they may be right—that a public role of any sort may be inappropriate.

Many say perhaps that there is some holiness in me, and attribute my merits to the grace of God, thinking me to be something when I am nothing. But others will think to themselves, "if this be a real servant of God [dei famula], let her be completely silent and not allow her name to be esteemed on earth"—not knowing by what goads I am being prodded to speak out. There are also some who would say that all those things they hear of me are a womanly fabrication or perhaps they will decide I am deluded by Satan. In these and other ways, my dearest, I am bound to be exposed to people's talk. And whence does this [happen] to me that I shall become known to anyone, I who have chosen to be hidden, and who do not think myself worthy that people raise their eyes to look at me? And it increases my anguish not a little, that the lord abbot has thought fit to commend my words to be written. For I, what am I, that anything should be remembered about me? Will this not be attributed to arrogance?[73]

On the other hand, Elisabeth feels compelled to communicate the visions. This is in part because some of her supporters—"certain of the wise" as she puts it—have urged her to do so for the good of others.

> But certain of the wise say to me that the Lord has not done this to me on account of me alone, but that through these things he provided also for the edification of others, because they seem to attain in some measure to the confirmation of the faith, and to the consolation of those who are troubled in heart because of the Lord. And for these aforementioned reasons, they reckon that the works of God should not be passed over in silence.[74]

But fundamentally she accepts the wisdom of this view because of supernatural signs—specifically because of the suffering that God has caused in her when she has declined or resisted making the visions public.

> I believe what they say to be true in some degree, on account of certain things that I will tell you: it happened several times when I was hiding in my heart those things which were shown me by the lord, that I was seized by such agony around my heart that I thought myself close to death; and when I revealed what I had seen to those around me, suddenly I was relieved.[75]

So it seems that God will not let her do otherwise than speak out. Nonetheless all the weighty objections to such a course remain intact: that is her quandary.

It is as a resolution to that quandary that the voice of Elisabeth here interprets Ekbert's presence at Schönau. She suggests, in the first place, that his purpose in moving to Schönau had to do with her visions. The passage begins:

> You ask me, brother, and you have come for this reason—that I relate to you the mercies of the Lord, by which he honored me in working in me according to the good pleasure of his grace. Indeed it is easy for me to give you complete satisfaction, for my soul too has long desired to confer with you about all these things, and to hear your opinion.[76]

She appears to be saying that Ekbert has come to Schönau—and lest there be any doubt that she is referring to his permanent move there and not simply a visit, she later refers to his "entry" (see the quotation below)—to hear about her visions and that she has not conferred with him earlier. This is, in any event, not quite accurate, since we know that he had already heard from her about her visions, had even begun to record them, before he came to Schönau as a monk. But the very inaccuracy, which serves to set his presence in relief against his absence, signals an intent to highlight his importance. His role, it becomes clear, is to decide which portions of her visions are to be made public and which not—and accordingly to resolve her dilemma.

> But I still reckon myself not at all sure what is best for me to do. For I under-stand how perilous it is for me to be quiet about the great things of God, but I fear that it will be more perilous to speak. For I know myself to have less discretion than I need to discern which of these things that are revealed to me it is right to speak of and which of them ought to be honored by silence. And behold, I am placed among all these things in peril of doing the wrong thing. For that reason, my dear, the tears do not cease flowing from my eyes, and my spirit is constantly in anguish. But behold, at your entrance my soul began to be consoled, and a great calm came over me.... And now, because by the will of the Lord you are brought to me from afar, I will not hide my heart from you, but I will open to you everything about me, both good and ill. From now on, what happens is at your discretion and the abbot's.[77]

Ekbert—along with Abbot Hildelin who, as the reigning authority in the mon-astery, must be mentioned but who otherwise does not appear to share Ekbert's role as direct examiner of the visions—will therefore provide sole "discretion," which she professes herself to lack, in the matter of revealing her visions. He is to be their arbiter.

So the words of the preface give Ekbert discretionary authority over Elisa-beth's visions, to decide whether they will be communicated. This was the au-thority he pictured himself exercising in the case of the vision about Potentinus, when he presumed to put the angel's words to the test.

Was it really Elisabeth's desire to accord such a role to Ekbert? Perhaps so, by the time the words of the preface were set down. But this introductory passage may well express the *result* of Ekbert's assertion of his claim to test the visions, such as appears in the Potentinus episode, rather than Elisabeth's original idea of things. Her letter to Hildegard of Bingen provides some evidence here. In that letter, which describes events that occurred in 1154 and 1155, before Ekbert's arrival at Schönau (and itself may well have been written before that moment since Ekbert at any rate is not mentioned), Elisabeth portrays her angel as, in effect, superseding human authority.[78] She tells Hildegard, from whom she had probably already received advice,[79] how she came to reveal to her abbot her minatory visions about a coming judgment, and the story involves a certain confrontation between her angel and the abbot, reminiscent of Ekbert and the Potentinus episode except that in this case the angel had the upper hand. It was her angel, in the first place, she says, who insisted to her that she must reveal her visions—first scolding her, then whipping her severely, and finally making her mute, until she gave the abbot the book of her visions (i.e., the ones that had so far been recorded by Ekbert and others) and told him orally about her revelations of a coming judgment. She asked the abbot to keep all of this to himself, but the abbot asked her to inquire of the angel whether he should reveal it; shortly afterward the angel replied in the affirmative. The abbot then publicized the visions, but when some of his hearers questioned their genuineness the abbot commanded her under obedience to demand from the angel whether he was a true angel or not. Elisabeth says she thought this demand "presumptuous," but she did as commanded. The angel became indignant and averted his face from her in subsequent appearances demanding that the abbot and brothers of the monastery celebrate several solemn masses in the angels' honor. The abbot complied, and when he was next invited by clerics to preach from Elisabeth's prophecies, he directed Elisabeth to ask the angel whether the prophecies were still to be preached. She received an affirmative answer for him, along with the admonition not to listen to the detractors this time.[80]

When this letter is compared with Elisabeth's introduction to the visions, the contrast makes Ekbert's discretionary stance all the clearer. It is true that in both cases it is the divine impulse that compels her to make her visions public. But whereas in the letter to Hildegard the angel is the final arbiter of what is revealed and the abbot is grouped with Elisabeth as recipient and conveyor of the contents of the visions, in the introduction the role of arbiter is Ekbert's. This is a role that, in the letter, she was not willing to give the abbot; the abbot's authority was relativized to the angel's. But now that Ekbert has arrived at Schönau—or so he wants his reader to believe—his authority is not to be relativized. Later in the Potentinus episode, when Ekbert is challenged by the angel, he does not back down.

Ekbert thus presents *his* role in Elisabeth's visionary enterprise as ultimately the role of director. This role was concisely summarized by Emecho, who says in his vita of Ekbert that Elisabeth opened to [Ekbert] in order everything that had happened concerning her, because she had bound herself more closely to him in love than to any of her other familiars. And he, diligently examining all the great works that our Lord was accomplishing in her, wrote down those things which he saw to be useful for the faithful, but those which would be of no profit for readers he remained quiet about.[81]

Emecho therefore saw Ekbert as actively controlling the access of Elisabeth's audience to her visions—a view consistent with Ekbert's own self-presentation in the visionary texts. But was it also the view of Elisabeth? To consider that question is to be confronted with the fact that although the Elisabeth of these texts is far from a mere invention of Ekbert, nonetheless it is Ekbert who composed the texts, and on the crucial issue of his own place in the events surrounding the visions he had every reason to convey his own view of things and—no doubt subtly—to suppress Elisabeth's if it should differ from his own. We cannot assume that it is simply Elisabeth's voice we are hearing in the introduction to the visions. Moreover, that the angel could try to challenge Ekbert (as regarding Potentinus) and that Elisabeth could on occasion demur from answering Ekbert's questions, suggest that his discretion over her was in fact hardly absolute.[82]

Clearly Ekbert is at pains to show the reader that he has matters firmly in hand in mediating Elisabeth's visions to her audience. In this sense Elisabeth has evidently—and if the introductory speech in the first *Liber visionum* truly represents her view, then also willingly—become subordinate to, dependent upon his judgments. And although only in a few passages does this dependence become explicit, still nowhere in the visionary records do we find a counterbalancing suggestion of any dependence of Ekbert on Elisabeth. Spiritual authority here is exercised in one direction only.

CONCLUSION

Ekbert the man of learning, the theologically trained cleric, who enlists Elisabeth's aid as a sort of researcher into the heavenly realms by posing various questions to her and who acts, with her approval and even gratitude, as sole gatekeeper between a fragile visionary and her audience: such is Ekbert as he presents himself in the collection of Elisabeth's visions. He does not belittle Elisabeth's powers, even though they are informal powers, derived from no office, lodged in no hierarchy. On the contrary, he earnestly promotes her reputation as a divinely graced visionary. But by the same token, and with that task

of promotion in mind, he also looks upon her as naturally subordinate to himself—that is, to his own powers of discretion, which are not informal at all but
rather derive from his status as a cleric and a man of learning, and which he
employs both to limit and to protect her.

Ekbert's stance toward Elisabeth is one that places her, ostensibly beneficent-
ly, in subordination to himself. But two elements of another possible, though
unrealized, stance are also present in these texts. One is that devotion to her,
apparent in *De obitu*, whereby he is not so much her protector and manager
as the recipient of her graces. The other is the brief occasional signal that Elisabeth's visionary world might not be entirely subject to his discretion after all,
as when the pouting angel declares that he "offends me and my brothers." Such
moments in the texts offer just a glimpse of a different kind of relationship
between a cleric and a visionary woman, one in which his own powers cannot
simply take precedence over hers but rather must acknowledge in her powers
some measure of independence, that is, arrive at some sort of balance with them
that acknowledges an authority that he cannot override. In Ekbert's case, the
glimpse is fleeting at best. But we get a better look at such a possibility in the
literary exchanges that were to take place between Elisabeth's mentor Hildegard
of Bingen and the monk Guibert of Gembloux just a few years after Elisabeth's
death, perhaps even before Ekbert had put the final touches on the collection
of her visions.

CHAPTER 3

A Shared Endeavor?

Guibert of Gembloux on Hildegard of Bingen

IN THE LAST TWO YEARS of the life of the abbess and prophet Hildegard of Bingen (1098–1179), the monk Guibert of Gembloux (c. 1125–1213) lived in her monastery. One of his several tasks there was to collaborate with her in producing texts of her visions, as Ekbert had collaborated with Elisabeth. But Guibert was no Ekbert: not only was his association with Hildegard of much briefer duration than Ekbert's with Elisabeth, but he neither possessed nor claimed, as Ekbert had done, the power to stand as gatekeeper between the woman and her audience. Hildegard was not his subordinate, and he did not imagine otherwise. Instead, he tried to think of Hildegard as his colleague in the monastic life; her revelations do not constitute his only point of orientation to her. Consequently, his writings to and about Hildegard, while acknowledging, even celebrating, her revelatory gifts, do not treat those gifts as a subject unto themselves but place them in the context of her whole monastic life, a life that he treats as exemplary and amenable to being shared. He presents himself as her colleague.

In the collection of Guibert's writings that was preserved at Gembloux, there is also a short treatise by Hildegard, the so-called "Vision Sent to Guibert," through which she responded, in effect, to Guibert's bid to be her colleague. It is a response in which Hildegard hints at an understanding of the relation between holy woman and attending cleric that was decisively different from Guibert's, but also from Ekbert's. She, as receiver of revelations, casts herself neither as the man's colleague nor his subordinate; rather, her own calling as prophet and his calling as priest (Guibert's priesthood rather than his monastic profession being the important point for her) occupy two distinct spheres, each with its own discrete definition, task, and authority—spheres that are to be neither merged nor ordered by rank.

These texts, therefore, present both Guibert's view of his relationship to Hildegard and a counterview of her own. The two do not directly debate each other, but still this question is clearly at stake for both of them: In what terms *other than terms of subordination* is the relationship between the man and the woman to be understood?

GUIBERT AND HILDEGARD

Guibert was a learned monk of literary bent.[1] Most of his writing that has survived is preserved in three codices that were produced at Gembloux in the thirteenth century and are now in the Royal Library in Brussels.[2] His literary output included two vitae of Martin of Tours and a vita of Martin's hagiographer Sulpicius Severus, but it was otherwise almost completely in the form of highly polished letters, written in a somewhat lugubrious style and full of learned allusions to both classical and Christian authors. Most are addressed to monastic figures, but some are to great secular clerics, most notably the Cologne archbishop Philip of Heinsberg and the Mainz archbishop Siegfried of Eppenstein.[3] In all, seventy-four of Guibert's letters survive, most of them in the form in which he himself collected and edited them toward the end of his life.[4]

From the letters, the major events of Guibert's life can be gathered.[5] He was probably educated in the external school of the abbey of Gembloux, in the diocese of Liège in the southern Low Countries, and at some point he became a monk at that abbey. With the permission of his abbot, he resided at Hildegard's monastery of Rupertsberg, near Bingen on the Rhine, from 1177 to 1180, in circumstances that I shall consider in a moment, and for eight months in 1180 and 1181 in Tours, where he made pilgrimage to the sites of St. Martin. After a fire destroyed the abbey of Gembloux in 1185 he traveled again to Tours, now to make his profession at the abbey of Marmoutiers, which had been founded by his beloved St. Martin, but then the Gembloux monastic community reconstituted itself and called him back. In 1188 or 1189 he became abbot of the nearby monastery of Florennes, but five years later he was elected abbot of Gembloux, to which he thus returned once more. In 1204 he gave up his abbacy to live out his years as a simple monk at Florennes.[6] There he died in 1213 or 1214.

It is also Guibert's letters that tell us about his relationship with Hildegard. He initiated his correspondence with her in 1175.[7] In his first two letters he expressed his admiration for her visionary gift, requested her intercessions on behalf of himself and others, and asked for specifics about how she received her visions.[8] When she replied within a few months fulfilling both requests, Guibert wrote her back to describe his own and others' admiring reactions to her letter.[9] The correspondence continued over the next two years, much of it centering on Guibert's request for answers to thirty-eight questions posed by the Cistercian monks of Villers on various obscurities of Scripture and divine dispensation—answers that he seems to have hoped would constitute a superior monastic alternative to the teachings of the schools.[10] He also visited her at the Rupertsberg at least once and probably twice in this period.[11] In the course of time he accepted her invitation to reside with her there. The invitation was contained, however, in a letter that he did not preserve, and so how she framed it remains obscure. He arrived there sometime in 1177, ostensibly to help her with her "books";[12] very likely, as Lieven van Acker has argued, this help included the task of compiling the so-called "Riesenkodex" (Hessische Landesbibliothek, MS 2), which appears to have been intended as a definitive collection of Hildegard's works.[13] But soon, upon the death of both Hildegard's brother Hugo, who had overseen the external business of the monastery, and an unnamed canon of Mainz, who had had pastoral care of the nuns, Guibert took over those tasks also.[14]

Hildegard herself was about seventy-seven years of age, with most of her life behind her, when she received Guibert's first letter. She had been an enclosed religious from her early childhood. It had been some thirty-five years since she had had the vision that inaugurated her public career as a visionary prophet, and she had already produced her three major literary works based on her visions, namely, *Scivias*, the *Liber vitae meritorum* (Book of the merits of life), and the *Liber vitae meritorum* (Book of the works of God). Guibert was therefore not destined to figure in the major achievements of her life. It is important to note, however that Hildegard had *never* countenanced a collaborator with the power to approve her visions and to stand between her and her audience. Her refusal to do so was no incidental feature of her visionary career but expresses the claim to direct divine validation that lay at its heart—a claim that, at crucial moments, had supported her resistance to the wishes of men of ecclesiastical authority such as the abbot of Disibodenberg or the cathedral chapter of Mainz.[15] Even the most important of the figures who preceded Guibert in assisting her—the monk Volmar of Disibodenberg, who died in 1173 and to whom she refers in each of her major works as a "witness" to the truth of her revelations, apparently in the sense that he had observed how the divine scourge of her illness had compelled her to write—never appears in the sources in any sense as her director, however highly she valued his encouragement and advice.[16] In this sense Guibert stood in continuity with her previous collaborators.

Guibert stayed at Hildegard's monastery until her death (29 September 1179) and a few months beyond it, during which time (as will be seen) he began, but did not finish, a vita of the saint.[17] But his departure seems to have marked the effective end of his active interest in Hildegard. Afterward he had little to say about her, although he corresponded with the sisters at the Rupertsberg until 1186. Only sometime after 1204, when he was in retirement, did he briefly take up again his vita of the saint—apparently, however, without advancing it toward completion—and he also made some changes, mostly stylistic, in the copy of the vita of Hildegard by Theoderic of Echternach that he received, in that late phase of his life, from the abbot Godfrey of St. Eucherius in Trier.[18]

GUIBERT AS HAGIOGRAPHER

Guibert began a vita of Hildegard, probably shortly after her death. He never finished it. Yet the vita contains enough of substance to suggest the main lines of Guibert's distinctive approach to the saint, especially when compared to the other hagiography about Hildegard that was taking shape at the time. What makes Guibert's approach distinctive is his emphasis on Hildegard's collegiality with others: for him, her monastic community is not a background against which to present her prophetic calling but instead is the central component of that calling.

In the form in which we have it, the vita forms the concluding portion of the letter Guibert wrote to his friend the monk Bovo of Gembloux soon after arriving at the Rupertsberg monastery in 1177. In theme, the vita fits well with this letter. The earlier passages of the letter glow with enthusiasm for both the Rupertsberg and its leader, whom Guibert describes in terms that suggest less a prophet than a model monastic superior in a model community, which he contrasts with Gembloux. "Here," he tells Bovo, "a wonderful contest of virtues is to be seen," between the obedient daughters and the mother Hildegard who, "expending herself from love, is always fully occupied with giving counsel to all who ask it, answering the most difficult questions for those who bring them forward, writing books, teaching the sisters, comforting the sinners who come to her."[19] Then in the vita Guibert relates, in sequence, Hildegard's oblation as a child at Disibodenberg under the recluse Jutta, Jutta's own strict commitment to the cloister, Hildegard's strong identification with this unworldly monastic community, her reluctant assumption of the office of *magistra* after Jutta's death, her exercise of wise and compassionate leadership, and her reliance on a certain monk of the Rupertsberg community (apparently Volmar, though here he is not named) when God obliged her to record her visions and make them known. The vita then ends abruptly with a description of the abbot's hesitation at an answer to her request for Volmar's aid.[20] In the vita, as in the previous portion of the letter, Guibert certainly understands her visions as marvelous and unique, yet he presents the visionary as first and foremost a nun and abbess, emphatically set apart from the secular world but not from her community.

Though the vita harmonizes nicely with the rest of the letter to Bovo, it almost certainly did not originally belong to it. When the letter makes its rather abrupt transition ("But enough of these things [*Et de his quidem hactenus*]") to the narrative of her life, its stated purpose to tell Bovo "how things are with me, and what is going on around me, and what are the virtues of the venerable mother Hildegard and the sisters serving God under her rule" has in fact already been fulfilled.[21] The paragraph that then introduces the narrative refers to her death as an accomplished fact, which suggests that the vita dates originally from at least two years after the letter.[22] In that case the vita preserved in the letter to Bovo is probably the very vita to which Guibert made reference in a letter that he wrote later, sometime after the saint's death, to her admirer Philip of Heinsberg, archbishop of Cologne. There we learn that during Guibert's stay at the Rupertsberg, while Hildegard was still alive, he had agreed to Philip's request that he write something about her. He says that he began the task only after she died, however, and that when he was obliged to return to Gembloux at the command of his abbot, whom he had been able to put off only as long as Hildegard had lived, he abandoned it.[23] This would have been in late 1179 or 1180.[24]

If, as seems likely, the vita preserved in the letter to Bovo is the vita of which Guibert wrote to Philip, then for us it acquires the added interest of having a direct connection to the project that would produce the definitive work of Hildegardean hagiography, the *Vita sanctae Hildegardis* compiled by the monk Theoderic of Echternach. In the letter to Philip, Guibert frames his explanation of his efforts at a vita by reference to two works about Hildegard by other authors. One of these was what he calls a "little book about her life [*libellus vitae ejus*]," which came to his attention when he finally began his research by questioning Hildegard's longtime companions. The discovery meant that he would no longer attempt a vita from scratch but instead would revise this *libellus*—a task that, he says, the nuns themselves urged upon him: "since it appeared that the style in which that book was written was humble, I was begged by a chorus of a great many of her daughters … that, by bringing together the things that were contained in that work along with anything that I might find that pertained to her particularly in the volumes that she herself had written, and adding her death, I might improve the words as far as I was able."[25] The second work that Guibert mentions is one that represented the completion of the task Guibert abandoned: after he had left for Gembloux, Guibert tells Philip, the sisters chose someone else to complete and revise the *libellus*, and that person finished the job—indeed, he adds magnanimously, did better that he himself would have done. He suggests that Philip ask the Rupertsberg nuns for a copy of the man's work.[26]

What were these two works? Who were the authors? Guibert says that the *libellus* had been composed by Hildegard's "first son," which would seem to refer to Volmar of Disibodenberg, and modern scholars such as Ildefons Herwegen have assumed that Volmar must have produced a vita that is now lost.[27] But as Monica Klaes has now shown, the task that Guibert describes is strongly reminiscent of the task Theoderic of Echternach undertook in the *Vita sanctae Hildegardis*, namely to complete an extant vita by one Godfrey who was, as is known from a later letter in Guibert's own collection, a monk of Disibodenberg who had died in 1176—a vita that Theoderic presented to his readers as book 1 of the *Vita sanctae Hildegardis*.[28] The sequence of events in Guibert's vita is indeed the same as in the opening sections of Godfrey's: her birth, her precocious asceticism in childhood, her parents' resolve to set her apart, her oblation at the age of eight, her subsequent upbringing under Jutta (*GGE* 38.103–224; *VSH* 1.1.1–1.2.20), and then her divine commission to record what she saw in her visions, the illness that attended her reluctance to do so, and finally the confidence she placed in a certain monk (presumably Volmar) about this matter, who in turn brought it before her abbot (*GGE* 38.371–450; *VSH* 1.3.1–10). (Guibert adds an account of Jutta herself and of Hildegard's election as her successor.)[29] It appears likely that the *libellus* that Guibert set about to revise was precisely Godfrey's vita, even though Guibert, disingenuously or not, attributed it to Volmar, and that even though Guibert's voice is not to be heard in the *Vita sanctae Hildegardis*, he nonetheless partook in the project that Theoderic brought to completion.[30]

Certain voices do resound clearly in the completed *Vita sanctae Hildegardis*, and these provide instructive points of comparison with Guibert. As Barbara Newman has recently pointed out, the work witnesses to three distinct perspectives on the saint's life: not only that of Godfrey's *libellus*, which forms most of

book 1, but also that of Hildegard herself in a series of twelve autobiographical
texts preserved by Theoderic and presented at intervals throughout books 2
and 3, and finally the perspective of Theoderic as it becomes evident in those
same books in his comments on Hildegard's narratives. Godfrey, for his part,
presents the saint as preeminently a recognized prophet whose gift was vali-
dated by miracles and approved by ecclesiastical authorities, most importantly
Pope Eugenius III, and who brought renown to both the Disibodenberg and
Rupertsberg monasteries.[31] As for Hildegard's first-person narratives—which
according to Klaes's hypothesis would have been found by Theoderic among
the materials that Guibert had collected in the research for his vita—it remains
obscure in what circumstances she produced them, and whether she intended
them to constitute a single work.[32] But it is clear that she was intent on presenting her own prophetic calling not in terms of official validation as in Godfrey's
narrative but rather in terms of her own experience and conviction, construing
her own illnesses and difficulties as, like those of Biblical prophets, seals of her
authority.[33] Finally, as for Theoderic himself, the compiler of the *Vita sanctae
Hildegardis* probably had not known the saint personally and, except for a series
of miracle stories in book 3, provided little information about her beyond what
Godfrey's vita and Hildegard's autobiographical narratives contained. Nonetheless, in his comments on those narratives he shows himself distinctively, as
Newman puts it, "less concerned with her ability to speak *for* God than her
privileged relationship *with* God, which is significantly gendered" so as to make
her a mystically privileged bride of Christ and accordingly anticipates an approach to female sanctity that would later become popular but that was alien to
Hildegard's self-understanding.[34]

Guibert's approach to Hildegard differs from those of all these three strands
of the *Vita sanctae Hildegardis*, in two important ways: first, her visionary gift
lacks the definitive place in Guibert's presentation that it has in theirs, and second, he accords a much more significant role in her prophecy to her collaborator Volmar.

In treating Hildegard's early years, the three strands of the *Vita sanctae Hildegardis* all take her visionary gift as their principal point of orientation. Hildegard is first and foremost a visionary. In the saint's own narrative of her early
life, as preserved by Theoderic in book 2, she preeminently explains herself as
such: "Wisdom teaches and directs me, in the light of charity, to say how I was
established in this vision"[35]—"vision" understood here in the generic sense of
the mode of constant supernatural sight that was, she says, implanted in her
before birth. She mentions the events of her life only as they touch upon the

manifestation of that visionary gift. She does not speak directly of her oblation or her early years under Jutta, and when she introduces Jutta it is as a witness to her visions: "for the fear that I had toward people, I did not dare to say how it was I saw; but a certain noble woman, to whom I was submitted in discipline, noticed these things and opened them to a certain monk known to her."[36] Theoderic, for his part, glosses her narrative at this point by casting Hildegard as the bride of the Song of Songs, but nonetheless like Hildegard herself he keeps his attention fixed on her visionary gift. Godfrey, in book 1, says more about her early years with Jutta, but he too is broadly concerned with explaining her visionary gift. He introduces Jutta as teacher, characterizing the extent of the knowledge she imparted as modest in contrast to the evident erudition of Hildegard's many literary works, and at this point he quotes her introduction to *Scivias* to the effect that her understanding of the Scriptures derived from her divine inspiration rather than from any human learning.[37] Godfrey proceeds then to speak of her growth in virtue in the monastery—invoking Jutta as a witness that in this respect she had advanced from pupil to teacher—and of her increasing physical illness which corresponded with an increase in spiritual fervor. Godfrey presents all of this growth specifically as preparing the way for the moment when she would receive the divine commission to make her visions known: "When her holy resolve had grown over many years, and she was intent on pleasing God alone, and the time was finally at hand for her life and teaching to be made known for the improvement of many, a divine voice came directing her not to delay in writing anything else that she would see or hear."[38]

Guibert's vita, in contrast to the *Vita sanctae Hildegardis*, does not take the saint's visionary gift as its beginning point. Instead he begins by treating her early years with Jutta in their own right and at length, discussing her visionary gift only afterward, against the background of those years. What he particularly stresses about Hildegard's years with Jutta is her effective separation from the world outside the monastery, and by implication her pure commitment to the monastic life. He points out that her oblation as a child separated her from her parents and siblings and "left her hoping in the mercy of God alone and casting not only her thoughts but her whole self upon him."[39] He proceeds with an extensive description—in effect a little vita, as Klaes has called it—of Jutta, establishing the older woman as a model of renunciation who rejected suitors and built a cell adjoining the male monastery of Disibodenberg that he likens, in its sequestration, to a prison or tomb.[40] He describes in detail the funereal rites by which the eight-year-old Hildegard joined Jutta in that cell, where they communicated with the outside world only through one small window, and he presents this *mausoleum* as maintained in its strict enclosure even when many new girls joined them.[41] Finally, after he has told of Jutta's death and Hildegard's reluctant assumption of her office (events not mentioned in the *Vita sanctae Hildegardis*) and spoken of the virtues—moderation, compassion, patience—that she displayed, Guibert comes to the moment of Hildegard's divine commission to make her visions known.[42] But since he has made no prior reference to her visions, the commission stands not an as episode in a visionary career but simply as the culmination of the monastic virtues that he has been describing:

> When she was still dwelling in the place of her conversion, some years after the death of Mistress Jutta she took, though reluctantly, the office of holy prelacy, God already arranging to divulge her merits, and to manifest her to the world and exalt her for an example to the praise of his name and the improvement of many, and the word of God was given to her, not as a nocturnal vision, but as an open rebuke to her, which directed that she declare in writing what had been divinely revealed to her, and hand it over to the church to be read.[43]

Only after these comments does Guibert turn back to the saint's childhood to describe the mode of her visions, and only then does he refer to her description of this commissioning in the introduction to *Scivias*—the description on which Godfrey, in contrast, had predicated his whole account of her early years.

The other major difference between Guibert's vita and the *Vita sanctae Hildegardis* is to be found in his treatment of the role of the monk-collaborator to whom Hildegard turned after she received her divine commission to make her visions known. All the strands of Theoderic's compilation make mention of this figure, that is, Volmar (although here he is unnamed). For Hildegard herself, in the autobiographical narrative preserved in book 2, he was a figure of encouragement and understanding, but she makes it clear that in the first place it was not because of him but rather because of her own "powers" that she overcame her reluctance to comply with the divine command:

> Then in the same vision I was obliged, by great pressure of pains, to make public what I had seen and heard, but I feared greatly, and was ashamed to bring forth what I had until then kept back. However my veins and marrow were then full of the power that I lacked from my childhood and youth. These things I made known to a certain monk, my teacher, who was of good con-

versation and diligent intention and like a stranger to the questioning habits of many people, for which reason he freely listened to these marvels. He, in admiration, enjoined me to write down the hidden things, until he could see what they were and whence they came. Understanding then that they were from God, he made this known to his abbot and from then on, with a great desire, he worked with me in these things.[44]

Theoderic, similarly, is at pains to give a negative answer to the implicit question whether the collaborator was in any way a source of the visions themselves:

> It is a great thing and worthy of wonder, that those things that she heard or saw in the spirit, in the same meaning and with the same words, with an upright and clear mind, she wrote with her own hand or made their contents known orally to one faithful scribe [symmista], who in the light of the art of grammar, with which she was unfamiliar, supplied cases, tense and gender, but in no way presumed to add or take away from her meaning or understanding.[45]

Godfrey, for his part, has less to say about the monk, mentioning him only in passing as the one to whom Hildegard first revealed the cause of her illness and who then told the abbot and thus began the chain of information that led to the Archbishop of Mainz and through him to Pope Eugenius, whose approbation of the saint Godfrey particularly celebrates.

Therefore in the accounts in the *Vita sanctae Hildegardis*, Volmar appears as instrumental in making Hildegard's visions known, but little more. Guibert, however, accords him a much more important role in her visionary career. He attributes her initial reluctance, in the wake of her commission, to her own lack of knowledge: she was terrified lest her pronouncements bring derision upon herself rather than instruction to others, and Guibert considers the fear well-grounded: "indeed, she was untaught as far as grammatical erudition went."[46] Enter Volmar:

> Meanwhile... there was introduced in the same monastery a sober monk, chaste and learned in his heart and wise in his speech, who, immediately when these things became known to him, freely consented to her desire and, showing a censor's caution, clothed her bare and unpolished words with the attire of a more decorous speech.[47]

The implication here is that Volmar represented God's own answer to her concern, and therefore that the involvement of others was not incidental to her fulfilling of her calling—a point that is underscored by Guibert's account of her subsequent train of thought as she came to the decision to reveal her visions. For he says that, among various biblical passages that would invalidate the excuse of human insufficiency in the face of God's call, she recalled the story of Moses, who, worrying about his "uncircumcised lips and lack of eloquence" took on Aaron his brother as communicative helper (Exod. 6:12, 30; 7:2).[48] And Guibert's mind is still on the importance of not going it alone when he then describes Hildegard approaching the abbot of Disibodenberg with her request for Volmar's aid, on the grounds that it would be presumptuous to make the decision by herself.[49]

In the end, what distinguishes Guibert's approach to Hildegard in this unfinished vita from the approaches of the writers of the *Vita sanctae Hildegardis* is his emphasis on the importance of her immediate community. He is less concerned than Godfrey or Theoderic or indeed Hildegard herself in staking out her charismatic distinctness from those around her and more concerned to place her within the context of her monastic community, to the extent of making her collaboration with others a necessary component of her calling. The idea that a visionary woman's gifts were essentially bound into the life of her community is not an idea that would catch on among later hagiographers of such women, especially male hagiographers. Nonetheless Guibert gave it considerable thought not only in this fragmentary vita but also in his correspondence.

GUIBERT AS COLLABORATOR

In the letters that he wrote to or about Hildegard, Guibert regards her in terms of the monastic calling she shares with him rather than in terms of a prophetic calling distinct to itself that would have set her apart from him and others in some definitive way. In this sense, he writes less as a devotee than as a colleague who shares in her work, and for him there is no question of a tension, fruitful or otherwise, between formal and informal powers, as though he and she were speaking or acting from distinct bases of authority.

Guibert displayed, to be sure, an intense interest in Hildegard's visions, especially at the beginning of their acquaintance. The visions were what brought him to her in the first place, and his admiration shines brightly in his first letters to her, where he declares her visions to be unprecedented marvels in both mode and content. There he compares her favorably with the female biblical prophets Miriam, Deborah, and Judith, who did not have access to divine mysteries as great as Hildegard's.[50] Nor, he writes, does he know of anything to equal either of the kinds of light that, in her first letter to him, she professed to see: one of these, the "shadow of the living light [umbra viventis lucis]," is constantly visible to her, and in this she surpasses the prophets of the Old Testament, such as Nathan or Elijah, whom the prophetic spirit sometimes deserted; and the other, more extraordinary, light, the "living light [lux vivens]" itself, which takes away her pains and makes her like a girl again, is something altogether unheard of.[51] He finds her gifts comparable to the great gifts of the Spirit at Pentecost, in the sense that she receives them not in dreams or in a trance but rather while she is awake.[52] Furthermore her prophecies cause her to transcend the limits of her sex.[53] For since the Spirit teaches her directly, she can rightly teach others and is therefore "unbound" from Pauline proscription on female teachers in the church, even though she obeys it in the strict sense that she does not address congregations in church buildings. And though she covers her head in keeping with the other Pauline restriction on women, still the fact that "matched with not just any man but with men of the height of eminence, she observes the glory of the Lord with unveiled face, is transformed in his image, from clarity into clarity, as by the Spirit of the Lord" makes the covering irrelevant.[54] Guibert grandiosely describes himself treating the famous first letter from her as a sacred object, even before he had read it: sensing that there was something *venerabile et magnificum* in it and, fearing the divine judgments it might contain against him, he placed it on a convenient altar, prostrated himself, prayed for worthiness and purification, and only then read it, proclaiming afterward that what he encountered there was "more the voice of the Spirit or an angelic tongue, than a human one."[55]

But even in the early letters, for all his enthusiasm about her visionary gift Guibert somewhat misses the point of Hildegard's own sense of calling; or anyway he has his own way of seeing it. Already in his first letter to her he admonishes her at length on the subject of sin, almost routinely as it would seem: she has her treasure in a fragile vessel (cf. 2 Cor. 4.7); she should remember that winds can fell not just twigs and reeds but large ancient trees; she should recall the biblical figures David and Peter, apparently as examples of how the mighty may fall; she should consider that even if her chastity is beyond question, there are other sins to worry about besides sexual ones. And then as if to make the point that susceptibility to sin is something they share, he bewails his own sins as well.[56] Similarly at the end of the letter in which he relates his exuberant reaction to her first response, he makes sure to refer again to her vulnerability to sin, telling her that he will cut short his adulation since she may rightly find in it a temptation to think too highly of herself—a temptation, he says, that he knows well.[57] His point is that she ought not let her virtue be undermined by the success and fame that her visionary gift has brought her. It is a point that, to be sure, Hildegard herself acknowledged in that same first letter to Guibert that he so celebrated, yet with an important difference of emphasis. For there Hildegard understands her insufficiency, or rather her acknowledgment of it, not so much as a bond shared with Guibert but rather as the condition on which her distinctive prophetic calling rests. Many other people have been given the grace of understanding divine mysteries, she says, but have failed in ascribing their understanding to themselves; it is those who "thirsted for wisdom from God and counted themselves as nothing," like the apostle Paul and the evangelist John, who become the "pillars of heaven." Accordingly, "I always tremble with fear, since I know there is no possibility of security in myself."[58] She thus evokes as her instructive examples of flawed saints not the fallen Peter and David, as Guibert had done, but rather John and Paul, whose openness to divine calling presupposed their *prior* weaknesses—not, in other words, to illustrate the danger of losing virtue once attained but rather to establish an appropriate awareness of her smallness or insufficiency as essential to her success. To put the matter that way certainly does not contradict anything Guibert has written to her but gives it all a different cast. For he has exhorted her to humility in a spirit of commiseration. He has pictured her weakness not as itself the key to the visionary gift that sets her apart from himself and others but rather as a condition shared with himself and others, a point of contact between them.

When Guibert, shortly after his arrival at the Rupertsberg, wrote his letter to Bovo of Gembloux—to which he would eventually attach his unfinished vita—to report "how I am doing, and what is going on around me, and the virtues of the venerable mother Hildegard and the sisters serving under her direction," it was exactly her points of contact with himself and others that interested him.[59] It is not that he exposes her weaknesses here; on the contrary, he praises her virtues. But the virtues he has in mind are not the marks of a prophet but those of a model monastic superior, devoted to the sisters of her community. Here he makes no direct reference to her visions, only to "writing books."[60] As for Guibert's own relationship to Hildegard, he writes in terms that suggest a reciprocity or balance of responsibilities: he benefits from her ministrations, as everyone else in the monastery does, but he also has something to offer, namely pastoral care for everyone and literary help for Hildegard.

I live with her in the beauty of peace and of all delight and sweetness. I am directed by her counsels, supported by her prayers, I press forward by her merits, I am upheld by her kindnesses, and daily I enjoy conversation with her. She wants nothing more at the present, as far as external things go, than that I might remain living in the house of the Lord that she rules all the days of my life, and that I might undertake both the spiritual care [interiorem curam] of her and her daughters, and the consideration of the books that she has written.[61]

Again, Hildegard the visionary appears only obliquely in the reference to "books that she has written," and insofar as he refers to himself as giving "consideration" to these at her wish, he implies that the visionary enterprise is something she somehow shares, or at least for which she asks assistance. As noted below, Hildegard was, or became, careful to limit his assistance, but here in Guibert's account there is no question of that. In his view her visions, to the extent that they belong in the picture at all, occupy a niche in the shared life of the monastic community.

Two years later, shortly before Hildegard's death, Guibert wrote another letter about the Rupertsberg monastery and his place there, but in this letter, in contrast to the letter to Bovo, Hildegard appears in an unflattering light. The letter is addressed to Ralph, a monk of the Cistercian monastery of Villers.[62] Several years earlier, Guibert had helped the Villers monks by prevailing upon Hildegard to use her visionary powers to provide answers to thirty-eight questions, mostly about obscurities or apparent contradictions in Scripture. Now Ralph has sent thirty-three new questions.[63] Stating bluntly that he cannot get the answers from Hildegard, Guibert lists the obstacles that prevent him. She is weak and ill, kept so by an angel who buffets her for the sake of her humility.[64] She is very old, and her many years of asceticism have consumed her body so that her flesh sticks to her bones. "From such an instrument, destroyed by the blistering of age and by the perforations of weakness, what you hear is groans, not gracious teaching."[65] And to cap it all, she is destitute of the help of her deceased brother Hugo who had been serving as provost and is compelled to take care of many details of the monastery that Guibert, not knowing the German language, cannot help her with, nor is the abbot of St. Disibod at all cooperative—with the result that she certainly has no time for searching out answers to questions. But even that is not the whole of it. Guibert goes on to suggest that she has never really had the time; for although she did reply to some of the earlier questions from the Villers monks, her answers, which anyway have been lost, were brief and insufficient.[66] The picture of Hildegard is of a sick, overwrought old woman. He concludes by recommending to Ralph and the Villers monks to take their questions instead to some learned French *magister*.[67]

Although the tone of this letter with its unidealized treatment of Hildegard differs strikingly from that of the earlier letters, still his view of her remains consistent at least in the sense that he had always stopped short of making her an object of devotion, even when he spoke of her in glowing terms. Indeed his major purpose in the letter to Ralph is to argue that it was never a mere personal devotion to Hildegard that brought him to her monastery. Unnamed critics had questioned his motives,[68] and Guibert answers them at great length. He admits that it was he who initiated his correspondence with her but argues that he did so to test her genuineness because he had found the reports of her hard to believe.[69] He describes his opening letter to her in terms of this diagnostic intent.[70] Just so, he accounts for his decision to pay a first visit on her by saying that he did not understand what she had written him and wanted to clear it up.[71] He portrays himself in the period of the early letters, therefore, not as an interested individual attracted to Hildegard but rather as a monk conscientiously concerned for rectitude. Then he protests that it was later not at his own initiative, but at Hildegard's, that he came to live at the Rupertsberg, for it was she who asked him to render assistance to her as Volmar had done before his death. Subsequently he only stayed, he says, because she pleaded with him to do so at least until she could get someone else to attend her.[72] Then two months later when he was about to accept an invitation to become a monk at the reform-oriented abbey of St. Amand, it was Hildegard and her sisters who refused to let him go.[73] Then the deaths of Hugo and of an unnamed monk who had ministered to the nuns obliged Guibert to assume their responsibilities and ensconced him further at the Rupertsberg through no initiative of his own.[74] When his own abbot came from Gembloux to fetch him back, it was once again not he but Hildegard, along with her sisters and the bishop of Liège, who stood in the way, prevailing upon the abbot to let him stay.[75] In this way he absolves himself of responsibility for his connection to the Rupertsberg: it was not from interested motives but entirely from disinterested ones, or because of forces beyond his control, that he came to Hildegard and stayed with her so long.

In the letters when taken together, it is hard to avoid the impression of a certain ambivalence or tension in Guibert: clearly he was, or had been, fascinated by Hildegard and her gifts, but he was at pains to minimize or rationalize that fascination, even at the end to deny it. Why? Perhaps the key lies in the very overkill of his long self-defense to Ralph, who himself seems to have made only the merest mention of Guibert's critics (though we should keep in mind that we know Ralph's letter only through the letter collection that Guibert himself edited).[76] The charge that goaded Guibert was that in leaving Gembloux and delaying his return he had been guilty of "levity" or "instability";[77] or that, as he paraphrases (or quotes?) his critics, he has "left the house of his own profession, in which he ought to have been making good on his vows and working for reform, and instead, eating another's bread without paying for it [cf. 2 Thess. 3.8], he lingers with weak women and makes jests, lusting with girls in the recesses of the cloister, and lives in idleness."[78] The charges imply, anyway, that his very attention to Hildegard was a breach of monastic discipline and that her prophetic gift drew his affections, sirenlike, in the wrong direction.

All of this touches a sore spot in Guibert. He is at pains then to justify his cohabitation with women and cites an abundance of biblical precedents, for instance of Christ's and the apostles' inclusion of women in their ministry.[79] One suspects from his indignation that he is not entirely convinced of his own innocence. This anyway is the heart of his concern to picture Hildegard as, for all her gifts, fundamentally just an exemplary abbess: he cannot quite come to terms with her exceptionality. The letters suggest that Guibert may have glimpsed in Hildegard something of what, in hindsight, we recognize as the potent generic figure of the charismatic female saint, who will be irresistible to so many later ecclesiastical men precisely in her charismatic uniqueness, her fascinating alienation from her own environment—and he is trying to turn away, even as he affirms Hildegard's visionary gift and the fruits it has borne in her writings.

The "Visio ad Guibertum Missa"

If Guibert finally shied away from presenting Hildegard in her uniqueness as a prophet, Hildegard herself had no hesitation in presenting herself so. In the "Visio ad Guibertum Missa," she sketches out to Guibert her own way of thinking about herself and about his relationship to her.

This "Visio" is an explicated vision that Hildegard addressed to Guibert, apparently during his stay at the Rupertsberg, although whether early or late in that stay is unclear. Here it becomes apparent that Guibert has asked for a more collaborative role in her literary work, a request that appears consistent with the collegial emphasis in his writings about her. Hildegard, in response, reflects not only on her own prophetic role in the light of Guibert's expressed desire but also his role as priest, in a way that implies that there is a precise distinction to be made between them which his request has misguidedly blurred.

The text of the "Visio" is contained in Guibert's letter collection, appended to the letter he wrote to Philip of Heinsberg about the project of a vita of Hildegard.[80] Guibert explains in that letter that instead of the vita that he never finished he is sending Philip this vision, which he calls a "letter full of wonderful instruction," as well as the account of a vision of St. Martin, which Hildegard also produced for Guibert: "Since I knew you to love her greatly, and yet I have not been able to satisfy you with an account of her deeds, at least receive some consolation from her words, which I am sending you: so read carefully not only a letter full of wonderful instruction but also a beautiful vision divinely shown to her of the excellence of St. Martin, both of which, carrying her meaning but written by my pen, she sent to a certain friend of hers."[81] He states outright that it is he who has recorded these texts, and, especially since in this text itself Hildegard permits him to give a literary polishing to such visions as she had specifically addressed to him, it is probable that some or many of the words and phrases here may be Guibert's and not Hildegard's. But in a broader sense the voice here, which both praises and chides Guibert and astutely defines her own prophetic calling, sounds forth unmistakably as Hildegard's, whatever stylistic revisions the text has undergone; it is possible to take Guibert cautiously at his word that he has preserved her "meaning."

The text ostensibly elaborates to Guibert a vision concerning himself.[82] Of the twenty-nine paragraphs of the letter in Pitra's edition, scholars of Hildegard have tended to pay attention only to the last five, in which her almost complete rebuff of Guibert's apparent request for an editorial role in her vision writing helps establish a basis for confidence that her visionary texts really convey her own words.[83] This is, to be sure, a point of great importance for the study of Hildegard's writings. But the letter also merits being read as a whole, in which case it becomes clear that those often-cited paragraphs serve as conclusion to a long didactic exposition—a "letter full of wonderful instruction"—tailored for Guibert.[84] The letter as a whole tells him his proper relationship to God and to others. Seen in that context, those final paragraphs, which correct what Hildegard considers his misunderstanding of herself, tell him how *her* relationship to God and to others is different from his own. In the letter taken as a whole, her understanding of those relationships finds expression in her treatment of his and her respective roles or callings—priesthood in his case, prophecy in hers. By portraying Guibert as a priest and then presenting herself as a prophet, she places the two callings side by side; although the comparison is not explicit, nonetheless her perception of their difference emerges clearly. Both priest and prophet serve as mediators between the human and the divine. The difference lies in the mode of mediation: whereas Guibert's priestly role positions him *between* God and humans and therefore separate from each, Hildegard's prophetic role identifies her *with* God, causes her literally to speak to humans *for* God.

Hildegard positions Guibert between God and humans by distinguishing him from both, setting him apart from (and effectively above) other people by virtue of divine favor but also apart from God by virtue of his human, therefore sinful, nature. As for setting him apart from others, she is at work on this already at the beginning of the letter, describing the vision that it ostensibly elaborates. That vision began, she says, with the personified virtues humility, obedience, and abstinence emerging from a cloud of fire to promise salvation to those perople, apparently including Guibert, who would persevere in them. Subsequently sparks flew out from the cloud to touch "many in our congregation," and finally a large spark touched the soul of Guibert, accompanied by a verse from the Song of Songs: "show me your face; let your voice sound in my ears; for your voice is sweet and your face is becoming" (Cant. 2.14).[85] She glosses the vision by telling him that God has been pleased with his habitual concern for salvation—for Guibert has "asked, and subtly considered, how the saints and elect of God … arrive at him"—and that he has done well to undertake prayer and praise of God in the monastic life.[86]

When, later in the letter, she comes to her most explicit consideration of Guibert as priest, she lays particular stress on his separateness from other people, using metaphors of clothing to make the point. She tells him that as a priest celebrating the Eucharist he officiates at the marriage between the believer and Christ, that is, between the *sponsa* and *sponsus* of the Song of Songs, and that as such he must preserve dignity and purity by wearing garments that are whole and clean, not appearing "with indecent, that is, common, attire that is torn or corrupted by the least stain."[87] Referring then to the parable of the man without a wedding garment, she makes the point a fortiori that his purity gains importance from his conspicuous placement between Christ and the believer: "If [the guest] could not hide amid the crowd of those attending such a great wedding, how will you—you who, in your ministry, must stand in the middle between the bridegroom and the bride, and extend to the bride the bread and cup which you hold in your hands from the bridegroom, and which the faith of believers understands to be set aside from other food?"[88] She adds that he must avoid intemperance in eating, drinking, and speaking, which would make him like the common throng and metaphorically deprive him of his clothing altogether, as in Exodus 32.6,25: "the people sat down to eat and drink, and rose up to play… and Moses saw that they were naked."[89]

Hildegard thus presents Guibert as someone divinely favored and set apart from others. But she also issues strong counterbalancing reminders of his sinfulness, both by warning him to keep it in check and by impressing on him his need for divine grace. She warns him at length against the danger of neglecting penitence and self-examination. The warning takes the form of a gloss on Song of Songs 1.7 ("If you do not know yourself, O fairest among women, go out and follow after the steps of the flock, and feed your goats by the shepherds' tents"), to the effect that without self-scrutiny he will find himself among "unstable and weak souls," will imitate the doctrine and example of the "irrational multitude," and will succumb to sensuality.[90] The possibility of repentance even if he falls into that danger (a possibility expressed by the beloved's position near the "tents of the shepherds," understood as priests) leads Hildegard to think of the return of the prodigal son (Luke 15), and she points to the older brother in the parable as a cautionary example of that "ignorance of the truth and of oneself," against which she is warning him.[91] Against such ignorance she prescribes a course of meditation on "the dignity of humanity's condition, the infidelity of its fall and the sublimity of its recovery"; she exhorts him to obey the Decalogue, to follow Christ's counsels of perfection, to renounce the world, to resist pride.[92] Then, when she is speaking more explicitly of his priesthood she says that his metaphorical garments should be bright (*candida*), meaning that he should be morally pure but that because of his own sinfulness, he must rely on God's purity to substitute for his own and therefore must pray for, as it were, God's clothing, "that the weakness of your nature might be worthy of being covered up by the vestments of his glory."[93] And when she exhorts him then to preach, she tells him he may depend upon God to supply his own inadequacies, in this case filling him with "the Spirit of wisdom, for the proclaiming of his praise in the midst of the Church, and for telling of his name to your brothers," which will be valuable to others even when his influence may seem small. She exhorts him to rely on God in the case of his own temptations. [94] Hildegard's picture of Guibert, then, which occupies the bulk of the letter, is of a figure set apart from, and in effect between, God and humans: a mediating figure, not incidentally a priest.

When Hildegard comes to speak of herself, in those final passages mentioned earlier, she sees herself also as a mediating figure, in the sense of making God known to humans. But there is a difference in the mode of mediation. She does not stand in a place of dignity between God and the believer, as Guibert does in conveying the sacraments, or preach to bring people to God as Guibert does. Rather, her words are God's *own* words. In this limited but potent sense she identifies herself with God, substitutes herself for God—as Guibert does not.

As already mentioned, it is Guibert's request for a role in her vision writing that, Hildegard says, has caused her to make these reflections on her own role. He has asked to "clothe" her visions in "more decent words, for since just as some foods, however useful of themselves, do not appetize if not cooked, also some writings, though they contain salutary directions, will be distasteful to ears accustomed to an urbane style if they are not rendered agreeable through some color of eloquence."[95] Hildegard does ostensibly grant his request and goes on to say that she accepts, "as you assert," that a "buffing" and polishing (rather than a fundamental change of meaning) is what Jerome accomplished by putting the scriptures, which were written in "uncultivated and simple style," into elegant Latin and that such a goal would be acceptable in the case of her writings too.[96] But she proceeds to place such drastic limits on her permission that she has all but withdrawn it by the time she has finished. For he is only to make such adjustments to visions that are "specially directed to you, or afterward to be directed to you." Of these, in fact, there are only two extant examples among all Hildegard's works, namely this letter itself and her vision of St. Martin.[97] Even so, he is not to alter the meaning of the visions.[98] And she is clearly uneasy about having made any concession at all. "For," she goes on to fret, "in my other, or former, writings I never granted this either to the girls who receive [them] from my lips nor to my uniquely beloved son of pious memory, Volmar, who carefully helped in these corrections before your time."[99] There is an unspoken question here: Why can Guibert not leave well enough alone, as Volmar did?

Hildegard then proceeds well beyond mere uneasiness about Guibert's request. She goes on not simply to excuse but even to defend the lack of eloquence that Guibert has wished to correct. It is here that she most clearly expresses her own self-understanding. She does so in terms consistent with the view she expressed in many other places in her work, that what proves her validity as a prophet is precisely her weakness as a human being.[100] She is like biblical writers, she says—like Moses and Paul and Jeremiah, who also lacked eloquence:

Nor let this defect of Latin eloquence that I suffer scandalize you, or any of my readers, because I am not given the faculty or competency of setting forth in Latin those things which are revealed to me or are commanded divinely to be put forth to be manifested through me—for the "intimus confabulator Dei" [Moses], profiting from ineloquence or impediment or lateness of language, received from God himself as interpreter his brother Aaron for supplementing his helplessness to the end of explaining the things for which he himself did not suffice; and Jeremiah, holy before he was born, testified that he did not know how to speak; and the "egregius praedicator" [Paul] not only asserted with his own voice that he was unskilled, not in knowledge, but in words [cf. 1 Cor 2.4], but also, as I have heard said, showed little care in his dictation.[101]

Moreover, such shortcomings in those who speak for God are not accidental. God sends infirmities precisely to those he has raised up. As for herself, from the time of her childhood, while God has been raising her up, apparently by granting her visions, he has also been striking her down, through an angel of Satan who caused her infirmity. She glories in this infirmity: "let the angel do what he will, nor spare it; I bravely give him my flesh to be sieved out, so that my spirit may be safe at the day of the Lord."[102] She feels for herself, as for Guibert, the necessity of stressing a distinctness from God, in view of the implicit danger of pride that a favored role—his or hers—might otherwise carry with it. But for her this is achieved not by a well-articulated mediatorship, a median mix of humility and purity, as in the case of Guibert, but rather a simultaneous embrace of the extremes of exaltation and debasement.

It is evident by the end of the "Visio" that she has been lecturing him on the proper understanding of her role as well as of his own. Then she concludes by exhorting Guibert once again to humility. Here, words that earlier on would have seemed but one more moral exhortation now carry the strong hint of a rebuke for overstepping. He has tried to associate himself with her by sharing in her visionary task. She tries to reformulate his association with her by specifying what she thinks should be *his* relation to the divine power from which her visions come. "If through the powers [*virtutes*] of which in the beginning I also declared myself to have seen the form, and heard the voices, you also wish to conquer and be crowned, humble yourself beneath the powerful hand of God, imitating the one who did not come to do his own will but was made obedient unto death." Her parting words concern abstinence from food, and given that he seems to have used the metaphor of food for the kind of literary revisions he has wanted to make, the words may suggest a double meaning: "since food does not commend us to God," for "the stomach is made for food and food for the stomach" (1 Cor.6.12), whereas God is "yesterday today and forever" (Heb. 13.8), let him castigate his body through abstinence, for abstinence makes one inwardly fat and well-fortified against all enemies.[103] Perhaps he should apply the lesson to his own relation to Hildegard? Let him cultivate his own priestly calling and not confuse his tasks with hers.

Guibert, in presenting himself as first and foremost Hildegard's colleague, had resisted the idea that she existed in some sphere separate from his own. But that is just the idea that Hildegard promotes in the "Visio." Not only are their spheres separate, but they are also carefully defined in terms of their distinct placement in relation to God and humanity and their distinct ways of mediating between the two. One sphere is that of priesthood, of the institutional office, in other words; the other is that of prophecy, informal in its dependence on God directly. The two potentially define a delicate balance that would depend for its vitality precisely on their distinctness from each other.[104] Hildegard, though in other respects quite different from the visionaries and mystics of the following century in her understanding of her task,[105] was anticipating things to come. For this is just the balance that would so fascinate clerics in their encounters with holy women a generation later.

CONCLUSION

If Hildegard's notion of the terms of her relationship with Guibert anticipates things to come, Guibert's does not. It is distinction, not overlap, between male and female roles that will dominate subsequent medieval male understandings of visionary women.

It may be that Guibert was neither unaware nor perhaps even displeased that there were standpoints different from his own from which to view Hildegard. He seems to have perceived that her most avid devotees came not from the monasteries but from the ranks of great secular clerics. In his letter to Philip of Heinsberg explaining why he did not intend to finish the vita of Hildegard that Philip had requested of him, Guibert says that he certainly understood Philip's desire for such a vita, for he had observed many prelates visiting Hildegard and of these it was Philip who came to her most often and with greatest devotion. And no doubt it was logical to commission a vita from himself, since he was in such a good position to gather information.[106] But in the course of his rather convoluted excuse, Guibert protests, among other things, that he lacks the erudition for the job. This is a topos of humility to be sure, not to be taken at face value. Nonetheless when he tells Philip that in asking him to write the vita, "putting aside the scholars (*magistri*) who were capable of the task, of whom there are many in your entourage, you decided to bestow it on me, an unlearned man of no significance," he has a real distinction in mind between his own learning and that of the learned seculars in Philip's employ.[107] In a previous letter to

Philip, recollecting how he had presented his work *On the Praises of St. Martin* to him, he had written that those secular clerics around Philip wanted to see it also, but that out of shame (*verecundia*) he had not shown it to them or even told them what it was, fearing that it would seem a "rude and impolite work to ears that were curious and accustomed to secular eloquence."[108] Now in declining to take on the task of writing a vita of Hildegard, Guibert hints that the vita is a task for those of "secular" eloquence, not for himself: Hildegard is perhaps not so much *his* saint to venerate, as she is Philip's.[109] At any rate, in his correspondence he was to have little more to say about her.

CHAPTER 4

James of Vitry and the Other World of Mary of Oignies

T HE FAMOUS VITA OF Mary of Oignies (1177–1213), written in about
1215 by the prominent cleric James of Vitry (1160/70–1240), takes us
away from the monastic world of the work of Ekbert and Guibert. Mary was
not a nun but rather a Beguine, a lay woman who embraced a "semireligious"
life, that is, a life in which she took on religious discipline without entering a
cloister or taking vows. Indeed the vita is our earliest full-scale hagiographical portrait of a Beguine, and it has long stood as an important document
of the momentous religious currents of the time, which were creating new
forms of devout life outside the traditional cadres.[1] James includes himself
as a character in the vita, and its noncloistered setting has important implications for his treatment of his own relationship to the saint, especially
when seen in comparison to the work of Ekbert and Guibert. By appearing
not as her colleague in a monastery, but rather as a priest in relation to a lay
person within the daily life of urban society, James emphasizes the difference between his role or status in the world and that of Mary, a difference
that corresponds to and reinforces the evident difference in their powers.
For James wants to explore the possible balance and interaction of informal
and institutional powers, and accordingly he treats the saint's charismatic
authority as occupying a sphere of its own in clear distinction from the authority of clerics, indeed rather as Hildegard had imagined it in her "Visio
ad Guibertum Missa." Thus, although James necessarily asserts that Mary's
powers do not conflict with the powers of clerics, still—in part, precisely in
order to insure their unique service to clerics—those powers also necessarily
stand outside clerical direction.

MARY, JAMES, AND THE *VITA MARIAE*

Mary of Oignies was born in Nivelles. She married at the age of fourteen and soon afterward she and her husband John both decided to embrace a life of celibacy. The two then served the leper colony of Willambroux near Nivelles.[2] Around 1208, with the permission of her husband and her confessor, Mary moved some thirty miles away to Oignies, a town on the Sambre, to live in a cell near the priory of its Augustinian canons. Other penitent women soon joined her there to form a small community of Beguines. She died in 1213.[3]

It was no later than 1211, and possibly a few years earlier, that James of Vitry settled in Oignies, where he eventually made his profession as a regular canon at the Augustinian priory.[4] By the time he arrived, James had studied at Paris, probably under the master Peter the Chanter, and possibly had served briefly as a parish priest in the French town of Argenteuil.[5] Exactly what brought him to Oignies remains unclear; it may have been the reputation of the Augustinian priory of St. Nicholas for drawing seculars to the religious life, or, as his admirer Thomas of Cantimpré thought, it may have been the reputation of Mary.[6] In any event, he developed a close tie to Mary while he was there. In the year that she died, 1213, or possibly earlier, James began to undertake preaching tours that were to make him famous as a promoter of the crusade against the Albigensians and of a new crusade to the Holy Land. He held the bishopric of Acre in Palestine from 1216 until he renounced it, probably in 1228, having returned to Europe permanently in 1225. In 1229 Gregory IX made him cardinal of Tusculum (today Frascati), and he spent the last years of his life in the papal curia. After he died in Rome in 1240, his body was taken to Oignies, according to his wishes.[7]

James completed the vita of Mary sometime before the autumn of 1216, when he sailed to Acre to take up his duties there.[8] By the time he wrote it he had established himself as a cleric of broad concerns and influence, and the work addresses two issues that were of pressing importance far beyond Mary's immediate region and circumstances. Both touched closely on matters of ecclesiastical authority. One was the question of the legitimacy of the Beguine movement. We know that in July 1216, James asked and received from Pope Honorius III official approbation of the Beguines not only in the diocese of Liège but also in France and the Holy Roman Empire;[9] although in the vita he never employs the term "Beguine," he probably has it in mind when he writes that "new names" were being attached to women like Mary as terms of derision.[10] Beguines, as people who embraced some elements of religious life but did not take vows or thereby conform to the assumed orders of society or fall clearly within the structures of ecclesiastical authority, elicited suspicion and distrust from clerics.[11] James's very project of presenting Mary as a saint was, in part at least, an attempt to tame and sanctify the public image of Beguines, in particular by pointing to the sexual abstinence that made her, though married, effectively a virgin and accordingly conformed her to traditional assumptions about religious life and by laying strong emphasis on her unqualified support for the preaching and sacramental ministry of priests.[12] The second issue was the perceived threat of heresy in western Christendom at the time. James intended the vita as a weapon in the anti-Albigensian cause on behalf of which he had recently undertaken an extensive preaching tour, probably in northern France and Germany.[13] Here he is explicit: he has undertaken the vita, he says in the prologue, at the request of the exiled bishop Fulk of Toulouse, and he addresses the work to Fulk with the stated aim of fortifying him against the heretics who had forced him from his diocese, by means of a portrait of this fervently pious lay woman of unquestionable orthodoxy, whom Fulk himself had visited and admired, apparently in the last days of her life.[14] James's evident concern to address both issues makes the vita stand as vindication and support of the authority of clerics in these important matters.

At the same time that James addresses such issues of large ecclesiastical significance, he also casts the vita in part as a testimony to Mary's place in his own life. He refers to himself throughout the work as a party to the events and circumstances he describes. Already in the prologue, addressing Fulk, who, he says, had traveled as though from Egypt to the promised land when he left his own troubled diocese and came into the company of devout people in "our parts," James avers that he knew the very women who impressed Fulk—not only Mary but also, for instance, an unnamed woman who could not be taken from her contemplation and another who lost consciousness in ecstasy twenty-five times a day without falling and injuring herself.[15] Then over the course of the work, in addition to a host of passages in which he describes events or interactions in the first person plural ("we sometimes reproached her," "we asked her whether the pain of her illness was disturbing her"), referring either editorially to himself or else collectively to the community of canons at Oignies (it is not always clear which),[16] James also frequently writes directly in the first person singular about his own experiences of Mary. He professes that "never in her whole life or conversation was I able to perceive even one mortal sin"; he reports that when he was having trouble learning to preach effectively, she received a vision that helped him identify his problem; he declares that she showed him the place where she had prophetically discerned she would be buried and that when the time of her death was close she told him she was bequeathing him personal objects (a belt, a handkerchief) that, he says, "are dearer to me than gold and silver."[17] And he is almost certainly referring to himself when he speaks of a certain preacher being given to her as a "gift" by God and when he describes her watching clairvoyantly from Oignies the ordination of "a certain friend most dear to her" in Paris.[18] The vita has, in part, the character of a memoir of his relationship with her, in which he gives the reader a calculated glimpse of her impact upon him—of his devotion to her as well as the desires and disposition that he brought to their interaction.

These two elements of the *Vita Mariae*—James's concern with issues of ecclesiastical authority and his personal witness to his encounters with the saint—are not mutually exclusive. They overlap most clearly in his accounts of her revelations, which play a large part in the vita. For James presents her powers to receive such revelations in such a way as to display not only their support of the formal powers of clerics but also their importance for his own spiritual well-being, for which, so he would have the reader believe, he frankly depended upon her. Such dependency finds expression in a remarkable reversal of roles: he pictures himself not directing her but rather taking direction *from* her—a reversal that is heightened in clarity by the contrast between his position in life as an influential cleric, a learned and well-connected preacher who (as the reader would know) was soon to be a bishop, and hers as a voluntarily poor woman of lay status who occupied no niche within the institutional structure of the church. But the reversal does not undermine his own authority or put him at a disadvantage. On the contrary, it both gives vivid expression to James's self-perception and desires and provides that those desires will be satisfied, making the cleric all the more confident in his tasks. For in picturing her as a sure discerner of the divine, he ascribes to Mary powers that he, for all his official importance, professed himself to lack but which are now exercised on his behalf. So it is that by the very contrast and reversal of roles between himself and Mary in the vita, James appropriates the effects of spiritual gifts that he does not possess—and so, through personal encounter, enlists informal powers into the service of institutional ones.

MARY'S REVELATIONS

The *Vita Mariae* consists of a prologue and two books. The prologue, which addresses the work to the exiled bishop Fulk, introduces Mary as an example of the extraordinary piety that, according to James, Fulk encountered among women of the diocese of Liège during his sojourn there. Book 1, ostensibly about her exterior life, describes, in sequence, her precocious devotion in childhood, her chaste marriage, her compunction and gift of tears, and then her disciplines of penitence, fasting, vigils, clothing, and manual labor. Book 2, ostensibly about her interior life, is organized rather loosely according to the gifts of the Holy Spirit, namely, fear, piety, knowledge, fortitude, counsel, understanding, and wisdom. Mary's revelations are reported throughout the vita, but especially in book 2, where, because these functioned for the benefit of others, James's presentation of the inner life in fact says a great deal about the outer life, that is, her place and importance in the world around her. As a receiver of revelations Mary here resembles Hildegard and Elisabeth, for all her obvious difference in circumstances and life story, and clues (to be noted below) suggest that the range of her subject matter may actually have extended, like theirs, to a wide variety of mysteries of the divine dispensation. But for purposes of his portrait James limits the scope of her revelations, minimizing those broader interests. Mary appears here, like James himself, mainly as zealous for souls; the focus of the great majority of her revelations, as he reports them, is upon particular people and their salvation. This is a focus that exposes her contacts with others in such a way as to support the work of evangelistically minded clerics like himself.

To be sure, revelations in aid of others are not the only feature of Mary's inner life that James reports. He claims for her a true contemplative union with God quite apart from such revelations. Already in the prologue, he makes a point of the raptures typical of the holy women of Liège generally: some of these women, he says, were so taken up in contemplation as to be silent for a whole day at a time.[19] Mary herself, as he writes later in the work, would go into raptures for weeks on end without eating.[20] And in the context of illustrating her "spirit of understanding," he describes a contemplative state that she often achieved: she "flew very high for a day at a time, sometimes even for several," and "beheld like an eagle the sun of justice," so that she was "purged from the cloud of all corporeal images, without any fantasy or imagination, and she received simple and divine forms as though in a pure mirror in the soul."[21]

Furthermore, not all her revelations were explicitly for the good of others; some of them serve rather as indications of her fecund inner life and the favor in which God held her, in a way reminiscent of visions of Elisabeth of Schönau. She saw visions of Christ in Gospel scenes on the appropriate liturgical feasts: Christ showed himself at Christmas as a nursing baby, at the feast of purification as a child offered to Simeon, and sometimes at Passiontide in his suffering.[22] Saints too appeared routinely on their feast days, passing their time with her as they had with Elisabeth.[23] Among those saints, John the Evangelist had particular prominence for her, as for many other female visionaries. He would visit her while she was eating, arousing her to a devotion that took her appetite away, and on one occasion he literally transported her cares to heaven: she "saw a certain eagle above her breast, which dipped its beak as though in a spring, and filled the air with great cries; and she understood in the spirit that the blessed John was carrying her tears and groaning to the Lord."[24] Also like Elisabeth, Mary had an angel appointed to her, although in her case not as a guide to the heavenly places but as a coach to regulate the severity of her devotion.[25] Heavenly visitations were, as for Elisabeth, more or less continuous: "hardly a day or night went by without a visit from God or his angels, or the heavenly saints."[26]

Apparently Mary's revelations, like Elisabeth's and Hildegard's, also included teaching on matters of doctrine or scriptural exegesis or obscurities of divine dispensation. James seems to have such teachings in mind when he writes of revelations that fairly exploded from her in spite of the humility that she otherwise displayed and that countered anyone's impression that she was giving herself airs. The substance of these teachings came to her when she was in contemplative ecstasy. James addresses Mary:

When the King would bring you into his winecellar, did you not sometimes cry out from drunkenness, 'Why do you hide yourself, Lord, why do you not show yourself as you are?' ... When the new wine seethed within you with fervent spirit, you would break open unless you could breathe it out; when you could not bear the conflagration of fire without evaporating, then finally from a pure heart, intoxicated, the truth was wrenched out; then, belching out marvelous and unheard of things from the fullness of the book of life, if we might only grasp them, you gave us many and marvelous readings, being suddenly converted from disciple into *magistra*. But when you came back to yourself, like a warrior drunk on wine [Ps. 77:65] awakening after a dream, then you kept quiet about what you said either because you had forgotten, or else, if you brought anything back to memory, because you were bewildered and ashamed, judging yourself a prattler and a fool; and, amazed at what had happened, begging forgiveness from the Lord.[27]

James gives no examples of these "readings" that made her suddenly a teacher, although in his account of the last days of her life he reports a series of teachings that evidently derived from revelations. There he pictures her on her deathbed improvising a remarkable song that lasted three days and three nights and touched upon several matters of doctrine and scriptural exegesis:

> She began her antiphon with the Holy Trinity praising at great length Trinity in Unity and the Unity in Trinity, and inserting marvelous, almost ineffable things into her song, explaining certain things from the divine scriptures and in a new and wonderful way subtly unfolding much from the Gospel, the Psalms, the New and Old Testaments, that she had never heard.[28]

As the song progressed she discoursed upon Christ, the Virgin, the angels, and various saints. She declared that angels derive their intelligence from the Trinity but their joy from the ascended body of Christ; she prophesied that the Holy Spirit would soon "send holy workers abundantly through the whole church for the profit of souls"; she provided extrabiblical details about the martyrdom of St. Stephen (Acts 7.54–8.1), namely that at the moment of his death God presented him with the bystander St. Paul "as a gift [*in munere*]" and that afterward at Paul's martyrdom he considered that the gift had been returned with interest (*cum fructu multiplici*). She also broached two questions that had in fact occupied Elisabeth, affirming in each case (as it happens) the view Elisabeth had held—that the virgin was assumed into heaven bodily and that the resurrections that occurred at the time of Christ's Passion were irreversible.[29]

But James does not accord such teachings much space in the vita. He clearly plays them down. We have seen that he suggests that she uttered them involuntarily, without knowing what she was doing. All specifics are saved for the deathbed scene, where he makes a point of the paucity of witnesses: from the second day of her singing, a Sunday, the prior of the canons, embarrassed and worried lest visitors to the church think her foolish, kept the door of the cell closed so that only he and her maid heard the song, and anyway they "could not understand many of the arcane heavenly things she said."[30] James conveys the impression that such erudite revelations accounted for a small part of her influence, although the fact that he reports them at all may suggest that they were well known and could not be ignored.

These magisterial revelations, however, are not the only sort of revelations that James reports of Mary. There are also others, much more numerous, that have a pastoral rather than magisterial function, in the sense of addressing the spiritual states of living people rather than questions of doctrine or exegesis. It is just prior to his exclamation about the irrepressiblity of her magisterial "readings," as quoted above, that he gives a summary description of these pastoral revelations:

From the abundance of her humility she always desired to hide what was in her. So it was that sometimes when she could not hide inside herself from the exultation of her heart, and from the fullness of grace, she would flee to a rural place or a thicket, so that, avoiding human eyes, she saved her secret for herself [cf. Isa. 24:16] in the ark of a pure conscience. But whenever she was compelled by the prayers of her friends, or sent by the Lord to anyone specially, or incited by a state of compassion to console the meek, she did report, humbly and bashfully, a few of the many things she was sensing. O how many times she said to friends: why are you asking me? I am not worthy to discern the sort of things you are seeking. How many times would she respond to the Lord, as though complaining: 'Why me, Lord? Send someone else [*mitte quem missurus es*; cf. Ex. 4:13]. I am not worthy to go and announce your counsels to others.' But, urged on by the Holy Spirit, she could not resist being of service by speaking out in a way that would profit others. For how many times did she alert her sisters to dangers? How many times did she uncover the hidden snares of evil spirits for her friends? How many times did she strengthen the timid, and those wavering in faith, by marvels of divine revelation? How many times did she admonish people not to act upon some thought that was only in their minds? How many times, by means of divine consolations, did she restore those who were almost hopelessly falling toward ruin?[31]

James proceeds then to scold her ironically for her timidity about making such revelations known for the edification of others, and it is then that he adduces the fact that she could not repress what she learned in her raptures as evidence that God himself would not let her be silent. The ordering of the passage implies that the pastoral revelations, as distinct from the magisterial ones, did not necessarily occur while she was in contemplative ecstasy but apparently came to her in a more routine fashion. They were, at any rate, more directly linked to her social interactions.

Such pastoral revelations, in contrast to the magisterial ones, appear in abundance throughout the vita, especially in book 2. They show Mary busy for souls in a variety of ways. In some instances the revelations informed her of the state of souls in the afterlife, usually so as to alert her or others to help them. In the chapter on her habits of prayer, for instance, James relates her vision of a crowd of hands raised as though in supplication and trying to prevent her from leaving her cell, with the accompanying revelation that "the souls of the departed who were being tormented in purgatory were asking for the assistance of her prayers, which like a precious perfume sweetened their torment."[32] In the chapter on her gift of piety, James tells the story of a devout widow of a merchant who, as Mary saw in a vision, went to purgatory after her death because she had not made complete restitution for goods she had been complicit in receiving fraudulently; Mary alerted others to pray for the woman and later received another a vision of her, this time pure and shining in heaven. In the same chapter she is also described at the deathbed of the holy man John of Dinant, where she saw John being received by angels and was informed that his virtues had been such as to relieve him from purgatory.[33] In the chapter on her gift of understanding, James reports that she saw the souls of the anti-Albigensian crusaders killed at the battle of Montjoie (1211) entering heaven directly.[34] In a similar vein in the same chapter, he reports her observing a cross descending upon a layman of Oignies on his deathbed—since although he had not yet gone on crusade he had vowed to do so—which foiled the demons roaring around him.[35]

In other instances, the revelations provided useful advice to the living. Two prime examples, to which I shall return, are a vision reported in the chapter on her gift of counsel, which helped James himself interpret problems he was experiencing with his preaching, and, in the chapter on her gift of piety, the story of a knight named Ywain of Zoania, whom she helped toward conversion and then prevented from backsliding, aided by revelations about his circumstances and mental state.[36] Also in the chapter on her gift of counsel, James pictures Mary responding to a cleric's query whether he should accept employment with a certain nobleman by reporting to him a vision of a black horse neighing in the direction of hell: she advised him against the move.[37] Similarly, as reported in the same chapter, when another clerical friend asked her whether he should keep a second benefice that he had taken on, she received a revelation telling him not to do it.[38]

There are also several instances in which revelations clued her in to the work of demons so that she could move against them to protect their victims or certify the victims' own efforts. In the chapter on her gift of piety, James says that she would often see demons try to trap people in scandals and would undergo long fasts to free the victims.[39] In the same chapter he writes that after she had prayed for a Cistercian monk who had fallen into despair because he was unable to attain the prelapsarian purity of Adam and Eve, she saw the monk give up "the obstinacy of despair and the blackness of sorrow and pain" in the form of visible black rocks falling from his mouth when he said the *confiteor* before the introit of the mass.[40] There are stories of her summoning demons who were vexing various people, for instance a story in the chapter on her habits of prayer in which a so-called noontime demon (about which, more below), "transfiguring himself into an angel of light as though under the form of piety," gradually seduced a canon into error. Mary had a revelation of the presence of the demon, and after the man resisted her warnings, she prayed until the demon himself was forced to appear before her to be confronted and dispelled.[41] In another case, reported in the same chapter, she summoned a demon who was vexing a Cistercian sister, and the demon appeared to her then apparently in defeat, wearing his interior organs on his shoulders. Mary dispatched him to deepest hell.[42] Or again, in the chapter on her gift of piety, she saw clairvoyantly from her own cell a crowd of raging demons around the deathbed of the sister of a canon of Oignies, hurried there, dispelled the demons, and later received a revelation that in life the woman had loved worldly pleasures inordinately and was enduring extreme punishment in purgatory.[43] In another case, as related in the chapter on her gift of understanding, she saw demons leave a woman at a moment when, as the woman later told her, she had triumphed over certain temptations.[44]

Mary's pastoral revelations, for all the varied situations that they speak to, have in common that they do not place her in conflict with the authority of priests. On the contrary they tend to support that authority specifically. Indeed, the danger of implying anything to the contrary helps account for the paucity of detail that I have already noted about Mary's actual teachings. And in the chapter on her gift of wisdom, James makes explicit what he sees as the harmonious relationship between her inner revelations and preachers' outward proclamation of the Scripture. These were both from the Holy Spirit and therefore in concord with each other, and there was no contradiction involved in the profit she accordingly derived from the work of preachers, even though the Spirit spoke to her inwardly:

> Although she was taught inwardly by the unction of the Holy Spirit and by divine revelations, still she listened willingly to the outward testimonies of the Scriptures, which are in concord inwardly with the Holy Spirit. For however much the Lord, illuminating his disciples inwardly, could instruct without speaking, outwardly however teaching by means of voice, he expounded upon the Scriptures to the ones to whom he himself said: "You are already clean according to the word which I spoke to you" [cf. John 13:10] Therefore from day to day, being washed increasingly by the words of Holy Scripture towards purity, she was also edified toward the adornment of her ways, and illuminated toward faith: if however it can be called faith in her, properly

speaking, because by the Lord's revelation she, equipped with the eyes of faith, saw invisible things as though they were visible [cf. Heb. 11:1].[45]

James goes on to report a set of revelations that affirmed the validity of sacraments. In observing the baptism of a child at a village near Nivelles, she perceived an evil spirit departing the scene when the child was catechized at the church door, and then at the font she saw the Holy Spirit descend.[46] Similarly she once observed angels rejoicing while priests celebrated mass, and at another time a dove descending over a priest celebrating; and she often saw Christ in the Host.[47]

So Mary embraces wholeheartedly the ministry of priests. Nonetheless, in James's very explanation of why she would not have done otherwise, as I have just quoted it, she also takes on a certain independence from priests. Her revelations, coming from the same Holy Spirit as the Scripture, cannot be contrary to Scripture or to the preachers to whom it is entrusted, and she is perforce devoted to them. On the other hand, this very way of putting the matter also ascribes to her an authority of her own that, even though it places her necessarily in agreement with the preaching of priests, nonetheless does not derive from them. For her revelations give her an access to the divine that was parallel to that of preachers rather that subordinate to them. In this sense, her authority and theirs occupied separate spheres. But how, for James, were these two spheres related in practice?

A Reversal of Roles

As I have already suggested, James presents Mary as a great supporter of priests and their ministry of preaching and sacraments. Her revelations about the spiritual state of specific people aided priests' work by bringing people to penitence and conversion, and it is not surprising to find her depicted as working in harmony with James himself, who, according to Thomas of Cantimpré, had been ordained at her urging.[48] She is not, however, subservient to him; for as has been seen, James pictures her exercising her visionary gifts in a fashion better described as parallel to the actions of priests than as subordinate to them. Unlike Ekbert of Schönau, James does not present himself to the reader as her director, except perhaps by implication in the brief references he makes to having heard her confession.[49] He appears instead as, in effect, a partner, whose actions for evangelistic ends are supplemented by hers. But there is also something more here. In various passages, James presents Mary's powers not only as discrete and authoritative in their own way but also as necessary for himself; indeed, he pictures himself here as, like many of the other people she encountered, personally indebted to her for the aid she provides him through her extraordinary gifts. This sense of indebtedness, in turn, causes him at times to represent himself frankly, even eagerly, as dependent upon her. At such moments he writes as though he and Mary had reversed the roles that Ekbert and Elisabeth had assumed—as though *she* were the director, and he the subordinate.

The *Vita Mariae* makes the distinction between the visionary and priestly tasks clear throughout. James is especially concerned to demonstrate that Mary respected and supported priests and did not presume to perform any task reserved for them. Just before accounting for himself as a "gift" to Mary, James has described her enthusiastic devotion to priests:

> During her final illness when she was already falling inwardly near death, and anyone gave a sermon to the people in the church [which was adjacent to her cell], her spirit revived immediately to the word of God, to death's dismay, and she pricked up her ears, prepared her heart and even commented on the sermon to those standing by her. And so much did she love preachers and faithful shepherds of souls, that when their labor of preaching was done she would embrace their feet with wonderful affection and kiss them for a long time even against their will, or else, if they drew away, cry out in anguish.[50]

When she experienced sympathetic illnesses on behalf of others, she would have a priest make the sign of the cross over the afflicted part, and the affliction would immediately subside.[51] When asked to identify the relics of an unknown martyr, she obliged with a vision in which the martyr appeared to her and identified himself by writing the letters "A.I.O.L" so that she could see them—but unlike Elisabeth and Hildegard in similar circumstances she could not by herself tell who this was, but applied to a priest, who identified the letters as referring to the ninth-century bishop St. Aiolis (Aigulf).[52] James pictures her receiving supernatural signs of the worthiness of priests[53] and making thorough confession to priests herself.[54] Probably we are witnessing James's concern here to vouch for the loyalty and obedience of Beguines, in the face of widespread suspicion aroused by their ambiguous status outside the structures of ecclesiastical authority.[55]

It is in the context of Mary's firm respect for priests that James depicts himself interacting with her. In a passage that follows closely upon his description of her devotion to preachers in general, he declares what he considers to be the true origin of his relationship with her (though the actual circumstances of their meeting remain obscure) and in doing so draws a distinction between her task in life and his own. He does not name himself, but it is probable that he has himself in mind.[56]

> Moreover by insistently imploring the Lord with tearful sighs, and with much prayer and fasting, she obtained that the Lord would compensate her, through another person, for the merit and office of preaching that she could not exercise in herself; and [thus] that the Lord would give her a preacher, as a great gift. Once this was given, although it was through him as though through an instrument that the Lord sent forth the word of preaching, still it was because of the holy woman's prayers that he prepared the heart, gave the body strength for labor, provided the word, directed his steps, and, through his handmaid's merits, provided favor and response in the hearers. For day by day, when he was at work preaching, she implored the Lord and the blessed Virgin by saying the Ave Maria a hundred times, just as Martin prayed while Hilary preached. And her preacher, whom she soon left behind by death, she commended most devoutly to God. For when she loved her own, she loved them to the end.[57]

James presents the "preacher" here as God's gift to Mary, granted to her in compensation for her ineligibility for priesthood. If, putting aside for a moment the conceit that he is a passive "instrument" made useful only through the actions of Mary, one asks only how he conceives of his and Mary's respective tasks here, the obvious answer is: he preaches, and she makes contact with God. This distinction calls to mind Hildegard's distinction between Guibert and herself in the "Visio S. Hildegardis ad Guibertum missa": the woman's charismatic gift exists in its own sphere, not confused with that that of the priest and—on the assumption of course, that her powers in no way challenge his—not placed under his direction.

It is without compromising this sense of a distinction of spheres that in some passages, including the one in which he presents her preacher as "gift," James describes her remarkable and unreciprocated spiritual effect upon himself and speaks of his relationship with her in a way that suggests a reversal of roles. But before turning to those passages in their own right, I call attention to an important element of the context in which they appear here, namely James's tendency to depict Mary as a woman with a penchant for producing spiritual effects in other persons, particularly men, who pointedly lacked the ability to attain those effects by themselves.[58]

A long conversion story of Mary's relative Ywain of Zoania, which James includes in the chapter on her gift of piety, is his most thorough treatment of Mary's talent for saving spiritually inept men. Ywain was a knight who, "being divinely inspired and aided by the holy woman's admonitions and prayers, left the world, and converted to the Lord."[59] In this case, leaving the world evidently does not mean entering a cloister but rather embracing a life of penitence while continuing to discharge secular obligations. As Ywain did so, he retained his need for Mary's "admonitions and prayers," to such an extent that his piety appears almost as more Mary's business than his own. After his conversion it was she who received a visit from a demon, who wailed, "You have done me great harm, for you have taken one of my special assistants away from me!"[60] Later, when Ywain was having a sumptuous meal at the house of a former associate and the demon had seized the unguarded moment to insert thoughts of illicit pleasures into his mind, it was not Ywain but Mary who put up resistance: she received a revelation of the knight's peril, sent a messenger to fetch him from his feasting, and corrected him with a thorough scolding. Always thereafter, whenever the pious Ywain was bruised by criticism or ridicule as he moved about in the world, she was supernaturally apprised of each incident at the moment it occurred so as to aid him with her immediate prayers, as she informed him to his comfort when he then "ran to her for solace."[61]

James evinces a certain sympathy for Ywain's situation, even his weakness. Of the knight's morally perilous association with his former creditor, James explains, "he could not easily remove himself from familiarity with one to whom he was tied by debts," and it was unavoidable necessities of business that put him in the way of his later perils.[62] He is a helpless figure but for Mary, lacking the wherewithal to direct his own spiritual life in a worldly context that he could not avoid.[63] James implies that at the house of the creditor Ywain did not know what was happening to him; his mind received the thoughts the demon placed there. But it was Mary who actually encountered this demon, and it was she who identified what was occurring as an episode of perilous temptation. Ywain, for his part, got the point only after she explained it, likening him to Lot's wife and the man of Jesus' parable who has looked back after placing his hand on the plough; "having come back to himself, he felt a salutary compunction at the miracle of such a revelation."[64]

In other stories, James makes clear that Mary's decisive influence was not a matter of verbal persuasion but came from her prayer or revelations or from her presence itself; her mode of influence was by implication discrete from that of a preacher, even if it served the same ends. An example is the story of an unnamed companion of one Guido, cantor of Le Cambre, who on a journey had made a detour from his planned route in order to visit Mary. The companion, "who did not yet know how much is conferred on pious spirits by visits and familiarity with good persons," derided him for wasting his time as though chasing after butterflies, and then, while Guido made his visit, his companion occupied himself elsewhere in idle conversation. Finally, bored, he returned impatiently to interrupt Guido, but in so doing he set eyes on Mary and was instantly transformed:

> And when he fixed his eyes on the face of the handmaid of Christ, suddenly and marvelously he was so changed in his soul, that he dissolved into copious tears, and for a long time afterward could hardly be moved from the place and from her presence. Although, ashamed, he wished to hide, he was watched by the cantor who, realizing what had happened, rejoiced and, with the tables now turned, laughed at his companion and said, "Let's go; why are you staying? Perhaps you want to drive away the butterflies." But he, after many sighs and tears, could barely be pulled away, and said, "Forgive me, because earlier I did not know what I was saying, but now in this holy woman I have experienced the power of God."[65]

No words of Mary are reported here; her appearance alone was sufficient to produce devotion in the man, all the more obviously for the fact that he himself had been busy talking. A similar case is that of a man described as "one of her principal friends" who was "tempted" by a "noontide demon who walks at noon in the shadows [cf. Ps. 90:5–6]," who masqueraded as an upright person, gaining his confidence by criticizing the man's vices and exhorting him to virtue and "giving promise of remedy so as to insert the poison the more secretly," by gradually mixing false counsel with true.[66] The Holy Spirit alerted Mary to the demon's deception, and she warned the man. When he would not be persuaded, undaunted she "took refuge in her accustomed weapons of prayer, and moistened the Lord's feet with her weeping[cf. Luke 7:38], and agitated heaven powerfully with her prayers." It was her prayers that forced the demon to appear before her and confess his identity, and later his deceptions became clear to the man he had molested.[67]

James's treatment of Mary as a rescuer of men also touches, lightly but unmistakably, on the peculiar implications of such rescue when the man is a priest—namely to raise the shadow of a doubt whether *she* really needs priests. It is not that he questions her dutiful obedience to priests or her (or his own) conviction of the efficacy of the sacraments or the importance of preaching—all of which he is at pains to establish. But in a passage I have already quoted, he asserts that, for all that she was devoted to preaching and received benefit from it, God gave her inward certainty of the things that others would have to take preachers' word for.[68] In another context he declares that it was out of humility, not necessity, that she accepted advice: "although she benefited by the familiar interior counsel of the Holy Spirit, and was sufficiently instructed in the holy Scriptures, nonetheless according to the abundance of her humility, lest she seem wise in her own eyes, she did not disdain to subject herself to the counsels of others freely and devoutly, renouncing her own will."[69] Her direct contact with God, moreover, gave her a certain prerogative over priests, as suggested by an incident in which an unnamed priest had criticized her for her excessive tears, admonishing her not to cry so loudly in church. Her response was not to confront him directly but rather to use her access to God to make the priest change his mind: she went off by herself and "procured from the Lord with tears that he would show the said priest that it is not in human power to hold back the impetus of tears when the waters are flowing by the violent wind of the Spirit." Then when the priest was celebrating mass later the same day, he found himself overcome by a flood of tears that soaked the altar linen. Afterward Mary came and made her point directly: "now you have learned from experience that it is not for humans to hold back the force of the Spirit."[70] Here the reversal is particularly clear: the priest had thought to give direction to her, but in the end she gave it to him.[71] The vita thus conveys a picture of Mary as rescuer of men, producing a salutary effect on them that they could not, or anyway did not, experience otherwise—an influence that did not challenge or supplant the work of priests, yet from which priests were themselves not excluded.

To turn back now to James's treatment of his own interactions with Mary: he counts himself among the men affected by her and pictures her as in some sense his own guide or director. In the passage quoted earlier in which he writes of the preacher—presumably himself—who is God's "gift" to her, he speaks of his preaching itself as an act of cooperation not indeed between Mary and the preacher but between Mary and God, with the preacher as their passive instrument. She is the soul of his preaching; at any rate, the very conceit of being a "gift" implies that he is not his own, but hers. There is a suggestion of reversal: she is the one who knows, the one in charge. To be sure, the conceit that his successes result entirely from her efforts is by itself a mere piece of hagiographical hyperbole, and perhaps not even a very remarkable one—a topos to be found also, according to James himself, in the tradition that Martin of Tours prayed for the preaching of Hilary of Poitiers.[72] But other passages reinforce the suggestion of reversal. In the chapter on her gift of counsel, he writes in the first person of an encounter between himself and Mary that shows him relying on her to correct a fault, or rather a set of faults, that had hindered his preaching.

> In order to relate the great deeds of the holy woman without regard for persons, I will not spare even myself, indeed I will relate a story of my own misfortune. When, though unworthy, I was beginning to preach the word of God to simple lay people, I was not yet practiced or accustomed to making sermons for the people, and I was always fearing failure because of a sermon's imperfection. I was collecting many things from various sources and, having brought them together, I wanted to make public everything in my mind.... And when, coming to myself after I had confused myself with such prodigality [cf. Luke 15:17], after the sermon I fell into a kind of weariness of spirit because of what seemed to me the disorder and jumble of much that I had said.[73]

He was too ashamed, he says, to explain his sadness to Mary or solicit her help, preferring to gain what solace he could from the routine congratulations of his hearers. So it was Mary instead who broached the subject. She told him of a vision of him as a hairy man being eyed by a prostitute who emitted a ray of light in his direction; upon hearing her description, he perceived that the hairiness signified the excess verbiage of his sermons, which had been oppressing him; that the prostitute signified his own pride in his preaching; and that the ray of light signified the compliments of his hearers, in which he was taking too much pleasure. He implies that the vision's effect on him was as a "cure": "I do not know by what praises to exalt you, O holy woman, you who know the secrets of God. It is not in vain that the Lord opened to you peoples' thoughts; to your prayers he conferred the power of curing lassitude."[74] James frames the story so as to emphasize his inadequacy: he did not know his own spirit until Mary instructed him, and so at heart he was not so different from the clueless Ywain in needing Mary to bring him into line. It is true that he shows himself working out the problem on his own. He, not Mary, articulates his malaise, and Mary's cryptic contribution only served as catalyst to his own understanding. Yet he presents the catalyst as something necessary. He pictures her, at any rate, as knowing him thoroughly: on her deathbed, in the course of intoning a prayer for him in his absence, as a part of her long "song," she recited his temptations and sins so accurately that the prior of the regular canons, who was present and happened to be James's confessor, later told him that she might as well have been reading his faults from a book.[75]

James's interest in such role reversal—that is, his interest in portraying Mary as director and himself (or another) as the person being directed—stands out with particular clarity when we compare the *Vita Mariae* with the companion piece that James's admirer, the prolific hagiographer Thomas of Cantimpré, wrote for it in 1231.[76] Thomas produced his *Supplement*, which he addressed to Giles, the prior of the canons of Oignies, ostensibly to record stories about Mary that James had omitted; indeed the work contains several new stories, including a few accounts of miracles and a long narrative of her interactions with an unnamed merchant who, like Ywain of Zoania, depended upon her as spiritual adviser.[77] But Thomas also shows great interest in James himself. He begins the work by accounting for James's arrival in Oignies as motivated by Mary, whose reputation, Thomas believes, had already reached him. Thomas says that she demanded that he stay there and "compelled" him to preach to lay people and was among those who urged him to become a priest. Then, "by the prayers and merits of the blessed woman in brief time he attained to such preeminence in preaching, that in expounding the scriptures and in confounding sins he hardly had any equal among mortals." After he returned to Oignies from his ordination in Paris, she kissed his footprints in the street, prophesying that "God chose him to be raised up gloriously among mortals, and is working wonderfully through him for the salvation of souls." She also prophesied that God would "raise him to the holy chair of a bishop overseas in the Holy Land."[78] Then long after her death when that prophecy had been fulfilled and he was bishop of Acre, she appeared to him, according to Thomas, at sea during a storm and assured him that she had assisted him with her prayers in all the intervening years.[79] All in all, Thomas confirms the picture in the *Vita Mariae* of Mary as a great supporter of James's pastoral activity. But Thomas stops short of describing the sort of reversal that, in James's own account, put him in a self-perceived position of dependence upon her. He refers to the passage about the preacher who was a "gift" to Mary from God in response to her prayers and whose ministry was dependent on her prayers. Thomas takes it as self-evident that the preacher is James himself but regards the passage as only an acknowledgment of Mary's wishes for him: "The servant of God … demanded of him by insistent prayers that he leave France behind and remain with the brothers of Oignies. This is what that venerable James is referring to in the book of her life when, suppressing his own name, he says that the Lord gave a certain preacher to his handmaiden, whom at her death she commended to the Lord with many prayers."[80]

In fact, Thomas pictures James as distinctly *not* subservient to Mary. He quotes her telling James in her appearance at sea, "you, a man of your own will, have never wanted to acquiesce to my counsels or those of others who love you spiritually, and you always have walked by your own rather than others' judgments."[81] Later, when after giving up his see and retiring to Oignies, he went off again to Rome at the behest of Gregory IX to become a cardinal—a departure that was a great blow to the church in the whole region of Lorraine according to Thomas, who takes him to task for it in the final paragraphs of the *Supplement*—Thomas depicts him acting specifically against Mary's advice as she expressed it in revelations both to him and to Giles. For better or worse, the James of the *Supplement*, unlike the James of the *Vita*, is unambiguously his own man.

By contrast, James's assertion that he was *not* his own, but Mary's—along with all his play with role reversal elsewhere in the *Vita*—is a statement of a different kind, a way of expressing a sense of self, in the context of his hagiographical purposes. No doubt it would not have been fitting for Thomas to suggest that the great preacher was Mary's puppet, a suggestion that anyway would undermine his own criticism of James as self-willed. But coming from James himself, the very figure of speech that he was not his own but Mary's, and the suggestion that Mary took charge where he and other men were stupidly oblivious to their own condition, become ways of expressing precisely a putative sense of something missing in himself, some spiritual resource otherwise essential to his calling. But such an admission of inadequacy does not damage him; on the contrary, her very devotion to priests makes it safe—his authority of office being perforce unquestioned—and beyond that, it is an admission made precisely to show that the inadequacy would be supplied. For Mary provides "her" preacher with just what he needs. Indeed, the picture of dependency hardly corresponds to the real external realities of James's considerable stature and influence (such as Thomas, for instance, witnesses to) but rather to, as it were, James's fantasies. She becomes a figure of wish fulfillment for him. In picturing her as sure discerner of the divine, he ascribes to her powers that he, for all his official importance, professed himself to lack; yet in picturing her as his devoted patroness, he appropriates the benefits of precisely those powers for himself.

In the vita therefore, the figure of Mary displays, for all her devoted obedience to and respect for priests, a certain functional independence from them, even a kind of superiority over them, born of her virtue and privileged contact with God. Accordingly, in his own case James pictures her as the very soul of his preaching. I have already suggested that James's notion of the division of labor between holy woman and cleric recalls Hildegard's in the"Visio."[82] But James's interest in that division obviously also differs from hers both in his focus upon the working interaction between the two and in the very lopsidedness of their relationship as he pictures it. Whereas Hildegard implied a functional equality between priest and female visionary, each with a discrete job to do, James pictures himself as needing Mary more than she needed him. The focus on Mary's virtue is, of course, de rigueur for a work of hagiography; still, it is remarkable, and not hagiographically necessary, that Mary should appear here as (such is his conceit) the essential actor in his own ministry. On the other hand, if in establishing Mary's virtues he exalts her above himself and in a sense above clerics in general, he also presents himself and other devout men as the peculiar beneficiaries of those virtues. The James who likes to present himself as subservient to this woman who was ostensibly powerless is in fact a man of great power, which his apparent subservience does not compromise at all.

CONCLUSION

The *Vita Mariae* gives expression to a notion of the relation between female informal powers and the institutional powers of clerics that will find expression many more times in the two centuries to follow: the notion that a woman may exercise powers discrete from, yet putatively not subordinate to, a cleric's own powers. For it is of the essence of James's portrait of Mary that though he as a man of office in the church can rely absolutely on the loyal Mary and her revelations, yet as far as those revelations go she is not under his direction. And so he does not picture himself testing her or mediating between her and her audience but instead presents her as a woman with powers that are, in their origin as well as their function, discrete from his own powers, even though they supplement and fulfill them. Accordingly, her powers fascinate him; indeed, he likes to think of himself as under their sway, finding in her a certain deeply desirable vitality and insight that, so he would have us believe, he does not find in himself. He also shows no hesitation in saying so, and perhaps here the very difference in their positions in life is important. James is not hindered from expressing his fascination by the monastic qualms of a Guibert of Gembloux about singling out a colleague in monastic life as an object of veneration, and he recalls instead that grand secular cleric Philip of

Heinsberg, who lacked any such monastic qualms that would have kept him from paying assiduous attention to Hildegard. James does all he can, in fact, to stress the discreteness of Mary's sphere of experience and action from his own, for it is on that discreteness that the fruitfulness of the relationship between them finally depends.

CHAPTER 5

Self and Saint

Peter of Dacia on Christine of Stommeln

S EVERAL DECADES AFTER THE DEATH of James of Vitry, another
northern cleric was also to write memorably about a Beguine whom he
himself had known. This was the Scandinavian friar Peter of Dacia (1230/40–
1289). The Beguine was one Christine (1242–1312), a woman who lived in the
village of Stommeln near Cologne.

There are striking differences between Peter's portrait of Christine and
James's of Mary. Most remarkably, revelations per se play only a small role in
Christine's life as Peter presents it. She therefore lacks most of the means by
which female saints were seen to influence others and accomplish good things
in the society around them.[1] In fact it was not as a person of active charity that
Christine attracted Peter's attentions but rather as a passive subject of raptures
and a victim of sensational attacks by demons—in which, for example, objects
would hurl themselves at her, excrement would fall upon her from the air, un-
seen forces would jerk her about, or bruises and lesions would suddenly mate-
rialize on her body.

Nonetheless, there is something strongly reminiscent of James not only in
Peter's choice of a Beguine as the object of his attentions but also in his way
of presenting her, and Peter's work significantly extends some of the important
themes in James. Central to Peter's interest in Christine are his sense of her stark
difference from himself and his conviction that her extraordinary contact with
God placed her in a sphere of experience outside either his own experience or his
potential oversight. This is a conviction that recalls James at precisely the point
where he differed most from Guibert and Ekbert. Indeed Peter develops the implications of this conviction further than James, considering more thoroughly
what was at stake for himself in his encounter with the woman who fascinated

him. His writings tell us not just about her but also, in considerable detail, about himself. He regards Christine's supposed access to God as the object of a deep desire of his own that his theological studies have left unfulfilled. He considers himself to benefit from her experience vicariously through the devotion she has elicited in him, which however also represents a sort of consolation prize, which he has accepted in lieu of that greater object of his own desire. He presents Christine as possessing a greater grace than he has himself, a foretaste of glory that has eluded him but *might have been his*; and thus he explicitly roots his fascination with her in a sense of his own spiritual deficit.

CHRISTINE AND PETER: LIVES AND SOURCES

Christine, who was the daughter of a farmer of Stommeln, lived a troubled life. When she was ten years old, she had a dream in which Christ told her that she would live with Beguines, and at thirteen, against her mother's entreaties, she left home and sought out a community of Beguines in Cologne. There she lived very ascetically, meditated intensely on the Passion of Christ, and began to undergo raptures, as it seemed to her, which, however, the other Beguines considered as evidence of insanity or epilepsy. It was after two years of this life that she began to experience visits by demons who put thoughts of suicide into her mind.[2] Apparently the Cologne Beguines rejected her around this time, for soon afterward she was back in Stommeln, where she was to live from then on, sometimes with her family and sometimes in the house of the parish priest, who for a time hosted a small community of Beguines to which she belonged.[3] After her parents' deaths (which had occurred by 1278) she and her brother Sigwin tried to keep the family farm going, but without success.[4] She continued all the while to experience extreme sufferings at the hands of demons until these came to an end, apparently suddenly, after an illness in 1288.[5] After this we know nothing of her except that she died on 6 November 1312.[6]

The Dominican friar Peter of Dacia met Christine during Advent of 1267, when she was living at the house of the Stommeln parish priest.[7] At that time Peter was a student at the Dominican *studium generale* in Cologne, which, along with its counterparts in Paris, Montpellier, Bologna, and Oxford, prepared select friars from throughout the order to serve as convent lectors in their home provinces and also represented the highest level of Dominican education.[8] He was from Gotland, the large island to the east of the Swedish mainland, and there he had served his novitiate in the Dominican house in the town of Visby.

He had been sent to Cologne in 1266, and he was to stay until the Spring of 1269, when he moved on to Paris for another year of study. On his first encounter with Christine, at a moment when she was enduring an attack by demons, Peter felt an immediate fascination. He developed a close relationship with her, visiting her thirteen more times (according to his later accounts) before his departure for Paris. Then, when he was in Paris he and she began a correspondence, with the Stommeln parish priest serving as scribe for Christine. On his way back from Paris to Sweden, he stopped at Stommeln for a few weeks, visited her several times, and received from her a "notebook [*quaternus*]" that contained the story of her life as she had told it to the priest at Peter's request. Peter spent the rest of his life in Sweden, where he served as lector first at the Dominican house at Skänninge until 1278 and then at that of Västeras before becoming prior of Visby in 1286.[9] Peter cultivated relationships with other devout women in his homeland—his correspondence mentions several, including one unnamed woman who had frequent raptures (possibly Ingrid of Skänninge who became a Dominican nun and was later beatified)[10]—but without diminishing his interest in Christine. He visited her twice on journeys abroad, once in 1279 and once in 1287, and kept up his correspondence with her until 1288, the year before he died.[11]

Most sources for the lives of Christine and Peter—and there is now a learned and thorough study on these by Christine Ruhrberg[12]—derive from a manuscript volume known as the *Codex Iuliacensis*, preserved for many years at Jülich and now at Aachen. The manuscript was produced sometime before 1325, very likely in the scriptorium of the house of regular canonesses in Stommeln (St. Cäcillien), and it belonged at some point to the canons of Nideggen, who are known to have transferred there in 1342 from Stommeln, where they had been founded in 1327.[13] The canons also possessed Christine's body, which was moved along with the codex to Nideggen, where the count of Jülich appears to have had an interest in her cult.[14] The codex has three parts. The first part comprises a work by Peter, entitled by its modern editor *De gratia naturam ditante* (On the enrichment of nature by grace), which consists of a poem in praise of Christine accompanied by a long and learned commentary. We gather from the correspondence that Peter brought part of this work with him on his visit to Stommeln 1179 and sent the rest of it there in 1181.[15] Over half of the second part of the manuscript is devoted to a compilation of texts that Peter himself arranged and edited. The texts, which (as will be seen later) Peter ordered according to a roughly chronological scheme, include nineteen narratives that he himself wrote to describe his visits to Stommeln over time, as well the "notebook" of Christine, and thirty-three letters (thirteen by himself, fourteen by Christine, and six by others of their circle).[16] A comment by Peter in one of his narratives shows that he had begun writing them by 1279, and he must have finished the work as a whole sometime after 20 August 1282, which is the date of the latest of the letters.[17] Peter's compilation is followed in the manuscript (though the scribe does not note the transition) by thirty-nine more letters (twenty-two by Peter, five by Christine, and twelve by others, all of which had probably been conserved at Stommeln) that do not belong to Peter's compilation and appear in no particular order. These include several letters that were written after 1282, among them one addressed to Christine from a Swedish friar announcing Peter's death in 1289.[18] The third part of the manuscript comprises narratives of Christine's sufferings between 1279 and 1287 as written by one "Master John," schoolmaster of Stommeln, whom Peter commissioned to take the place of the parish priest, after the latter's death in 1277, as his correspondent and Christine's confidant.[19]

All of these texts have relevance to what follows, but my main concern will with the second part of the *Codex Iuliacensis*, especially the texts of the compilation edited by Peter. I will ask first how Christine herself appears in her own words, then how Peter positions himself in relation to her, and finally what meaning he attaches to Christine in the context of his reflection on himself.

An Attenuated Mysticism

In the letters and narratives in the second part of the *Codex Iuliacensis* that purport to be by Christine herself—fourteen letters addressed to Peter, the autobiographical notebook produced at his request—as well as the series of accounts of demonic vexations that the third part of the manuscript comprises, we find descriptions of her experiences. The voice that speaks in the texts is, to be sure, not purely Christine's own. All of them were ostensibly dictated to others, including the parish priest, the schoolmaster, and a certain Friar Lawrence.[20] That these men had a hand in the composition is evident from the lapse of some of the texts into the third-person singular in their references to Christine, from the variation in styles,[21] and from two notable passages in which the schoolmaster hints strongly that he himself, not Christine, has supplied the words he is writing.[22] The texts that emerge from this apparently collaborative enterprise present her as someone whose inner life was dominated by demons and the troubles they inflicted upon her, and it is the description of those troubles that dominates these texts.[23] They do portray her as having an extraordinary experience of God that was far from incidental to her inner life. But even so, about the actual content of that experience—what she perceived or felt or learned—the texts are remarkably vague and laconic.

It was in the context of her friendship with Peter that Christine told him the details of her life. The letters and narratives give no evidence that she held the belief, otherwise so typical of mystical or visionary writers, that God was pressing her to disclose her experiences. Rather, it was Peter who pressed her. To be sure, she was willing to respond, especially in the early years of their acquaintance. Already during his visits of 1267 through 1270 he began asking her for her own accounts of what had happened to her,[24] and his letters from Paris show him keenly interested in whatever she could tell him on the subject.[25] She appears to have been extremely gratified by his attentions, declaring in an early letter that among all her acquaintances, he alone understood her and that "there is no one whom I would be more willing to have present in my troubles, because you were always prepared to come to me when I was in tribulation."[26] Two of the four preserved letters she wrote him during the course of his year in Paris consist of long, detailed serial accounts of her most recent experiences, dominated by her encounters with demons.[27] When, still in Paris, he wrote asking her to produce a "notebook [*quaternus*]" of writings "concerning your state,"[28] she replied that she would do it for him, indeed that it was only for him that she would consider doing such a thing;[29] then at the very end of his visit to Stommeln on his way back to Sweden, as Peter reports in his account of that visit, she presented him the notebook, a day after telling him that at their very first meeting she had heard the Lord telling her that Peter "is, and will be, your friend, and will do many things for you; but you also will do for him something that you will do for nobody else. And know, that he will remain with you in eternal life."[30] In her next letter, after he left again for Sweden, she thanked him for his good will ("you have always turned everything to the good, in the way of a friend easily discerning my intention") and declared that she wanted to reveal many more things to him, which she had not revealed to anyone.[31]

Nonetheless, her subsequent letters show her often less forthcoming about her supernatural experiences than about other matters such as the misfortunes that followed the financial ruin of her father and her desire for Peter's help in bringing her brother Sigwin into the Dominican order.[32] In the last few years of his life we find Peter (in letters that are not in his edited compilation) lamenting that he heard nothing but complaints from her, reproving her for not delivering secrets that she had promised and, after his last visit to Stommeln in 1287, commenting bitterly to her that she should not expect so many letters from him, since she seemed to think him, as he told her, "unworthy of your secrets."[33] Even so, most of her letters do contain at least some allusion to the experiences he wanted to hear about, and over the period of a year or two after his 1279 visit to Stommeln, when he had exhorted her to inform the schoolmaster about "her status,"[34] the schoolmaster sent him three letters full of Christine's purported accounts of her intimate experiences[35] and also undertook for good measure his own collection of such accounts, which would eventually form the third part of the codex.[36]

The theme that predominates in all the texts purportedly by Christine is that of her suffering at the hands of demons. I shall return to it in a moment, but I note first that for all the predominance of the demonic theme, her self-revelations are framed by reference to her privileged access to God—either visionary, mystical, or both—so as to suggest that the vexations would not have occurred had she not been favored with such access. This framing is particularly evident in the "notebook" she gave to Peter in 1270. There she prefaces her stories of the demons' trials with an account of the events of her early life, beginning with a vision that she received at the age of ten in which Christ asked for her "allegiance [*fidem*]," then proceeding to describe her strenuous asceticism among the Beguines of Cologne in her adolescence and a vision she had then of Christ's Passion. These events establish her devotion and privileged experience of God prior to the onset of the demons' vexations two years into her sojourn at Cologne.[37] Peppered among the vexation stories themselves, which then account for the bulk of the remainder of the notebook, are references to paramystical experiences that remind the reader of the virtue or divine favor that has drawn the demons' hostile attention to her in the first place: the appearance of the Christ child in the priest's hands at the elevation of the Host,[38] the sound of presumably heavenly singing,[39] a sensation of the crown of thorns descending upon her head and afterward the appearance of stigmata on her hands and feet,[40] a dream in which Christ exhorted her to patience and called himself her bridegroom,[41] a visit from Christ commending her faithfulness and pledging his own.[42]

Not only in the notebook but also in the letters, she reports that the demons prevented her from receiving Communion or from experiencing the raptures that typically followed Communion—for instance, that once after a demon had terrorized her with a hot iron, she took Communion and then went to her habitual place east of the altar where she would often experience her raptures, but nothing happened.[43] Particularly in the late letters recorded by the schoolmaster, she appears in triumphant ecstasy after each extended bout of trouble with a demon. Thus after a series of tortures late in Advent of 1279, as the schoolmaster puts it, "that sweetest bridegroom, taking up her blessed soul, transported it to the secret marriage bed of his most beloved heart, where divine consolations gladdened her in the same measure as the multitude of her preceding afflictions."[44] All of this suggests that Christine's letters and narratives are intended to present her to the reader as, amidst all her troubles, not just a virtuous woman but more precisely a woman who had experienced extraordinary supernatural graces arising from a direct experience of God: when the demons are shown unleashing troubles upon her, they do so to divorce her from those graces. Mysticism, in the sense of extraordinary immediate consciousness of God, is an essential if largely implicit element in the portrait of Christine that emerges here.[45]

But for all the importance the texts attach to the divine favor that Christine supposedly possessed, and accordingly to her ecstasies, still they say remarkably little about what she was supposed to have experienced in those ecstasies. Only the schoolmaster makes any real attempt to supply the lack, and he does not tell us much of substance. He uses the language of bridal mysticism, but rather vaguely, as when referring to "consolations" of the "bridegroom" in Advent 1279 in the passage quoted above, or when reporting that on the following Maundy Thursday she received "a precious vision of her bridegroom and profound joy in her heart"[46] and later at the Nativity of the Virgin was taken into his "marriage bed" where "divine consolations gave her ineffable joys matching the multitude of tribulations that had preceded them"[47]—a statement that is, at any rate, not directly attributed to her. As for the account in the 1270 notebook of her first direct encounter with Christ, remarkably Christine recalls no joy or sweetness, gives no hint of the bride's delight in the bridegroom; on the contrary, she says that the vision made her anxious because of Christ's apparently unexpected prophecy that she would live with Beguines. Indeed, even though the recollection of this vision at the end of the notebook appears to refer to it as a betrothal, Christ as she quotes him makes no explicit allusion to marriage but only asks her allegiance.[48] It is true that an interpolated comment from Peter in the *Codex Iuliacensis* declares that when he visited her almost a decade later in 1279, she said that Christ's presence had been so glorious in the vision as to make her rapt for three days and nights afterward—but such an experience does not belong to the notebook itself, at this or any other point.[49] Similarly, in the description of her sojourn at Cologne, another interpolation from Peter informs us that she had later told him that she experienced raptures there, for which reason the Beguines thought her either epileptic or insane, but once again this is Peter's interest showing; the notebook itself describes no raptures.[50] In the other letters the substance of the ecstasies is described only obliquely as "consolations."

But if in Christine's letters and narratives her heavenly consolations appear only vaguely, by contrast her demonic tribulations appear in considerable precise detail. These tribulations are her great subject, her almost constant theme. Her early letters to Paris already describe a large number and wide variety of attacks by demons: they appeared to her, she says, in physically intimidating and often violent ways, as when a demon terrorized and then injured her with a hot iron over the course of several weeks or, more bizarrely, assaulted her and others with a severed human head after frightening them by peering at them through its eyes,[51] but they also, more subtly, put troubling notions into her mind—for instance, that she was offering her prayers in the name of a demon or that not only her confessor but even Christ himself was unworthy of her.[52] In her long-term recollections in the notebook of 1270 she again tells tales of both overt violence[53] and mental trials, though here it is the latter that loom larger, as she tells how demons suggested to her the idea of killing herself so as to get to heaven; caused her to doubt whether God created the world or cared for her;[54] made her consider Christ's Passion a fable of clerics; tempted her with thoughts of wealth and of the pleasures of married life; threatened to spread a rumor that she had borne a child;[55] caused her food, and even the Host itself at mass, to transform into toads, snakes, or spiders;[56] and made her surroundings appear to ignite in flames when she tried to pray or make her confession.[57] Then in her subsequent accounts, and especially in those recorded by the schoolmaster, the physical violence predominates: she tells of demons singly or collectively pulling her upward by her hair,[58] making her unable to keep her tongue in her mouth, giving her convulsions, piercing her hands and feet with twigs, suspending her from trees,[59] appearing as a horse to trample upon her head, severing various of her body parts (later restored by angels), stripping her naked to expose her to the elements,[60] hanging her by hooks,[61] tossing her between themselves like a ball, pricking her with sharp instruments, and threatening or assaulting her en masse in the form, variously, of wolves, cats, dogs, and lascivious men.[62] So it is that her tales are mostly of her troubles, and spectacular troubles they are.

The letters and narratives ostensibly by Christine, then, are only minimally mystical in the sense of expressing a direct consciousness of God. We could say instead that they express a direct consciousness of demons. Why should the texts be so reticent about her experience of God, given that the demons postulate their attacks upon it and that the trances that gave occasion for it figure so prominently? An obvious explanation, likely in itself, is that the historical Christine had little to say about any such experience, perhaps even that apart from the urgings of Peter and the efforts of her collaborators she would not have claimed it at all. Thus those collaborators had little to go on. But if that is so, then it is all the more remarkable that Peter should have been so keen on soliciting and preserving Christine's demon-filled tales. For, as will be seen, Peter presents Christine precisely as enjoying that mystical encounter with the heavenly bridegroom about which she says so little of substance in her letters and narratives; all the more remarkably, he uses those very letters and narratives to make his point.

PETER AS HAGIOGRAPHER

Peter's narratives meticulously describe nineteen visits he made to Christine over many years.[63] He also combines those narratives with the texts already examined, as well as letters of his own and a few others from members of their circle, to make the compilation that forms over half of the second part of the *Codex Iuliacensis*. We can discern him at work therefore both as author and as editor; in both roles he is also a hagiographer, in the sense of attempting to present her, throughout, as a person of virtue and favor in the sight of God. But neither his narratives by themselves nor the texts of the collection as a whole add up to a vita of Christine in any conventional sense;[64] instead they make for an idiosyncratic kind of hagiography that borders on autobiography or personal memoir on the part of the hagiographer.[65] For Peter's principal means of demonstrating Christine's sanctity is to present himself as a person convinced of it; his account of her is first and foremost an account of himself, as he watched her and interpreted what he saw. And given Christine's notable silence on the matter of her own encounter with God, the person whose religious experience finds by far the most explicit expression here is not Christine but Peter.

Peter calls attention to himself as eyewitness and interpreter not only in (as will be seen) his own letters and narratives but also in the way he frames the collection as a whole. In the prologue he declares that he will be recalling the working of God's grace in things that he himself has witnessed.[66] He arranges the texts of the collection then in a series of blocks of text: (1) narratives of his initial thirteen visits to Stommeln in 1267 through 1269,[67] (2) fifteen letters from the time of his stay in Paris in 1269 and 1270,[68] (3) narratives of three visits he made to Stommeln in 1270,[69] (4) Christine's notebook,[70] (5) seven letters from the period of 1270 through 1279,[71] (6) narratives of three more visits he made to Stommeln in 1279,[72] and (7) nine letters from the years following those visits.[73] By this arrangement Peter situates the letters within the chronological series of events that his own narratives make explicit. He also prefaces some of the texts in each of the blocks of letters with comments in the first person, referring to the circumstances in which he received or wrote a given letter or explaining why he has grouped certain of them together.[74] He also interpolates such first-person comments at intervals within the very texts of Christine's early letters and notebook, glossing her accounts of events with his own observations or with reports of what she or others have told him. So, for instance, he interrupts the text of letter 4, in which Christine tells of a demon terrorizing her with a hot iron after she has received Communion, to relate remarks made to him later by the parish priest to the effect that in other instances she had been undisturbed by demons after Communion and to describe the appearance of her wounds after this episode. He also interrupts the notebook, after Christine's tale of having wounded herself with a knife to distract her mind at the prospect of being raped, to say that he, Peter, had seen the knife and a rag soaked with blood from the wound.[75] He keeps the reader aware of himself as witness, even when the texts ostensibly present the voice of Christine.

Within the collection thus assembled, Peter is the one who, in his letters, describes and appraises those putative encounters with Christ of which Christine herself says almost nothing. It is in his second letter in the Paris correspondence (letter 5) that Peter stakes out this role for himself. Responding to her comment that no other man could comfort her as he did, he tells her that it is her affection for Christ, not for himself, that he wants to hear about.

> I have never intended to concern myself with, or even acknowledge, your affection toward me, but rather, as far as I knew how, I have labored by my words and demonstrations so that you would take all your affection to Christ, and transfer your embrace to him, calling him your bridegroom joyfully and without fear—and, with that same inner joy, laying claim to him not just in word but in fact.[76]

He proceeds to devote the rest of the letter to her encounter with Christ. He exhorts her to consider often, love deeply and desire fervently that which is so victorious as to triumph over natural things, so close to you as to lead your exterior senses inward, so delightful as to make it oblivious or rather insensible to itself, so joyful that it cannot be contained, but rather issues in actions it wishes to be hidden from everyone—a joy that in any case not only gladdens you, in whom it both shows itself, and infuses itself deeply so as to fill and inebriate and pour forth from you, but has also gladdened me, not in small measure or only once, but many times, though I am unworthy and placed in a far off region of dissimilitude.[77]

But none of the preceding or subsequent texts—either Peter's narratives or her own letters—have shown her expressing the joy he claims to have perceived in her. As he proceeds to rhapsodize on her nuptials as the bride of Christ,[78] who becomes present in her heart and her intellect, assuages her fears, subdues her pride, and so on,[79] to speculate whether she is in the body or not during her raptures (2 Cor. 12:2–3), to affirm that Christ is present in her as she is in Christ (Gal. 2:20),[80] and to construe her stigmata as signs of this presence,[81] his language, ideas, and images display no apparent debt to Christine's own, as least as far as we can see from the writings attributed to her.[82] In another of his Paris letters he comments extensively on three brief phrases at the end of a letter of hers—"I am not able to write of the state of my heart," "I complain of the absence of my beloved," "nonetheless a little bit of light shone forth"[83]—which appear to represent the meager extent of what Peter construes as her mysticism. (In fact in the letter in question Christine is arguably more explicit about her affection for Peter than about her experience of Christ; in response, as elsewhere, Peter discusses their mutual affection in terms of its origin and purpose in God.)[84] In subsequent letters he continues to think of her as the bride of Christ, who has entered the bridegroom's wine cellar (cf. Cant. 2:4.),[85] and demonstrates as a result the virtues of patience, prudence, discernment, wisdom and joy[86]—and in imagining her putative experience as bride, he uses her as a way of attaining to Christ vicariously, as will be made clear below.[87]

If Peter's letters therefore show him at work to expose Christine's experience in a way that she herself had not done, his narratives, especially the early ones, place himself even more conspicuously at center stage: here the prevailing evidence of her sanctity consists of nothing so much as the movements of his own soul. These narratives show him carefully observing a succession of wonders that occurred in her person in order to register their effect upon himself.

That the wonders associated with Christine were *observable* is crucial to the narratives. For here, as in her own letters, we learn little of Christine's inner thoughts or feelings, or her rapport with Christ in its own right; rather, the reported events are external ones, occurring in or around her body and open to view. When Peter first met her at the house of the parish priest of Stommeln during Advent of 1267, he observed the jerking of her body, as though some force were thrusting her backward where she was sitting. He also observed wounds that appeared in her feet, and later that night when he and others kept vigil with her he received from her hand a hot nail which, as she said, the demon had used to wound her.[88] When he came back for his second visit, during Lent of 1268, he watched her as she went into a trance while someone was singing the hymn *Jesu dulcis memoria* and observed in minute detail the course of the trance over several hours' time, as she first groaned and sobbed, then began to breathe less frequently, eventually began to tremble, then by turns was quiet, prayerful, and anguished.[89] When he visited her on 23 March, just before the feast of the Annunciation, he observed on her left palm a figure of something like "a cross adorned with beautiful flowers," and on 14 April, just before Easter, he came again and saw her face bruised like Christ's, and another mark on her hand.[90]

In subsequent visits that year he observed her again in rapture: on the feast of the Dominican saint Peter Martyr (April 29), when he noticed a sweet fragrance about her; during mass at Pentecost (June 2), when a book she had lost came hurtling through the air at her from, as its foul smell indicated, a demon; on the feast of Mary Magdalene (July 22), when the sudden stiffening of her body trapped the hand of Peter's companion Friar Albrandino (who had been doubting the reports of her raptures) against a wall; and at the feast of All Saints (November 1), when Peter and Albrandino heard a strange song emanating from her chest while she was unconscious.[91] Then in two memorable visits during Advent, Peter witnessed the most bizarre of her trials (at least among those anyone beyond Christine herself claimed to have seen), when human excrement began to fall out of thin air. This was the work of a demon, whom only Christine could see, though others could hear him, and the excrement dropped not only on her but also on those, including Peter, who stood around her while she lay in bed in her family's home, and while the figure of the cross on her hand evidently triplicated itself.[92] Finally, before leaving for Paris in Eastertide of 1269, Peter visited her during Lent, when he observed a sort of dew to appear on her clothing while she prayed; he visited her again at Easter when he witnessed another episode of falling excrement and watched her once more in rapture, as fresh blood flowed from wounds on her head and feet.[93]

Central to Peter's accounts of these marvels is his attention to his own reactions, his quickened devotion. He begins his account of the first visit by commenting that as a child he had delighted to hear of the "life and character, passions and deaths" of the saints, Christ, and the Virgin and he had had thoughts of renouncing the world. Among these thoughts a desire emerged, that God might grant the grace

> to show me some one of his servants, in whom I might learn the ways of his saints not just through words but through deeds and examples sure and clear; to whom I might be joined and united in heartfelt love; whose actions might instruct me; whose devotion might kindle me and rouse me from the torpor that had oppressed me since childhood; whose conversation might enlighten me; whose friendship might console me; whose example might clear up all my doubts, especially about the ways of the saints.[94]

This desire had remained unfulfilled for years, he says, until God "unexpectedly showed me a certain person in this way, whose countenance and speech together have gladdened me, not just when present to view but also when recollected in memory."[95] He had been alerted by others before he encountered her that he might see something "extraordinary or marvelous"; and when he did finally have his first sight of her as she was being thrown against the wall, he did not share the dismay of the others present: "I alone was inwardly consoled and filled with a certain unaccustomed joy, and was suspended in a state of amazement."[96] From that point on through the accounts of the subsequent visits, Peter repeatedly stresses that the wonders he observed had the power to arouse his devotion. In the visit on the feast of the Annunciation when he first saw the figure of a cross on her hand, he says that he perceived it with his eyes, "but its power I perceived within my heart, for from that moment it became more familiar to me to meditate on the cross and the crucified one."[97] Similarly in the account of the following visit, when he observed the bruises on her face, he says, "at that repeated sight there came a certain stupor and admiration to my eyes, and a wonderful compassion toward the suffering Christ was born in my heart; and I do not know if from that day to this anything of what I have seen, heard, read, or written has so penetrated my heart and poured the Passion of Christ into it."[98] After the visit when he observed the soiled book that flew at her through the air of the church, Peter says that for four days, he as well as his Dominican companion Gerard and the parish priest, who had both witnessed the event too, felt a "special joy."[99] In the Advent episodes of flying excrement, Peter pictures himself and his Dominican companions as strangely edified by what they saw; Friar Wipertus, commenting on how the demon has drenched his new white scapula with filth, comments, "I am also drenched in my heart with a great joy that I have otherwise not known and so cannot stop myself from laughing."[100] Peter remarks that everyone around Christine, including himself, was without fear when in the room with her, even during the demon's rampages, but became fearful upon leaving.[101]

Peter's attention to his own reactions to Christine's "wonders" is such that at points he seems to be marveling less at what he has observed in her than at its effect on himself. Of course her virtues were not irrelevant, and the connection between the three sorts of observable wonders in Christine—demonic vexations, raptures, and signs of the Passion—seems clear enough: as a person of virtue who experienced a mystical consciousness of God (thus the raptures) she was targeted by demons for special trials (thus the buffetings and the excrement), to which she responded with heroic patience (thus the signs of the Passion). But Peter seems hardly interested in exploring this connection, which remains largely implicit. In the account of the first visit, for instance, he presents his own response to Christine as something that was without evident explanation—as a sort of miracle that God was working in him when he observed her rather than as his own devout response to the spectacle of her virtue: "for nothing was thus outwardly brought to the senses, that could cause such an inward joy. Indeed as I have said, the presence of the demon was felt close by, its rage was feared, the sorrow of the family was heard, and the sadness of the girl could be observed; and among these things, I ask: whence could have come the joy and such an unwonted change?"[102] He does refer to her evident virtue: "at these things I began to be astonished not only that amid such blows and such troubles I did not hear any groan or sob from her, but also that in neither words nor actions did she give anyone a sign of distress, not to mention impatience; rather she remained motionless, without murmur or complaint."[103] But he loses track of this thought almost immediately, as he proceeds to describe her "sighing as though some unusual affliction had come to her"[104]—surely a sign of distress—and anyway avoids attributing his unwonted joy to the observation of her virtuous patience. When, at the end of the account, he reflects back on the course of events, he says nothing about her virtues but much about what was happening within himself. In a complex thought, he says that he hopes that because of that night at Stommeln—as his own equivalent of the night when Judas left the disciples, the night when the Virgin bore the son of God, or the moment when Christ was resurrected from the dead—he himself might lose his tendency to faithlessness and his own soul might be renewed to new life: "and therefore I wanted to witness and attend the marvels of God that were being shown clearly and in so many ways in the aforesaid person, to whom already my soul was joined in the spirit of truth and the love of sincerity to such an extent that I could hardly think of God without remembering her."[105]

Peter's way of writing about Christine is therefore to write about himself. He is determined to place himself in full view. What remains for us to consider is the meaning she held for him.

WEDDING GUEST AND SISTER OF THE BRIDE

Peter professed to experience in Christine's presence an unwonted devotion that came as an answer to prayers of long standing. Since she did not presume to teach or otherwise direct him, there is no show of role reversal here like that between James of Vitry and Mary of Oignies. Nonetheless, Peter's descriptions of Christine's effect on him recall James's descriptions of those men whom only Mary could cure of spiritual torpor: here again a holy woman acts, even if inadvertently, from a sphere of authority distinctively her own, possessing a divine favor inaccessible to others, notably men, who derive a benefit from it through the devotion she inspires. What is new in Peter is his thorough exploration of that benefit and of how he acquires it: he attempts to state in theological terms what he believes to be extraordinary about Christine, to suggest why those extraordinary qualities draw him to her, and to examine how they affect him when he is with her. In all of this Peter is comparing himself with Christine and finding himself deficient in the supernatural grace he sees as characteristic of her life. Accordingly he presents her not just as object of his admiration but also as token of his shortcomings.

Central to Peter's understanding of Christine are those things he observes in her that he considers to be outside the realm of nature. I have already observed that he is not so much interested in her patience or charity as in what he regards as wonders (*mirabilia*), such as raptures and the signs of Christ's passion that appeared on her body; what constitutes these things as wonders is, precisely, that they do not obey the normal ways of nature. In his account of a visit in June 1269 when Christine, in a rapture, trapped the hand of his companion Friar Albrandino against the wall with her stiffened arm, Peter reports Albrandino reasoning that since the pressure he felt from her hand lacked tension or movement it was "not natural" in origin but rather "supernatural."[106] In Peter's first description of one of her raptures—this one occurring in Lent of 1268 at the parish priest's house in Stommeln—he says that Christine

> was taken [*rapta*] by such a departure of mind [*excessum mentis*] that all her senses ceased their working and her whole body hardened and she gave no sign of sensible life, and—to add to the astonishment—what it was that had drawn her spirit could not be discerned. While these things were happening I wept for joy, as I admit, and was astounded by the marvel and I gave thanks to the Giver for the gift of such divine outpouring; for I attributed none of this to nature or to human activity, but recognized with reverence the divine presence in this event. ... And seeing therefore that no mortal human could have arranged this, I judged it to be what I have read about in the Apostle: "if we depart from our mind [it is of God]" [2 Cor. 5:13], for it seemed to me that I had not seen anything else like it, and I began all the more excitedly to consider what was happening, and pay attention to her words, and ponder her movements and actions, and commit them to the depths of my memory, because I attributed all these things to the privilege of an extraordinary grace.[107]

Here "nature" and "human activity" are contrasted with "the privilege of an extraordinary grace." That her rapture was *not* natural—a point reinforced by the attendant marvels that Peter is careful to note in his other accounts of raptures, such as a wonderful fragrance, a book suddenly flying through the air toward her, a sweet voice coming from her chest, the appearance of a dew on her pallium that has healing powers, the mysterious appearance of wounds on her body[108]—implies for Peter that in the raptures some unusual version of divine grace must be manifest.

Though they are evidently not natural, these phenomena attending Christine are, in Peter's view, thoroughly explainable. In the poem and accompanying commentary that comprise the first part of the *Codex Iuliacensis*,[109] he accounts for them with theological precision, in terms that owe much to the thought of Thomas Aquinas, whose lectures he must have heard in Paris in 1269 and 1270.[110] There he identifies the grace that was at work in her raptures and stigmata as a certain "privileged grace [*gracia privilegiata*]," through which "it is given to certain people to have, by means of rapture, a foretaste" of heavenly beatitude.[111] He distinguishes this "privileged grace" from other categories of grace, such as the grace accorded humans in their created state (*gracia condicionis*), the grace by which Christ was incarnated (*gracia assumptionis*), the grace by which we are made righteous in God's sight (*gracia iustificationis*), or rewarded in heaven (*gracia glorificacionis*).[112] Those other categories illustrate the principle that "grace enriches nature"—which, as Monika Asztalos has pointed out, is Peter's equivalent of the Thomistic axiom that "grace perfects nature"—by the fact that their effects improve the workings of nature but do not contradict or surpass it.[113] So, for instance, Christine's own ascetical disciplines and her way of life in general, which involve no actions or events that are not explicable by natural causes, illustrate such ordinary workings of grace, (especially, it would seem, of *gracia iustificationis*):

> Mos, os, cor, cultus, cibus et gradus, actio, vultus!
> Ieiunat, vigilat, patitur, pugnatque triumphat!
> Ornat naturam virtus naturaque curam
> istis ostendit propriam, quas gloria pendit.

> Her way of life, speech, feeling, demeanor, her food and gait, her activity,
>   her countenance:
> She fasts, keeps vigil, suffers, fights and triumphs!
> Virtue adorns nature and nature shows its proper care
> for those things on which glory depends.[114]

But by contrast, the "privileged grace" at work in Christine's raptures and the marvelous signs that attend them produces effects that are not recognizably within the realm of nature but rather "surpass" it. In lines parallel to the preceding ones, the poem proceeds to describe what happens in her raptures:

> Raptus, amor, placor, ardor, odor, livor et cruor, angor!
> Eructat, iubilat, subridet, deficit, orat!
> Istis natura gaudens superat sua iura,
> hoc ultra votum prebet quia gracia totum.

> Her rapture, love, contentment, ardor, fragrance, her bruises and blood,
>   her anguish:
> She gushes, shouts for joy, smiles, withdraws, entreats!
> Rejoicing in these things, nature surpasses its laws,
> And grants what is beyond its promise because all is by grace.[115]

Peter does not quote the maxim "grace enriches nature" in reference to this "privileged grace," to which it evidently does not apply, since the effects of this grace are not natural, as he has been so intent to point out.[116] But it is also important to note that Peter, the pupil of Aquinas, is unwilling to characterize any effects of "privileged grace" as being in conflict with or defiance of nature even when they are evidently not natural; indeed, he pictures nature in these verses as being in willing collusion even with this kind of grace whose effects "surpass" it. This suggests a concern to present the grace at work in her raptures, however extraordinary its effects, as manifesting the same harmonious divine disposition toward the world as any other sort of grace would manifest.

In theorizing about Christine's grace, Peter does not wish simply to come to an understanding of what happens to Christine; he also wishes to experience it in his own right. So in letter 10, from Paris, he imagines a conversation with Christ in which he asks about Christine's obliviousness to everything, indeed even to herself, when she is in her raptures. These, as we know from the poem, he considered to "surpass" nature in the sense of not being bound by its laws. But, he asks Christ, does the rapture not *violate* nature, in the sense of severing the bond between the body and the "rational spirit" that was established at creation? Christ tells him no, and that what he, Christ, intends in such a case is not to sever the body from the spirit but rather to "convert and attract to me the body whose senses have been prone to evil since adolescence, so that, once my spirit has been tasted, all flesh would seem insipid"[117]—in other words, not to forsake the body at all but rather to improve it. "In this way," says Christ to Peter, "I draw the spirit to me, marked by my image, and through it I will take to myself that clay that is composed of all the elements, so that, just as corporal and spiritual things are created by me, thus both of them according to the means possible for them are beatified in me and alienated in a certain way from themselves, so as to be transformed in me."[118] What the rapture displays, then, is really nothing other than Christ working to sanctify the whole person experiencing it: but then how could Peter not wish such sanctification for himself? So he tells her that he would like to undergo raptures just as she does: "Who would grant it to me that the Omnipotent would hear my desire, that I might live in the way or, as I would more truly say, in the divine gift, in which you live, when you depart to hide yourself in the hidden divine face, and find protection in the tabernacle from the human crowd and contradictions of tongues [Ps. 30:21]?"[119] Here we see him not merely holding Christine up as an object of his wonder, but also—perhaps more profoundly, at the heart of that wonder—wishing to be like her.

To wish to be like Christine, however, is to set himself up for a comparison with her that exposes him in his own eyes as severely deficient. So it is that in letter 10, from Paris, immediately after expressing that desire for rapture and wishing that he might "participate in this [Christine's] way of life even in some remote way,"[120] Peter proceeds to imagine himself as a third party to her marriage with Christ. He has anticipated this image in an earlier Paris letter (letter 5) in which he wrote of himself as a guest at the wedding who was privileged "to enter the bridal chamber with duty and reverence, and to listen intently and devoutly to the wedding song," or, barring that, at least to hear about the bridegroom from the bride.[121] But here the image becomes more complex, and he makes himself out not simply as an observer of the marriage but rather as someone with more intimate involvement as well. He does begin by placing himself again as observer: "with what affection," he exclaims, "would I take pleasure in the joining and intimacy, the conjunction and the combined rejoicing of you and your beloved, the two whom I so love and desire, and who are even dearer to each other, when from you I would hear your vows of devotion, words of delight, sounds of obedience, prayers of expectation, the joy of acceptance, of exultation, of enjoyment, the desire of continuation, the sigh of separation and the tears of desolation!"[122] But then he explains his presence at the wedding not as that of a guest but as that of a rejected bride, apparently Leah, to whom, in the biblical story (Gen. 30), the patriarch Jacob preferred the more beautiful Rachel. It is Christine who, like Rachel, has attracted the husband's—the heavenly bridegroom's—affection; Peter asks rhetorically whether he should not be "indignant and spiteful at that person, however formerly beloved, who snatched me from me my husband" and whether—here recalling the strategy of Leah, who lured Jacob temporarily from Rachel's bed to her own with a bribe of mandrakes—he should dare to say to Christ, "come in to me, because I have bought you with a price [Gen. 30:16]?"[123] But the answer is of course no; he lacks the substance of the figurative bribe, namely "purity and love, devotion and honest conduct, continual and fervent conversation, sublime and affective contemplation."[124] At any rate his "sister" Christine is more acceptable to the bridegroom, being beautiful in virtue and fecund in good works whereas he is not, and so it is hardly a surprise that he experiences no raptures.[125]

His professed sense of inferiority to Christine in turn leads Peter to speak of his devotion to her, which however has a certain edge to it, a tone of concession. Still in the role of Leah, he asks: If he cannot either entice the bridegroom or rightly complain of being ignored, what can he do?

What therefore remains for me, older in years and already unsuccessful in marriage—because I am cold in heart, wrinkled in face, poor in income, sterile in childbearing and, overshadowed by my younger sister, an object of disdain—except to avoid displeasing the one whom I have not deserved to please? I know what I will do: I will show myself familiar with my sister and devoted and obedient to her husband, so that she might at least tell me something about her flood of joys and her secrets, and that he might come the more freely, frequently, festively and familiarly, when in one of the sisters he finds the marriage bed prepared and in the other a ready obedience of the body, and in both the desire of devoted expectation. I will therefore please the bridegroom with prayers, please him with gifts, please him with dutiful works; and I will say to him, so that I might more easily allure him, please him better and draw him more strongly, "I have a more beautiful younger sister; go in to her, join with her, embrace her," so that the memory of me will not be removed from his affections.[126]

In his picturing here of the triad consisting of himself, Christine and Christ, at least two different movements are evident. On the one hand, he seems to be saying, in an almost pandering way, that he will find merit with Christ by presenting Christine to him, and on the other hand, he says that he will learn of Christ by associating himself with Christine. In either case, Christine serves him as a means to bring himself closer, in some sense, to Christ. But in either event by casting himself as Christine's sister and thus identifying himself much more closely with her, he imagines himself not simply as her admirer but, at a deeper level, as her losing competitor, and thus he highlights his own inadequacy as all the more striking because he is without the excuse of a generic difference. To put the matter another way: he is not a favored outside observer, brought in to see the wedding, but rather himself a humbled insider, a failed bride, living with the conviction that in theory he could, and perhaps should, have been as acceptable to Christ as Christine—a conviction that then tends to make him display his difference from her the more strongly, and to add a touch of shame. In his last letter from Paris, he laments that "amid such great devotion on the part of so many [people he has encountered] I am dry, amid the fervent love of so many I am cold, amid such energetic activity I am subdued, and amid such strict religion I do not fear to behave laxly."[127]

This avowed sense of inferiority on account of his failure to (according to his later explanations) soar like Christine beyond the limits of nature seems to have been at its most acute in the early years when Peter was a student, although he never lost that sense entirely. In letters written much later, after his 1279 visit to Stommeln—and in the context of commiseration about her family's hardships—he can think of her and himself in terms that suggest something more like equality. He imagines her married to himself as well as to Christ ("you who are dearest to me and are through divine love betrothed both to God and to my soul, pray the Lord that we keep the chaste faith of this betrothal and that we might know the pledge of our love to be undiminished")[128] and discerns "a certain similarity in us—a similarity to the eternal fellowship and intimate love of the saints."[129] He speaks of being joined with her, "though far apart and dissimilar in daily activity, in one bond of friendship."[130] But when, even in those late letters, he turns his attention back from the matter of her friendship to that of her putative mysticism, he can again compare himself to her in markedly negative terms, as when he pictures her dallying with Christ in a paradise from which he has been excluded.[131]

Peter's self-perceived lack of the grace that would allow him to proceed beyond nature into the immediate presence of God is thus closely bound to his professed devotion to Christine. Since such a grace was so famously the prerogative of women in this period, it is perhaps unsurprising that when Peter tries to imagine his own prospects as a candidate to receive it, he thinks of himself as a woman, a bride. But by his own account he is a singularly unsuccessful bride. He presents his experience of interaction with Christine, whether in the role of inferior sister or that of wedding guest, as the closest he will come to the divine presence that eludes him.

CONCLUSION

Peter's work—including his own narratives and letters as well as the collection that brought these together with the writings of Christine—presents therefore a picture not simply or even primarily of Christine in her own right but rather of himself observing her and pondering what he observed. Christine, as a saint whose putative favor with God produced little fruit in the form of active charity or useful knowledge of any sort, is an improbable candidate for a hagiographer's attention. But the very paucity of her evident contribution to the world around her helps Peter keep his gaze fixed upon the narrow field of his own interaction with her. The narrowness of that field of vision in turn allows him the liberty of extending its depth, and it is the depth of his gaze that gives these writings about some highly circumscribed interactions of an otherwise obscure Beguine a broader significance, at least in terms of the themes of our study. For in observing himself with Christine, Peter explores his own response to that aspect of a holy woman's life which also most fascinated the male confidants of other holy women in this period—namely, the direct contact with God that placed her in a sphere of her own, outside his control or direction. That exploration leads him to recognize at the root of his fascination a desire that has unmistakable parallels in other men's writing about such women, though it was perhaps never expressed so boldly as Peter expresses it. This was the desire not simply to be edified or informed but to possess for himself what the woman possessed, and thus even, in a sense, to *be* the woman.

CHAPTER 6

Hagiography and Theology in the *Memorial* of Angela of Foligno

I T WAS PROBABLY AROUND 1297—a decade or so after Peter of Dacia, in Sweden, sent his last letter to Christine of Stommeln—that an anonymous Franciscan friar far to the south in Umbria completed his *Memorial* of the woman we know as Angela of Foligno (d. 1309). The *Memorial* presents this woman's account of her life, principally her inner life, as told to the friar. She begins that account by telling of her conversion to penitence and voluntary poverty, and then she speaks of the revelations she received and her increasingly profound mystical experience.

Throughout the work the friar includes, in his own voice, abundant commentary not only about his interactions with Angela but also about his role as her literary assistant. In fact his place in the record of her experience is rather like the place Guibert of Gembloux had wished to have in the literary visions of Hildegard: he appears not simply as Angela's admirer and beneficiary but also as her genuine collaborator, whose contributions become a substantive part of the literary product. The friar stands finally *with* Angela in the text of the *Memorial*. He looks together with her toward God, in a theological enterprise. In presenting her as a theologian and in according himself a role in her teaching, the friar introduces elements not present in the work of Peter of Dacia and James of Vitry, and in this sense the narrative of the *Memorial*, as it proceeds, moves in a direction that is different from theirs. Fundamentally, nonetheless, the figure of the friar here belongs to the hagiographical world of Peter and James, rather than that of Guibert, or of Ekbert of Schönau. For he shares with Peter and James an acute sense of the otherness of the woman about whom he wrote, a conviction that she spoke from an experience of God which he could in no sense share or supervise and which remained, for all of his efforts, finally beyond the reach of his words. For the friar it is, paradoxically, precisely *from* that conviction that the possiblity of true collaboration arises.

THE MEMORIAL

The *Memorial*, which exists in several fourteenth- and fifteenth-century manuscripts, presents Angela's life and experience in the form of a rather complex narrative that is examined in greater detail below.[1] The work constitutes the first of the two parts of the so-called Book of Angela, the second part being a miscellany of teachings (*Instructions*) ascribed to her.[2] As for dating, the text of the *Memorial* mentions the pontificate of Pope Celestine V, who was elected 5 July 1294, as having begun shortly after the start of one of the late phases of Angela's experience, the sixth "supplementary step" (see below), which lasted for two years; and the so-called *Testificatio*, a short text probably dating from 1308 and 1309, which appears at the head of the *Memorial* in three fourteenth-century manuscripts, declares that the cardinal James Colonna read and approved it "before he fell into scandal with the supreme pontiff," a phrase that apparently refers to his conflict with Boniface VIII, which began 10 May 1297. The work was probably completed, therefore, sometime shortly before the latter event.[3]

A very little is known of Angela from other sources. There is one known reference to her in a contemporary text outside the Book, namely an acknowledgement by the spiritual Franciscan author Ubertino da Casale of her influence upon him in the prologue to his *Arbor Vitae*, from 1305.[4] There exists also a report of her death, on 4 January 1309, in the oldest surviving manuscript of the *Memorial* (Assisi, Communal Library 342), in the form of a scribal note placed in a way that suggests the event may have just occurred when it was penned.[5] But otherwise, information about Angela comes from the texts of the Book, indeed, for all intents and purposes, exclusively from the *Memorial*.[6]

As the *Memorial* presents her, Angela was a lay penitent. We can place her, that is, within the broad penitential movement of the time in Italy, a movement similar to that of the Beguines of the north both in the extensive involvement of women and, more generally, in the impetus to express strong religious devotion and commitment outside the cloister.[7] She was a married woman when she converted to a life of penitence, but before long her husband, mother, and sons all died, in answer, as we are told, to her prayers.[8] This freed her to embrace poverty by disposing of her property, which she had already begun and now continued in stages, although she appears to have remained in her own house instead of joining one of the several communities of penitents then coming into existence in Foligno, as in other Italian cities.[9] As is typical of the hagiography of Italian penitent women (and again like that of the northern Beguines, for instance the vita of Mary of Oignies) the *Memorial* pictures Angela as displaying a profound, even obsessive, devotion to the Passion and the Eucharist and exercising prophetic gifts.[10] We also see her performing works of charity for lepers and for the poor.[11] And like many other female penitents and Beguines, she came into close contact with mendicant friars, in her case Franciscans. She appears to have taken a vow as a Franciscan penitent; the friar who wrote the *Memorial* pictures himself taking responsibility for her supervision.[12]

So much the *Memorial* tells us about the external events and circumstances of Angela's life. But the work is particularly remarkable for what it does *not* tell us. It maintains a strange air of anonymity. The friar refers to Angela never by name but instead by variations of the epithet "*fidelis Christi* [Christ's faithful one]" and, once, "L," possibly for the diminutive "Lella."[13] He also avoids attaching names to most of the minor figures mentioned in the narrative, never names Foligno as the city that provides the work's main setting,[14] and gives very few details that would aid in dating events or otherwise putting them in context. M. J. Ferré, in an article in 1925, reasoned from apparent clues in the text to establish "the principal dates" of Angela's life, including 1248 as her birth year, 1285 or 1286 as the year of her conversion, and 1291 as the year of the journey to Assisi that led to her collaboration with the friar.[15] For a long while scholars tended to accept Ferré's dates as though they were established facts. But in a provocative article from 1995, Jacques Dalarun points out the tenuous basis of most of Ferré's dates and suggests that the *Memorial* may be essentially resistant to such an attempt at dating, for its obscurity regarding place and time appears to be quite deliberate.[16]

It is indeed not only the identity of Angela that is obscure here, but also that of the writer. He refers to himself only as "*frater scriptor*" ("friar-writer," "brother writer") or (once) "Friar A."[17] He calls himself a kinsman of Angela and also her confessor and adviser, but he remains mute about the circumstances of his life beyond his encounters with her.[18] Later traditions that name him "Arnold" have no basis in the sources, and it is not at all clear that he is to be identified with the bishop's chaplain to whom Angela first confessed after her conversion, as has often been assumed.[19]

Why the obscurities? Apparently there was a need for secrecy. The connection between the *Memorial* and the spiritual Franciscans may possibly be a key here. The names that do figure in the sources about Angela suggest the connection: Ubertino was a leader among the spirituals, Cardinal Colonna a friend to the cause, Celestine V one of their heroes. Given the persecution that at least some groups of the spirituals were undergoing, the friar and those around him may have thought it best to keep the figures of the *Memorial* anonymous, if this indeed was the company they kept.[20] The *Testificatio* also suggests a perceived necessity for secrecy, even as it shows an evident concern for institutional approval that places its audience within the order: after the reference to Cardinal James Colonna, it declares that the work was also approved by eight "famous" friars who had served in positions of authority in the order, but who, contrary to what we might expect from such an endorsement, are not named.[21] The fact that at some point the *Testificatio* itself was erased in the Assisi manuscript suggests, furthermore, that the evident need for such endorsement itself came to be considered something to hide. Nonetheless, the exact relationship of the *Memorial* to the ideas and programs of the spirituals remains less than clear. Comparison, for example, between the *Memorial* and work of Ubertino of Casale has not shown close similarities in either tone or ideas.[22] As David Burr has pointed out, there is little indication in the *Memorial* of a polemic against the rest of the order such as was typical of the spirituals; if caution about its reception was indeed the reason for the secrecy, the latter may well be explainable apart from Angela's association with the spirituals per se (whatever her actual relations with them), simply on the basis of passages in the *Memorial* that in themselves could be seen to push against the bounds of orthodoxy.[23]

Whatever the reasons for the anonymity of the *Memorial*, the friar presents in fact a vivid picture of Angela's relationship with himself, *as it pertains to the writing of the work*. He does so in two ways, both of which recall James of Vitry and Peter of Dacia and yet also show him going a step beyond them in a way that pushes beyond hagiography per se. In the first place, he addresses frequent first-person comments to the reader that serve to frame his presentation of Angela in terms of his own perceptions. This is reminiscent of Peter, yet these perceptions do not serve primarily to establish the woman's sanctity as Peter's do; rather, they are the friar's attempt to mediate to the reader the substance of what Angela has said, and in this sense he presents himself not merely as devotee (though he does not cease to be such) but also, simultaneously, as a pupil or coworker, attempting to articulate, in his own avowedly imperfect way, the truths he has heard from her—finally to the extent of representing the entire work as such an attempt rather than as simply the product of Angela's dictation as it may seem on first impression. In the second place, he reports, as though at

a remove, his many interactions with Angela during the time when she was telling him of her experiences. These interactions show him, like James and Peter,
admiring a woman whom he perceives to abound in graces, which confront
him with the limits of his own powers or knowledge and also provide the means
to extend those limits in some measure; and yet the friar's very admiration and
his very sense of difference from her, and his conviction that she had some vital
grace lacking in himself, cause him to report, at her leading, a certain transcendence of that difference. By that transcendence the two of them become two
subjects, two souls coming to knowledge of God as they try to find words for
her inexpressible experience. For in the universe of the *Memorial,* experience of
God is of all things worthy of pursuit, and its achievement worthy of veneration. But that achievement brings with it a strong message that knowledge of
God is not finally to be entrusted to the human understanding or enclosed in its
human exemplars—a message that we can well imagine to have been congenial
to the Franciscan spirituals in their resistance to Pope Boniface's mobilization
of papal authority against them. It is, anyway, in the context of the friar's very
recognition of the otherness of the saint that her otherness is transcended; the
oppositeness of saint and venerator fades just when it is being highlighted, and
the common ground on which they stand comes into view.

THE VOICE OF THE FRIAR

Two human voices speak in the *Memorial.* One is the putative voice of Angela,
which tells of her "experience and the doctrine of that same experience."[24] The
other voice is that of the friar, heard at frequent intervals, telling of the circumstances in which he listened to her and of his interventions and his struggles
to understand her. The friar's comments in his own voice interrupt Angela's
narrative; the work would be much smoother to read, and less complicated, if
Angela's voice stood alone—as is the case in the so-called minor recension of
the *Memorial* (probably originating, as Emore Paoli has shown, in the circles of
the Modern Devotion in the Low Countries in the fifteenth century) in which
omission of the friar's interventions serves a broader program of emphasiz-
ing Angela's asceticism and minimizing her more controversial mysticism.[25]
But those interruptions are, for the friar himself, an essential element of the
work. By means of them, as will be seen, he takes what would otherwise stand
as a straightforward, if remarkable, piece of autohagiography from Angela and
obliges the reader not to accept it at face value but rather to read it as a flawed

product of his own efforts to mediate between her experience and the reader. What constitutes the core subject matter of the *Memorial* is therefore not just the *substance* of the mystic's message but also its *reception*—the way in which listeners, here represented by the friar, will understand it.

As Beatrice Coppini has pointed out (drawing on the narrative morphology of Gérard Gennette), the voices of Angela and the friar define, respectively, two "levels" of the narrative of the *Memorial*. At the first level is the voice of the friar, who, describing the circumstances and substance of his interactions with Angela, addresses himself directly to the reader. The voice of Angela, then, conveying her "experience and doctrine," speaks at a second level of the narrative in the sense that she addresses her narrative not to the reader, but rather to the friar himself, putatively in the course of those interactions that are the subject of his own narrative.[26] Formally, therefore, his narrative contains hers within it. It is true that the *Memorial* begins with the second level of narrative rather than, as one might perhaps expect, the first. For after the opening statement in which the friar, with no reference to himself, declares that "Christ's faithful one [*fidelis Christi*]" had identified, "as found in herself, thirty steps or changes that are made by a soul advancing in the way of penitence," the voice of Angela immediately relates, in short order and with only brief interruption by the friar, the first nineteen of these "steps" and the beginning of a twentieth.[27] But then the voice of the friar intervenes to establish the foundation of the first level of the narrative, by giving an extended account of how, at the point in her life marked by that twentieth step, he came to hear and record what she said, including her retroactive description of the steps about which we have already heard.[28] It is here that he identifies himself as her kinsman and confessor and explains that in their hometown sometime after she had embarrassed him by shrieking and crying out inconsolably in his presence on a visit to the basilica of St. Francis, at Assisi, he "obliged" her to reveal her experiences, intending to discern if there were a "malignant spirit" at work. But as he listened to her, he became convinced that her experience was really of God and began making the record which would become the *Memorial*.[29] After this explanation, the narrative returns to the second level—to the voice of Angela, that is—which goes all the way to the end of the work with her detailed description of the remaining steps of her spiritual life (organized by the friar into seven rather the expected ten and, to avoid confusion, designated by editors as "supplementary" steps) but with continual reversions to the first level, as the friar again and again interpolates his own comments. These draw the reader's attention away from Angela's narrative itself to his own interventions and his attempts to come to terms with what she has told him. In this back-and-forth switching between the levels of narrative, the friar keeps himself, and the processes of his understanding, before the reader's eyes.

When considered in its own right without reference (for the moment) to the friar's interruptions, the narrative at the second level—that is, Angela's narrative—stands as a piece of hagiography. That is to say: it focuses upon her person to document her virtues and the favor that God has shown toward her. It is, in effect, a saint's vita, and the fact that the voice of that very saint presents it, though unusual, is far from unique in the period.[30] The story is of a woman who, in the context of a life of penance and poverty, received revelations and experienced mystical states. It unfolds progressively. In the first twenty steps Angela describes the deepening of her penitence, from conviction of sin, confession, and recognition of grace, to a greater knowledge of self, a desire to follow in the way of the cross and therefore in poverty, and tentative consolations in the presence of God.[31] Then in the supplementary steps, while continuing to develop those penitential themes, she begins to speak of receiving direct messages from God (variously the second or third persons of the Trinity) and feeling the presence of God immediately through her senses.[32] Accordingly, a major theme throughout the supplementary steps is that of discernment: she worries about being "deceived" in thinking her experiences are from God[33] and reports receiving various assurances, including several revelations of Christ's partiality toward her over other people,[34] but also, in the mystical flights of the final supplementary step, a sure if temporary sense of security.[35] She also, beginning in the third supplementary step, reports revelations of a discursive sort—for instance, a parable to illustrate who are God's "own children" (those invited to share the cup and plate of their host at dinner) and another to suggest how Christ in his divinity could experience human pain (a nobleman had his house destroyed, though he himself was not injured).[36] In the later steps she also describes intimate physical encounters with Christ—he embraces her inside her soul, she enters into his side, she kisses him within his tomb on Holy Saturday[37]—and vivid visions of his poverty and passion.[38] In the last step, she relates profound encounters with God, whom she perceived within a darkness that was beyond all understanding, beyond images or ideas, beyond even love.[39] In the midst of all this, she also reports revelations received for others: she answers questions posed of her (Can God be "known in creatures?"[40] How is Christ's body simultaneously present on all altars?[41]), tells a certain friar of his impending reappointment to the post of guardian,[42] and addresses an admonitory parable to the friar-writer himself, likening him to a negligent schoolboy.[43]

There are also points in the *Memorial*, particularly in the late supplementary steps, when the narrative of Angela pushes momentarily beyond hagiography per se. These are the moments when, instead of simply reporting the revelations and mystical states that come to her, she pauses to reflect upon them, to generalize and formulate teachings of her own about the nature and knowability of God. Already in the early steps, in worrying about the genuineness of her experiences, she remarks often on their inexpressibility ("it seems to me that all the things we might say are as trifles, because this was something else than could be expressed; and I am very much ashamed to speak more"),[44] posing questions of God about the revelations she has received,[45] and drawing conclusions of her own—as when, in the fourth supplementary step, God shows her his power and his humility, and in both cases we hear her response: in the first case to observe that the world is pregnant with God and in the second to examine herself and find only pride.[46] But the reader sees her reflecting on her experience especially in the late steps where, in extended passages, she temporarily ceases narrating her experience per se and speaks discursively to questions or problems that the experience has raised. Thus in the fifth supplementary step, when the friar has asked her how she discerns the presence of God ("the pilgrim") in the soul, she responds with an extended discourse saying, for instance, that God can be present in the soul without the soul's awareness, that the proper proof of God's presence is the soul's lack of fear, that the sweetness of God can be believed only by one who has experienced it, and that the more one feels the presence of God the less adequate are words, even the words of Scripture, to express it—all of which she asserts not as revelations she has received but rather apparently as conclusions that she herself has reached.[47] The same is true of the discourse that follows on "the ways ... in which spiritual persons may be deceived."[48] Then at the beginning of the seventh step, after speaking of the experience of seeing God in "darkness [*tenebra*]," she begins making comparisons with her previous experiences to explain how the encounter with the darkness involved a more profound knowledge of God, beyond devotion or love, and in any case distinct from and far greater than her erstwhile exalted visions of Christ.[49] She considers at length the ineffability of this most exalted state in which she is completely alone with God and beyond all creatures.[50] In such passages, Angela has ceased, in effect, to be her own hagiographer and speaks instead as theologian, not presenting herself per se, that is, her virtues and experience, but rather expounding upon, in their own right, the ideas that her experience has suggested to her.[51] In these instances, the friar allows us to hear her as she speculates and teaches—exactly what James of Vitry was reluctant to do in the case of Mary—and the work shifts from a piece of hagiography in the strict sense to something more like a work of mystical theology. This is, to be sure, a smooth and natural movement, in the sense that the very experiences on which Angela the theologian reflects appear in the text, in themselves, as evidence of Angela the saint; yet it makes for a kind of a hybrid of genre.

Such is the substance of the second level of the narrative, the voice of Angela. If its mix of (as I have put it) hagiography and theology gives the narrative at that level a certain complexity in its own right, that complexity is increased by the frequent interruptions of the voice of the friar—that is, the frequent reversions to the first level of the narrative. For the friar's long description of the event at Assisi and its aftermath, and then his interpolated references to his exchanges with Angela in the course of her narrative, raise doubts, often in strong terms, whether what the reader has been hearing is precisely Angela's voice.

The friar makes insistent reference to this inaccuracy of the narrative at its second level, ascribing it to various causes. Sometimes the press of circumstances made him hurry in recording what she said so that he missed part of it. In the second supplementary step, for example, when Angela has reported a revelation declaring that no one can be excused for failing to love God, the friar injects the comment that he did not take note of everything she said because he was rushing.[52] In the following step, he says that he condensed, "because of hurry [*propter festinationem*]," her teaching about how the divinity of Christ can have experienced the suffering of his humanity.[53] The reader is therefore left to wonder what may be missing here. Later, at the beginning of the fifth supplementary step, he explains that because of the "prohibition of the friars"—a hint that suggests some difficulty with his own superiors over his attentions to her, otherwise unexplained—he had to rely on a "small boy" to glean from Angela what turns out to be a passage of several pages of her narrative. The passage, which includes her accounts of visions of Christ's poverty and his Passion, and the pain she felt in observing them, is, the friar says, so "meagerly and badly" written that Angela urged him to destroy it; apparently having ignored her advice, he has copied it out into the *Memorial* just as he received it (though translating it from Italian to Latin), since he does not understand the words well enough to guess how they ought to be revised![54] Elsewhere he makes it clear that even when he has heard her directly, he has had trouble understanding her. In his general description of the project of the *Memorial* he says that he was like a "sieve," unable retain what she told him, and he cites as evidence various critical responses she has given him to what he had written on the basis of their sessions:

And this may somewhat show how I was not able to grasp anything but the very obvious from the divine words [spoken by her]: once, when I had written correctly what I had been able to grasp from what she said, I read back to her what I had written so that she might tell me what else to write, and she said that she was amazed that she did not recognize it. And another time when I read to her so that she could see if I had written well, she replied that I spoke dryly and without any flavor, which amazed her. And another time she explained: "through these words I remember the ones I spoke to you, but the writing is very obscure because these words that you read to me do not explain the things they refer to, and so the writing is obscure." And another time she said: "you have written down the lesser things, and things that were nothing at all, but of the precious thing felt by the soul you have not written."[55]

Elsewhere she declares repeatedly that what he has written is true but nonetheless defective.[56]

All of this would seem to undermine the reader's confidence in the narrative of Angela, and indeed that seems to be the friar's intention—or at least, he wishes to undermine confidence that it *is* Angela's narrative, that it is what *Angela* said. The narrative calls attention to itself, in other words, as the *friar's* narrative.[57] In effect, he makes clear that the words are his, and not necessarily Angela's, and that, in this sense, he himself is the writer of the *Memorial*. The second level of the narrative, though based on what he heard from her, nonetheless stands as his composition; moreover, he is at pains that we should know this. He may seem to state the contrary in describing his procedure in writing:

I wrote with great reverence and fear so as to put in nothing of my own, nor even so much as a word [*dictio*] that I had not been able to grasp correctly from her as she was speaking, as though from her mouth, and did not write anything after I had gone away from her; and even when I was sitting with her, I made her repeat to me several times the statement [*verbum*] I had to write down.[58]

But he cannot mean that the words he wrote were the very words she spoke, for immediately he goes on to report comments from Angela, which I have quoted already, that imply the contrary: that in hearing him read what he had written she did not recognize what she had said and, more precisely, that though "through these words I *remember* the ones I spoke to you, still the writing is very obscure."[59] Later he will comment, about a certain set of sayings, that the words she actually spoke were "more in number, and more efficacious, and full of light" than the ones he has written,[60] and he will report her telling him something about divine justice that she could not entirely explain and accordingly he could not "grasp [*capere*]" to write—implying that writing was for him not simply a matter of transcribing her words but of somehow translating them into his understanding.[61] The distinction between her words and his own is so clear here that he can hardly be unwittingly, let alone deliberately, undermining his own self-presentation as a careful scribe.[62] Instead it would seem that for him there was no contradiction implied in claiming to present a woman's revelations accurately yet in fact placing his own words in her mouth.

Indeed, in the very midst of his avowed inadequacy as a scribe, the friar makes a high claim for his own role in his collaboration with Angela. For though, as we have seen, he makes it clear enough that the *Memorial* is his own composition, he also asserts often, on Angela's authority and God's, that the *Memorial* is a "true" account of her experience and teachings. He quotes Angela to this effect repeatedly, in the context of those very criticisms from her which, as I have already suggested, serve to acknowledge him as writer. Once when he read to her what he had written, "she said that I had written truly but in a way that was abbreviated and reduced ... and it was said to her in revelation that I had written everything truly and without lies, but they were written with great defect."[63] On another occasion similarly "she said that what I had written was not immediate [*actatum*] but on the contrary dry and remote [*deactatum*] although she confirmed that I had written the truth."[64] And at the end of the *Memorial* Angela reports a revelation from God certifying the truth of the whole work: "The whole of this writing is written according to my will and comes from me, that is, it proceeds out of me."[65] In all of this, where exactly the "truth" takes over and the defects leave off is finally obscure. It is clear that one of his supposed defects was to have left things out; thus he quotes Angela saying with evident reprehension, that he has omitted some of what she said, as when she tells him, "you wrote about the lesser things, and about what is nothing at all, but of the precious thing that the soul felt you did not write anything."[66] But the fact of the revelation of the *Memorial*'s "truth" makes these questions finally unimportant; for the narrative of Angela *as he understood it*—which is finally, as the first level of narrative establishes, all the book tells us—itself has the divine blessing.

The fact of the two levels of narrative gives the *Memorial* a certain disjunctive quality and may leave an impression that the work is at cross-purposes with itself. For really only one level of the narrative—the second level—responds directly to the task of the work as stated in the prologue, namely to expose the "experience and doctrine" of a certain person who was faithful to Christ. The other level, namely the one articulated in the friar's voice, continually interrupts the flow and even *appears* to subvert that task—and would do in actuality, if it were not itself also, by divine declaration, "true." But in fact the very disjointedness of the *Memorial* exemplifies and develops its mystical doctrine and provides the work no small part of its power as an exposition of the contradictions inherent in attempts to articulate knowledge of God; in that sense, the unease that the narrative's discontinuities may provoke in the reader is consistent with the writer's purposes.

THE FRIAR AS DEVOTEE AND COLLEAGUE

Within what I am calling the first level of the narrative the friar presents himself to the reader in two ways. As already noted, he speaks as the narrator who informs the reader about the nature and genesis of the text itself. But he also appears as a character in the story he tells—a character who speaks not to the reader but rather to Angela, with whom he is pictured interacting in his role as audience and secretary for her putative words, which constitute the second level of the narrative. I turn now to consider the picture the friar thereby creates of his interactions with her. That picture shows him adopting a stance reminiscent of James of Vitry and Peter of Dacia: he casts himself as witness to Angela's privileged intercourse with God, a third party who both admired and drew upon the graces that he perceived in her and that he found lacking in himself. He appears as convinced of a great gap between her and himself. Yet the relationship between saint and collaborator develops over the course of the *Memorial* into something strikingly different from what we found in Peter and in James. The difference derives not so much from the friar's depiction of himself as from his depiction of Angela: she appears not just as an oracle of God's revelations or a receptacle of the graces the friar admires but also, especially in the final steps of her experience, as a theologian, who reflected *upon* those revelations and graces. When engaging in such reflection, she removes herself from her position at the center of the friar's field of vision and places herself instead by his side, contemplating the divine *with* him, aware beyond all things of the ineffable transcendence of God, a move that pairs the two of them as mere creatures. Throughout her account of the steps of her experience, the friar pictures himself retaining a vivid appreciation of those privileged graces that made her hugely different from, and superior to, himself. But given her stance toward him, the difference between them increasingly displays itself not in terms of a stark otherness—as the difference between discrete spheres of experience—but rather in terms of the mere, if great, distance between points within a common sphere.

The friar depicts himself as her unswerving devotee rather than her spiritual director, from a particular early moment onward. At the time of his encounter with Angela in Assisi, and just afterward, he indeed thought of himself as directing her: at first, scarcely containing his shame on her behalf, he commanded her not to come to Assisi anymore and told her companions not to bring her, and later at Foligno he

> advised and obliged her to tell me everything and [said] that I wished to write it all down so as to be able to consult about it with some wise and spiritual man who had never known her. I said that I wished this, so that she would not be deceived by any evil spirit, and I tried to inspire fear in her by telling her stories of many persons who had been deceived, which showed how she also could be deceived.[67]

And so it was as a wary judge of her experience that he began to record what she told him. But soon the tables turned. As she told him things that he had trouble taking in, he received a sign, in the form of an unspecified "new and special grace of God which I had never experienced before." This brought on a "great reverence and fear" in him such that he began to act as a reverential secretary rather than a judge: he became careful not to add any comment of his own to what she said or to presume to write from memory when she was not present.[68] From that point onward in his narrative we are reminded of the role reversals in James's vita of Mary. The friar makes no more allusions to the hypothetical wise consultant or to the possibility of a demon, and he no longer presents himself as telling her what to do. It is almost as though her own access to the divine had made his direction unnecessary or inappropriate. Angela, for her part, makes her own authority clear: she asserts more than once that when she spoke to him it was not at his command but at God's, and once she receives a revelation criticizing his negligence in cultivating the gifts God has given him.[69] The friar does make references to his priestly attentions to her, but these point precisely to her holiness, as when she made a confession so perfect as to convince him that he could not possibly be "deceived" about the divine origin of her experiences, or when after giving her Communion he asked what extraordinary graces she received in partaking, or when, apparently in his capacity as confessor, he prevented her from injuring herself in her ascetic zeal.[70]

In the accounts of the first four supplementary steps, in which Angela still appears as more of an oracle than a theologian, the friar's stance as admiring devotee casts him as a third party observing the interchanges between saint and God—rather like Peter in his accounts of visits to Christine, although here the interchange is much more open to view and the friar assumes a more active role. Typically in Angela's narration of these steps, she reports her relations with God in the form of conversations, in which she has solicited or responded to divine "locutions" that have instructed or consoled or admonished her. The friar, for his part, presses her at intervals for details or clarification of these reports or introduces a question of his own[71]—requests that she usually passes along to her divine interlocutor, who replies either directly or by engaging her in more conversation, which she again reports to the friar.[72] In the account of the first supplementary step, for example, she responds to the friar's demand to know what happened to her at Assisi by telling him about her conversations with the Holy Spirit, who came to her first at a crossroads on her journey to the town. The Spirit promised, she says, to remain with her until her second visit to the church of St. Francis—where its departure was to trigger her public grief—but also to attend her later on and professed love for her "more than any other woman in the valley of Spoleto." The Spirit corrected her when she construed the assurance of divine favor as a promise of freedom from mortal sin and sought to allay her suspicions of demonic deception, for instance by telling her "I am the one who was crucified for you."[73] When the friar asks how the voice could be that of both the Holy Spirit and the crucified one—of two different persons of the Trinity at once—the voice instructs her to recall to him a locution that she had already reported having received prior to her journey to Assisi, which told her specifically that the whole of the Trinity would come into her, and to counter-question the friar so as to lead him to the conclusion that the persons of the Trinity would be able to speak to her interchangeably: "Ask him, Friar A., why it is that it was said to you that the Trinity had already come into you."[74] It is true that Angela is never *merely* an oracle; here as elsewhere in the *Memorial* she insists upon understanding what the divine voice says before she passes it along. When he asks her, for instance, why God permitted humans to sin and then underwent suffering on account of what he had himself permitted, she responds ultimately by telling him of relevant revelations she has received, but she reports these as responses to a process of critical questioning that she herself had addressed to God.[75] And when the friar asks for an explanation of how Christ's "true children" find sweetness in tribulation—a point made by the divine voice—she explains this by means of examples from her *own* experience, telling him of the sweetness she felt when persecuted by "friars and continents" and when drinking the bathwater of lepers.[76] Yet even in those examples, as throughout the first four supplementary steps, with their alternating divine and human conversations, her implied task is to discern what the divine voice says; she alone hears it directly, and her role is to convey the substance of what she has heard.

But then in the fifth, sixth, and seventh supplementary steps, in which Angela speaks of her most profound mystical experiences, the voice of God rather suddenly recedes from its central place in her narrative. It is in these steps (and indeed already at the very end of the fourth, when she begins to speak in earnest of describing the indescribable)[77] that she appears most clearly in the role of theologian. She does report divine locutions here and there in these steps,[78] and in one long passage in the last step she quotes a series of exchanges between herself and Christ on the subject of the Eucharist.[79] But for the most part she now tries to articulate, patently in her own words, what she herself perceived or learned through her visions and extraordinary states of consciousness. Thus she begins the fifth supplementary step by telling the friar the conclusions she drew from several visions in which she observed Christ but did not (with the exception of her encounter with him in his tomb on Holy Saturday)[80] explicitly interact with him: that his poverty was profound and shocking, that his divine power remained nonetheless apparent, that his foreknowledge of the extent of his persecutors' intentions increased the horror of the Passion, that the Virgin herself could not express the extent of the horror.[81] She comments on her perception of divine love, likening it to a sickle that appears to recede from her in the very process of coming nearer.[82] She generalizes from her experiences to list seven signs that tell her of the presence of God ("the pilgrim") in the soul and to give a rather technical account of how pious souls may deceive themselves.[83] She interprets her struggles with temptation in terms of a conflict between a particular vice and a particular virtue (though she leaves both unspecified).[84] And at great length she tries to describe her experience of God "in darkness [*tenebra*]," the depth of which ruled out any divine self-expression through words or images, so that she is clearly not conveying God's revelations per se but rather her own analyses and insights, as she makes comparisons among her various other experiences to suggest the great profundity of this one[85] and in general tries to find words to impress its very ineffability upon the friar.[86]

It is the receding of the divine voice in those late supplementary steps that causes the shift in the friar's role to which I have referred: from now on, he appears in a certain sense on a level with her. I do not mean to suggest that he begins to consider himself her equal; her authority to speak still comes from her extraordinary access to God, which he never shares. Yet she is *teaching* here—not simply conveying divine messages but rather attempting to make herself understood through articulating her own ideas, and his questions and "resistances" help the process along. That is the shared enterprise: he helps her to teach. Near the beginning of the account of the last supplementary step, for instance, the friar reports himself asking her a question that he says he has found in Augustine, whether "the saints in heaven stand or sit." The question evidently invited the kind of oracular response he had received in the fourth supplementary step when he asked how a certain "tribulation" had conveyed "grace" to her, and she had then received a response for him from the divine voice ("say to that brother, 'why is it that in tribulation she loved not less but more?'," etc.).[87] But here that voice does not speak. Instead she says that she entered a state in which, as she will eventually tell him, she possessed a knowledge that was total yet inexpressible, being manifested in "darkness [*tenebra*]."[88] In saying this she arguably responded to his question, although indirectly and inconclusively, by implying that to perceive heaven truly was to recognize the question as unanswerable. But if so, the response was not God's but Angela's, expressing an insight she had deduced from her experience. When the friar presses her—"when I, the friar, resisted her about the aforesaid darkness and did not understand"—she explains by comparing this perception of the divine in "darkness" to previous, and evidently clearer, visions of God that, she says, were inferior to what she saw now, as part is inferior to whole—implying that it is the very comprehensiveness of her present vision of God that makes it both authoritative and inexpressible.[89] Thus she explains herself without a speech from God. In a similar vein later in the same step, when she has said that her soul veritably "swims [*natat*]" in delight in the presence of God "because love is measured and the spirit is given in measure," the friar "resists" again, objecting that such a notion contradicts Scripture (e.g., John 3:34: "It is not by measure that he gives the Spirit" [RSV]). In response she once again reasons from her own perceptions, this time to place herself more carefully within the limit of correctness that he has pointed out for her: "It is true what he [John] says, that God does not give the *Spirit* in measure, but nonetheless my soul swims and delights in the fact that God gives to his Son and all the saints in measure."[90] Though her insights emerge from an experience unique to herself, still they

---

are in principle accessible to the friar's understanding just as to hers. In this way—and by virtue of her action rather than his own—she has become his fellow traveler.

Nowhere in the *Memorial* does this collegiality between Angela and the friar appear so clearly as when he and she discuss the very experiences that he does not share with her. Angela makes clear again and again that the *sine qua non* of her mystical experience is its inexpressibility. She tells him that she finds the greatness of her experience of divine "darkness" to consist in its transcendence not only of words but also of feelings, and she labels attempts at description of such experience of God as outright blasphemy. And, most suggestively, she uses this notion of divine indescribability to place the truth of such experience beyond the words of Scripture itself, as when saying that one can "babble something" about Scripture by way of explanation, but about these "ineffable divine operations … in the soul, nothing can be said or babbled in any way."[91] Yet exactly for that reason, to speak of her experience at all she must find some way of expressing the *concept* of inexpressibility so as to be understood, and it is the friar who, in his account of their interactions, obliges her to see this point. In discoursing on the presence of the "pilgrim" in the soul, for instance, when she says that God's "embrace" is such that no one who has not experienced it could believe it, the friar "resists" her: "and when I the friar resisted her about whether it could be believed, she replied, perhaps such a one could believe some of it, but not in the same way."[92] In that same discourse, when she tells him that the degree to which God surpasses description varies inversely with the intensity of the devout person's feeling, he again "resists" her and she reasserts her point by telling him that if he had had her experience of God he would not be able to preach at all but would have to dismiss his hearers, telling them, "go with God, for of God I can say nothing."[93] He pictures himself obliging her, in other words, to think about how her concept of the inexpressibility of God is to be *conveyed* so as to be understood; though the advice to dismiss his hearers is perhaps hardly practical, still it shows her placing herself in his position, imagining a congregation, and thus thinking of her ideas in relation to the people to whom they are presented. Here she stands with him imaginatively. Indeed she may do so, at least implicitly, throughout the *Memorial*, in the sense that they both struggle, though at different levels of sophistication, to put ideas into words with similarly partial success. Already in the second supplementary step, Angela told him that the divine voice had informed her that though "all that I have said of myself, and that you [the friar] have written of me," was true, yet "what I have said was defective and what the scribe wrote had limits and defects."[94] They share the task—and the ultimate inability—to express what could not be expressed.[95]

A certain collegiality therefore emerges between Angela and the friar here in the friar's *Memorial,* a suggestion of shared task, a companionable turning to the divine. But as we have seen, it emerges not in spite of the extraordinary divine favor that places her, in the manner of Mary of Oignies or Christine of Stommeln, in a sphere of experience of her own that he does not share—and that indeed makes her a sort of opposite to himself—but rather *because* of that favor. For it is in and through that divine favor and the experience it entails for her that, in the friar's account, Angela comes to the heightened perception of the transcendence of God that, for all her powers, places her not in world apart from him but rather at his side, grasping with him for words.

CONCLUSION

So the Angela of the *Memorial* stands in a privileged relationship to God in which she receives the favor of experiences that are rare or even unique to herself, which, however, put her in the position of grasping for words about God, a position in which she knows herself to be not so different from the friar or any other rational creature, for that matter. If there is a salubrious irony here, it is one that extends to the heart of the message of the *Memorial* as well. For the openness of the divine invitation to all people and the universal ability of humans to respond to that invitation are important themes of her revelations: "No one," says the divine voice, "will have an excuse not to be saved, because nothing more is required than what a sick person would do toward a physician, that is, to make the illness known and be willing to do as directed";[96] or again, "I have called and invited everyone to eternal life; those who wish to come, do come, because no one can claim the excuse of not being called."[97] Nonetheless Angela passes these sayings to the friar and their readers precisely on the basis of the claim of a privileged access to God that few others shared; the nonelitist message that the call of God gives privilege to no one over anyone else relies, for its authority, on the presumption of her own privilege as a person uniquely favored by God through all the means that the friar has been so careful to document—the revelations, the declarations of love, the gift of an extraordinary awareness of God's presence.

The hagiography and theology of the *Memorial* are, in any event, firmly connected. For it is only because she has been established as one whose virtue gives her an immediate consciousness of God that Angela, being a woman excluded from the teaching office, can acquire the authority to speak as theologian. She speaks ultimately from a sphere of authority that is her own as a charismatic visionary. As for the friar, he proclaims the experiences of Angela the visionary saint to be beyond his comprehension, while at the same time articulating the substance of these experiences to the reader in words whose inadequacy becomes permissible on the basis of what Angela the theologian says about the essential inexpressibility of the experiences. Even should the theology here interest us more than the hagiography, the latter remains the basis of the *Memorial*'s claim to be true. The relationship between saint and devotee produces the foundation that underlies and supports the work and its ideas.

CHAPTER 7

The Limits of Religious Authority

Margaret of Cortona and Giunta Bevegnati

A T ABOUT THE TIME that the anonymous friar of Foligno produced Angela's *Memorial*, not far away in the Tuscan town of Cortona a Franciscan named Giunta Bevegnati was writing a vita of the lay penitent woman known as Margaret of Cortona. In Giunta's *Legenda Margaritae* we have, once again, an account of a lay woman of semireligious status living in the midst of secular society, by a cleric who, having met her in the course of his ministry, recognizes in her an extraordinary access to God and holds her in awe. The triad of woman/Christ/cleric also appears clearly here, for Giunta not only describes Margaret's relations with Christ but includes himself in the narrative as well.

That is the familiar threesome. What is new here is how explicitly, in picturing it, Giunta addresses the question of the relationship between the woman's informal powers and the man's institutional powers. For even in James's vita of Mary, where, as I have suggested, we can pose that question and find answers, still the question itself remains largely implicit. By contrast, the *Legenda* of Margaret can be read as an extended meditation on the interrelated authorities of prophecy and priesthood. For Giunta these are elements of a system of authorities of which he is constantly aware.

Giunta presents that system in a perceptive and sober way. For him its most salient feature is precisely the limitation it imposes upon all human authority. The boundaries not only of the cleric's powers but also of the woman's stand out distinctly, and he shows himself aware of the bounds of any claim to exercise power on God's behalf, whether through official functions or through extraordinary charisms. In the realm of the *Legenda Margaritae*, such exercise has its place, but only under a strict subordination to the mandates of the gospel, which in the end lead the principals away from the exercise of power rather than toward it.

Giunta, Margaret, and the *Legenda*

Margaret came from the town of Laviano near Perugia, in Umbria.[1] As a young woman she lived in the Tuscan town of Montepulciano for nine years, apparently unmarried, with a man of substance by whom she had a son.[2] Upon her lover's death, she tried to return to the house of her father but was expelled at her stepmother's urging.[3] It was as an "illegitimate widow," therefore, a person of marginal status, that she migrated to the town of Cortona in Tuscany. We do not know for sure when she came to Cortona or how old she was at the time. Taken in by two noble ladies of the town named Raniera and Marinaria, she supported herself and her son as a midwife[4] and underwent a conversion to a life of austere devotion, becoming a lay penitent or *pinzochere*, and thus a part of the important lay penitential movement of the time which produced, as we know, many female saints.[5] Giunta says that in 1277 she entered the Franciscan Order of Penitence, or Third Order, receiving her habit from a Friar Ranaldo, the guardian of the Franciscans for the territory of Arrezzo, in which Cortona is situated.[6] Afterward she lived in a cell near the friars' church in the midst of the town and then, from about 1288, in another cell on the hill overlooking it.[7] Though she lived reclusively, she also showed an active concern for the city. She served the poor both by acts of charity to individuals and by establishing a hospice,[8] and she took an interest in settling the local factional quarrels that were typical of Italian communes at the time.[9] Like Angela of Foligno, she certainly had contact with some of the spiritual Franciscans, including Ubertino of Casale, but the extent to which she shared their views is far from clear.[10] She died in 1297.

About Giunta Bevegnati we do not know very much, but the *Legenda* and some other surviving documents allow a few glimpses of his life. He was probably a native of Cortona, for his name appears among the Cortonese signatories of a legal instrument dated 18 August 1258 documenting an agreement between their city and Perugia. In that document he is not yet designated as a friar, a fact which led his eighteenth-century editor to suggest his age as eighteen, in which case he would have been born around 1240. But that is hardly certain.[11] Sometime later as a friar of Cortona, he appears to have been active in peacemaking as well as preaching and hearing confessions.[12] It was as a friar that he had close contact with Margaret, mainly prior to 1290. In that year he was reassigned from Cortona to Siena, where he stayed for seven years, returning to his native city just before the saint's death.[13] His own death occurred no earlier than 1311, when his name appears on a legal document concerning the Franciscans in Cortona.[14]

Clues about the date and circumstances of Giunta's *Legenda* emerge from his so-called "Testimony of Authenticity," a brief text that prefaces the *Legenda* in the fourteenth-century manuscript conserved in Cortona that forms the basis of the modern critical edition by Fortunato Iozzelli.[15] Here Giunta says that the friar and inquisitor Giovanni Castiglione, who was Margaret's confessor and (as he will say later) sometime guardian of the Franciscans of the territory of Arezzo, commissioned the work and then also "saw" it.[16] Castiglione apparently died no later than 1290, and thus Giunta had already begun the work by then—although it must have been an unfinished version that his superior saw, since the vita as we have it mentions the latter's death and indeed extends to Margaret's death and to the miracles beyond.[17] In any case, Giunta finished the work well before 15 February 1308. It was then that, as the "Testimony" reports, the papal legate Napoleon Orsini formally approved the *Legenda* and encouraged the copying and "preaching" of its contents. This took place in a ceremony in the palace of the politically ascendant Casali family of Cortona, who were promoting Margaret as patroness of the town and associating her with their own Ghibelline interests.[18] Giunta also names ten friars, including several officials of the order, who had already read and approved the work—a statement reminiscent of the analogous testimony at the head of the *Memorial* of Angela, though with the significant difference that here the readers are all named; Margaret's cult was clearly already a public affair at the time the *Legenda* received its official approval.

In form, the *Legenda* stands as an elaborate catalogue of Margaret's virtues. Giunta intends, as he says in the prologue, to "pluck out ... certain flowers from the wonderful life of Margaret who, with the greatest devotion to God, did severe penance in Cortona."[19] He plucks without any evident attempt to place the events of her life in sequence, though he does typically link those events to the liturgical feasts.[20] After the scene that pictures her receiving the habit of the Order of Penitence of St. Francis in 1277 (chap. 1) and a summary account of her asceticism (chap. 2), the remainder of the work presents and illustrates (often rather loosely) the list of her virtues—first, fasting and devotion to poverty (chap. 3), then humility and contempt of self (chap. 4), patience and devotion to Christ's Passion (chap. 5), prayer and devotion to preaching (chap.

6), purity of conscience and devotion to the sacraments (chap. 7), zeal for souls (chaps. 8 and 9), and holy fear (chap. 10)—before accounting for her last days (chap. 11).

As for its content, the *Legenda* is remarkable for its focus on Margaret's *inner* life. No doubt the virtues in question could be demonstrated by accounts of her actions and behavior as witnessed by those around her, and such accounts are not entirely lacking here. But Giunta devotes the bulk of each of the chapters not to what he or others witnessed but rather to what, putatively anyway, he could have known only from Margaret herself: her personal interactions with Christ. He describes at length what she said to Christ and what he said to her; in each chapter, it is her conversation with the Savior that constitutes the main evidence to establish the virtues in question. So: her humility appears when she protests her unworthiness and receives expression of Christ's favor;[21] her apostolic calling finds expression when Christ tells her she will be a "star for the world" or "new banner" to attract sinners to conversion by her penitent example;[22] her extreme fasting comes to light through Christ's reported instructions to her about food;[23] her prophecies consist in pieces of knowledge she is shown receiving in her encounters with Christ, whether about the state of souls, unworthy priests, or the prospects for peacemaking in Cortona.[24] To what extent Giunta based these reported exchanges on what she really said to him, and to what extent they display his own imaginings, is uncertain. But they serve to center the action of the vita firmly within Margaret rather than in the external world she inhabited, even in matters closely affecting that world.

The *Legenda* is also remarkable for what Anna Benvenuti Papi has called its "Franciscanity."[25] Giunta was much more concerned to make Margaret out as a glorious representative of the Franciscan order, than to picture her as the patroness of the town. (The "Testimony" does indeed show that the work was employed to promote her local cult; however, as Joanna Cannon has argued, it probably had much less influence on the cult than the murals painted in the Church of St. Margaret in the early decades of the fourteenth century, seen by every pilgrim, which focused on her public ministry and lacked the Franciscan emphasis of the *Legenda*.)[26] The opening scene of the *Legenda*, in which Margaret receives her habit from Friar Ranaldo, sets the tone, and the work as a whole presents her as a towering example and patroness for Franciscan penitents—a new Magdalene, a model lay penitent, engaged in a life of profound humility in the midst of the urban scene and committed to the life of the city.[27] As such a figure, she has, for Giunta, a place next to Francis and Clare themselves: "'you are [Christ tells her] the third light given by me for the order of my beloved Francis: for in the order of the Friars Minor he himself is the first light, in the order of nuns the blessed Clare the second light, and you in the order of penitents the third.' "[28]

Giunta also pictures her as faithfully obedient to the friars themselves and on intimate terms with them. All the way through the work, the friars recur as subject of her interchanges with Christ: she intercedes for them, and Christ for his part gives her many revelations destined for them both individually and collectively. He tells her repeatedly to speak to no one but them and declares that it is he himself who has entrusted her to them.[29] In part, Giunta's continuing emphasis on her Franciscan connection suggests an attempt to reassert the order's claim on her, in light of the evident fact that when she left the immediate vicinity of the friars' church for her cell on the hill in about 1288, she removed herself from their influence, at least to some degree. For there in her last dwelling place, she received the permission of the bishop to repair the nearby church of St. Basil, and the pastor of that church, one Ser Badia, who was not a friar but a secular priest, became her confessor; and when she died, her body remained, to Giunta's dismay, at St. Basil's and thus outside the friars' jurisdiction.[30] Why, and indeed to what extent, she actually dissociated herself from the friars is not clear. She may have made the move to the last cell, as Mariano D'Alatri has argued, in order to distance herself from the friars in light of the criticisms that, as Giunta reports, were made of her in the Franciscans' chapter, probably in 1288, and that were the occasion for a directive from the guardian to limit Giunta's own visits to her to one per week.[31] It may also be that in a broader sense, as Daniel Bornstein has suggested, she had a "desire for independence" in conflict with the friars' authority over lay penitents, an authority strengthened by the bull of Nicholas IV, *supra montem* (18 August 1289), which placed them unambiguously under the friars' control.[32] But whatever the extent of her real separation from the friars, Giunta works hard to downplay it and demonstrate an ongoing connection.

Giunta inserts himself into the vita in the role of close associate of the saint and eyewitness to her life, and he presents his own relationship with her as the focus of her relationship with the Franciscans. Giunta makes clear that it was Castiglione who served as Margaret's chief director, and only after his superior's death did he himself take over that role, which he can have had for no more than two years (since he was transferred from Cortona to Siena in 1290). Yet he also pictures himself associating closely with her during Castiglione's lifetime and consulting with him about her.[33] It is Giunta's own interaction with the saint, not Castiglione's, that the reader is given to observe. Without giving any indication of when he first encountered her or dating his interactions with her, Giunta calls himself her "confessor" or "governor" (*baiulus*) throughout the vita, conveying imprecisely the impression that he knew her well for a long time and heard her confessions, perhaps even from her earliest association with the friars. Accordingly, his self-inclusion underscores the very strong Franciscan element in the vita, and, unlike the presence of Angela's friar in the *Memorial*, Giunta's presence places his priesthood within the purview of the *Legenda*, thus bringing the coordination of their respective priestly and charismatic roles into view.

So the *Legenda* pictures both her inner relationship with Christ and her outer relationship with the Franciscans, Giunta in particular. I shall consider each of these two aspects of the work in turn. But they are hardly mutually exclusive. Not only are concerns of the friars always entering into her conversations with Christ, but, more profoundly, both her interior relations and her exterior relations bear directly upon what can be seen as a single overriding question, namely, that of the nature and scope of her spiritual authority.

MARGARET'S ENCOUNTERS WITH CHRIST

Giunta clearly presents Margaret as someone in privileged contact with the divine: an ongoing conversation between Christ and Margaret wends its way through the *Legenda Margaritae* and accounts for the bulk of the work. What Christ tells her in the course of that extended conversation includes many individual revelations for the benefit of other people, in the time-honored tradition of late-medieval holy women. Giunta places almost all of these, however, in a single chapter (the ninth, of which I will have more to say below). By contrast, the rest of the revelations conveyed by Christ typically have Margaret herself for their subject: he speaks to her about her virtues, her shortcomings, her relationship with the friars, and especially her relationship with himself. And a particular theme of these is the problematic nature of her supernatural graces. That is: even while continuing to grant her privileged access to himself, Christ repeatedly directs her energies and interest *away* from the exercise of that privilege and instead toward her own penance and suffering, as these serve both her own salvation and, by example, the salvation of others. Thus here the granting of the woman's special status, which is the basis of her informal powers, brings with it a critique of her very embrace of that status.

It is important to note here that Margaret appears throughout the *Legenda* as a figure of imperfection rather than perfection. Christ frequently calls her attention to the sins she continues to commit. "The desire that you have for me," he tells her, "is welcome to me; nonetheless you offend me venially, because, from fear, you experience distractions of your mind through the things you see and hear, when you should be thinking only of me."[34] Similarly, he tells her, variously, that she commits venial sin by complaining and feeling sorry for herself, that she serves her neighbor for her own purposes rather than for Christ's honor, and that when she prays for the recovery of a dying infant she shows a lack of regard for Christ's redeeming sacrifice.[35] For Giunta, she is, to be sure, heroic in virtue. But her surpassing virtue is humility, and he does not mind pointing out that she has due cause for it: she is above all a penitent sinner.

Accordingly, although Christ's speeches to Margaret present her as a chosen vessel—for instance, like Angela, as the woman he loves more than other women[36]—still the chosenness is almost always linked directly to humility, in such a way as to make a point of his grace and by implication her shortcomings. His declarations of favor elicit her protestations of inadequacy, which he does not contradict. When she tells him, for instance, that she cannot think of anyone since Adam whose sin has been worse than her own, Christ only bids her "remember that I can give my grace to whomever I please" and reminds her of the Gospel examples of Mary Magdalene, the Samaritan woman, the Canaanite woman, the publican, the disciple Matthew, and the thief on the cross.[37] The point is not her virtue but precisely her repentance, and his own mercy. Just so, when she tells Christ that she considers herself unworthy of mercy and that she would throw herself into a fire rather than think otherwise, he replies that, after all, no one is worthy, that his mercy is entirely his own affair:

> And I say to you, that if all the purity of the angels and all the saints who are in heaven and on earth were put together, if I did not condescend to them, it would all be nothing in comparison to my manifest purity. Did I not descend, daughter, to take on the flesh of the Virgin Mary … ? I did it, O my simple one. Did I not come down to permit myself to be touched by sinners and to live and eat with them?[38]

Although the *Legenda Margaritae* relates a few miracles that Margaret performed during her lifetime,[39] on the whole it is not miracle, but rather penitence, that demonstrates her chosenness. As Giunta puts it, Christ "does not say to those who love him, learn of me to raise the dead, or to walk with dry feet upon the water, or to heal lepers or give sight to the blind, but rather, 'learn of me because I am meek and humble of heart [Matt. 11:29].'"[40]

Christ can therefore show pleasure at Margaret's humility. At other times, however, he shows displeasure at her desire for his presence—a displeasure that suggests, on the part of Giunta and perhaps Margaret herself, a certain caution, even ambivalence, about the fact of her supernatural favors. For Christ criticizes her for occupying herself too much with the pleasure of his presence, when she should be out courting tribulation:

> Whenever Margaret, servant of God, believed herself to receive the sign of a
> new consolation from the Lord, she said first inwardly, "what will the Lord
> give me now?" The Savior criticized this thought, saying, "why do you try to
> measure infinite wisdom? Never dare to impose a limit on my works; survey
> my works but do not touch any of them. Rather, if you wish to attain what
> you desire, run by the way of the cross and in that way you will surely attain
> the great gifts you are hoping for."[41]

He takes her to task for wanting to be "satiated" with him all the time, for acting like a child who will not leave its mother's breast.[42] She wants to "make a paradise on earth [*in terra facere paradisum*]" just as Peter did when he asked to set up tabernacles on the mountain of the Transfiguration (Mark 9:5)—but he will not grant her wish as he did not grant Peter's.[43] And when she complains of a lack of "sweetness" (*dulcedo*) from Christ, he tells her not to expect it and calls up the example of the Virgin at the Purification, who felt no joy because she understood Simeon's speech (Luke 2:34–35) as prophesying the Passion.[44] The contrast between Christ's own pain and the spiritual pleasure she derives from his presence is a frequent theme of his speeches: to wish to be able to rely on the joy of his presence would be to turn her back on the Passion, even on the Incarnation, and decline to imitate him, for he in his sufferings had lacked any consolation at all.[45]

In keeping with these criticisms of her expectations, when Christ exhorts her to imitate himself in suffering he often makes the point that such suffering requires her to do without consolations. It is true that this is not absolutely always the case: in one passage, he keeps a promise to fill her with "delights" to counter the devil's temptations to corporeal pleasures, and in another the anxious but salutary fear that she often felt is said to be mixed with "sweetness" (*dulcedo*).[46] But for the most part her sufferings exclude such sweetness. In one exchange, for instance, after Christ has told her that no one laments his Passion as much as she does, that she suffers just as he has suffered, and that her suffering will increase, he also denies her request for his "grace" toward her to increase with her tribulations. He tells her that, in view of her stage of advancement, he will instead absent himself from her, as a function of her imitation of him: "'just as I subtracted and hid my power in the wood of the cross, so I have hidden myself from you so that your reward might grow and that you might know what you are by yourself without me.'"[47] Similarly, in a moment when she says she feels great spiritual joy, she asks why that moment was preceded by a long period of anguish and fasting in which he absented himself from her, and Christ responds that he wanted her to do as he did in the time after his baptism.[48]

So Christ's exhortations to Margaret, as Giunta relates them, address her attitudes, her motivation. But that is not all; they also have practical implications for her place in the world around her. For Christ impresses upon her the imperative to offer herself—or rather allow herself to be offered—for the service of others. He frequently complains to her of the sins of her contemporaries; "never since the act of redemption," he tells her for instance, "have so many gone to the agonies of hell as have gone recently."[49] She is to suffer for the sake of those sinners; in the day of judgment, "all those who have done penance on account of what they heard and saw of you will rejoice at the labors and hardships that you now suffer."[50] It is true that Christ frequently adjures her not to associate directly with "secular" persons, but rather to give all her attention to the friars, who are to be the mediators of her example to the world—a point to which I shall return.[51] But even so, he makes clear that the salvation of sinners ought to be her main motivation. He berates her when this is not so: "'weep,'" he tells her, "'for your own disobedience, because you have not obeyed me in fishing for souls, for it is not that I need them but rather that they need me, their true and highest good.'"[52] When she begs to "taste more fully the joy of [his] presence," he criticizes her attachment to himself as a selfish attachment: "'Your sense of taste is unhealthy, because the graces with which I have honored you I have not given for your self, but rather for love of those who, to the full extent of their abilities, do not desist from doing everything they can to put me back on the cross. Yet I myself, in paternal devotion, descend to them mercifully in every way.'" He goes on then to criticize her for ignoring the friars too, and ends by accusing her: "'You do not care for anyone, Margaret, except yourself.'"[53]

Thus for all the intimacy and implied privacy of his encounters with her, Christ uses those encounters to articulate a vocation for Margaret that is not contemplative but active; he pictures her even as a kind of public figure. Like her suffering itself, her public role is framed as an imitation of Christ: "'I was a delight to the eyes of my disciples,'" he says, "'and so are you to the eyes of creatures, because I will make you a light to show how to penetrate the darkness.' "[54] Accordingly, at times he speaks of her life itself, rather than anything she might say, as constituting her witness to the world: " 'I tell you that you are the new light, illuminated by me, which I have given to this world.... . Have you not, daughter, deprived yourself of all the delights of the world for love of me? Have you not chosen to bear all agonies for the love of my name? Have you not enclosed all the poor in your heart, on my account?' "[55] But at other times it sounds as though she is supposed to speak of Christ in words as well. For he tells her that just as her life itself spoke out against him prior to her conversion, so now she will speak out for him:

> "Daughter, you have said that my love for you constrained me to suffer and that I did whatever I did out of zeal for your souls. And you know that just as I came with great anguish seeking you, thus you must come with great bitterness and afflictions seeking me. Prepare yourself therefore for the greatest distress: for just as your life of vanity once called out against me through the tongues of those who murmured in towns, woods, fields, meadows and villages, so may you not cease to proclaim the events of my Passion in order and the fact that in this life I always lived in labors and hardships for the love of humans. Whoever shall presume to murmur about this offends me seriously and you shall please me. Proclaim therefore, daughter, that, seized by love of you, I came down from the bosom of the father into the womb of the Virgin mother when she called herself the handmaid of the Lord. Proclaim the marking of the circumcision, the adoration of the magi, the offering in the temple into the hand of my old Symeon, the persecution of Herod, and the flight into Egypt [etc., through the events of his life].... And I want you to say at each of these worthy works of mine that it was love of souls alone that inclined me to do all of these things."[56]

These words sound like a charge to speak in public; a few pages earlier Giunta has related that once, in public view in the friars' church, she experienced a vision of the events of Good Friday and gave a running description of it for public consumption.[57] Giunta also says that she wished to be strictly enclosed in her cell rather than to frequent the friars' church any more, in part "because devout ladies stood around her ... and often impeded her prayers by their talking," but that Christ would not hear of her thus hiding herself.[58] And once, apparently again in the friars' church, she modestly begged her observers to leave her so that they would not see "the ardor she conceived at the gifts and consolations promised to her" by Christ—who however immediately threatened to cease speaking to her if they were to leave, "since I would make of you a mirror for sinners" and therefore he wanted her observers to see everything.[59]

It is in terms of this apostolic role that Christ has given to Margaret—her vocation to convert sinners by her example—that Giunta sees the importance of her contact with the friars. For beyond such instances as I have just mentioned, when she is on immediate display, it is the friars who are to be the mediators between her and the world at large. Here, it will be recalled, Giunta's view is probably not that of Margaret herself, who seems to have eventually separated herself somewhat from the friars. But be that as it may, Giunta makes the friars essential actors in the drama of her life. He reports Christ telling her not to speak with anyone except the friars and not to go anywhere outside her cell except to the friars' church.[60] And he presents the friars, for their part, as the ones who will preach about her so as to convey her example to sinners. When she complains that the Franciscans do not allow her the solitude she wishes, Christ tells her they are right to show her off: "they do not place you [in solitude], daughter, because you are a star newly given to the world for bestowing sight on the blind, for bringing wanderers back to the right path and for raising up the lapsed from the burden of their sins. You are a new banner rallying sinners back to me, a banner under which the penitent pour out abundant tears and sighs."[61] By making her known, they help fulfill her apostolic calling—or rather, as Christ says to her, it is they who are like the apostles and she, once again, who is like himself, in such a way as to invite the imitation of others in turn, through the medium of the friars' preaching:

"I will give you my apostles the friars minor, who will preach the things happening to you just as the apostles preached my Gospel to the people.... I tell you that, although I cannot grow or change in myself, still through the example of your life and through my gifts which will be working in you, I will be exalted through imitation of [your] life by those who now scorn me as little and weak, and multiply their vices and neither love me nor praise me but blaspheme against me by word and deed."[62]

So it is that Margaret's conversations with Christ, as Giunta spins them out, signal her intimate and privileged awareness of the presence of God and yet at the same time direct her *away* from such divine intimacy toward the world outside her, toward suffering and service, the latter specifically implemented by the friars. The theme of the relationship between inner and outer life is a familiar one in the hagiography of semireligious women; it is present, for example, in

James of Vitry's construction of his vita of Mary of Oignies. In Giunta's work there is in that relationship a certain fundamental tension not explicitly evident in Mary, a tension that becomes evident in the occasional scolding from Christ that exposes Margaret's desire for his presence as potentially excessive and self-ish. That tension, in turn, expresses a paradox of mystical theology reminis-cent of the great Beguine theologians of the period, most notably Hadewijch of Brabant: a sense that the true presence of Christ is to be found precisely in his absence and in the suffering that absence entails, a suffering that makes possible a deeper conformity to him and a closer experiential knowledge of the self-emptying that was essential to the Incarnation.[63] Here Giunta's hint of such a paradox suggests also an ambiguity in Margaret's own authority to speak as a holy woman with a privileged knowledge of divine things. For it raises the question of whether perhaps she ought to have renounced that authority itself, which, as the voice of Christ makes clear, is subject to critique.

A System of Authorities in Practice and Theory

The *Legenda Margaritae* presents the familiar triad of woman/Christ/cleric, but in a new guise. Here it is not mainly a matter of Giunta as the third party de-voutly observing the privileged relations between the loving pair Christ and Margaret, even though the work is suffused with his reports of Margaret's con-versations with Christ. Nor is it a matter of Giunta functioning as the saint's intellectual colleague, paired with her in observation of the divine in the fashion of Friar A. and Angela. Giunta is not particularly interested, that is, in the rela-tion of a couple to a third person. Rather, each of the three figures stands alone, as it were, in relation to each of the other two, in such a fashion as to show the ways in which each possesses and exercises distinct authority in relation to the others. So we observe Giunta performing his priestly function toward Margaret and Margaret exercising her charismatic powers for Giunta and on his behalf, each at the separate behest of Christ the director and in a mutually edifying way: the threesome thus models that great desideratum, a balance of priestly and prophetic authority. And not only do they model it in their words and actions, but Christ also provides a running explanation, in exhortations to Margaret that offer a kind of blueprint for this balance of authorities—which accordingly appears here not only in practice but also in theory.

Giunta pictures himself exercising pastoral care toward Margaret, not only in giving her the sacraments but also in disciplining, guiding, and comforting.

There is no hint here, as in James's account of Mary, or even Friar A.'s account of Angela, that priestly ministrations may be unnecessary or beside the point; Giunta clearly presents Margaret as needing him. It was Giunta who, apparently toward the beginning of her years in Cortona, heard her general confession, which took her eight days to make and which, Christ told her, was the condition for her being called his (Christ's) daughter.[64] After she had had herself led around on a rope in Montepulciano by a servant whom she had directed to denounce her aloud as having once "wounded many" there through her worldliness, it was Giunta who, "reflecting on the daughter of Jacob" (i.e., Dinah, [Gen. 34]), he forbade her any more such displays.[65] He also kept her, on pain of losing him as her confessor (a point to which I shall return), from making good on her plan to protect others from her beauty by deforming her own face.[66] When he found, as he says, that she was in the habit of saying the Pater Noster, Ave Maria, and Gloria Patri six hundred times daily, he tried to moderate her behavior by telling her that a constant desire for Christ and meditation on the Passion were themselves a form of prayer and that in any case mental prayer was superior to vocal prayer.[67] He instructed her about the ways of demons.[68] He tried to moderate her austerities in other ways too, for instance by arranging an anonymous gift of firewood after she had given her own to the poor and was doing without, or—though unsuccessfully—by exhorting her to take food.[69] He reprimanded one of her companions who had been maligning her.[70] He reports himself comforting her, indeed sending her into a rapture (*excessus mentis*), by reading Scripture to her, or speaking to her of heaven. And once he cheered her by reading "from the divine promises made to her"—presumably from his own notes about her experiences or even some version of the eventual vita itself.[71] Giunta is also willing to let the reader see him responding to her saintly behavior in terms that suggest not just a devout admiration but also a frank concern to restrain or manage. Thus one Friday, at the Franciscans' oratory, while in full view of the congregation, she experienced an unfolding vision of the events of Christ's Passion, crying out in sorrow to the edified onlookers at each turn in the story. At mass on the following Sunday she continued the performance, interrupting Giunta's sermon by asking in tears (echoing the Magdalene, John 20:11–15) "if I [i.e., Giunta] knew the crucified Lord, and where had I put her master?"—evoking the tears of the rest of the congregation as well. He replied firmly, assuring her of Christ's presence, "both to put confidence into her heart that she would find her master again, and to prevent the preaching of the word of God from being impeded"—quieting her and restoring his own control of the situation.[72]

As for Margaret, Giunta shows her often exercising her charismatic powers or influence specifically in coordination with his own ministry, either to supplement or inform it in particular cases, especially those involving the hearing of confessions and the mending of quarrels. He says that she often revealed to her acquaintances their intimate sins, exhorting them to make confession, and she would also tell Giunta about "this or that sin, of this or that person," which had not been adequately confessed. He for his part then went and ferreted these out in confession: "In order to expel these things from their consciences, like a midwife I carefully, with cautious interrogation, found the things that those confessing to me had, for shame, never dared confess."[73] He says in one passage that she was reluctant to reveal certain people's sins that had been revealed to her, on the grounds that she did not wish to judge anyone besides herself, but he warned her that not to reveal them would be "contrary to the will of God and the good of her neighbor" and in any case that he did not mention her name to the persons in question but elicited the confessions from them by targeted questioning.[74] In one case, however, Margaret appears as anything but reluctant to inform. This was the case of one of her own devotees, a woman who confessed regularly, but who—so Margaret tells Giunta—omitted to mention a multitude of sins including vanity, false testimony in court, excessive love of husband and children, insufficient love of others, hypocrisy, gluttony, and a perverse desire to be rewarded for her charity.[75] The mending of quarrels, apparently among the families of Cortona, seems to have been one of Giunta's major concerns, and he attributes its impetus to Margaret, or rather to her relaying of Christ's wishes. He reports Christ telling her to comfort him, apparently in view of the discouragements of the task, by reminding him of how the Gerasenes caused the Savior himself to leave their town (Mark 5:17). She assured him of continuing grace for his efforts during some unspecified demonic trial and exhorted him on Christ's behalf to keep preaching peace, in such a way as to suggest that she saw herself too in the role of peacemaker—for she worried at her own presumption, and received divine assurances.[76] She also appears to have called him back to Cortona for some task of peacemaking there while he was living in Siena.[77]

In addition to such messages about particular pastoral cases, Giunta also pictures Margaret giving him messages that concern himself and his vocation as a friar. He is not the only friar whom he reports receiving such messages; indeed, the advising of Franciscans from supernatural sources—generally to prod them to greater zeal in exercising their duties, but with sensitivity to their individual gifts and problems—appears here as one of her principal activities.

To a Friar Philip who had doubted whether he had adequate understanding to interrogate penitents, Margaret relayed Christ's word that he should stop worrying and interrogate all penitents, even if he should hear a thousand confessions in a day.[78] Similarly, to a Friar Benignus who had feared to celebrate Mass too frequently, she conveyed Christ's permission to do so as often as he wanted, as long as he first made full confession. And to an unnamed friar who wanted to receive the sacrament daily but was too timid to receive it at all, she passed along Christ's permission for daily Communion if he would only be more zealous in his speech.[79] She gave the message to a Friar Conrad (probably Conrad of Offida, prominent among the Franciscan spirituals) to turn himself over to Christ's will, and she told a friar who had asked her to pray that he might not acquire any more administrative burdens than he already had, that Christ was pleased with his reluctance to accumulate power (*"fuga praelationis"*), but wanted him to remember the importance of obedience.[80] She gave Castiglione Christ's endorsement of his zeal as confessor and preacher and recommended the example of Francis of Assisi who made a penitent woman carry a cow's intestine on her head through the streets.[81] In his own case Giunta describes Margaret giving him Christ's warning to refuse the Eucharist to anyone vainly curious, unready to die, or without fervor—implying apparently that he had been lax; after Giunta himself had told Margaret not to send any more penitents to him for confession since "he did not wish to clean so many stables in one day" Christ had her tell him that confession was not a matter of cleaning stables but of " 'preparing a place for me in souls.' "[82] Christ also exhorted Giunta, through Margaret, to greater zeal; told her to advise him to seek the sympathy of a superior who had apparently misunderstood him; warned him against seeking fame; promised him "a great gift of grace" on the basis of her merits; expressed his own sympathy (born, as he said, of his earthly experience) at Giunta's not being appreciated by others; and counseled Giunta to remember, in hearing confessions, the extreme offense he himself takes at sin.[83] And while Giunta was staying in Siena she wrote him a letter dictated, as she said, by Christ, advising him, "when you preach to the people, present yourself to sinners as tractable and human, and in your warnings against sins, mix into your words my clemency for sinners, which I give freely to the sinner who returns."[84]

In the interaction of Giunta and Margaret in the *Legenda*, therefore, it would appear that Giunta provided pastoral services to Margaret, and she served as a bearer of supernatural advice and direction to him. I note that the dynamic here is not that of a role reversal of the sort found in, for instance, James of Vitry. It is true that Margaret's oracles sometimes criticize Giunta, but there is no question here of the directee becoming the director or of the priest attributing any aspect of his priestly activity to the penitent. The two figures' respective roles remain clear and intact. Nonetheless, although—or perhaps in part because—there is no reversal of Margaret and Giunta's roles here in the *Legenda*, there is yet a certain tension between those roles. It is a tension that evidently has much to do with Margaret's debated relationship to the Franciscan Order, which I discussed earlier. For there are several clues that from Giunta's point of view Margaret did not adequately reveal herself to him as her confessor and director and that he and Castiglione opposed her decision to relocate herself to the cell at the fortress overlooking the city—a decision in which, however, she persisted. But it is important to see that Giunta labors to present these tensions as though they were resolved, and he does so in the person of Christ, who, lecturing both the saint and the friars about their respective requirements of each other, effects a compromise between them. By articulating the compromise in Christ's voice, Giunta presents the envisioned balance between their roles as divinely ordained—as no mere expedient faute de mieux, but rather the proper state of things.

It is as part of such an overall view of the situation that Giunta presents Christ as frequently criticizing Margaret for holding back her self-revelation from Giunta, in such a way as to underline his authority and importance as priest and director. For instance, he describes Christ directing her to make confession daily to a "certain friar," perhaps himself or Castiglione, to whom she has been reluctant to confess, "sometimes because she felt greater shame before that confessor, and sometimes because he confronted her more than other confessors did."[85] He also quotes Christ asking her why she did not pass on to Giunta all the things divinely revealed to her.[86] On another occasion, he says, Christ did not speak to her in his customary way after she had received the Host, and in response to her question whether the cause may have been some unconfessed sin, Christ replied that it was because she had been slow to comply with Giunta's direction that she should partake of the Eucharist, and he continued: "I command, that whenever your confessor directs you to do anything, you obey him, because I will endow his spirit with the light of special grace in everything concerning your life."[87] In the same vein, when Margaret asked Christ if she offended him by her frequent partaking, Christ replied in the negative by commending Giunta for having recommended it.[88] In another passage Giunta says that once when she was not feeling her customary spiritual joy, he advised her to go ahead and confess and receive Communion even if it did not mean receiving consolations. Later Christ spoke with her and among

other things reproved her for forgetting about Giunta during her sweet collo-
quies with himself and purported to have been speaking through Giunta in the
latter's earlier words of advice;[89] in ensuing conversations he continued to take
her to task for not thinking enough of Giunta or the other friars—for which
fault she then repented.[90] The inclusion of these passages, of course, suggests
strongly that Giunta and the other friars did not have the hold on Margaret
that they wished to have. On the other hand, perhaps precisely because of that
fact, such passages also nicely crystallize a view of what the holy woman *should*
render the priest, namely, a thorough obedience and a devoted intercession.

But Christ, in the *Legenda Margaritae*, not only reproves Margaret for inadequate attention to the friars; he also reproves the friars for inadequate recognition of Christ's direct claim upon her attentions. Here again, the passages in
question appear to be putting the best interpretation on a situation that was not
of the friars' choosing, in this case Margaret's removal to the cell overlooking
the town. As Giunta tells the story, Christ informed her one day that he did not
wish her to stay in the cell she was living in at the time, which was the one near
the friars' oratory. He went on to say that even though she would remain under
the Franciscans' care (although presumably with much reduced attention to
her, as I have suggested), they would oppose the move both because the new cell
was far from them and also because they feared that someone other than themselves would bury her (which, Giunta adds, is just what later occurred) and
consequently have benefit of the custody of her body. But the move, he said,
was his own will for her, and he had a higher claim on her than did the friars:

> "Daughter, the friars say they put much labor into you, and that is true; but I
> have redeemed you at a dearer price, and I have labored harder for you. And
> although I have made them your exterior teachers, I myself am and have been
> your interior teacher. I have made myself your guide, mercifully deigning to
> lead you out of the deep abyss of this world and of your miseries. For I was
> at the root of your conversion, all of your living is by my rule, and I shall be
> the means and end of your salvation. I led you to this cell, in which you have
> offended me little, and served me much."

She should therefore tell Giunta and Castiglione not to impede her.[91] Here the
figure of Christ is articulating a classical "mystical" statement of a direct obedience to God that takes precedence over anything else, including human authorities, clerics though they be.[92] His order here is certainly in tension with,
if not in contradiction to, his erstwhile direction to Margaret to be obedient to

Giunta and the friars: now she is to disobey them. But on the other hand, since it is Christ who issues both directions, the message here is that any tension or even contradiction is by definition transcended—that in the saint, obedience and service to that figure of priestly authority, the confessor, can exist side by side with obedience to God born of a direct divine encounter.

Thus the configuration of the triad of woman/Christ/cleric here shows three figures of spiritual authority: the cleric who directs souls and dispenses the sacraments on the basis of his office, the woman who conveys to others her unique and useful knowledge of divine things on the basis of her unmediated contact with the divine, and Christ who commands and transcends them both. Christ's authority is, no doubt, without limits, but the man and the woman, though they serve each other, also check each other. Each marks the boundary of the other's authority and points up its limits. This picture evidently corresponds to a historical situation in which Margaret had some degree of independence from the friars. But as a hagiographical picture, Giunta's version of this triad rationalizes that independence in such a way as to respect the legitimacy and discreteness of her powers but nonetheless bring them into coordination with the powers of the priest.

Conclusion

There is thus a limit to Giunta's authority over Margaret in her life as he recounts it, and there is a also a limit to Margaret's mysticism itself. What sets these limits, in Giunta's way of thinking, is the consideration of utility, specifically in the matter of saving souls. It is when Margaret shows signs of hiding her light under a bushel, withholding her salutary example from the gaze of sinners, that Christ begins to frown at her delight in him and threatens to withdraw his presence; just so, her revelations to Giunta and the friars, and their proper interest in her, extend only to what they need to know to do their evangelistic job. Beyond the limit of such usefulness, Giunta seems to say, we must leave the heavenly other world to God and pursue a holiness that, in its suffering and self-denial, belongs completely in this one.

Described that way, Giunta's conviction of the limits of religious knowledge and authority brings to mind his contemporaries and fellow Franciscans Angela of Foligno and the friar who collaborated with her. It is true that the supernatural graces of the Angela of the *Memorial* are hardly utilitarian in the manner of Margaret's; Angela travels well beyond the realm of mere evangelistically useful information and far into the mysterious and inexpressible heart of divinity itself, calling into question the very possibility of preaching about God. Still, in the *Memorial* as in the *Legenda Margaritae* the figures of that familiar threesome—holy woman, Christ, cleric—point up, by their assorted words and deeds, precisely the restrictions that arise for the human experience of the divine even as the possibilities of such knowledge are explored. And in each of these cases, for all the celebrity of the woman's holiness and for all the humility, industry, curiosity, suffering, or longing of both the human parties, still all of the busy talk and action shows the divine partner remaining just beyond grasp or comprehension. In effect, then, these Franciscan presentations of the relationship between holy woman and cleric assert the freedom of God from the constraints of human understanding and accordingly the provisional nature of human religious authority.

CHAPTER 8

Hagiography in Process

Henry of Nördlingen and Margaret Ebner

M ARGARET EBNER (1291–1351) was a nun of the Dominican convent
of Maria Medingen near the Danube town of Dillingen in Swabia, one
of the many Dominican convents in southwestern Germany where, in her time,
the mystical experiences of nuns were being recorded in remarkable numbers.[1]
It was in 1312 that Margaret entered a period of illness that led to supernatural stirrings: visions, voices, and extraordinary states of mind. These continued
over many years. It was probably in 1332 that Henry of Nördlingen (d. after
1351), who was a secular priest from her region, paid a visit to the convent and
began to take an interest in Margaret. He encouraged her to record her experiences, which she did in the work known as her *Revelations*. Henry also kept up
a correspondence with her for most of the remaining nineteen years of her life.
Fifty-six of his letters to her survive.

In the letters, Henry appears to us as yet another cleric writing about a
woman whom he believed to have extraordinary access to God and attributing to her a sphere of authority distinct from his own. Margaret, it is true, was
a Dominican nun in an intensely devout cloistered atmosphere rather than a
lay penitent or a Beguine living in a city like the women whom I have already
discussed. But Henry himself, like James of Vitry, Peter of Dacia, "Friar A.," and
Giunta Bevegnati, had an active ministry in secular society, which seems to have
encouraged him to consider, in hagiographical form as they had, the distinction
and interplay between an exceptional woman's authority and his own.

Henry approaches this topic in ways similar to the others: he articulates his
own shortcomings by idealizing Margaret, solicits her revelations, and claims to
depend on her for the exercise of his ministry. But his letters are distinctive in
that they open a wider window than those other texts on the contexts in which

his thinking about the woman developed, that is, the events and situations that affected him as he was writing to her. In doing so, the letters reveal that Henry's understanding of Margaret and of his relationship to her as a figure of access to God was far from static but rather developed over time, in close interrelation with his other experiences, and that it was taken over by Margaret's cult, in which he had a formative role. The literary expression of Henry's encounter with the holy woman and her powers thus does not appear here as an accomplished fact; the reader watches it taking form.

The Letters

The fifty-six extant letters of Henry to Margaret date from the period between about October 1332, when he first met her, and the spring of 1350, the year before she died. They are each relatively brief, varying in length, in Philipp Strauch's edition, from eleven lines to a hundred forty-two. They are highly personal in tone—Henry addresses particulars of Margaret's experience and assumes a certain intimacy with her—in contrast to the more detached homiletical letters that his sometime friend Henry Suso was writing to nuns of his own acquaintance at about the same time.[2] The letters are among the earliest such personal letters in German that have survived.[3]

The source for Henry's letters to Margaret is a collection of correspondence extant in a single copy in the British Library (Add. 11430), in a codex devoted to texts concerning Margaret. The first of these texts is a copy, in a sixteenth-century hand, of Margaret's own *Revelations* and of an intercessory prayer of her own composing, which she had called her *Pater Noster*. Then comes the letter collection itself in another sixteenth-century hand, beginning with a notice to the reader that declares that Margaret Ebner was a nun who had lived a holy life in the cloister, that God had begun his special work in her in 1312 (as the *Revelations* say), that she died in 1341 (*sic*), and that the letters were sent to her by her "faithful spiritual father, named Master Henry of Nördlingen, a devout and blessed man and a particular friend of God, who was given and sent by God to her and to others of God's children, and to whom she, in the love of God and at the inspiration of God, revealed her life and being and what God had done with her, and she received advice and help from him, etc."[4] The collection includes, interspersed among Henry's fifty-six letters, one letter from Margaret to Henry, eight to Margaret from other people in Henry's circle, and two from Henry to other sisters at Medingen. The codex contains two other texts, placed after the letter collection: copies, in a seventeenth- or eighteenth-century hand, of two late seventeenth-century published devotional biographies of Margaret. The codex appears to have a Medingen connection: on its first leaf is a line drawing of Margaret's tomb there, and the exemplar of its text of the *Revelations*, as Strauch showed, was the text that was produced within two years of the saint's death and preserved at Medingen.

The letters have a hagiographical character. In most of them Henry develops at length the theme of Margaret's favor in the sight of God, casting her as a bride of Christ and himself a wretch by comparison. We do not often think of hagiography as something addressed *to* a saint, in what is ostensibly a personal letter, framed as exhortation and advice. But in that exhortation and advice, the focus is unmistakably on her extraordinary grace, her exceptionality, her holiness. And Henry apparently had a wider audience in the monastery as well, to which he was surely speaking by implication, including one Elisabeth Schepach, who would eventually become prioress and thus, as Ursula Peters points out, appears in a position analogous to the superiors of some of the other southern German Dominican monasteries at the time who encouraged the collecting of hagiographical texts about sisters within the convents, the so-called sisterbooks. Thus probably with encouragement from within the Medingen community, Henry is providing that community with texts that call attention to the saintliness of one of their own. The London manuscript itself, as Peters has pointed out, demonstrates how those who venerated Margaret might use the letters for hagiographical purposes: for there the letters do not stand on their own but serve to provide contextual details of the otherwise rather imprecise picture of the saint's life as given in the *Revelations*. Their prefatory note forges the link, and it is worth remembering that this is the only context in which we know for sure that the letters were available to a reader.[5]

The letters can thus be read for hagiographical content. Yet it is important to note that the letters are not *only* about Margaret and her favor in the sight of God. They also witness to many events, circumstances, and people in Henry's life, many of them not directly related to Margaret; it is exactly those other elements of the letters that allow us to place Henry's thinking about Margaret in a context—to see not just the hagiography here, but the *making* of the hagiography. Peters rightly points out that the letters are problematic as historical sources if we are asking about the actual relations between holy woman and priest—the terms of their friendship and content of their interaction—precisely because of their hagiographical intent. They are not meant to document those relations so much as to make Margaret out as a saint—a rather different purpose. Thus Peters argues, for example, that in casting himself in his letters as a "homeless cleric, financially troubled and consumed by secular as well as pastoral business," in contrast to the holy Margaret who is his haven of peace, Henry is employing a "stylized" hagiographical theme to highlight the virtues of the saint, rather as Thomas of Cantimpré did in his descriptions of the busy James of Vitry in the *Supplement* to James's vita of Mary of Oignies. It is a topos, in other words; it is a function of Henry's interest in making Margaret out as a saint and is not to be trusted to bear the weight of an analysis that aims at charting the terms of the actual relationship between a devout woman and her clerical advisor.[6] This is an important point. But conversely, if we aim instead precisely at charting the way in which Henry made Margaret out as a saint, about how and why and in what circumstances over time he did so, then the texts tell us much, indeed especially when they are conveying hagiographical topoi, and they do so with important support from their nonhagiographical elements.

HENRY'S LIFE IN THE LETTERS

In the next section of this chapter I will consider the letters' hagiographical themes, with particular attention to how Henry presents himself in relation to Margaret. In the present section, by way of establishing the context in which he articulates those themes, I examine what the letters say about Henry's life and circumstances. The story that emerges from them is of a gregarious and ambitious secular cleric from Swabia who spent a dozen years in self-imposed exile, mostly in the city of Basel. There, as a popular preacher, he cultivated a wide circle of pious friends, into which he also drew Margaret, through the letters.

A few words are in order first about the dating of the letters and about their form. We owe the dating to Strauch. As found in the London manuscript, the letters are undated and evidently do not appear in chronological order.[7] (I shall consider the ordering of the collection itself in the last section of this chapter.) Strauch was able to establish dates or at least chronological parameters for all of the letters but two (55 and 56), and he arranged them in the roughly chronological order in which they appear in his edition. Subsequent scholarship has generally accepted his dating.[8] As a group, letters 1–22 are the least precisely datable; all of them show Henry still living in his homeland of southern Germany, so as to place them before December of 1338 when his exile (to be considered below) began, though in these cases his comments about external events afford few other decisive clues for dating. But afterward, beginning at the time of the exile, or actually a few months before, as exile appeared on the horizon, and continuing through the rest of the correspondence, Henry was to say much more about what was happening around him, making possible a somewhat more exact dating of most of the remaining letters (23–54).

The literary form of the letters itself suggests a distinction between the respective topics of Margaret's holiness and Henry's activities. As Debra Stoudt has shown, the letters generally follow the five-part program prescribed by the high-medieval Latin *ars dictandi*: *salutatio, captatio benevolentiae* (expression of good wishes), *narratio* (the principal matter of the letter), *petitio* (request of the addressee), *conclusio*.[9] The opening sections of the letters are almost always devoted to Margaret's holiness. In the *salutatio* Henry typically "offers" her an edifying image or idea or a pledge of his own faithfulness, and in the process asserts both her special relationship with Christ and his own unworthiness: "To the virgin, who is invited to the table of the eternal banquet ... her poor unworthy friend, whom she knows in a way that he does not know himself, offers faithfulness and truth, love and peace, joy and delight."[10] In the *captatio benevolentiae*, he expresses wishes for her, or gratitude toward her, in terms or images that refer, directly or indirectly, to her mystical experience: "My beloved in God, my soul wishes for you ... some of the beloved blessing which is poured forth from the father through his son Jesus and through Mary ... in which your demanding heart and your loving soul and your thirsty spirit can overflow in all the abundance of God."[11] And in the first part of the *narratio* (which follows no single formula) he continues with exhortation, advice, or reflection about Margaret's relationship to God in terms that develop the themes sounded already in the opening sections. But then, with occasionally an "amen" or "*pax tibi*" to signal the end of his train of thought on spiritual matters, he usually proceeds with a second part of the *narratio*, in which, in much less florid language, he brings out the more mundane matters that are on his mind: news about himself, messages from other people, comments on gifts he is sending her, discussion of the prospects for visiting her, and so forth. This latter part of the *narratio* varies in length; Stoudt finds that most of the letters "devote between one-fifth and one-third of their total content to private matters," though in a few cases these account for the bulk of the letter.[12] Henry also often includes a *petitio* or request of Margaret at some point in a letter (though not necessarily in the prescribed fourth position) and ends with a formal *conclusio*, most often in the form of a blessing.[13]

The letters that date from Henry's years in his homeland, prior to the summer of 1338, show him in close relationship not just with Margaret but with others as well. Henry makes as yet little reference to his own activities or movements, beyond a few visits to Medingen, an extended absence from the region—probably for a sojourn in Avignon from late 1335 to early 1337—and a journey (perhaps it was the return from Avignon) that brought him through Neuhofen and Speyer.[14] But he makes abundant reference to particular people. He greets other Medingen sisters by name, especially Elisabeth Schepach ("my faithful one"), who will later become prioress of the convent, and makes frequent reference to gifts he is sending either to Margaret or to others: a tablecloth, a head cover, candles, various books, lengths of cloth, pots of mustard.[15] He also makes a point of mentioning friends outside the monastery, whom he considers to be Margaret's friends as well. The person most frequently named is his mother; he passes along her greetings in several of the early letters, and on at least two occasions he mentions that she was to visit Margaret in her own right.[16] He also mentions, and conveys greetings from, two other women who appear to have been close to him: an "Irmel" whose family name he does not give, and Euphemia Frick ("die Frickin,") a particularly beloved friend who will be at his side in the Basel period and afterward.[17] He asks prayers for an unnamed friend in the Cistercian monastery of Kaisheim, with which he apparently has close ties, passes on a revelation from an anonymous "friend of God in a cloister,"[18] and tells Margaret about a nun named Ellin von Crewelsheim of the Cistercian convent of Zimmern who, like herself, underwent periodic silence in her suffering and who has told him to greet Margaret for her.[19] His own wide acquaintance is evident here, as well as his desire to incorporate Margaret within it.

Henry's abundant references to specific people and his concern to connect Margaret to his broader circle of acquaintance would remain constant features of the correspondence. But in several letters in the summer and fall of 1338 (letters 23–29), he also tells her much more about his own movements. Ten years earlier, after the German king Louis the Bavarian had had himself crowned Holy Roman Emperor at Rome with the support of the Italian Ghibellines, Pope John XXII had placed Germany under interdict, and priests were therefore forbidden to administer the Eucharist in normal circumstances. But on 6 August, 1338, the imperial Diet in Frankfurt declared the interdict invalid, requiring priests to ignore it.[20] Henry, loyal to the pope, did not intend to comply, and he writes Margaret in August or early September that he expects to be forced into exile, and that he has asked for protection from the leading people of his hometown of Nördlingen and from Christine Ebner of the Dominican convent of Engelthal at Nuremberg, all of whom expressed their sympathy but could not give him refuge.[21] His own affairs were complicated by the offer that his friend the Cistercian abbot of Kaisheim had made to him earlier in the summer of a benefice, the parish church of the town of Fessenheim, for which, however, there was a rival candidate put forward by a competing interest, so that Henry was obliged to canvass support for himself.[22] In the fall he obtained a date (October 22) to appear before the bishop of Augsburg, who would decide the matter.[23] But we never hear what happened at Augsburg, for by the time he writes his next two letters (31 and 32), one shortly before the following Epiphany and the other in Lent, the only thing on his mind is his exile, which has now begun: he has looked unsuccessfully for refuge at Constance and then at the cloister of Königsfelden in Aargau, before finally finding his safe haven at Basel, where the papal interdict continued in effect.[24]

Henry wrote several letters within the first few months after settling in Basel in early 1339 (letters 32–35), in which he continues to tell Margaret of his activities and to include her in his ever-widening circle of friends. Gone now is the dire tone of the letters of the previous year, and he is clearly thriving. He has obtained lodging in the Hospital, he says, and is regularly preaching there to appreciative hearers. He has become a celebrity: "the best people in Basel come to my preaching, from among the poor children of God and the rich, from the men and the women, from the priests, monks, brothers, burghers, canons, nobles, and common folk… God gives the people a wonderful inclination toward me, and I toward them."[25] He finds himself hard-pressed by demands on his time,[26] is showered with offers of other positions,[27] and feels the jealousy of the Basel clergy.[28] As always he is cultivating friends, and now he uses the term "Friends of God" to refer to a particular group or network of people he is encountering regularly.[29] Prominent among these is Tauler, who was also in Basel because of the interdict and who himself had earlier accompanied Henry to visit Margaret. (He mentions Henry Suso as well, though their friendship appears to have diminished.)[30] Henry continues to show his strong personal attachment to Margaret. He requests a nightgown of hers and then reports himself wearing it.[31] Henry also thinks of her as one of the "Friends of God," who "all press so strongly toward the one whose name is so deeply impressed in you, in whom alone is to be found what in truth was always present in the Father,"[32] and they ask her, through him, to write to them.[33] And in a letter affirming Margaret's decision to take Communion in spite of the interdict—saying that, in her extraordinary case, Christ invited her to "eat with" him as in the biblical story Ahasuerus had invited Esther, that is, because she "ruled with" him (cf. Esth. 2:16–18)—he thinks of the others as well: "I would not dare to hinder such strong and sincere desire in God and toward God, either in you *or in any other friend of God*."[34]

After these first few months in Basel the surviving letters become sparse for a time. He wrote one, probably in 1340, to explain that he was unable to make the journey to visit Margaret (letter 36), and two more in late 1341 in the wake of the visit he finally did make in November of that year (letters 37 and 38), and then there are no surviving letters that clearly date from 1342 or 1343.

In late 1344 the correspondence revives, and there are thirteen more letters before his departure from Basel in 1347 or 1348 (letters 39–51). In these later Basel letters, Henry still appears as a busy cleric with broad contacts. But both in what he says about his activities and in what he asks of Margaret, the focus of the letters has shifted. He still continually mentions old friends and names new ones, including a lay woman named Margaret of the Golden Ring, who herself wrote a surviving letter to Margaret Ebner.[35] He still speaks of the press of work, and in one particularly introspective letter he reflects on his evident successes, musing that he does not recognize in himself the grace that others say they receive through him.[36] But he no longer seems interested in telling her of the circumstances of his ministry. What may have occasioned the resurgence of his letter writing (although there may well have been letters, now lost, that would fill the gap) was something new, namely the project of Margaret's *Revelations.* It was probably in a visit of October 1344 that he had asked her to undertake the work, and in a letter before Lent of 1345 he puts the request in writing: "I desire also, as I have already asked of you, that, God willing, you write for us, in an ordered way, the changes that God has worked in you."[37] Then in a dramatic letter sometime later that year, he acknowledges receipt of the first installment of the work: "What should I write to you? Your God-speaking mouth has made me speechless."[38] Afterward he urges her to send him more,[39] and (as I shall suggest later) it is probably not incidental that throughout the remaining Basel letters his reflections on Margaret's special status with God become more focused on her role as a source of revelations, an oracle. He casts her in that role also in the matter of relics: in 1346 he sends her some of the relics he collected on a trip to Cologne and Aachen and asks her to pray for a revelation of certitude about others, especially a purported finger of St. Agnes, which he mentions in four separate letters.[40] He writes her about business and literary matters as well: he alerts her to money he has raised for a building project at Medingen,[41] asks her for copies of works of Thomas Aquinas,[42] and sends her his translation of the *Flowing Light of the Godhead* of Mechthild of Magdeburg, which, he says, took him two years of work.[43]

The last three of the datable letters (52–54), which show that he had left Basel, strike a tone reminiscent of the letters that had preceded his arrival there.

He still speaks of friends—Euphemia Frick leaves with him, and his mother also, who, however, was soon to die[44]—and he sends another gift.[45] And he reminds Margaret again to send him more of the *Revelations*.[46] But his focus now once more is on the changes in his own life. Why he left Basel is not entirely clear, though the letters suggest some possible reasons: in the last Basel letter, in late 1347 or early 1348, he wishes for a quieter life and also notes with alarm the proximity of the plague, and in the first letter after his departure, written sometime in 1348 or 1349 from the Alsatian town of Sulz, he says he has decided that "my work is needed more elsewhere than in Basel."[47] But he says no more about what occasioned the decision. It is also not clear what position or status he had then in Sulz, where he says that he finds himself still too attached to the memory of Basel and considers himself to be undergoing some sort of persecution at the hand of others: Christ, he says, "pushes me, along with his lambs, among the wolves [cf. Matt. 10:16], some of whom bite me furiously and attack me hatefully and mock me wickedly."[48] He apparently did not stay in Sulz long, for sometime in 1349 he writes that he is he is now wandering from one city to another, preaching, "without a sure stopping place in a convent," and asks her advice as to how vigorously he ought to preach about coming tribulations that, he says, had been prophesied by Hildegard of Bingen.[49] Then finally, no later than the spring of 1350, in his last datable letter, he writes her happily that he is on his way home, bearing relics for her.[50]

We know a little more of Henry after the moment of that last letter, but not much. One of the other letters in the letter collection, from the abbot of Kaisheim to Margaret, establishes that Henry did visit Margaret in Medingen in 1350, and we know that in the following year he spent three weeks with Christine Ebner at the monastery of Engelthal.[51] But the rest of Henry's life, as well as the time and circumstances of his death, remain obscure.[52]

HAGIOGRAPHY IN CONTEXT

I have already noted that Henry begins every letter with reflections upon Margaret's holiness. His exhortations, wishes, words of praise, and meditations on that subject, as he proceeds from *salutatio* to *captatio benevolentiae* to *narratio*, are extensive and in many cases account for the bulk of the letter. Throughout the correspondence, he keeps her on a pedestal, professing his own unworthiness in contrast. That is a constant. But even so, Henry's image of Margaret in these passages undergoes an evolution that the letters themselves allow us to place in the context of the unfolding events of his life. At first, before the crisis that led to his exile, he focuses almost exclusively upon her experience of God in its own right. But from the time of that crisis onward, as his own concerns and the circle of his friends come more fully within the purview of the letters, he pictures her increasingly as not just a person of mystical experience but also an intercessor for himself and others and, especially in the late letters, as a source of revelations. Her significance, therefore, widens perceptibly, so that she begins to appear as not simply an exemplary friend of God but also a saint with a following.

When Henry addresses Margaret on the subject of her relationship to God, he proceeds by invoking a profusion of images.[53] His repertory of these—a repertory shared in great part with the German mystical writers of the period and in many cases rooted in more ancient traditions—is too large for a comprehensive survey here, but I point out a few of the more prominent images, or complexes of images. He often writes of the divine as "flowing" toward or into her, as when he wishes for her that "he [Christ] would overflow into your heart, so that you would enter again into him and there would know as you are known, and love as you are loved; and that you would receive from the heart of Jesus Christ the very best benefit that has ever flowed out of the marrow of the sweet love of God in a spirit that burns with love."[54] He also frequently employs images of light to refer both to the divine itself and to her encounter with it, as when he wishes for her that God would "enlighten you in your inner humanity and show you himself in the abyss of his eternal brightness," or when he imagines the grace of Christ coming to her "in the emission of eternal light that breaks forth from the bright countenance of God into you and lifts you up into itself."[55] He regularly imagines Margaret as bride or consort of Christ, telling her for example that he is addressing "the one who is cleansed through the love-rich blood of her bridegroom, the one who has nested so fully in the wounds of her beloved, and who lies in the bridal bed, that is, in the secure chamber of his heart, which is surrounded by sixty strong men [cf. Song of Songs 3:7]."[56] He suggests more than once that Christ is being born within her, and he otherwise routinely sets up parallels between herself and the Virgin: "I desire for you the joy in your loving heart, which Mary received when she had her first sight of her child in eternity"; she must put the Christ child in the "crib of your devout heart."[57]

It is important to note that Henry's focus in these passages is not on exegetical or theological themes per se but on Margaret herself, that is, on her person in its exceptionality and holiness. In that sense, he is not writing letters of spiritual advice, let alone theological argument, so much as he is, in effect, producing hagiography, and this fact separates him from the great German mystical writers of the period, for all his sharing of their language and imagery. Unlike Mechthild, Eckhart, Tauler, and Suso, Henry neither implies a claim to mystical experience in his own right nor develops any sustained or focused doctrine about God or the soul or the encounter between the two. Also unlike them, as Grete Lüers has shown, Henry sometimes employs images of established mystical import not for their metaphorical power to express the truth about God or the soul or the divine encounter but rather as a "literary device [*Stilmittel*]" for rhetorical effect, as for example when he writes of Margaret drinking and being submerged not in the "sea" of God—an image that the other writers employed to express the divine limitlessness and by implication the mystery of mystical union—but rather in "the rolling waves of the fatherly mercy."[58] Instead, as becomes especially clear when the letters are compared to the *Revelations* (to be examined later), Henry's use of the mystics' repertory of images serves to elevate Margaret by highlighting the exceptionality and the divine favor that her experiences imply. For example, in the *Revelations* Margaret herself associates her periods of involuntary silence with pain, anxiety, and thoughts of the Passion, but for Henry her silence becomes a condition for ecstatic mystical union, as when he wishes that the grace of Christ in her might "become a supernatural silence that surpasses all created understanding in the peace of God and in the emission of eternal light.... Then, like St. Paul, you know not where you are or what has happened to you, when you are returned again to us and to yourself."[59]

It is in the context of this constant interest in Margaret's holiness that Henry steadily asserts his own insufficiency or inferiority. Well over half the letters begin with some *Demutsformel*, or self-deprecating epithet for himself as a part of the salutation: "to the chosen child of God ... I, a friend undeserving of her and her devotion, offer what I am and have in God"; "to the humble handmaid of God, her unworthy friend offers Jesus Christ."[60] And throughout the correspondence he draws contrasts between himself and Margaret, setting her holiness into relief against his own insignificance. He scolds her for declining to "deplore my faults" and therefore depriving him of the benefit of her intercessions with her beloved Jesus.[61] He implores her to ask God to punish him and bring his rebelling heart into subjection.[62] He tells her he is amazed that she, as someone who experienced the constant presence of God, would deign to take notice of a mere sinner such as himself.[63] He protests the kind things she has said about him and affects to doubt that he can be of any use to her.[64] He pictures himself as a "poor kitchen boy" who has no right to approach the bride of the king.[65] The thought of her graces makes him think about his own sins, and her revelations make him think about his own lack of insight.[66] This abundance of humility in the letters has fueled the negative assessment of Henry's character that prevailed for a long while among scholars. For Richard Schultz, for example, Henry was a person of "weak, sentimental and indecisive character without a pronounced self-understanding," subservient to Margaret, who was "the stronger personality and driving force" in the friendship.[67] Yet in the light of Henry's evident main intent to evoke a picture of Margaret's mystical graces and holiness in these letters, the tendency to self-abasement must appear less as a personal deficit than as a familiar hagiographical strategy. For we are, after all, in well-worn hagiographical territory: Henry is exploiting the conceit of opposites—of the woman as grace filled, the man as graceless—that had such strong appeal for male hagiographers and presumably their readers.

Henry's focus on Margaret's holiness, paired with his self-deprecation, is the great constant of the correspondence, a *cantus firmus* that continues strongly throughout. But above that foundation, new elements emerge over time in his thinking about her. In late 1338, when (as we have seen) he begins to say more about his own circumstances, he also begins to make an explicit connection between Margaret's powers and his own needs and desires. She is now not only the one whose grace he exalts in contrast to his own gracelessness; she is also now his intercessor and coworker, his helper in bearing his burdens. In a letter (28) written in Augsburg as he awaited the day of his hearing before the bishop, he tells her:

> I have been before the princes of this world. They make me an outlaw, so that I no longer have a sure place in the land, unless I am willing also to sing [Mass]. . . . Pray to your mighty beloved Jesus Christ that he might have mercy on me in all things, as he knows my poverty, and that he teach you what I ought to do and what I ought to leave alone. Greet all our faithful ones! Pray God for all my enemies! Write me on God's behalf what is necessary for me.[68]

He casts himself already as an exile, bereft of help, relying on her for her prayers, and wanting a revelation from her. Then the next year, when his period of exile has begun in earnest and he is deep in pastoral tasks at Basel, he combines his complaint of overwork with an appeal for her help: "by great constant work of preaching and hearing confession, I am drawn out of myself, so that I cannot attain inward devotion," he tells her, and so "I lay on you the heavier part of all my sorrows. For you have so much more love than I do, and can bear that much more than I can.... And therefore you shall more justly enjoy the fruits of my work, as you planted them more lovingly and truly than I did."[69] The conceit here recalls James of Vitry: the woman's prayers merit the credit for the man's pastoral work. And throughout the Basel years, and afterward as well, his requests for her intercessions remain a feature of the letters.[70]

Another element begins to appear in Henry's picture of Margaret later in the Basel period, after he receives the first installment of the *Revelations* in 1345: now, in addition to everything else, she becomes for him an oracle, a source of revelations. Of course this is not totally new; already in his first letter from Basel he had asked her on behalf of "our dear father Tauler and other friends of God, that you write us something collectively, as your beloved Jesus inspires you, particularly about the state of Christendom and of the friends who suffer severely because of it."[71] And it is clear from earlier letters that he was already aware of at least some of what would become the contents of Margaret's work.[72] But now her prophetic abilities become a major focus of his interest, as he exhorts her to "write out for me zealously what God has given to you to say, and collect every last bit of what you have perhaps forgotten or have not yet written down."[73] He begins pressing her for revelations to identify relics.[74] He also develops a new image for her that shows her not interceding *for* others so much as conveying something *to* them: in the letter following his acknowledgement of the *Revelations*, he imagines her as the bride who emerges from the wine cellar of the king (Cant. 2:4), where she has drunk the "wine of the Holy Spirit," and then offers her breast to himself and others who have been waiting for her.

> You may say with joy: "the king has brought me into his winecellar" [cf. Song of Songs 2:4], and there you seek and discover how sweet the king is, there you drink the delightful wine of the Holy Spirit in abundant plenty both for yourself and for others, for from your motherly full maidenly breast, cheerfully and obligingly, you are able to suckle us poor thirsty ones who have waited outside the cell with great longing for your return.[75]

This image of Margaret as a holy wet nurse for the faithful appears twice more in Henry's late letters from Basel.[76] The image is yet another example of Henry's use of the language of the German mystics for purposes different from theirs, that is, for hagiographical purposes. Eckhart, Mechthild, and others had written of the suckling of faithful souls, but either at the breast of the Virgin (as an implication of the soul's identification with Christ) or at the breast of Christ himself (following the supposed example of John the Evangelist at the Last Supper), whereas what Henry wants to represent is not the soul's direct experience of God but rather the saint's mediation, her ability to convey the fruits of an experience of God that belongs to her alone rather than, even in theory, to her devotee.[77]

One more element is also added to the picture of Margaret in the letters of the Basel years: an increasing sense that she is a figure of significance for many others besides Henry himself, a saint with a public. As we have seen already, the early Basel letters show him bringing knowledge of her into his own widening circle of associates. Later on, after he has begun receiving the *Revelations*, it seems no accident that when Henry imagines Margaret outside Christ's wine cellar, it is not just to himself but to "us" that she offers her breast, "us" being presumably all who would read her or hear of her. In letter 45 he also introduces another image that suggests a specific awareness of her public when he exhorts her to keep praying for certain people, to "draw them with a new loving earnestness from your heart into the merciful heart of Jesus Christ, such that through your heart they move into his heart." He continues:

> What I have pursued and obtained in Christ I bring to you as to the favored and gracious spouse of the son of the eternal emperor, for her to offer up devoutly through the will of her beloved for his honor. Oh! dearly beloved of God, do not let go the leash of the poor brute of a hunting dog that belongs both to you and to him, until you bring it home with you.[78]

Here Henry sees himself as Margaret's and Christ's faithful dog, hunting for people whom he then brings to her so that she may offer them on to God. It is an image of himself as subordinate, and in that sense like the image of the little kitchen boy, though here it stands not in contrast to her so much as in association with her (though to be sure it suggests no equality between them) in ministry to others.[79]

Therefore, though Henry is consistent both in his admiration of Margaret's holiness and his corresponding self-abasement, the letters do suggest a development over time in his image of Margaret: she becomes increasingly not just a subject of admirable mystical experience but also a figure of useful charismatic powers. The letters, with their abundance of information about Henry, suggest that this development reflects changes in Henry's own life and situation. As noted above, the letters suggest too that other people around them shared his interest in Margaret and thus that, in some small measure at least, a cult was developing around her outside the Medingen convent as well as within it.

Another trace of that cult is apparent when one turns from the individual letters of Henry to the letter collection as a whole. But it will be helpful first to consider the relationship between the letters and the other major text of the London manuscript, Margaret's *Revelations.*

HENRY AND THE *REVELATIONS*

The letters assert that Henry encouraged Margaret to write the *Revelations*, and the London manuscript pairs the two works together. The *Revelations* are indeed remarkable for complementing the letters: they are vague where the letters are specific (especially about relevant events and people in Margaret's and Henry's world of acquaintance), and specific where the letters are vague (especially about the particulars of Margaret's mystical experience). This is not accidental. If, as the letters suggest, Henry was advising Margaret on the *Revelations* during the years of the correspondence and furthermore had her audience in mind (in Medingen and perhaps beyond) when he wrote his letters—the same audience as for the *Revelations*—then the *Revelations* and the letters do not represent entirely separate hagiographical projects but rather parts of the same one; in effect, they divide up between them the subject matter relevant to presenting Margaret as a figure of exceptional holiness. And if so, then the figure of Henry himself becomes, as Peters has noted, the link between the two, just as the London manuscript would have it. It is true that he appears in different guises in the two works: in Margaret's, the device of his inferiority unsurprisingly disappears and instead she expresses reverent admiration for him in his own right. But this very feature of the *Revelations* serves to recommend the letters to the reader, even as the letters serve to recommend the *Revelations.*[80]

The *Revelations* relate Margaret's experiences from 1312 to 1348. Overall, her subject is the supernatural favor she received from God in and through illness and suffering. She begins with the onset of an illness in 1312, during which she became aware of her own spiritual condition.[81] As the illness continued over many years, removing her somewhat from the daily disciplines of the cloister, she devoted herself to interior prayer and cultivated a devotion to the Passion—focused at first upon crucifixes, which she liked to embrace—and a concern to intercede for "poor souls" in purgatory, from or about whom she also received revelations.[82] Then on a Shrove Tuesday (in 1335, by Strauch's reckoning) a new element of experience appeared: on feeling God's "grasp" upon her heart, she began to speak out uncontrollably.[83] Such periods of "speaking" (*rede*), in which she repeated the name of Jesus and exclaimed her devotion for him, became a regular feature of her life and were soon typically preceded by what she called the "binding silence"—periods of increasing duration in which she was in great pain and unable to speak as she thought about the Passion of Christ.[84] Later, during a Lenten season (in 1340 if Strauch is right), such thoughts would often cause her to break out into similarly uncontrollable "loud cries" (*rüefe*),[85] and she also began to experience "thrusts" against her heart. In one instance the cries and thrusts coincided with a swelling of her body, to suggest the labors of childbirth.[86] After acquiring a statue of the infant Christ which she liked to clasp to her breast (with, on at least one occasion, the physical sensation of nursing),[87] she began as well to have supernatural conversations with the Christ child. He revealed to her, for instance, that he had been fully formed at conception, that St. Joseph had held him during his circumcision because his mother was overcome by sympathetic pain, and that he had pulled the hair of the three kings.[88] She also quotes his comments on other matters, such as his own favor toward her, the ills of Christendom in general, and the prospects of the soul of the emperor Louis the Bavarian in particular, about whom Margaret always showed special concern.[89]

Scattered through this running narrative of her experiences are some fifteen passages that refer to Henry. He makes his first appearance about a fifth of the way through the book: she reports that God's "true friend"—she always refers to him by this epithet or some variant of it—visited her, comforting her in her grief over the death of a convent sister to whom she had been close. She records seven more pastoral visits from Henry, spread over the next fifteen years.[90] She mentions him in other contexts as well: when recounting how she began to write the work itself, apparently in Advent of 1344, she says that she acted at Henry's request;[91] at other points she recalls her desire to tell him about the extraordinary things happening to her and her regret at his absence from her;[92] at still other points she mentions revelations that she received about him, and in one case a dream in which he appeared to her and received her pledge of cooperation.[93]

The importance of Henry as a figure in the *Revelations* is consistent with what the letters tell us. The letters suggest that already several years before receiving the work from her he had commented on accounts she had sent him of some of the experiences she was to cover in it—later perhaps to be preliminary drafts for the work itself—and at least once he returned to her a "finished" version of what she had written, from which it would seem that they already had some idea of a literary product.[94] Then in his letter acknowledging receipt of the first installment of the *Revelations* (which Strauch dates to 1345), we find him implying that he intended eventually to edit it: "I do not dare either to add or take away anything either in Latin or in German, until I read it over again with you and understand its truth anew from your own mouth and your own heart."[95] His letters, as we have seen, show him expressing great interest in her relationship to God and encouraging her longings. Her conviction of God's "grasp" on her heart in 1335, and the ensuing grand expansion of her repertory of paramystical experience, appear to have occurred only after the beginning of her friendship with Henry.[96] Also, her conversations with the Christ child, and more generally the interest in the Savior's childhood that she says accompanied her efforts to write her book, owe something to the influence of Mechthild of Magdeburg's dialogues with Christ in *The Flowing Light of the Godhead*, of which Henry sent her his own High German translation; echoes of Mechthild's imagery are to found throughout the *Revelations*.[97]

Henry's actual appearance in the *Revelations*, however, is rather different from his self-presentation in the letters. Here he is anything but a wretch; for Margaret he is someone with a holiness of his own. As a kind of addendum to a dream she had of Henry asking her "to cooperate with him in faith," her beloved deceased sister appears to her and says, "'Have no worry about him. If there is anyone on earth who leads the life of the apostles, it is he.'"[98] Another revelation tells her that Henry is being given Christ's humanity as a protection against "natural weakness" and that he is also given Christ's divinity in the sense that Christ will "draw him into the Incomprehensible Essence of my Holy Godhead in which he shall lose himself out of love for me";[99] or again, Christ tells her, "He leads a truly authentic life that upholds my honor."[100] She also presents him as her unique confidant, the only person who could relieve the loneliness that set in early in her illness when she learned that she could not depend upon others but only upon God.[101] In the days just after the "speaking" first came upon her, she says, "in all the mysterious ways [*unkunden wegen*] that I had to go, I had no one, except the truly faithful one whom God had given me in His dear Friend. I received powerful consolation from his words and life all the time, so that I often wondered about it myself."[102] She calls him her teacher, but says nothing about what he taught her, nor does she refer directly to the correspondence.[103] Rather, she claims a kind of spiritual balm from him, an immediate infusion of grace, as when at their first meeting he told her to "give" him the dead sister for whom she was grieving, and she felt the grief diminish.[104]

When he visited again on All Saints' Eve of 1334, she was in grief for another sister, but "immeasurable grace coming from him enlightened me and an inner delight of true sweetness proceeded from his words, so that the yearning arose in me to speak with him about all my concerns." Afterward in the night she could "scarcely wait for daybreak in order to visit him again," and she felt herself to be receiving "a great gift from the gentle richness of God," namely a joy that endured "for a long time" and a "lightness of body" that gave her the sensation of floating.[105] He is "the Friend of God, through whom the grace of our Lord always increased in me."[106]

If Henry appears here not as her hagiographer but rather as her colleague or companion in sanctity, such a role appears to qualify him exactly to be her hagiographer. For he is sharing just that part of her life in which she otherwise stands alone and is therefore the one who really *knows* her, a trustworthy person, genuinely worthy to promote her sanctity. The immediate context of her dream of Henry, mentioned above, was her "desire to know what true love for God is": one day while praying her *pater noster*, she says, she received an inward response that God would fulfill the desire, but moreover in such a way that "the whole region would come to know of it." This, however, "alarmed" her, for it was enough for her that no one would know about it except "a true friend of God." The theme of broader public knowledge disappears from the passage at this point as she reports that God gave her the dream, in which Henry appeared and "desired from me, that I take him into my confidence. I said, 'I will gladly do that, if your intention is God's honor,' and he answered that he had no other intention, as, since then, I have found to be true, for I recognize in him a true, guiltless life."[107]

Margaret and Henry in the Letter Collection

I turn, finally, to the letter collection in the London manuscript, which sets these complementary texts, the letters and the *Revelations*, side by side. In doing so, the manuscript also gives expression to Margaret's cult in a way that extends beyond the glimpse offered by Henry's letters in the later Basel years. For in addition to appending the letters to the *Revelations*, the manuscript also obscures the letters' context in Henry's eventful life and accordingly makes it difficult to read them as about Henry in his own right. Now Margaret appears decisively as the central figure and Henry as her satellite.

It is the ordering of the letters in the collection that keeps the story of Henry's life from claiming the reader's attention.[108] The very first letter that appears there (*l* 1) is the letter in which Henry, writing from Strassburg, declares himself "speechless" at the draft of the *Revelations* that he has just received from her—the letter that appears as letter 41 in the edition of Strauch, who dates it to 1345. Next (*l* 2) comes the letter Henry wrote in 1348 or 1349 from Sulz (letter 52 in Strauch), in which he presents himself as an itinerant priest in hostile territory, who has left behind the comforts and support of Basel and relies on her prayers as he attempts to do the work of God in the midst of persecution. The letter that follows (*l* 3) is one of the Basel letters again (letter 47 in Strauch), written in 1346, in which he contrasts her with himself—his own "sick eyes are so unable to see the clear sun of divine truth"—and calls her the "doctor of his wounded heart." Then comes Strauch's letter 25 (*l* 4), one of the crisis letters of 1338, in which Henry speaks of canvassing support for his claim to the living of Fessenheim. This is followed by the early (pre-1338) letter that is letter 1 in Strauch (*l* 5), in which he refers to a recent visit to her and her distress at parting. And so on: the collection continues to jump back and forth between the periods of Henry's life. We cannot be entirely certain how deliberately it jumps. But the very thoroughness with which the collection mixes up the chronology suggests the strong possibility that the letters had been conserved in something more like the order in which we find them in Strauch, in which case the compiler of the collection was intentionally obscuring the chronology.[109] It is also possible that the letters were not conserved in order, were already thoroughly jumbled, in which case the chronology was already obscured by the time the compiler took them in hand.[110] But in either event, that compiler is clearly not interested in establishing the sequence of events in Henry's career, and the reader unaided by Strauch would be hard-pressed to figure it out.

Henry's own story being thus obscured, his relations with Margaret loom the larger in their own right; the compiler wastes no time in exposing all the major themes. So it is that already in those first several texts in the collection we find expression of Henry's interest in the *Revelations*, his high estimate of Margaret's holiness, his own self-abasement, his concern to include her among his friends, and his sense of himself as an exile cast loose upon the world and in need of her prayers. There are no major themes that remain to be introduced after those initial letters; the remainder of the collection displays no evident scheme of organization or thematic development. And so for all the liveliness of some of the individual letters, the collection as whole has a static quality, standing as a sort of icon of the holy woman accompanied by her dependent clerical admirer, with their friends arranged around them.

That literary icon seems to have served the cult of Margaret specifically by pointing beyond itself to her *Revelations*, providing *her* writing, that is, with a firm context without the distraction of Henry's own story and thus making a bid to help establish her significance both within and beyond the monastery. The collection thus serves to fill in the blank spaces around the *Revelations*, that is, to give Margaret's writing, as Peters has put it, a "public" character that it otherwise lacks.[111] For read by itself, Margaret's work is a record of the intensely personal experiences of a largely isolated nun, and the people around her, all unnamed including Henry himself, remain somewhat shadowy. But the letters give names and personalities to those figures, especially Henry, and they serve to fix Margaret's place within a particular social and religious context. That context includes not only Henry and his friendship group but also the Medingen convent itself. For Henry's frequent affectionate and approving references and messages to the Medingen prioress Elisabeth Schepach in his letters to Margaret (a letter of Henry directly to the prioress being also included early in the collection [*l* 10]) help make Margaret's writings into "an official document, whose origin the Prioress supports with her powers"—a document that is in this sense like the famous contemporary "sister books" in which other German Dominican convents of the period preserved the vitae of their nuns.

Conclusion

Henry's letters show him attributing extraordinary powers to Margaret, contrasting himself with her, and in general treating her authority to speak as something valid yet different from his own. This is the familiar stance of clerical collaborator toward holy woman, here glimpsed exceptionally, however, as it took shape over time and helped to inform her cult, which then also made its own use of Henry.

A remarkable feature of both the letters and the *Revelations* is that Margaret does not appear as having detractors who need to be answered. In this she is unlike Angela of Foligno and Margaret of Cortona in their respective vitae, and indeed unlike most other women in the hagiography of the period. Perhaps it is the very fact that Henry is *not* on the defensive for Margaret that allows him to bring his reflections about her so naturally into the context of other matters and move so freely among the things that are on his mind—and accordingly to place her sanctity, and his own relation to it, against what is for us an unusually spacious and detailed background.

The expansive quality of these sources is something that will not arise again in this study. The cases examined in the next two chapters reflect the atmosphere of increased suspicion about holy women that will be evident around the end of the fourteenth century in some important quarters; a corresponding defensiveness on the part of their male confidants will be the order of the day.

CHAPTER 9

Managing Holiness

Raymond of Capua and Catherine of Siena

T HE LAY PENITENT CATHERINE of Siena acquired a reputation as a holy woman in the 1370s, amid turbulent political events in the Italian peninsula in which she played a role. She died in 1380. Then in the years between 1385 and 1395, her sometime confessor Raymond of Capua wrote his monumental vita of Catherine, the so-called *Legenda maior*. By that time Raymond was master general of the Roman observance of the Dominican Order, and he wrote the work as part of a Dominican effort to see her canonized.

In the *Legenda maior* Raymond makes the most of his own relationship with Catherine during her lifetime. He inserts himself continually as a figure in the narrative, placing himself at her side as much as possible, connecting himself with events in her life, telling the reader what he was thinking as he interacted with her. The *Legenda maior* represents in fact a kind of a summing-up of the themes and trends that already described in male hagiographers of holy women over the preceding two centuries. For Raymond shows himself acutely aware of the distinction between the institutional powers of clerics and the informal powers of holy women, and he explores the relationship between the two through the medium of his own personal experience, like those other writers but, ostensibly anyway, in a manner more precise and calculated than anything discussed so far. It is especially through Raymond's exploration of these concerns, moreover, that they find their way into future hagiography. For the *Legenda maior* as a hagiographical account of "a holy woman and her confessor" was to become an important model for the centuries that followed, when such confessors were to become common figures in hagiography.[1]

But if Raymond's work summed up for posterity the concerns and interests that he shared with the self-referential male hagiographers who preceded him, still there is also something missing from his work that we have observed in at least some of those others. For if the very precision and calculation of Raymond's self-inclusion in Catherine's life is recognized—his careful positioning of himself so as to stand as the crucial person in divulging the details of her inner life, and in this regard her necessary point of access to her audience—it becomes difficult to sense the personal immediacy to be found, for instance, in the letters of Guibert of Gembloux or of Henry of Nördlingen or even in the hagiographical narratives of James of Vitry or Giunta Bevegnati. We have here instead an effort at self-depiction that, though every bit as self-aware as those of his predecessors, is arguably less self-revealing.

CATHERINE AND RAYMOND

It was probably shortly before 1 August 1374, that Friar Raymond of Capua took up a new position as lector at the Dominican convent of Camporeggi in Siena. On that date his name first appears on an official document of the house, after the names of the prior and the subprior; it is absent on a similar document dated two months earlier.[2] A bull of Gregory XI addressed to Raymond two years later tells us that at some unspecified moment the master general of the Dominicans, Elias of Toulouse, had appointed Raymond to attend closely to the lay penitent woman Catherine of Siena. The appointment was very likely what had prompted Raymond's restationing in Siena in 1374, and in that case Elias probably made it at the order's general chapter meeting in Florence in May of that year, which we know Catherine also attended.[3] What is clear, at any rate, is that Raymond's relationship to Catherine was to be an official one, mandated by the authority of his order.

By 1374 Raymond of Capua was a seasoned friar who had already held several positions of responsibility. Born around 1330, a member of the noble delle Vigne family of Naples, he was the son and grandson of counselors in royal service. He probably studied at Bologna and made his profession as a Dominican at Orvieto sometime between 1345 and 1348. His subsequent movements are unknown until 1363, when he became rector of the convent of Dominican nuns at Montepulciano, not far from Siena. He remained in Montepulciano until 1367, and it was there that he first tried his hand at a vita of a holy woman, in this case the convent's founder Agnes (d. 1317).[4] During Urban V's abortive attempt to return the papacy to Rome (1367–70), Raymond served as prior of Santa Maria sopra Minerva, the Dominican house at Rome. Then in 1373 we find his name on a document as regent of the Dominican house at Florence,

Santa Maria Novella. Probably this was the position he left in 1374 when he moved to Siena.[5]

By 1374 Catherine herself, the daughter of a Sienese dyer named Giacomo Benincasa and his wife Lapa, had become well known not only in Siena itself but also well beyond it. She was, like most of the other holy women of the Italian towns at the time—like Angela of Foligno or Margaret of Cortona—a penitent or *pinzochere*, a devout laywoman who undertook religious discipline without becoming a cloistered nun. Unmarried and about twenty-seven years of age at the time Raymond assumed his new duties in Siena, she had been for several years a member of the *mantellate*, a group of such female penitents affiliated with the Dominicans. Her particular fame derived from the remarkable force of her personality and the scope of her active life. Although she had a reputation for having spent several years in silent seclusion in her family's home as a younger person, by 1374 she had been out and about for some time, caring for the sick and poor, making peace among Sienese families, and promoting the idea of a new crusade in the Holy Land. And there had developed around her a "family" of devout people who revered her as "*mamma*" and acted as her helpers and companions.[6] Her influence extended also beyond her immediate circle. She had already exchanged correspondence with at least two high papal officials and had written to Gregory XI himself about the project of a crusade.[7] Earlier in 1374, around Palm Sunday, the pope had sent Alfonso of Valdaterra, the confessor of the recently deceased prophet Bridget of Sweden, to visit Catherine. Alfonso, as she reported in a letter to her own confessor at the time, solicited her prayers for the pope. But in view of Catherine's later activities, we can surmise that Alfonso was probably also charged to discern if this charismatic woman could become, in effect, a successor to Bridget as a prophet in public support of Gregory, who himself was pursuing the goals of a crusade and (on his own terms) a pacified Italy.[8]

What exactly was the task to which Elias appointed Raymond? The minutes of the chapter meeting have been lost. But in a later request to Gregory XI for papal confirmation of the appointment, Raymond apparently gave an account of Elias's action, the substance of which appears in the bull mentioned above, in which Gregory granted the request. There it is noted that Elias had entrusted to Raymond the "care [*curam*]" both of Catherine and of such of her companions as he and she together would choose from among her sisters, the Dominican penitents at Siena. The bull also says that he was to serve as "director [*magister*]" of Catherine as well as the companions, "so as to guide and correct them [*ut eas videlicet regeres et corrigeres*]." As to why Elias judged this necessary, the bull says that he acted after considering that Catherine "had concerned herself productively with the salvation of souls and the passage beyond the sea, and other matters of the holy Roman church." He ostensibly wanted to aid her public ministry, "so that the benefit of souls would not be in any way hindered," and, in referring to the "passage," he shows his interest in the crusade project.[9] He also, no doubt, intended to make sure that she stayed within the bounds of orthodoxy and of the church's interest. And given the pope's evident knowledge of Catherine and Alfonso's visit shortly before the chapter meeting, it seems likely that Gregory himself had a hand in the matter. Raymond's appointment therefore signaled official encouragement of Catherine's emerging public role in "matters of the holy Roman church."[10]

Catherine's efforts on behalf of the Roman church came to full flower in the years that followed. The project of a crusade was always on her mind, but for her, as indeed for the pope, it was also firmly linked with two other goals, namely, the return of the papacy from Avignon to Rome and the pacification of Italy, then torn by conflict between many of the city-states and the pope. All her major activities reflect these three concerns in one way or another. She was clearly much less a prophet, in the sense of a medium of supernatural revelations, than Gregory XI wanted her to be, although revelations and ecstasies were to figure prominently in her posthumous reputation. It was mainly, rather, by her own efforts of persuasion that she promoted her causes among those she considered to be in a position to do something about them.[11] Though the actual extent of her influence in the great affairs of the day is still a matter of debate, there is no doubt that she poured prodigious energy into the task, through a constant stream of letters and a series of missions that took her outside Siena for several long periods.[12] She spent most of 1375 in Pisa, promoting the crusade project. From June to October of 1376 she was in Avignon, where she attempted to mediate between the pope and the Florentines and urged the pope's return to Rome, which was anyway imminent (he embarked upon it in September). After passing much of 1377 in the countryside around Siena, in part to reconcile factions of the Salimbene family, she traveled to Florence sometime in the early months of 1378, at some personal risk, to encourage elements in the Guelph party there who were favorable to reconciliation with the pope, and she stayed in Florence through the death of Gregory (27 March) and the subsequent proclamation of peace (28 July). She returned briefly to Siena, but traveled again to Rome in November 1378 in the aftermath of the beginning of the Great Schism after the contested papal election, to support Urban VI over against his rival Clement VII, who was about to set up the papacy again in Avignon. Catherine remained in Rome, occupied in passionate advocacy and prayer for the Urbanist cause, until her death on 29 April 1380.

As for Raymond's part in these activities, though by his appointment he was indeed Catherine's "director," and in the *Legenda maior* he emphasizes his own role as her confessor, the sources overall give the impression that he functioned preeminently as her companion and collaborator. Over a period of three and a half years from his arrival in Siena in 1374 until his appointment as prior of the Dominican convent of Santa Maria sopra Minerva in Rome in January 1378, he seems to have spent much of his time either attending to Catherine or else undertaking missions related to her and her causes. He accompanied her during her sojourn in Pisa in 1375, heard confessions there from people whom she had brought to penitence, and in June of that year took a letter from Catherine to the English mercenary captain John Hawkwood, who had brought his dangerous unemployed army near the borders of Florence, proposing that he commit himself to the projected crusade.[13] In 1376 Raymond preceded Catherine to Avignon by several months, conveying a letter from her to the pope, and then stayed with her through her time of residence there and her return journey at the end of the year. He was with her again in the Sienese countryside in 1377, and when he traveled to Rome late in that year he conferred with the pope about the mission she would soon undertake to Florence.[14] Others of her "family," including her long-term confessor Bartolomeo Dominici, certainly knew her better, and for a longer period of time, than did Raymond. But exactly because of his stature and official standing, it was through Raymond as through no one else that she gained a place in the great events of Christendom. In this sense he was her major collaborator. In the last two and a half years of her life, he apparently did not see her at all except perhaps briefly in December of 1378 after she arrived in Rome, if he indeed had then not yet left on the first of two abortive attempts to travel to France to plead the Urbanist cause before the French king Charles V.[15] But even so, they kept in touch, and, as will be seen, Catherine's letters to Raymond in those final years of her life suggest a strong continuing bond between them.

When Raymond began to write the *Legenda maior* in 1385, five years after Catherine's death, he was still acting in an official capacity. For he was by then master general of the Dominican Order, or rather of the portion of it loyal to Urban. (His former superior Elias of Toulouse, who headed the portion loyal to Clement, was now his adversary.) He had been elected on 12 May 1380, only days after the saint's death, and was to remain in the office until his own death in 1399. Spurred on by some of the surviving members of Catherine's "family"—especially Thomas of Siena (in later tradition often called "Caffarini"), who served as Raymond's scribe in the last stages of writing and was later to become the great promoter of Catherine's canonization (which, however, was not to be achieved until 1460, long after the death of all her associates)—Raymond wrote the work over a ten-year period, finishing it in late 1395.[16] As master general, he was inevitably immersed in the affairs of the order and the politics of the schism during the whole period of the writing, and he clearly had them in mind as he wrote. Thus, as Robert Fawtier pointed out, the vita served to associate Catherine with the cause of the Urbanist papacy, the observant reform of the Dominican Order (to which I shall return), and perhaps also the prospective papal approval of the order of Dominican penitents (the so-called third order); it is possible that he was deliberately trying to give his Dominicans a stigmatized saint to compare with the founder of the Franciscans.[17] In Raymond's hands, at any rate, the project of promoting Catherine as saint became inescapably a matter that concerned the Dominican Order itself.

CATHERINE IN THE *LEGENDA MAIOR*

In the *Legenda maior* Raymond portrays Catherine in a way calculated to justify her "apostolate," her active involvement in society and in the great matters of Christendom.[18] That activity was problematic, as Raymond was acutely aware. The problem was inherent in the very idea of the semireligious life for women in the late Middle Ages, that is, the idea that lay women could adopt religious disciplines while remaining in the secular world, whether they were northern Beguines or Italian lay penitents like Catherine. The tensions involved are by now familiar to the reader, most explicitly from the case of Margaret of Cortona. For women's activity outside home or cloister went against the deep grain of societal assumptions about their place in society, even as the demands of the gospel, especially as mediated by preachers from the mendicant orders, appeared to draw them there. Maiju Lehmijoki-Gardner, in her study of late-medieval hagiographical works about Italian Dominican female penitents, including Raymond's *Legenda*, has shown that the mendicant hagiographers themselves displayed marked ambivalence about the proper role of women and accordingly "a bifurcated conception about the penitent women's presence in the world," portraying them "as physically present and active in the society, but mentally inhabiting the transcendent world." Catherine exceeded all the rest in the degree of her involvement in the public sphere, since the others' influence beyond the home, except for works of charity, was generally limited to letter writing and private advice.[19] Raymond therefore could not justify her behavior simply by pointing out the good she did. He had to establish her presence in the "transcendent world" as well, and that presence, as he seems to have thought, had to be extraordinary in direct proportion to the extraordinariness of her activity in society. So he portrays her in the *Legenda maior* as a figure of simultaneous action and contemplation, on a heroic scale.

A brief overview of the work will give us our bearings. Raymond himself divided it into three parts, ostensibly according to chronology, as he explains at the end of the prologue: part 1, in twelve chapters, about her childhood and youth up to and including the moment of her dramatic spiritual marriage to Christ; part 2, also in twelve chapters, about the public period of Catherine's life, from the immediate aftermath of that spiritual marriage until her final days; and then part 3, in six chapters, about those final days.[20] But if we view the work in terms of its argument overall, it divides more naturally into two sections, with the dividing point in the exact middle of part 2, between its sixth and seventh chapters. For from the beginning until that point (1.1–2.6), Raymond traces Catherine's personal formation, which in his account establishes her relationships with God and the world—and thus the foundation of her apostolate, her public ministry—ending with her so-called first death, when she literally expired and was resurrected, so as to be made fully ready for the public ministry that would follow. The whole of this formation clearly occurred, in Raymond's telling, well before he came on the scene as her confessor, and the "death" experience, which he says he heard about from her earlier confessors, marked the clear and firm conclusion of that formative period. Then the remainder of the body of the work (2.7–3.5) proceeds to describe her public ministry directly (including however many retrospective references to earlier events), with chapters on her various miracles in life, the events of the last two years of her life, her death, the content of her book the *Dialogue*, and the miracles after death. Finally in an epilogue (3.6) Raymond argues explicitly for her canonization based on the quality of her patience, understood as the endurance of adversity, which increases precisely as one's involvement with human society increases. In terms of overall structure, leaving aside the epilogue, the work is a two-stage presentation of Catherine as a public figure, with the first stage laying the foundation for, and in effect justifying, the second. The second stage actually abandons chronology as an overarching principle of organization, there being no remaining progress to trace.

This apparent finality of Catherine's early process of formation alerts us to Raymond's care to justify her apostolate. For precisely in making the mystical death a "once-in-a-lifetime" turning point for her, as Karen Scott has shown, Raymond was able to present "the holiness of her subsequent activism as that of a mystic already entirely possessed by God and dead to herself"—a person kept alive solely for purposes of that apostolate and thus an anomaly, not to be judged as one would judge other people.[21] Raymond's intention becomes the clearer, as Scott has also shown, when we compare his picture of Catherine to her own self-conception as this emerges from her letters. In the letters Catherine appears oblivious to issues of gender in relation to her calling and neither asserts her equality to men nor, conversely, claims for herself the divine strength expressed in female weakness. Raymond makes both these claims for her in the *Legenda*, typically putting them in the mouth of Christ addressing the saint. And Catherine calls little attention to the supernatural events in her life, saying nothing, for instance, about her spiritual marriage to Christ or her gift of stigmata, both of which occupy an important place in Raymond's argument for the legitimacy of her calling.[22] Particularly telling is Raymond's use of two letters that Catherine sent him from Rome in the last months of her life, in which she wrote metaphorically of returning her heart to God, to whom it belonged, and described a recent "death" experience in which she had left her body. He includes both the mystical death and exchange of hearts (which he interprets literally) in his narrative, but instead of placing them in her last months, he moves them back into her crucial early formative period, so as not to allow the possibility that in the time of her apostolate she had any perfection still to attain.[23]

As for the early formative period itself, it is there that Raymond finds and charts the perfecting of her sanctity in the parallel enlargement of her inner and outer lives. He advances the narrative of her formation at a series of crucial points with stories of encounters with Christ, each more extensive than the last, in which she is rewarded for the virtues she has thus far attained and is spurred on to new ones. The first of the encounters is the six-year-old Catherine's vision of Christ enthroned in a "beautiful palace" in the sky above the Dominican church in Siena (1.2). This was, says Raymond, a favor in response to her precocious early asceticism, and it also spurred her to greater austerities and finally to take the vow of virginity that set her in conflict with her family over their desire to see her married.[24] Then, after she triumphs and takes the habit of a Dominican tertiary, the visions multiply, with Christ beginning to act toward her "as teacher [*praeceptor*]"—"either," as Raymond reports her telling him, "by inspiration or else by appearing clearly and talking with me, just as a moment ago I talked with you," so constantly that "you could hardly find two people, who had such constant conversation with each other as she had with her bridegroom."[25] Then after a series of trials that includes a period in which Christ has appeared to withdraw from her, he comes back again to visit her either by himself (saying the Psalms with her) or with saints in tow.[26] At length Christ marries her, appearing to her in the company of saints and the Virgin and putting a ring on her finger that she, but only she, can see there ever afterward.[27] Christ does this, he says, in response to her desire to "attain a perfect degree of faith," and it signals now a greater involvement with the world around her, toward which Christ pushed her "but without withdrawing divine conversation from her, which indeed increased in its measure of perfection."[28]

Thereafter, frequent ecstasies accompany her first efforts to involve herself with others by doing servile chores in her parents' house, "for the memory of the holy bridegroom had only to refresh itself to that holy soul for a little while, and she drew back from her bodily senses as far as she could, and her bodily extremities, that is, her hands and feet, contracted."[29] Raymond then proceeds to report two series of charitable acts, to poor people and sick people, respectively, each series being crowned and completed by a revelation betokening some new grace: Christ in the first instance appears (as to Martin of Tours) wearing a tunic she had given to a pauper and gives her certainty about her own salvation. In the second, after she has confronted her own revulsion at the caviling, sick *mantellata* Andrea by drinking pus from Andrea's putrefying breast, he invites her to drink from the wound in his side from which he promises great "sweetness [*suavitatem*]."[30] This vision in turn inaugurates the final phase of Catherine's development. Now, as her activity in the world intensifies, her most spectacular encounters with Christ occur: he removes her heart and replaces it with his own, appears to her frequently during Communion, gives her sublime new visions, endows her with his own will in place of her own and then the stigmata (invisible to others, like her ring), and finally grants her request to feel the pain of his sufferings—thus causing her "death," in which she spends four hours with him in heaven before returning to life.[31] The encounters with Christ, therefore, reward her for virtues she has thus far attained and spur her on to new ones, each set of encounters somewhat grander or more profound than the previous one, precisely as her engagement in the world around her widens.

Raymond's interest in defending Catherine's apostolate is therefore of a piece with his interest in her inner life. He is asserting the necessary pairing of contemplation and action, the simultaneity of the inward life of love for Christ that finds expression in the spirit and the outward life of love for neighbor that finds expression in the body. A key image for him is that of grace overflowing.

At least four times in recounting the aftermath of her drink from Christ's side, Raymond explains that such an abundance of grace has now been poured into her spirit (*mens, anima,* or *spiritus*) as also to flow over into her body.[32] This conceit allows him not only to maintain the priority of spirit or soul to body (which he is everywhere concerned to do) but also to treat her corporeal and spiritual lives as entities that, though firmly connected (through the receipt of graces) are also firmly discrete (as separate vessels). The physical effects of these overflowing graces are two: a disappearance of her need for any food at all and a concomitant expansion of her scope of activity (a combination that calls to mind the classic symptoms of anorexia nervosa).[33] She not only lacks the need but also the ability to eat, says Raymond, a fact that he attributes to the drink from Christ's side and thereby to extraordinary grace: "from that hour the body, feeling the overflow [of grace], never took food as previously, nor could it."[34] As for the expansion of activity, it is a matter of associating herself indiscriminately with men as well as women for purposes of their souls' salvation and thus, in principle at least, a removal of any gender-based restraint upon her ministry within her society. Christ tells her, "'your heart will be so powerfully kindled toward the salvation of your neighbors that, forgetting your own sex, you will almost completely change your customary conversation and you will not avoid the company of both men and women as you are used to doing: indeed for the salvation of the souls of both you will put yourself forth with all your might in any labor.'"[35] The spiritual effect of the drink is to make Christ almost constantly visible to her, both in increasingly frequent ecstasies and also, it would seem, in the midst of her conscious actions: "For the Lord began from that moment not only to show himself to her openly and with familiarity, not only in secret places, as he had used to do, but also in public ones, when she was in motion as well as when she was standing still."[36]

In tracing Catherine's inner formation on a track parallel to her outer formation, assuring the reader that Catherine's apostolate did not draw her away from the "transcendent world"—that she was at least as much a part of that world as if she had been a cloistered nun—Raymond is writing from a perspective typical of mendicant friars. For friars did not so much invent a new ideal of the Christian life as live out ancient monastic ideals in new settings, that is, in the midst of secular society. Earlier vitae of female penitents by mendicant authors show a similarly acute interest in establishing their saints' ascetic credentials.[37] For example, the Franciscan Vito of Cortona (d. ca. 1250) wrote in his vita of the Franciscan tertiary Humiliana dei Cerchi of Florence (d. 1246), who lived an ascetic life in her father's house, that it was by the command of God that she stayed there instead of entering a cloister, so that because of her example "no one from the least to the greatest might have any excuse from serving God at home and in secular dress."[38] And I have already shown how Giunta Bevignati depicted Margaret of Cortona's exemplary penitence and ascetic self-denial as a visible "banner" to help the friars in their urban evangelistic work of rallying sinners back to God.[39]

If Raymond is innovating, the innovation lies not in this fundamental "both/and" character of his idea of holiness—the firmly linked dichotomy of ascetical prayer and charitable action—but rather in his characteristic pushing of both sides of that dichotomy just as far as he can make them go. Thus Catherine is an ascetic contemplative on a grand scale, one whose heart and will have been exchanged for Christ's very own and who has progressed so far into heaven that her body on earth needs no food; at the same time she is a charitable activist of the greatest consequence who works for the benefit of others not simply by offering a salutary visible example but by teaching, counseling, and interceding at every level of Christian society, including the most exalted. This simultaneity of action and contemplation gets its strongest expression in Raymond's account of Catherine's four-hour "death" as the event that completes her formation. It is the logical conclusion of the development of her inner life in the sense that it results from the sufferings that in turn have proceeded from the enhanced closeness to Christ brought on by the drink from his side; as part of her response to Raymond's inquiry as to what she saw in the afterlife, she tells him, "you may take it for certain that my soul saw the divine essence, and this is why I am so impatient about remaining in this prison of a body."[40] In this event, for Raymond, the formation of her outer life finds its completion, as Christ, in sending her back to her body, commissions her to leave her own home:

> The salvation of many souls requires that you go back, and that you no longer hold to the way of life you have held until now, nor will you any longer make your cell your home; indeed it will be necessary for you to leave even your own city for the salvation of souls. I, moreover, will always be with you and I will lead you here and there; and you will carry the honor of my name and the instructions of the Spirit before persons small and great, lay people as well as clerics and religious: for I will give you a mouth and a wisdom that no one will be able to resist [cf. Luke 21.15]. I will lead you before the bishops and others who govern the churches and the Christian people, to confound the pride of the strong by means of the weak, as is my way.[41]

This is Raymond's definitive statement of her apostolate, in the sense that there will not be any more widening of its scope. Catherine is now fully formed, in both her inner and her outer life.

For Raymond, therefore, Catherine's extraordinary supernatural graces both validate and necessarily accompany her extraordinary role as apostle; both aspects of her life together make up his portrait, each being equally essential to it. It remains to be asked how Raymond places himself in this carefully structured account of her life—how he presents his own role in life in relation to hers. Catherine's letters provide, first, a useful point of comparison to show how the saint herself thought about her relationship with Raymond.

CATHERINE ON RAYMOND

Among Catherine's surviving letters are seventeen that she wrote to Raymond, more letters than she sent to any other single correspondent. These are mostly hortatory in character: intently focused upon the life of active charity in herself and others, Catherine scolds and encourages Raymond toward greater zeal, love, courage, and self-sacrifice. She has almost nothing to say in these letters about Raymond's priestly functions, and she gives her own prophecies and visions a low profile; and so the question of the proper relation between distinct spheres of authority hardly occurs to her at all. She does often think in terms of a three-way relationship between herself, Raymond, and Christ—the familiar triad of woman/Christ/cleric—but so strong is her fervor to identify Raymond and herself together in their desires and actions that the threesome is always on the verge of collapsing into a mere pair.

Catherine shows little interest in Raymond as priest or figure of authority in these letters, and one would hardly guess from them that the pope had appointed him as her director. It is not that she challenges his authority but that she does not particularly express herself as someone under his care, except perhaps in her last letter to him (February 1380), when she calls him "father of my soul" and laments his absence as she feels her death approaching.[42] Nowhere does she ask his advice or refer to his instruction or aid. She writes of him as her confessor only in the context of telling him once that she has had a revelation in which Christ superseded him by granting her direct absolution of sin.[43] In three letters of uncertain date she exhorts him to be a good pastor, but of a flock (probably the friars of Santa Maria sopra Minerva in Rome) that apparently does not include herself, and even so she says nothing specific about pastoral functions and instead issues her usual exhortations: he should not be afraid, he should be solicitous for souls, he should identify himself with Christ.[44]

Though Catherine does not write to Raymond explicitly as to a priest—or anyway a priest under whose direction she stands—she herself does appear as something of a prophet, making mention of her revelations in eight of the seventeen letters.[45] Nonetheless, unlike Hildegard she does not frame her letters as explicated revelations but rather employs the revelations for emphasis or illustration of some urgent theme that she is otherwise developing in its own right.[46] In letter 219, for example, written in April 1376 to encourage Raymond at Avignon where she was soon to join him in the role (as she thought) of peacemaker between the pope and the Florentines, she begins by urging him to be united with Christ, "nailed to the cross," "bound" there, "set ablaze in the gentle Jesus," by "the wood of self-knowledge," and so on, and only then tells him her striking vision of a great procession of people, including herself, entering the side of the crucified Christ and a subsequent reassuring conversation with Christ, which betoken a good outcome in the cause of peace that they both serve.[47] There was indeed more to the vision, she says, but she intentionally leaves it out: "there were such mysteries as words can never describe, nor heart imagine, nor eye see. Now what words could ever describe the wonderful things of God? None from this poor wretch! So I'd rather keep silent and give myself completely to seeking God's honor, the salvation of souls, and the renewal and exaltation of holy Church."[48] In the midst of letter 104, a letter of uncertain date in which she addresses Raymond twice as a "negligent son" and lectures him on virtue and the necessity of "diligence" (*sollecitudine*) in seeking it, Catherine reports almost incidentally a snatch of dialog between herself and God who tells her " 'render honor to me, and hard work to your neighbor,' " with the implication that Raymond should do likewise.[49] In letter 273, perhaps the most famous of all her letters, probably written in June 1375, it is ostensibly to underscore and elaborate her impassioned wish that Raymond and the others of her group be "drenched" and "drowned" in Christ's blood, willing to embrace suffering and martyrdom, that she tells of the execution of an unnamed man, probably one Niccolò di Toldo who had been accused at Siena as an agent of the papal governor of Perugia, and she describes her vision of Christ receiving his soul after she herself has received his severed head in her hands and been splattered with his blood.[50] And in her last letter to Raymond, already mentioned, she frames her account of her temporary "death," in which Christ enjoined her to a new intensity of single-minded prayer for the church in those early days of the schism, as an exhortation to Raymond to give himself up also for the church.[51]

Catherine's stance toward Raymond in these letters typically combines sharp criticism and strong empathy. Whatever his official authority over her, she writes rather as a mother to a son, assuming both a deep connection with him that transcends any difference in activity or circumstance and yet by the same token a prerogative to command and reprove. All of this is present in the chiding letter 344, written at the end of July or beginning of August 1379.[52] The previous December, Raymond had embarked on his embassy to Charles V of France, but had returned in mid-journey upon being informed that partisans of the Avignonese papacy planned to ambush and capture him.[53] Catherine had written at the time scorning his lack of courage,[54] and now she is still calling him to task, in response to a letter he has apparently written her in the meantime. She begins, however, by accusing herself of the same reluctance to embrace martyrdom of which she has accused him, and she asks him to pray that "you and I together may drown ourselves in the blood of the humble Lamb." And in a rare moment of explicit affection she appeals to "a very close and special love between us, and one which is so faithful that it can neither believe nor imagine that the other could want anything but our good."[55] Raymond, as becomes clear, had worried that her love for him might have diminished.[56] This she denies vehemently, and in the same breath she renews her rebuke: she loves him as she loves herself and consequently could not want "anything other than the life of your soul"—therefore she could not ignore the "lack of faith" that he had shown in abandoning his mission. It is her role to chide him: "When your own faults are pointed out to you, rejoice, and be thankful to the divine Goodness who has appointed someone to work on you and keep watch for you before him."[57]

It is this sense of close identification with Raymond that makes it hard to apply the old Hildegardean role distinction between priest and holy woman here; for she is always collapsing their roles into one, joining herself to him, or him to her, before God. In letter 226, in which she claims to have had a prior revelation of certain unspecified good news that Raymond has since conveyed to her (very likely the election of Urban VI in April of 1378), she tells him that she has prayed for his presence as confessor but that Christ made known to her that he was giving her himself instead, granting absolution to Raymond as well. Thus woman and erstwhile confessor are paired together in the role of penitent.[58] We see a similar dynamic in her account of Niccolò di Toldo's execution in letter 273. There she describes her vision of Christ receiving the dead man's soul:

after he had received his blood and his desire, [Christ] received his soul as well and placed it all-mercifully into the open hostelry of his side.... As for him, he made a gesture sweet enough to charm a thousand hearts. (I'm not surprised, for he was already tasting the divine sweetness.) He turned as does a bride when, having reached her husband's threshold, she turns her head and looks back, nods to those who have attended her, and so expresses her thanks.[59]

In this extraordinary image, Catherine casts herself as friend of the "bride," who has prepared "her" for the wedding and now receives graceful thanks. And Catherine's preceding descriptions of her ministrations to Niccolò—how she visited him, apparently the day before the execution, and on the day itself took him to mass where he received Communion and expressed his devotion to her as well and then joined him at the block—make this triadic image poignant. But Catherine's imagination will not allow her to remain a mere observer, and typically she pushes on to identify herself, and by implication her addressee Raymond, with the executed man. She says that after Communion preceding the execution she "sensed an intense joy, a fragrance of his blood—and it wasn't separate from the fragrance of my own, which I am waiting to shed for my gentle Spouse Jesus." And when she waited for him at the place of execution, "I knelt down and stretched my neck out on the block, but did not succeed in getting what I longed for up there."[60] Given that the letter has begun with the wish to see Raymond and others in his circle "drenched" and "drowned" in the blood of Christ, clearly she means for Raymond to share in her desire to be the bride of Christ rather than only an attendant at the wedding. She anyway shows no interest in any distinction of roles between them.

RAYMOND IN THE *LEGENDA MAIOR*

In contrast to the terms of relationship implicit in Catherine's letters, Raymond in the *Legenda maior* pictures himself and the saint in distinct roles. He emphasizes her supernatural powers, and in his own extensive appearance in the vita—he alludes to himself on almost every page—he puts particular emphasis on his own priesthood, especially his role as her confessor. He also uses the distinctness of their roles to exploit the irony of reversal, in a manner reminiscent of James of Vitry, making a point of receiving direction from the woman to whom he was supposed to give it. But here the irony is not intended to suggest much about the inner man. For however evident the sincerity of the devotion Raymond manifests toward Catherine throughout, it is not his own need or longing that he purports to express in the *Legenda maior* so much as his clear-headed intention to prove her sanctity against her detractors. Even when he is depicting himself, that is the task he has in mind.

Raymond intended the *Legenda maior* to justify an unusual and controversial kind of sanctity. He sets an argumentative tone by his many explicit replies to Catherine's unnamed critics, especially after he has begun to recount her activities outside her home. He devotes one long set of rebuttals to people who objected to her extreme fasting, pointing out comparable examples from early monasticism and calling attention to her accompanying virtues as proof against the devil.[61] He makes another long reply to those who, as he thinks, misunderstood her prophecies of the imminence of the crusade that she zealously promoted: she never fixed a time, he says, or claimed that she herself would necessarily participate.[62] He responds in another extended passage to criticisms that she partook of the Eucharist too frequently: here he argues from Scripture and tradition in favor of the practice of frequent Communion and tells of miracles that attended her partaking.[63] Shorter replies to critics are scattered through the work.[64]

The argumentative quality of the *Legenda maior* helps explain Raymond's care to include himself in the text: he claims for himself the role of source or witness in support of the case he is making for her. Raymond's intentional citing of his sources is a remarkable feature of the work; he promises at the outset to provide a list in each chapter of the people who gave him his information. He keeps the promise for the first eighteen chapters with only one exception, although only sporadically thereafter.[65] In these lists he gives himself a prominent place, either as direct recipient of Catherine's confidences or as eyewitness to events. He also frames the work itself in terms of his role as witness: in the first of two prologues, after likening Catherine to the revelatory angel seen coming down from heaven in the twentieth chapter of the biblical book of Revelation, he proceeds to liken himself to John the Evangelist, the supposed recipient of the vision. Here he would have it that Catherine had chosen *him* as her confessor so that he could "participate in and know the secrets that God had conceded or revealed to her," and that accordingly she even called him John, apparently with the biblical vision in mind, "because of the secrets she revealed to me."[66]

In this way Raymond stakes Catherine's sanctity to a considerable extent on his own veracity as a witness, and it is not surprising to find him using his own putative experience to counter the doubts he anticipates in his reader. For instance, at the point in the narrative when Catherine, after receiving her habit, begins to experience revelations from Christ, Raymond responds to his imagined reader's wariness about the validity of such revelations by telling two stories about his own wariness. In one of these, he says he devised a test for her powers, asking her to pray not only for divine indulgence for his sins but also for some proof that her prayers had been heard—a "seal in the manner of the Roman curia [*more curiae Romane bullam*]," as he puts it—which he afterward received to his satisfaction during a conversation with her when he found himself suddenly in tears from a vivid sense of the mercy of God and the depth of his own sin.[67] In the other story, he suddenly saw her face transform itself into the face of "the Lord"—"an oblong, middle-aged face," as he says, with a "wheat-colored beard"—at a moment when he was doubting the truth of her words to him.[68] In a similar vein he relates two eucharistic miracles that he alone witnessed. In one of these, he saw a Host he had consecrated for Catherine rise up of its own accord toward the paten he was holding. In the other, when he was celebrating mass unaware of Catherine's presence in the back of the church, a small fragment of the broken Host fell, as he thought, onto the Communion cloth, but he could not find it there or anywhere after the mass was finished. When he discovered that Catherine had been present, he pressed her until she told him that Christ himself had brought her the fragment so that she could eat it. He accepted this explanation, he says, reflecting that indeed there had been no breeze to blow the Host to her, that he himself had looked too carefully to miss it if it had really fallen, and moreover that Catherine was strangely unperturbed about the whole matter, which would not have been the case if the fragment had truly been unaccounted for.[69]

It is in the role of confessor that Raymond the hagiographer makes the most use of himself as witness, for this allows him to vouch for the truth of Catherine's rapports with Christ, so essential to his case for her sanctity. Thus he could claim to know directly through her confession that Christ taught her personally all she knew and said the Psalms with her, that the Holy Spirit directly revealed to her as a child the stories of the lives of the desert fathers and other saints, that when Christ commissioned her to go out of her cell he recognized her grief in leaving it behind, and that when she first left the cell she felt an excruciating pain in her heart.[70] Broadly, his accounts of what she said in confession or other personal conversation introduce a subjective dimension into the narrative, claiming to expose her desires or feelings or ascetical practice and explaining her own perspectives. It was in confession, for example, that she told him of her childhood desire to be a friar, and thus male, or at least to pretend to be a monk as did the legendary virgin St. Euphrosyne. It was also in confession that she told him of her revulsion at the smell of meat, of her disregard of what people said about her, of the continual pain in her side from Christ's passion, and of her daily discipline with an iron chain.[71] The examples could be multiplied; the vita is suffused with confidences of this sort. Raymond the confidant is present at every turn even if sometimes he is scarcely noticeable.[72]

In certain passages that include Raymond as witness, however, he is very noticeable indeed, especially when he shows himself interacting with her. Here role reversal is the norm: Raymond the director and confessor typically becomes Catherine's pupil and the recipient of her rebukes. In the episode already mentioned when she obtained Raymond's "bull" of contrition, for example, he became in a certain sense her penitent.[73] On another occasion, when he had fallen asleep as she discoursed at length on some devout topic, she "made a loud sound to wake me up, saying, 'can it be that for the sake of sleep you would lose something good for your soul? Am I speaking words of God to the wall rather than to you?'"[74] Another time, when she was trying to eat something so as not to scandalize the critics of her fasting, he told her to ignore them, but she instructed him instead on the usefulness of taking such "murmurings" to heart—instruction to which, he tells the reader, he wishes he had paid more attention.[75] He also says she would read his thoughts and reprove him:

I know for myself, and I confess before the whole church of Christ militant, that when she often reproved me for certain thoughts that were at that moment turning in my head, and I (as I do not blush to declare for her glory) wanted to excuse myself by lying, she replied to me: "why do you deny the thought that I can see even more clearly than I see you who are thinking it?" And after that she added very profitable teaching concerning the matter at hand, which she demonstrated by her own illustration.[76]

Although Raymond typically tells the stories of role reversal in a self-deprecating way, it is important to note that he stops short of picturing himself as dependent upon Catherine. In this he stands in contrast to James of Vitry, Peter of Dacia, and Henry of Nördlingen, all of whom cultivated the idea that the women about whom they wrote provided them something they needed but were unable to obtain on their own. James, for example, described Mary of Oignies's vision of himself being wooed by a prostitute as a revelation of his shortcomings as a man and a preacher, of which he was otherwise unaware, with a corrective effect.[77] But by comparison, Raymond's story of Catherine reading his thoughts does not contain any revelation, and he does not imagine that she knows anything about him that he himself does not. He does not need her for self-knowledge; when she produces his "bull" of contrition, he does not present it as something he cannot have otherwise. The point is to establish *her* powers. Though in the process he may expose his own foibles, as in the mind-reading episode, there is no conceit here that he particularly relies on her to make up for them, or for that matter to supply any other need of his own.

Indeed, Raymond's self-portrayal here is that of a man assured of his own authority and in control of himself. An example is the interchange he had with Catherine, in confession, about an episode in her early life when she had acquiesced to her sister Bonaventura's attempts to dress her up and make her pretty. Here Raymond shows himself allowing Catherine to turn the tables on him by lecturing him in the confessional, and yet he keeps her squarely in his sights as object of analysis. He says that whenever she made general confession to him, "she always accused herself very harshly with sobs and tears" and claimed that this particular sin of adolescent vanity was worthy of eternal punishment. He pressed her however, to see if the sin was really as she claimed: did she either intend or desire to break the vow of virginity that she had already privately taken by that point, and had she really been trying to make herself pleasing to men? No, she said. He then asked her why she thought the sin was grave, and she replied that she had loved her sister "excessively, and that it seemed to her that at that moment she had loved her more than God." When Raymond responded that even so, without "vain intention" she was not really violating divine precepts, Catherine exclaimed, " 'O God, what sort of spiritual father have I got now, who excuses my sins?' " and lectured him some more on the depth of her sinfulness. "I," says Raymond, "was obliged to be quiet."[78] But then he goes on to tell the reader that he as her confessor had found her to be not only without mortal sin but almost without any sin at all. In other words, he has not wavered in his assessment of her, and the story itself in fact supports his position. We are not told anything revealing about Raymond or his stake in the relationship with Catherine; the whole episode illustrates only Catherine's perfection.

Raymond offers glimpses, as well, of interactions between himself and Catherine without the role reversal or the inequality implied by it—intimations of partnership between them, male priesthood and female apostolate complementing each other.[79] He describes, for instance, hearing the confessions of those converted by Catherine's preaching, as he had special papal permission to do.

We stood, my associates and I, frequently without food until evening, nor could we hear all those confessing. And such was the pressure of those wanting to confess that many times I was weighted down and annoyed by the excessive labors. But she prayed without ceasing, and as a victrix exulting over her prey in the Lord, directed her other sons and daughters to hand on to those of us who had the net what she captured and sent to them.[80]

He also describes collaborating with Catherine in the conversion of the banker Nanni di ser Vanni, who, as Raymond would have it, endangered the city by carrying on many quarrels and who later became an important member of her "family."[81] At the urging of Catherine's admirer William Flete, Nanni came to visit Catherine at a moment when Raymond was present at her house but she herself was not. Raymond sent a messenger for her and tried, a bit comically, to keep up a conversation to prevent the uneasy Nanni from leaving again. He was on the verge of failing when Catherine herself arrived. At first unable to talk Nanni into terminating his quarrels, she then entered into an ecstasy and, as she said, convinced God to do it instead—so that by the time she came to her senses, divine forces had brought Nanni thoroughly to peace. She directed him to confess his sins to Raymond.[82] Raymond also tells a story of Catherine curing him of the plague so that he could pursue his ministry. This would have been in Siena in 1374 when he intentionally stayed in the city in time of plague: "I decided to expose my body to the peril of death for the salvation of souls and not to avoid any sick person.... considering the truth that Christ is more powerful than Galen, and grace than nature, and noting that, while others were fleeing, the souls of the dying remained without counsel and help."[83] Catherine helped him, and when he began to experience symptoms of the disease in his own body, he managed to drag himself to the place where she was living, and while she sat next to him for half an hour he felt his symptoms gradually disperse—after which she charged him to get back to work.[84]

I have suggested that to whatever extent Raymond appears in the *Legenda maior* as Catherine's pupil or subordinate, in fact he pictures himself standing all the time very much on his own authority. The technique of pursuing his aims precisely through depicting himself as inferior to figures who personify those aims seems to have been standard fare for Raymond; his surviving writings in support of the observant reform movement in the Dominican Order suggest an instructive parallel to his writing in support of Catherine. As master general, he initiated the reform in a decree approved by Boniface IX and dated 1 November 1390, during the period when he was writing the *Legenda*. The chief thrust of the decree was to establish one congregation in each province of the order that would obey the order's constitutions strictly.[85] Raymond was almost obsessively committed to this reform, which, though finally only minimally successful, consumed much of his energy in the last ten years of this life.[86] But he adopted the conceit that he instigated it not out of his own conviction (which anyway he makes clear) but rather at the behest of the reforming friar Conrad of Prussia and other friars who wanted it. That is what he says in a letter to the cardinal of Ostia, Philip of Alençon, whose patronage the opponents of the reform—in the name of moderation and unity—had tried to enlist in their support, specifically that he initiated the reform in response to Conrad's request, "considering that a friar helped by a friar is like a strong city."[87] One might of course speculate that it was a necessary convention to attribute his work to a request, rather like a treatise writer. But in another section of the same letter to Philip, Raymond makes clear that he himself could not claim to be a thorough adherent of the reform. There he admits the truth of his opponents' accusation that he himself did not fast as the friars of the reform houses did, which made him appear hypocritical in requiring establishment of observant reform in each province, and although he claims that he suffers from physical inability to fast, he admits that his many efforts to overcome it have come to naught.[88] He therefore must stand a little to the side; he supports the holy reformers without himself claiming to be one.

Standing thus a little to the side of those who embody his aims seems to be a characteristic Raymondian strategy for achieving them. No doubt he really was physically unable to fast and embarrassed about his inability. But what has not been noticed about his letter to Philip is that the admission of his weakness becomes the very lynchpin of his defense of the reform. For the crucial passage comes when, after making his admission, he goes on the attack against his opponents on the basis of his own shortcomings. His admitted imperfections establish his humility in contrast to the pride evident in his opponents' defiance of him and thus establish his authority over them in the measure of his "weakness," in the fashion of St. Paul's self-justification to his Corinthian detractors (2 Cor. 12:1–13; "when I am weak, then I am strong," v. 3); forced by his opponents, as he says, to speak "foolishly" (cf. 2 Cor. 12:11), Raymond asserts his own humility and, in contrast to them, his own history of obedience to superiors.[89] The Pauline assertion of strength from weakness also appears at other points in Raymond's writings. He wrote, for instance, to the Dominican reform leader John Dominici, likening him to Paul, who suffered at everyone's hands to confirm his charity; in an open letter to the friars who had embraced the reform, he quotes Paul warning them not to yield to the temptation of thinking of themselves as something when they are nothing (Gal. 6:3) and tells them that what he fears on their behalf is pride.[90]

A similar strategy underlies his self-inclusion in his portrait of Catherine. For here too there is clear calculation in his tendency to deprecate himself.[91] In a passage in the epilogue, Raymond lumps together all Catherine's previous superiors and associates in religion as having failed her.

> Before I came to know this holy virgin, she could hardly perform one act of devotion in public without suffering calumny, impediments, and persecutions, mainly from the very ones who had the most responsibility to protect her and encourage her to such acts. Nor is it any wonder, because … unless spiritual persons completely extinguish their own love of self, they fall into worse traps than carnal persons.[92]

Here Raymond, the same Raymond who has highlighted his own weaknesses in his encounters with Catherine, asserts that it was only with his own arrival on the scene that she finally had proper direction. Has he then extinguished his own self-love? This suggests a proud humility indeed, and at any rate shows a director very confident of his powers and his place in the holy woman's life.

Things to Come

If Raymond is confident of his authority in his presentation of Catherine, though, we must remember on the other hand that he also considers himself to have much reason to assert that authority. The vita is indeed an answer, written large, to an implicit question: Was she a genuine, as opposed to a false, saint? The long replies to detractors suggest the importance of this question for Raymond, as well as his extreme care to name witnesses, as does the epilogue that reviews the details of the vita to conform them to the most canonizable standards. The *Legenda maior* was to become the main item in the literary tool chest of that broader movement to canonize her that was put into motion by Thomas of Siena, who had pressed Raymond to finish the vita and who instigated and closely managed the so-called Processo Castellano, the canonization hearings held in 1411 that produced a collection of depositions by those who knew Catherine.[93]

Thomas of Siena, indeed, was even more attuned than Raymond to the potential audience for Catherine's sanctity, addressing its every need. He produced an abridgement of Raymond's work, taking out some of the abundance of detail to make it more accessible. He also produced a supplement to Raymond's work to make sure that there was a record of the details Raymond had *not* included.[94] And to provide Catherine's admirers a supplementary model of Catherinian sanctity that invited imitation more unambiguously than the saint herself, he wrote a vita of a young female penitent named Mary Sturion of Venice, herself a devotee of Catherine, who displayed all of the saint's virtue of love for God and neighbor but none of her supernatural revelations or miracles. In this vita Thomas himself appears as Mary's confessor, Raymond-like in witnessing her seeming transcendence of the need for a confessor even as he received her total obedience.[95] But what is most to the point here is that, as Antonio Volpato has argued, Thomas's efforts to promote Catherine display a subtle change that reflected a concern to make her more defensible, in the decades that followed the completion of Raymond's work: perhaps in recognition that Catherine's prophecies were vulnerable to the very sort of criticism Raymond had had to fend off, Thomas began to emphasize Catherine's role not as a prophet pure and simple so much as a *teacher*, whose teaching, though indeed divinely inspired, was comparable in substance and consistent in content with that of the Scriptures and the church.[96]

The climate for holy women was changing. It is true enough that the question of genuineness or falsity is implicitly at stake in most saints' lives, and certainly most of those discussed in these pages, and in that sense that the *Legenda maior* is hardly unique. For instance, in Peter of Dacia's narratives of Christine of Stommeln there are many replies to detractors. But the unguardedness of Peter's personal witness, that naive self-revelation that the reader may find charming or distasteful, suggests that the question of genuineness, with its natural tendency to inspire caution and a defensive posture on the part of the saint's partisan, is not so close to the surface, or so all-motivating, as it is for Raymond. By the time Raymond wrote the *Legenda maior* and Thomas began to promote it, the age of the cleric who, in promoting a holy woman, felt relatively safe in expressing his own longing, exploring his own shortcomings, and in general wearing his heart on his sleeve was beginning to go into eclipse as the question of genuineness became more pressing.

CHAPTER 10

Revelation and Authority Revisited

John Marienwerder on Dorothy of Montau

J OHN MARIENWERDER (1343–1417), dean of the cathedral chapter in the Prussian town whose name he bore, became the confessor of Dorothy of Montau (1347–1394), a lay woman originally from Danzig, three years before her death. After she died he wrote several works of hagiography about her, in which he made extensive reference to himself and his interactions with her, in the process developing familiar themes and motifs: he employed the conceit of role reversals and thought ostensibly in terms of two spheres of authority, his own and hers. But as in Raymond's work on Catherine, so here as well, the question of the holy woman's genuineness has acquired new prominence. John's caution about Dorothy's genuineness substantively affects his depiction of her: he introduces a distinction between God's action in her and her own understanding of that action with a frank assertion of the possibility that she could be, in particulars anyway, mistaken about it. This distinction somewhat undermines the two-sphere schema, whereby a clerical writer liked to imagine a woman's authority as discrete from his own, and it increases the importance of John as a supervisor and judge who has the responsibility to discern the mistakes. In this sense, though the tone and themes of John's work remain reminiscent of James of Vitry, his own position here in relation to the holy woman recalls Ekbert of Schönau.

RECLUSE AND CONFESSOR

Dorothy was born in 1347 in the village of Montau on the Vistula, where her family were prosperous farmers. In 1363, when she was sixteen, she married Adalbert Swertveger, a wealthy armorer of Danzig. By Adalbert she had nine children between 1366 and 1380, all but one of whom had died by 1383. Dorothy was pious and ascetic already as a child and became increasingly so during her years of marriage. Exceptionally devoted to the Eucharist, in 1378 she began experiencing raptures, for which at first her husband beat her, accusing her of indolence in her housework. But in 1380 Adalbert took a vow of marital chastity together with Dorothy, and in 1384 they went on pilgrimage to Aachen and Finsterwald. In the next year, she believed, Christ took out her old heart and replaced it with a new one, and she began to hear the voice of God daily. In the next few years she made more pilgrimages, including a journey during 1389 and 1390 to Rome without Adalbert, who died in Danzig during her absence. Even before setting out for Rome she had felt the need for an expert spiritual director, and her longtime confessor Nicholas Hohenstein had recommended John. Finally in May of 1391 she traveled to Marienwerder, the seat of the west Prussian diocese of Pomerania, to confer with him for a week. In September of that year, having aroused suspicion of heresy at Danzig in the meantime (of which I shall say more) she returned to Marienwerder for good. The next January she began relating her revelations to John, and in March she petitioned for a cell—that is, to become an anchorite or recluse, the first ever in Prussia, as far as we know.[1] The cathedral chapter directed John to determine her aptness for such a life, and he tested her for a period of more than a year. Finally, on 2 May 1393, she entered her cell, a small room attached to the outside of the south wall of the cathedral choir. There she lived for the last fourteen months of her life, receiving Communion and telling her visions and other experiences to John daily, through a window that also gave her a glimpse of the altar. She died on 25 June 1394 at the age of forty-seven.[2]

When Dorothy first met him at Marienwerder, John had only fairly recently left the academic career to which he had given most of his adult life. As a youth he had studied at the cathedral's school, then in about 1365 he enrolled in the University of Prague, where he stayed for more than twenty years as student and teacher, receiving his baccalaureate in the arts faculty in 1367, the degree of master of arts two years later, and sometime before 1384 that of master of theology, having become a disciple of the famous nominalist theologian Henry Totting of Oytha. The university, which the emperor Charles IV had founded in the Bohemian city in 1348, was dominated by scholars and pupils from German-speaking regions in the years of John's residence there, but this domination was a source of long-standing conflict, and finally episcopal decrees in the early 1380s limited membership in all but one of the university's colleges to Bohemians. Appeals were sent to Rome—John's name is on one of them—but these were returned at the end of 1385, and there ensued a large-scale departure of Germans, John among them. Thus at the end of 1386, accompanied by his colleague John Rey-mann, John Marienwerder left Prague and returned to his hometown. There, in 1387, he joined the Teutonic Order as a priest (having been ordained in 1373), resigned his Prague positions, and became a canon of the cathedral. The next year he became the dean of the cathedral chapter, a position that he retained until his death. At about the same time, Reymann (who was eventually to be bishop of Pomerania) became provost of the cathedral and was also to hear the confessions of Dorothy.[3]

After Dorothy's death, John wrote an astonishing amount about her in short order, all of it more or less clearly in service of the cause of her canonization, which he and others energetically promoted (though the cause languished after a few years, and Dorothy was not to become officially a saint until 1976).[4] John's first efforts, within a year of her death, were two letters to Rome giving an ac-count of her sufferings and visions to the procurator of John's own Teutonic Order, which governed Prussia at the time, asking him to petition the pope to open an inquiry into her sanctity. (This was part of a larger campaign; in a coor-dinated effort only shortly afterward, in September 1395, all the major Prussian dignitaries, including all the bishops and the highest official of the order, sent letters to the pope promoting Dorothy.)[5] John seems to have recast each of his two letters separately as a little vita; late in 1395, he combined the letters to make a slightly longer vita (*Vita prima*) and the next year wrote another (the so-called *Vita Lindana*) that was longer still, in eighty-seven chapters.[6] Then between 1397 and 1404 he produced his monumental trilogy, based in large part on his ex-tensive record of what he had seen and heard from the saint: the massive *Vita Latina* in seven books (245 chapters); a collection of the visions she experienced on feast days known as *Liber de festis*; and the *Septililium*, a compilation of seven tractates on Dorothy's virtues and graces.[7] He also produced a vita in German, which drew its content from the *Vita Latina* and the *Septililium*.[8] This body of work was complete by the time the canonization process began in earnest with hearings in Marienwerder from 1404 through 1406, and its influence is evident in the records of those hearings, in the witnesses' frequent references to the books of John, quite apart from the fact that he himself gave extensive testimony. He probably also supplied the official "articles" themselves, that is, the compilations of putative facts of her life and miracles that informed the questioning of wit-nesses. For many of these articles show verbal similarity to his works.[9]

John's self-inclusion in these works tends to be dispassionate, but it is also extensive. John's typical procedure in writing is analytical and impersonal; he establishes distinctions, sorts Dorothy's experience into categories, and leaves his own immediate reactions and feelings out of the picture, not incidentally referring to himself always in the third person, as "the confessor." In this respect he stands in sharp contrast to Raymond of Capua, who was anyway not particularly impressed by *doctores*. Raymond moved the *Legenda maior* along by stories rather than analysis and used his accounts of his own reactions to Catherine as a way of persuading the reader of her sanctity. John instead relies on the weight of the facts themselves, sorted into large piles, to do the persuading. Nonetheless, he includes himself constantly in his narratives, making himself nearly as ubiquitous in these works as Raymond is in the *Legenda maior*. Dyan Elliott has argued that John wanted to establish his own connection, through Dorothy, to the divine reality to which she witnessed and thereby establish himself as "spokesperson for and ultimate authority on" her: this is one reason why the reader sees him at every turn—a constant presence that also serves as a reminder that he, not Dorothy, is the writer of these texts.[10] He also displays that interest in the interplay of spiritual authorities that has been the constant among the writers I have discussed in these chapters; John's very adoption of a stance of scientific objectivity has the effect of giving considerable focus and clarity to his picture of that interplay, in which he is a necessary partner and consequently a necessary object of his own observation.

Dorothy and Christ

Dorothy's direct relationship with Christ is John's principal interest in these writings. She was, in effect, the opposite of an apostle on the Catherininan model: in her case the personal presence of Christ made her a recluse, drawing her away from her social world rather than toward it.[11] Thus John focuses the narrative of *Vita Latina* on the emergence and intensification of her contacts with Christ over time, in and of themselves, and he treats her revelations as the fruit of these contacts as they develop.[12] He interprets her reception of the revelations as analogous to a process of learning from books. That interpretation allows him, in turn, to bring a critical stance to bear on her relations with Christ throughout the work, pointing out their limits and therefore the possible limitations of the revelations themselves, all without, in his view, detracting from her sanctity.

Her experiences of the presence of Christ, according to John's account in the *Vita Latina*, began when she was seven years old, during her convalescence from an accident in which boiling water scalded her whole body: "during that whole time, the all-powerful Lord, most faithful consoler of the afflicted, supported the blessed one by his visits, increasing the desire of that afflicted girl for himself to such an extent that from that moment until the end of her life her virtues never decreased but rather continually increased."[13] Later, from about 1378, some of these experiences took the form of raptures, in which, for an hour or more at a time (as respite from her "labors, afflictions and conflicts in marriage"), she would be in a state of "sleep," and the Lord would "murmur" to her, and she would have a foretaste of heaven.[14] But as yet she did not receive revelations per se.

The revelations began only later, as a part of the major change in Dorothy's life brought about the "extraction" of her heart. This event occurred about 25 January 1385; when she was at the high altar of the Church of the Blessed Virgin in Danzig amid a press of other worshipers she entered a rapture and felt her heart being removed and replaced with a new one, "a mass of flesh, all on fire."[15] At the same time, Christ endowed her with many of the varieties of *caritas* that John would record in the *Septililium*.[16] She received new understanding: "in that moment ... she was more completely instructed in the life of the saints than if she had studied under a learned person for a whole year."[17] It was then also that Christ told her to make painstakingly detailed confessions of her past life, which she proceeded to do for the next five years, in order to achieve a greater perfection and renunciation of the world: "being married, she did not completely adhere to God or totally leave the world behind, because of her household concerns and her dealings with earthly society. On that account, the Lord sent her the Holy Spirit to reprove her and teach her how she had offended the Lord."[18] Then too her desire for the Eucharist began to increase.[19] And it was as part of these other developments that she began to experience supernatural visitations. The day after the extraction, the Virgin Mary, in response to her prayers to be shown her son, placed the Christ child in her arms: the first, apparently, of her many encounters with Virgin and child that John will eventually report in *Liber de festis*.[20] John now uses bridal language for what happened during her ecstasies, suggesting a new intimacy with Christ: she was granted "now his kiss, now his embrace, now his murmurings, now the interior of his chamber."[21] And so it was that the revelations began as well: Christ began to speak to her on a daily basis, for instance, teaching her to be more passive in prayer and castigating her for her sins: the beginnings of the boundless divine loquacity toward her that John would later patiently record.[22]

If the extraction of Dorothy's heart brought her to one new stage in her relations with Christ, her entrance into the anchorage some eight years later brought her to another stage, the final one. There was no great change in the volume of her divine visitations, which were already by then coming in a virtually constant flow (although her "consolations" increased, especially in the form of visions of saints, who sometimes crowded her cell), and John continued to record them just as he had done for a year and a half by that time.[23] But Christ now moved to exclude everything else but himself from her affections. She had a later revelation that he had caused her to choose the anchorage instead of journeying to Jerusalem as she had considered doing (perhaps in imitation of Bridget of Sweden, whom she admired)[24] so that she not receive consolation from anyone but himself.[25] Another revelation told her that when she took Communion in the anchorage, no one else was to be present except the person bringing her the Host, "so that you might be alone with me; and for this, give me thanks that you are able to be thus separated from people!"[26] And John tells of a long visit that Christ and the Virgin made to her in the anchorage in December and January of 1393 and 1394, in which the Virgin scolded her for talking too much to others and not giving her attention exclusively to Christ, who added, " 'How do you dare avert yourself from me and my Mother and turn yourself to creatures, when day and night, and without pause, you can hear my voice, my admonitions, my inspiration?' "[27] At times, she signaled her attentiveness to Christ in a way that suggested her independence of the confessor (a complicated point to which I shall return), as when she received a revelation to remind John that she would have Christ even if she had no man to depend on.[28] When, prior to entering the anchorage, she expressed a wish to die, Christ presented the prospect of the anchorage as a concession to her desire: "For I wish to remove from you some of the miseries of this life…. All that happens in the world can happen just as well without you and without your care and anxiety. And so, humbly and in tears, you must ask me to arrange a little dwelling place for you, in which to be able to praise me with complete adoration, and end your life in my good favor."[29] Just so, at her entrance Christ told her to contemplate his glory "as though I wished already to say to you, "behold all things are ready [Luke 14:17]"—that is, to invite her already to the heavenly banquet.[30]

Within this narrative of Dorothy's increasing intimacy with Christ, John portrays her as a *learned* woman, whose knowledge, though different in content from what a scholar derives from the study of books, she nonetheless acquired in an analogous process. Early in the prologue, after a complex opening passage in which he calls her an eagle—like John the seer of the Book of Revelation, and like God himself (Deut. 32:11, Ezek. 17:3)—who in her flights encountered the "hidden things of God [*divinitatis archana*]" that found expression in the teachings of the *Septililium*, John comments on how she acquired her knowledge:

> She did not extract the above-mentioned things [i.e., her teachings] from the great, that is, the common, rules of the dialecticians or from the commonplaces of the rhetors or from the sayings of physicians or their principles or those of the other liberal arts, whose spirit is one of vanity and presumption. Often they suffocate their readers and hearers since they are puffed up and do not "take every thought captive in obedience to Christ" [2 Cor. 10:5] and to that "teaching which accords with piety of doctrine" [1 Tim. 6:3]. But this wise woman took these things from a heavenly original and from the book of life, which is the virtue and wisdom of God—a book that (as I would say) is written from within through a disposition toward its original, and from without through a revelation to the mind. And if it is for wise persons to know all things, and to search for their own sake to understand difficult things with certitude and in terms of causes, she moreover understood the ultimate causes of her philosophy, and thereby the principles by which she studiously gave herself to the one in whom all the treasures of wisdom and knowledge are hidden—not however for her own sake, but in order to know him alone.[31]

Here, though asserting Dorothy's wisdom to be superior to that of scholars, he nonetheless implies a generic similarity between them: like the wisdom of scholars, which comes from the study of human books, her wisdom also comes from the study of a source, in her case the "book of life," that is, her experience of Christ.[32] John develops the parallels. He notes, for instance, that she underwent rigors analogous to those of conventional study. Thus once in Danzig when she heard a preacher disparage "certain people" who "presumptuously dare to say that they are taught by God alone, when they have not put any discernible labor into studying," she thought how "simple" the preacher was to imagine that people who are taught directly by God do not labor: for to be taught by God one must be "inflamed with love" for God, which presupposes the labor of renouncing earthly loves, of avoiding errors, of repressing desires, all of which requires compunction, sighs and groaning, and constant anxiety to remain upright. In sequel to this thought she received a revelation from Christ that in fact "those who learn from God have a heavier burden than those who study books," since books can be put aside but the flame of love for God cannot.[33] In another revelation (echoed in many others) Christ identifies himself as her teacher [*magister*] and tells her that when she speaks of having a master who imparts high truth and teaches her to avoid sin, people may think she means her confessor, that is, John, whereas she knows she really will mean the Lord himself.[34] Indeed toward the end of her life when John undertook to teach her something of the Trinity, the Lord took exception, telling her that if he had wanted her to explore that deep subject, he would have taught her himself.[35]

John's treatment of Dorothy as a person of learning carries with it a certain ambiguity. On the one hand, since Christ himself is her teacher, her learning is of course superior to other learning. On the other hand, since it is generically like other learning, in the sense of depending not only on the knowledge of the teacher but also on the efforts the student, it is therefore subject to the same possible limitations, the same fallibility. Both points merit consideration.

John in fact devotes a chapter of the first book of the *Vita Latina* (1.4) to the superiority of Dorothy's knowledge (*noticia*) over other knowledge. He is typically precise in his use of terms, and although he does speak of Dorothy's knowledge as "divinely infused [*divinitus infusam*]," he clearly does not think of her as a mere blank slate for God to write on. Nor does he present the effects of her knowledge as supernatural or miraculous. Rather, he is interested the process of her learning, specifically in how she appropriated what she knew from God. He characterizes her knowledge as having both affective and intellectual components, that is, as comprising both love (*dilectio*) and understanding (*cognitio*), each of which was increased by action of the other.[36] Thus constituted, her knowledge "exceeded science [*scientia*] that was humanly acquired," specifically in two areas, in which, as Christ told her, she had much to teach to those two erstwhile men of learning, her confessors John himself and Reymann.[37] One of the two areas was a certain spiritual discernment.

> She knew how to point out the ways that lead to eternal life, and how to walk in them. She recognized the extent of the efforts needed for cleansing a soul, and what was called for to live an upright life. And she perceived what was to be loved and hated in a human soul, and what stood between the soul and God, whether worthy of hate or love [Eccles. 9:1].[38]

John gives as an example her assertion that no one in an entire Danzig parish of more than one thousand people knew the state of his or her own soul, or greatly desired the Eucharist. The example recalls the topos of the saint's ability to intuit the state of souls; yet here it is presented as a matter not simply of supernatural intuition but also of informed diagnosis. As for the second area of her superiority, her "knowledge of the distinctions between modes of loving and between spiritual feelings [*caritatum differenciam et spiritualium sentimentorum noticiam*]," John gives no example.[39] But these distinctions are exactly the subjects of the first and third tractates of the *Septililium*, and there it is clear that, though divinely revealed, the distinctions between types of infused love, and between varieties of Eucharist-related feelings, and the definitions of other movements within the soul make for a finely tuned vocabulary for precise description of mystical experience. John himself uses them as such in his extended descriptions of her experiences both in the *Septililium* and in *Liber de festis*. All of this suggests that though Dorothy's learning has a directly supernatural origin, it looks like, and competes on the same plane with, human learning.

As for the potential fallibility of Dorothy's reporting of what Christ told her: this follows from John's very conception of her as Christ's pupil. For pupils do not always learn their lessons exactly. It is true that John construes almost every dictum she addresses to him as a divine oracle from Christ himself, with the typical opening words, "say to your confessor." And he reports that she told him often, "When I sit near you and say things about my Lord, you must not think that I have conceived these things myself or drawn them out of my own intellect, but I have the Lord in me, putting the words in my mouth directly and uttering them through me.... Frequently when you come to write, I do not know what I ought then to say, and if the Lord did not instruct me and put the words in my mouth I would not be able to say anything."[40] Such a statement may seem to imply an assertion of the "verbal inerrancy" of what she says. But repeatedly John's reports undermine any such implication. For instance, he says that Christ would continually repeat what he had told her already so that she would retain it until the time came for the confessor to make a record, which suggests that her own memory was a factor in communicating the revelations. Her will was a factor too: there are several examples of her declining, out of humility or forgetfulness, to pass on revelations as directed, and Christ enjoined her to be sure not to reveal anything she was not specifically directed to reveal.[41] John also implies that he himself had a role in finding the right words: once, he says, the two of them "wrote with laborious difficulty ... discouraged at not finding apt words to express the revelations they were recording."[42] And once she failed the test of Scripture to which, as John already makes clear at the beginning of the prologue and repeats thereafter,[43] all her teachings must be submitted: this was when she reported a revelation that during the Passion Christ had particular pain from the wound in his side—a wound that, however, as

John pointed out to her, was inflicted after his death. The explanation for the error, as she learned from Christ afterward, was not in the revelation itself but in her understanding of it; he had not been speaking of the spear wound but of a spiritual wound, which he felt in his body even though it was not physically inflicted upon him. John gives the story as an example of an occasion "when she either did not plainly express what the Lord directed her to, or did not say it as she ought."[44] Thus the fact that the Lord put words into her mouth does not seem to have guaranteed that they would come out again exactly as they went in. In this case upon exit they had acquired a bit of subtle explanation that was not properly part of the revelation.

In the course of his accounts of her revelations, John issues frequent reminders that what she has been relating to him may not be precisely what Christ wished her to tell. For example, on one occasion Christ delivered a lengthy speech about the benefits she had received from him, and he told her to ask her confessors if they had ever heard of any of the saints being as graced as she was and asked her if he had ever withheld any good thing from her (her answer is no)—all to make the point that she had not adequately expressed these things to her confessor.[45] In another instance, in one revelation in *Liber de festis*, Christ remarks to her that the two revelations that preceded it were, in the form written down by John, incomplete: "concerning the benefits given to you, you only spoke of the more obvious things [*grossiora*], and omitted the things that were more spiritual, valuable and useful."[46] Here it is significant that the blame falls on her, rather than on the clerical scribe, as in the case of Angela of Foligno. The idea that she bears the responsibility rests in turn on the assumption that the process of communicating what she has experienced—and accordingly assimilating and putting it into words—is a process that occurs in *her*, the human and fallible Dorothy, and therefore her revelations themselves, in the form in which she expresses them, are open to criticism.

Dorothy therefore is for John certainly a bona fide holy woman, possessing a hard-won and now meticulously documented intimacy with Christ and experiencing frequent encounters with him, and yet what she says on the basis of those encounters is also open to prudent questioning. It is well to note that in John's accounts the problems he sees in her revelations do not always point to errors. For instance, another revelation concerning the wound in Christ's side, this time reported in *Liber de festis*, describes an interchange with Christ in which she asks whether after the Passion the spear that entered his side reached his heart. She is given a vision in which she can see that his heart was unwounded. John's response to this revelation is to point out that Bridget of Sweden has had a vision of his wounded heart, and he tells her to ask Christ about this discrepancy. But Christ's response this time does not say that Dorothy misunderstood; instead, he declares that not all recipients of revelation need agree. "You and your father confessor must not worry needlessly that the revelation given to you by me do not always accord and harmonize with other revelations. For the holy evangelists, who wrote my deeds and words, all of whom were present at them, in everything have not agreed."[47] Thus she did not get the revelation wrong (even though the evangelists' discrepancies themselves remain unexplained here). But on the other hand she *could* have gotten it wrong, as in the case of that other revelation about the spear wound, when John's question led to a correction.

The Question of Authority

Therefore John asserts both the truth of Dorothy's revelations and her fallibility in understanding and communicating them. This double aspect of Dorothy has implications for her relationship with John himself. On the one hand, the fact of her revelations gives her, in his eyes, the familiar informal power of the holy woman to speak from an authority distinct from the cleric's authority and, within its proper limits, places her frequently outside his direction. On the other hand, however, her imperfection implies that she also needs his direction even in matters having to do with the revelations, and he frequently pictures her receiving it. This combination of elements makes for a complex picture of her relations with John, as, at points, his own authority extends into the erstwhile proper territory of the holy woman.

The recognition of that well-established territory, that is, the assumption that Christ had a claim on the woman that made her independent in certain specific ways from the cleric's authority, is indeed evident in much of John's work. In one revelation Christ says that John is the "mediator and suitor [*mediator et procus*]" who brings him, in the form of the Eucharist, to Dorothy, but that afterward he and she "woo [*procare*]" each other without mediation.[48] Twenty weeks before the end of her life, for instance, John and Reymann tried to persuade Dorothy to tell her life story to them (presumably in greater detail than John's writings convey) so that they could eventually edify others by means of it. And, though she did not want to accede to this wish, she also did not (as he says) dare contradict the confessors' arguments, and so she prayed to Christ, who in turn recalled her whole life to her mind but then forbade her to reveal it so that in the end she refused the confessors' request.[49] In another instance, she declined to confess one day because Christ had not instructed her what to say.[50] It is in this same vein that in her last days, after John begged Dorothy to foretell the precise time of her death, so that he could be present, Christ told her to refuse the request: let him see the glory of God in some other way.[51] Thus Dorothy, or rather Christ through Dorothy, often had the last word.

It is consistent with Dorothy's authoritative stance here that she often appears as more savvy than her confessor about his own spiritual state, and she instructs him accordingly. She revealed, for instance, her knowledge of a "sin of incontinence" that John had committed in adolescence, including details such as when he had started and stopped and how little resistance he had put up to temptation.[52] She had passed onto him a revelation from Christ about a priest "already twenty years in the priesthood," apparently himself, from whom Christ had been keeping himself distant.[53] Once she told him of a vision of his own guardian angel, who appeared "amicable" but reluctant to give him all the protection he might.[54] Perhaps she was commenting on the spiritual implications of the very detachment that we ourselves may sense in the coolly observant John; in her last days, when she reported to him that she saw the heavens open and he expressed the wish to see this himself, she replied that his desire was not intense enough.[55] And in another revelation, Christ told her, "nothing harms your confessor so much as this, that he does not see me acutely. For if he were to see me well with the eyes of his soul, then my goodness, as he would then recognize it, would draw him to me wonderfully"; for a remedy he prescribed a greater zeal for souls in purgatory.[56] All of this insight for the cleric's benefit is reminiscent of Mary of Oignies. John, however, expresses no sense of his own need or desire for it in the fashion of James, except in one instance. This was when Dorothy reported to him a revelation about himself, namely, that he loved her and would choose to lack everything else in the world rather than lose her: John writes that at that moment he realized that he had indeed had precisely this thought and that if he were free of his vow of religion, he would go wherever she was, to serve God with her and receive her consolations.[57] But this startling self-disclosure appears in passing, and otherwise he records her many insights about himself without comment.

Dorothy also instructs John and Reymann about their work as confessors. These instructions can be in the form of supposedly edifying advice, as when she tells him and Reymann that their service to the Lord is like the action of shooting a bow, in which they must be so intent on their task as to forget about the possibility of injury to themselves as they undertake it.[58] But she can also give specific instruction about issues or cases. For instance, on the question of who qualifies for frequent partaking of the Eucharist—an issue which had been highly controversial at Prague when John taught there, and which Dorothy herself had raised both at Danzig and now at Marienwerder, where John eventually allowed her to commune daily—she received a revelation for John, essentially confirming his own policy: "no one ought to partake of me frequently, without already having excellent knowledge of me, and fervently burning with desire."[59] Dorothy also received revelations about the sins of people who came to give her alms, and she passed the knowledge along to John.[60] She received similar revelations concerning the confessions other people had made to John and his proper course of action. One woman, it seems, was confessing only her lighter sins and neglecting the more serious ones and also wasting John's time by remaining undecided as to what she would confess; John should point out the more serious sins and should also insist that she prepare for confession.[61] In another case she gives John a detailed critique of his handling of a woman who confessed having inadvertently crushed her child: he has not denounced her sin harshly enough, and when she demurred at the public penance he required of her (a fast), he did not censure her strongly enough, with the result that she was more distressed at the punishment than at her own crime.[62] She also criticizes him more generally for spending too much time hearing confessions (including the confessions of two particular women who, if they need instruction so badly, should be sent to hear sermons instead!) and sometimes missing Mass as a result.[63]

In other instances, she voices her criticisms of John while in the role of penitent. In an incident in *Liber de festis* she told John that on the basis of her visions of Mary and Christ, "I would wish to wrap the Lord Jesus in richer garments and words, than you will do" the next day, which was the feast of the Annunciation, when he was set to preach. She seems to have meant both that the Holy Family should not be represented as poor (a point that she also makes elsewhere) and that the events should be described in more elaborate detail. But John replies warning her against pride: "Watch out lest from this some empty glory arise, or lest it proceed from some selfish complacency. For vainglory tends to lie in ambush within good works."[64] She submitted to this rebuke from the confessor in penitence, but afterward she received another revelation, showing herself uncowed: even if he had committed to memory all that was in the Gospels about the Virgin, still "you would not yet speak of her as accurately, as if you had seen her with your own eyes."[65] In other words, Dorothy as visionary is a better witness to the Virgin than John, as mere reader of Scripture, and thus his criticism of her was misplaced. Elsewhere in *Liber de festis* John reports himself criticizing her when she made confession "with such great impatient love and in a love that was inebriated and discontented" to a greater extent than ever before, and he exclaimed that she should be patient. When she replied that she could not bear the bridegroom's absence patiently, he scolded her, charging her to await the good pleasure of God. But later, Christ vindicated her in a revelation, approving the impatience of her desire for himself and for eternal life.[66]

There are also some instances of outright role reversal where Dorothy gives direction to her director. I have already mentioned that on occasion John pictures her as teacher to himself and Reymann. The irony is that both were men of great academic distinction. She was literally teaching the great teachers, and John makes sure to call attention to the point. Her field of instruction appears to be that of mystical experience, for in this, as Christ tells her, she leaves the confessors speechless, since they themselves "cannot talk about spiritual hunger, about the joy and savor of the spirit, about the sweetness of the kisses and the delight of the embrace, about the spiritual birth, and about the exclamation of the heart, so precisely and distinctly as you."[67] There are, it is true, only a few cases in point when she conveys to the confessors anything that sounds much like doctrine: once she passes on to John from Christ a lengthy teaching, ostensibly in response to the confessors' desire to know what was required for a person to "be splendidly fit for me,"[68] and at the end of her life she gives them an speech of advice on discerning whether they have made spiritual progress.[69]

Thus John represents Dorothy as having an authoritative voice of her own, based on an intense rapport with Christ that was independent of her subordination to himself. But he could also represent her as clearly under his direction, and in need of it. Again in these cases, John the author is very much the thorough observer, interested in exposing the wide range of their interaction.

John's accounts of how she came to him as her confessor suggest already one important element of her subordination to him, namely his own learning. The story as it emerges from the vitae and from his testimony in the canonization process begins with disturbances she created in Danzig before she actually met him. The problem stemmed from her intense inward experience, he says: in church she not only laughed uncontrollably for joy but also went into raptures that kept her from hearing the bell and rising at the elevation of the Host.[70] Evidence from witnesses in the canonization process makes it clear that she was publicly suspected of heresy by several clerics at Danzig—possibly the shadowy heresy of the "Free Spirit," as Anneliese Triller has suggested in view of her apparent disregard for the sacrament.[71] John surely knew of the suspicions of heresy, and though he never refers to them explicitly in his own writing, he does at least refer rather vaguely to threatened censure in the *Vita Latina*, speaking of detractors who were "not enlivened but rather poisoned (*non vivificati sed veneficati*) by the fragrance of her sanctity," but in the German vita alluding to an official inquiry.[72] The canonization witnesses appear to place the public suspicions of heresy in the summer of 1391, whereas John places the difficulties prior her journey to Rome, which has the effect of presenting Dorothy's request to her confessor Nicholas Hohenstein for a learned director, and his referral of Dorothy to John as a person able to "resolve difficulties and doubts," all as a response to detractors. Here, in other words, was an attempt to engage someone who had the expertise to keep her from any more such scrapes, someone "wise in the eyes of God and people, to whom she might safely reveal the hidden things of her heart."[73] It is ambiguous here whether the usefulness of the adviser's wisdom lies in keeping detractors at bay or in helping her change herself so that she would have no more detractors. Perhaps both: either way a man of learning was the key to keeping her from the vulnerable position in which she had found herself. She then saw John in a vision, he says, so that she recognized him two years later, after her pilgrimage to Rome, when she finally journeyed to Marienwerder.[74]

In practice, John does not precisely picture himself resolving Dorothy's difficulties and doubts. But he certainly does not belittle his authority as Dorothy's confessor, and he frequently pictures her submitting herself to him in obedience. In part, such scenes serve the familiar hagiographical purpose of framing humble perfection, rather as does Catherine's similar obedience in the *Legenda maior*.[75] For instance, it is to demonstrate her humility that John quotes Christ directing Dorothy to confess the presumption she had displayed in coming to Marienwerder, to consider herself worthy to speak with him, whereas "now I do not esteem myself worthy even to see you."[76] Or again, he shows her complaining to Christ that he, John, is too easy on her and asking for a revelation to pass on to him directing him to require more rigorous penance—a request that, even though Christ refuses it, demonstrates her zeal.[77] But John's authoritative stance as her confessor is not simply a matter of providing, in the fashion of Raymond, a foil for her perfection. He also pictures her shortcomings that called for correction.[78] Thus she took an extraordinary vow of obedience to him in July of 1392, after several months in Marienwerder, ostensibly at the insistence of Christ who told her that she would be so joined with John that they would have between them only one will—namely John's.[79] And the vow appears not as a sign of virtue so much as a concession to the weakness of vacillation.

The Lord, wishing to stabilize the spirit of the bride, who had been fluctuating in the meantime whether to remain with the confessor or to leave him, directed her to make a vow that she would never wish to leave her confessor in her lifetime. And in directing her thus, he showed her the royal way leading to eternal life, as though to say, "do not fear that this vow will be an impediment to you; rather it will advance you to heaven." ... And then it appeared to her, as the Lord afterward said to her, that the vow bound her so strongly to remain with her confessor, that it was as if they were joined in matrimony.[80]

Christ later revealed to her that "because you have done this thing for me, you may be confident in me without worry. For I wish to help your confessor to be able to have charge of you in a sound way."[81] In other instances, her confessions appear as evidence not of virtue possessed but of virtue wanting. Christ frequently directs her to confess her own shortcomings, especially in *Liber de festis*, where it is a question of her lack of preparation for various feasts and her unworthiness in comparison with various saints.[82] John also depicts himself providing the sacrament of penance to her once in her anchorage after she has given in to the temptation of desiring some "delicate" food that had been inappropriately given to her.[83] To be sure, in portraying Dorothy as making genuine use of a confessor's services John is not undermining his own hagiographical intentions; especially in view of the rumors of heresy at Danzig, her obedience to authority and willingness to be corrected were important virtues to tout. Nonetheless, especially in comparison with previous clerics' representation of themselves and holy women, it makes for a picture of interaction that is somewhat more complicated.

An indication of John's critical distance from Dorothy even amid his efforts to demonstrate her sanctity is Dorothy's frequent reporting of Christ's attempts to help her convey her revelations to John in a way that will cause him to take them seriously. Quite a few revelations thus take as their subject the conveying of revelations. She received revelations telling John not to worry about what others will think of what she says and, when he was becoming tired in the evenings from transcribing the wax tablets on which he had written them, a revelation to the effect that John could moderate the pace of his work since she would not be dying immediately is followed by another revelation telling him not to involve himself in other activities so as to give the writing project all his attention.[84] Other revelations tell John to be sure to note this or that, for instance to be sure to include all of Dorothy's teaching about *energia*, the inward spiritual exertion that exhausted her—teaching that, Christ says, he has never before revealed.[85] Dorothy also reports revelations in which Christ strategizes with her to influence her confessors: to tell them that her copious tears are a sign of the plenary indulgence Christ has given her for her sins,[86] to make sure that they see her crying so that they will believe the extent of her tears,[87] or, when she was waiting for approval of her enclosure, to tell them that it would be good for them as much as for her, implying that otherwise it would be held against them all at the last judgment.[88] And she is to make sure not to let them think the revelations are her own idea: " 'It is not fitting,' " he tells her, " 'that the provost and the confessor reckon that *you* are saying this thing that they are writing down, and that they perceive as coming from me. For I myself am speaking, I myself am working, I myself am causing it to be said.' "[89] For a work of hagiography to raise the possibility, even obliquely, that her promoters would think otherwise—quite apart the evident insecurity on Dorothy's part—suggests at least an undercurrent of caution on the part of John.

CONCLUSION

Like Raymond writing about Catherine, John depicts himself as Dorothy's venerator even in the midst of exercising direction over her, and, as in Raymond's work, the directed woman frequently becomes, herself, the director. But the limits of her powers are also quite clear, not simply in the sense that she, like all orthodox holy women, gave the institutional powers of priests their due but also in another sense. For in John's perspective there was a significant ambiguity in the exercise of her powers themselves, which arose from the distinction between Christ's intention and her own understanding. That ambiguity introduced the possibility that she, even within the proper sphere of her powers, misunderstood the divine meaning, which John the learned cleric could perceive; consequently, at a certain point the distinction between the two spheres became less clear-cut than before.

John is the last major medieval example of a hagiographer who both collaborated closely with a female saint and made himself a conspicuous figure in her life so as to treat his interaction with her as an essential part of his proper subject matter. It is probably no accident that the absence of such figures in the hagiography of the ensuing years coincides with that increasing suspicion of the potential power and influence of holy women in the wake of the Great Schism, to which John Gerson gave famous expression at the time of the Council of Constance.[90] Vitae of holy women would continue to be written in the fifteenth century, but for hagiographers the idea of placing one's *self* in such a vita appears to have lost its appeal for a while. A more prudent detachment from one's subject became the order of the day; and perhaps that detachment is already present in John's reticence to expose his own feelings and reactions to Dorothy directly, for all his thorough inclusion of himself in his narratives.

CHAPTER 11

Authority and Female Sanctity

Conclusions

S USPICION ABOUT THE POWERS of holy women appears to have been
on the increase at the turn of the fifteenth century. In Raymond of Capua's
writing about Catherine of Siena and John Marienwerder's about Dorothy of
Montau, a concern whether the women's experiences and powers were genuinely of God lies close to the surface. It is not that such a concern was itself anything new in the years around 1400 when Raymond and John were producing
their works of hagiography. André Vauchez has pointed out, for example, that
already a century earlier, as the popularity of visionary and prophetic saints increased, canonization processes had begun to show evidence of concern about
the genuineness of saints' experience in life, as distinct from that of their posthumous miracles;[1] indeed in almost all of the hagiographical texts examined
here, even the ones composed as early as the twelfth century, such concern
is evident in some measure. But in comparison to the writers of those earlier
texts, Raymond and John focus their attention more sharply on countering
doubts and suspicions about the women and their powers. Those doubts and
suspicions accordingly become more conspicuous. Only a few years afterward,
at the Council of Constance in 1415, the chancellor of the University of Paris,
John Gerson, would write his *On the Testing of Spirits*, questioning the revelations of Bridget of Sweden whom the council was considering for sainthood.
He appealed to any "hearer or consultant" of such a woman *not* to "praise"
or "applaud" her but rather to "resist her, upbraid her harshly, scorn her"
for her pride in thinking herself different from other Christians. Later Gerson
would make an only slightly veiled denunciation of Catherine as well.[2] And
as recent scholarship has made clear, in the fifteenth century the practice of
"discernment of spirits" as theorized by Gerson and others left less and less

room for the possibility that women could be inhabited by the Holy Spirit and made more room for the alternative interpretation that the spirits who spoke through women were demonic—thus helping open the door to the charges of witchcraft that were soon to proliferate.[3]

In hagiography, amidst this atmosphere of heightened suspicion, the portrayal of female saints' relationships with male confidants was to become much more focused on the realm of sacramental confession. This focus is already clear in Raymond of Capua and John Marienwerder, who present themselves in their works preeminently as confessors to the women under their care (in Raymond's case, all the more insistently for the notoriety of Catherine's public activity). The earlier authors in this study, by contrast and with the exception of Giunta, had remarkably little to say about the women's confession per se, and some did not even mention hearing it. The confessional was not the central reference point for the action of any of the earlier vitae. James of Vitry, for example, may have at times been "confessor" to Mary of Oignies, but the fact is largely irrelevant to his presentation of her or himself in her vita. But Raymond's and John's strong concern to answer doubts about their subjects' genuineness caused them to emphasize their own role as confessors: they highlighted their ability to witness to the women's orthodoxy and holiness by relating what they heard in the rigorous and all-revealing forum of confession. Such attention to sacramental confession would also be the wave of the literary future of female saints' male collaborators, beyond the limits of our study: a strong tradition of male confessors as confidants and hagiographers of female saints—with Raymond's vita of Catherine serving typically as a model—was to thrive in Italy as well as among the French and Spanish on both sides of the Atlantic from the early sixteenth century well into the eighteenth century.[4]

If the last writers in the sequence studied here are different from the others in their sharpened focus on the saints' genuineness, they do not differ in their fundamental concern about the issues of religious authority posed by the coexistence of informal and institutional powers. What were the limits of the cleric's authority, and what lay beyond these limits? It is in terms of such issues that, by way of conclusion here, I want to summarize and reflect on the preceding chapters. I shall take two approaches. The first will be to consider the nine cases in sequence over time as my chapters themselves have done, to present them as an unfolding experiment about the nature and limits of priestly authority. The second will be to suggest what idea of female sanctity these texts collectively share, in addressing that fundamental question of religious authority. In both cases, the authors will appear as witnesses to an extended moment in the life of the late-medieval church when clerics could have enough confidence in their powers to entertain the question of the limits of clerical authority and, in answering it, to find some room for experiment. It was a period in which the danger of a threat to that authority was not yet such as to demand the repression of the charismatic powers that demonstrated its limits and facilitated an exploration beyond itself.

Two Spheres of Authority

In all of the nine cases discussed in this book, the male authors pictured their female subjects as claiming an authority of their own to speak and be heard, and to affect the lives of others—an authority based upon their own evident extraordinary access to God, especially in visions, revelations, and ecstasies. That was their great point of fascination for the men. It was an authority that, as the men found it possible to believe, derived directly from God rather than from the possession of any ecclesiastical office. It legitimated the women in the exercise of "informal" powers: to verify and convey arcane knowledge, to perceive the state of souls, to intercede with God for those in need, and also, in certain circumstances, to teach. The question at stake for the men about the women's authority was how to position it in relation to their own, which typically derived from their status as officeholders in the church and gave them the exercise of their own powers, in preaching, administration of sacraments, official teaching, and hierarchical jurisdiction. How were the two kinds of authority to coexist?

In the men's approach to that question over time, the nine cases here have suggested a kind of trajectory. After some initial experimentation, the women's authority emerged in the early thirteenth century as something remarkably discrete that, for a while, both interacted with and complemented the authority of clerics. Then at the end of the fourteenth century, it receded again somewhat in an atmosphere of distrust, and this particular long literary experiment in the balance of authorities came to at least a temporary end. Here I retrace that trajectory.

The earliest of the cases I have discussed here are those of Ekbert of Schönau and Guibert of Gembloux, in the second half of the twelfth century. Both wrote about holy women in a way that exposed and explicitly reflected upon their own personal encounters with those women, although in the matter of authority, they adopted different ways of thinking about their own relation to the women's charisms. Ekbert considered his visionary sister Elisabeth to be under his direction and made a point of his authority over her. For though her visions were surely her own, and there is no question of his having invented them, still he presented himself as exercising firm control over the visionary enterprise: he not only influenced the visions' subject matter by his promptings but also tested them for authenticity, decided which of them to publish, and recorded and collected them himself. Guibert, on the other hand, claimed no such authority over the commanding figure of the abbess Hildegard of Bingen. Instead he tried to picture her visionary gift as a function not only of her status as someone favored by God but also of the monastic calling that he himself shared with her, and in this way he sought to justify his own bid to correct and edit her visionary writings as an act of collegiality. If Ekbert considered the visionary woman's authority as subordinate to his own, Guibert by contrast wanted to think of himself as sharing in the woman's visionary enterprise by virtue of the commitments of their shared way of life.

Neither Ekbert's nor Guibert's approach to the women's charismatic authority, however, was to carry the day among the men who wrote first-person accounts of their relations with holy women in the two centuries to follow. The approach that was to prevail, rather, was one that treated the official authority of the man and the extraordinary charismatic authority of the woman as discrete entities: each appeared effective in its own right without trumping, or being trumped by, the other. Hildegard herself seems to have anticipated such a view when she responded to Guibert's desire to edit her visions by distinguishing his role as priest from hers as visionary in a way that avoided overlap or rank ordering. Such an approach, when it came into its own in the writings of male hagiographers in the thirteenth century, was to hold obvious dangers in the sense that it meant recognizing something in the women's experience and witness that was legitimately beyond their own reach and supervision. They knew that they had to be able to assume such women's loyalty to the church's priesthood and its doctrines, or else this approach to authority would become—as later on it did become—untenable. But it seems to have been exactly that prospect of encountering something legitimately beyond them that made holy women figures of fascination for clerical men, and the fascination accounts in no small part for the substance and depth of the men's writing about the women.

James of Vitry's vita of the Beguine Mary of Oignies, written in the early thirteenth century, stands as the first thoroughgoing attempt by the confidant of a holy woman to explore the idea of her charismatic authority as something discrete from his own priestly authority. In James's account, Mary displays access to supernatural sources of knowledge as Elisabeth and Hildegard had done, but

James makes knowledge of a speculative or doctrinal sort much less prominent in his account of her than in the accounts we have of the visions of Elisabeth and Hildegard; conversely, James emphasizes knowledge affecting the salvation of individual souls. For him, that latter knowledge makes Mary the invaluable partner of priests, who discerns the states of souls and works tirelessly to bring those souls to repentance, thus opening them to the preaching and sacraments of the church. James must make a particular point of the noncompetitiveness of this partnership and of her devotion to priests. For her supernatural knowledge, as something inaccessible yet desirable or even indispensable to priests, would indeed be dangerous if she were to stand against them in any way, and there are hints that for all her extreme veneration of priests, she was in a certain sense independent of them herself, knowing already from her divine sources, for instance, anything they would have to tell her. But by establishing that veneration beyond any doubt and thus heading off any possible sinister implications of her powers, James is able to exploit the very discreteness of his and her respective spheres of authority. He perceives such discreteness as something in the interest of both the church and himself in the sense that it clarifies both the need and the means by which he can complete or perfect his own priestly ministry—and perhaps even his own selfhood. To write of it becomes a way of both acknowledging and making up for the limits of formal ecclesiastical power—of exploring the relationship between the authority of office and what lay beyond it.

Such exploration of the limits of official authority was to be a primary concern of the subsequent men who reflected on their relationships with saintly women in the thirteenth and fourteenth centuries. But before preceding to recall those other works, I want to dwell for another moment on the differences between Ekbert and Guibert, on the one hand, and James, on the other. All three shared, to be sure, a deep fascination with the women's charisms as something immensely attractive that they themselves did not possess. But it is of no small importance that James, as the first hagiographer to picture himself with a holy woman in terms that express the two-sphere approach to the question of authority, should be a cleric, with an active ministry in secular society, and the woman in question should be a layperson. Whereas Ekbert and Elisabeth, and Guibert and Hildegard all shared a common monastic profession, James and Mary did not; the fact that they stand instead in roles in life that are very discrete helps James present their species of authority as likewise discrete. Mary indeed appears in retrospect as one of the earliest examples of the "new" female sanctity of the thirteenth century (as discussed in chapter 1), typified by profound devotion to the Eucharist and to the Passion of Christ and, in imitation of Christ, an unrestrained embrace of suffering. Her own ostensible lack of status and power in James's account (even though the social status of her family was probably high), increased both the evident anxiety and pathos of that suffering and the significance that both she and her admirers attached to her embrace of poverty and the life of the apostles. In other hagiography in this period, as well, women were typically (though not exclusively) lay people, especially Beguines and other penitents, who in this sense, like Mary, stood in stark contrast to the male clerics whose authority derived from their place in the institutional church. And that stark contrast consistently underlies the imaginative sorting-out of authorities into two spheres by James's male literary successors in the sequence of collaborations between clerics and holy women that I have discussed in this book.

Those later collaborations show something of the variety of the possible implications of the two-sphere model of authority that thus made its full debut in the literary imagination of James. The case of the Dominican friar Peter of Dacia, writing later in the thirteenth century about the Beguine Christine of Stommeln, presents a remarkable exploration of those implications for the self-understanding of the man, at least as he chooses to present it in the context of a hagiographical text. The theme of the cleric's self-understanding had already figured in James's vita but, by comparison to Peter anyway, with little elaboration. Peter expresses a sense of something lacking in himself that makes him unable to experience the closeness to God that he attributes to Christine. This sense consequently draws him to her so as to allow him to taste what he desires, if only vicariously, and at the same time confronts him all the more directly with his conviction of his own inadequacy. Peter, moreover, is a person of learning—he met Christine while he was a student at the Dominican school at Cologne—and he makes use of theological categories, which give him a vocabulary to explain or rationalize Christine's gifts. But he also considers his learning to be powerless to satisfy his deep desire for devotion and immediate experience of God, and the unlearned Christine has what he wants. The meaning Christine holds for him, then, lies in her considerable power to represent the boundary and limits of his own calling. And the irony is not incidental that she who possesses this power is, in every worldly sense, a helpless and even pitiful figure who has no power at all.

In the *Memorial* of the Italian penitent Angela of Foligno, written around the turn of the fourteenth century by the anonymous Franciscan Friar A, the two-sphere model finds yet another expression, this time with emphasis not so much on the subjectivity of the cleric, but rather on a set of fundamental theological questions, concerning the knowledge and knowability of God. Angela had prophetic powers to discern the states of souls and other particulars of God's dispensations, but the emphasis in the *Memorial*, which strengthens as the work proceeds, is on the directness of her encounter with the very being of God. The sort of knowledge that she and the friar are most concerned to articulate is not of the comparatively practical sort—whether magisterial or pastoral—conveyed by Mary of Oignies. Angela's concerns are more profound and speculative, as she attempts to say something true about God's nature and accessibility. Here the work is marked by a profound ambiguity: Angela, as the one who articulates this knowledge, does so not as an oracle—not, that is, as a mouthpiece of God—but rather as an interpretive observer of her own experience. When she observes this experience and interprets it, she ceases momentarily to speak as a person of charismatic powers, or rather these powers become the object of her analysis and thus are no longer the condition of her speech itself. At that point she speaks not in the mode of a prophet but in effect in that of a teacher, and the powers she exercises are not dissimilar from those of her male clerical collaborator. In this way the boundary between the two spheres of authority becomes evidently blurred even though the object of her understanding is still accessible to her only as the fruit of her informal and charismatic powers. But Angela and the friar both presuppose the distinctness of her charismatic authority from any authority that he may possess, and therefore they work from the two-sphere schema, even as they experiment with its limits.

In the early-fourteenth-century vita of the Franciscan penitent Margaret of Cortona, written at about the same time as the *Memorial* of Angela, Margaret's sometime confessor Giunta Bevegnati evolves a picture of her, and of her interactions with himself, in which the question of authority takes on a slightly different guise. There is little in Giunta of the sort of autobiographical witness to the meaning of the saint for himself found in Peter, nor is he interested in speculative theology in the fashion of Friar A. For Peter and Friar A, the two-sphere schema stood as an implicit assumption. But in Giunta it becomes explicit, an important part of the proper subject matter of his writing. He is conscious of the question of the proper relationship between the authority Margaret derives from her direct contact with Christ and the authority he himself and his fellow Franciscans of Cortona derive from their priestly office, and he has Christ address the question in imagined interviews with Margaret. The question is far from merely abstract; the actual relations of Margaret with the friars served to pose it. For though the precise facts remain somewhat obscure, it seems that she removed herself from their supervision late in her life. She did this, according to Giunta, against their wishes but at Christ's command. Thus he acknowledges limits to the authority of the friars and has Christ establish a balance between institutional and informal powers whereby they mutually correct and inform each other and become together a sign of the contingency of all human powers and the transcendence of the divine will.

As in Giunta's vita of Margaret, so too a few decades later in the letters of the fourteenth-century secular priest Henry of Nördlingen to the Dominican nun Margaret Ebner we have a picture of the broader, and in their case we might even say "normal," context in which cleric and charismatic woman could function and interact over time. Henry's letters display his rapports with Margaret over a twenty-year period in his own life. Like James of Vitry and the friars Peter, A, and Giunta, he takes the two-sphere approach to female sanctity. He admires Margaret and articulates his own sense of deficiency as he considers the supernatural grace that he finds in her, and he registers fascination with her revelations and in general her access to the realm of the divine. But the quotidian quality of many of the letters makes it possible for us to see all of this as but one aspect of a wide-ranging friendship. He tells her of his other friends and other concerns and of the events of his life, and he conveys as well some of the particulars of the everyday affairs of her monastery. Margaret's revelations, though extraordinary to be sure, are not miracles reported for their own sake but events that take their place easily within the otherwise ordinary round of daily life, in a manner like that of other Dominican women described in the convent "sister books" of the period.

It is, I suggest, in the famous vita of the Dominican penitent Catherine of Siena by the friar Raymond of Capua, written just before the end of the fourteenth century, that, within the sequence of texts studied here anyway, the two-sphere model of religious authority comes into its full maturity. Raymond pictures himself prominently as a party to interactions with Catherine in which she has access to the divine in a way that he does not and that, as he would have it, supply deficiencies in himself. His descriptions of these interactions recall our previous authors, even though he shows more reticence in exposing his own desire or longing. Raymond includes himself as a character in his hagiographical work about the saint with particular thoroughness: he stands in the frame of reference in almost every scene, continually presenting himself to the reader as the medium through whom the reader is viewing Catherine. In that sense he is like the comparably self-referential Peter of Dacia. But unlike Peter, whose focus of attention tends to migrate from Christine to himself, Raymond manages in and through his inclusion of himself in the narrative to keep his focus on Catherine and her mission. In his many appearances, he is her partner in that mission for the salvation of souls and the peaceful unity of Christendom.

If Raymond's vita of Catherine represents a maturing of reflective writing on female saints by their male collaborators, it also however hints at a change in the conditions that had made the experiment of such writing possible in the preceding two centuries. There is a polemical tone to Raymond's vita of Catherine, and its argument against detractors is a central feature of the narrative. The importance he attaches to that argument helps explain the paradox of Raymond's simultaneous personal reserve and ubiquity in the text: he uses himself as a tool for Catherine's defense but keeps his guard up as one would naturally do toward an audience one expects to be suspicious. In retrospect, it is clear that the detractors represent early evidence of the suspicion of visionary women such as Catherine and their supposed role in the Great Schism, to which Gerson was to give expression not many years afterward. Raymond, it seems, cannot make the assumption of the legitimacy of the charismatic authority of the woman he is writing about with quite the same ease as did the writers discussed in earlier chapters.

The same is true in the last of the writers examined here, the theologian and cathedral canon John Marienwerder, who, around the beginning of the fifteenth century, wrote several works on the recluse Dorothy of Montau, whose confessor he had become at the end of her life. John, to be sure, still gives expression to the two-sphere model. There is some reversal of roles, in the sense that Dorothy can be seen directing John: she intuits and receives revelations about his sins and shortcomings and informs him of these, somewhat as Mary of Oignies did for James of Vitry, and she even teaches him, as he reports, about spiritual discernment. Like Margaret of Cortona and Mary of Oignies, she intuits the sins of others, specifically other of John's penitents, and advises and criticizes him on his handling of them. And she receives some revelations criticizing his handling of herself. John also shows an explicit awareness of the "system" implied by the two spheres of authority rather as Giunta did; he pictures Dorothy and himself in a certain balance of authorities. But there is a difference: now Christ is less the transcendent figure who legitimates and relativizes the two types of authority, as in Giunta, but rather a kind of ally of Dorothy who coaches her to help John get her revelations right, and in the process appears curiously untranscendent, as though he were but another party interested in Dorothy. The system of authorities appears to lack some of its own sure rooting in the will of God. And although Dorothy's seclusion from the world stands in contrast to the apostolic activity of Catherine of Siena, John's treatment of her stands, like Raymond's of Catherine, as a sign of the receding of the propitious moment for the self-referential male hagiographer. It would not be quite true to say that John's attitude toward Dorothy brings us full-circle back to Ekbert, as though he had put the woman unambiguously under his supervision. But still there are signs that point in that direction, the most significant of which is his introduction of the idea that Dorothy's access to her visions is analogous to his own access to books. This analogy introduces the possibility that she may be in error; and John can give examples of her misunderstandings. He is therefore at some pains to establish that everything she said has been tested against Scripture.

. These texts open up, therefore, a realm of male clerical imagination that appears to have come into its own in the thirteenth and fourteenth centuries, whereby clerics envisioned a range of possibilities of encounter between two discrete and gendered spheres of authority. This envisioning makes clear what an important place women could occupy in clerics' thinking about their own authority. Clearly women's very exclusion from church office was a crucial factor in establishing them in this place. Dyan Elliott has shown with great insight how in these same centuries, in the context of the strict enforcement of clerical celibacy brought about by the Gregorian Reform, the figure of the "priest's wife" loomed all the larger in the clerical imagination for being suppressed in actuality, indeed took on a kind of demonic power that eventually merged her with the figure of the witch.[5] The place of the female saint in that clerical imagination was certainly not so sinister, indeed ostensibly not sinister at all, but there was a similar dynamic at work: for it was the exclusion of women in one space that made them reemerge significantly in another one. In these hagiographical portraits the woman's total lack of the authority attached to clerical office makes her a powerful signifier of the limits of that authority. It would seem, though, that the positive possibilities of such signifying receded somewhat, and gave greater place to the more sinister images of supernaturally powerful women in the clerical mind, as the fifteenth century progressed. It is then that clerics become more cautious about placing themselves as characters within their narratives of saintly women and accordingly making a proper subject of their own interactions with them. Thus after John Marienwerder the experiment came to a pause before resuming again in the early-modern period, when Raymond of Capua's vita of Catherine of Siena would exert widespread influence on hagiographers.

COLLABORATOR-HAGIOGRAPHERS AND THE
IDEA OF FEMALE SANCTITY

What then can be said about female sanctity, as an idea, in these texts? Clearly it is an idea that belongs to the monks and clerics who wrote the texts, not an abstraction that exists apart from them, and as much recent research has made clear, it would be an error to assume that what male authors tell us about women when we cannot otherwise hear the women's own voices is more or less what the women would have told us about themselves. The concerns and desires particular to those male authors do not simply shape or influence the idea of female sanctity here but lie at its heart, even create it, and they must constitute a starting point for any effort to describe it. Even so, however, that idea is not a mere solipsism or fantasy, nor is it merely a tool to subordinate the women to the men. It is rather an attempt to take seriously—to articulate the significance of and in this sense to imagine—what were, in their devotees' view anyway, the real powers of the women. The men accomplished this by thinking in terms of partnerships that, to be sure, did not undermine clerical authority yet that also acknowledged and explored the limits of that authority.

A major element in the men's imagination of that partnership, as this emerged over time, was their conviction of the women's stark difference from themselves. They typically articulate this difference in terms of contrast or opposition: the woman displays an extraordinary access to God that the man considers himself to lack utterly, and usually, as a corollary (or an assumed precondition) of that access, she also displays virtues that he likewise lacks, often in the form of endurance of physical austerities that mirror the Passion of Christ. The man's sense of these contrasts becomes then the sine qua non for his concept of his partnership with the holy woman, articulated as a partnership of opposites. Such heightening of the contrast between himself and the woman was not, indeed, the only possible means for such a man to ponder a partnership with charismatic women. Both Guibert of Gembloux's attempts to blur, or anyway downplay, the distinction between Hildegard's visionary efforts and his own efforts to assist her, and Ekbert of Schönau's confident and relatively unambiguous assumption of the role of his sister's director suggest other ways of thinking about partnership, at any rate in twelfth-century monastic circles. In the texts of this study, the contrast first comes clearly to light in James of Vitry's vita of the Beguine Mary of Oignies, in the early thirteenth century. But then it finds expression in all the texts thereafter (though on occasion less rigorously, as in Giunta's vita of Margaret), reflecting, as I have suggested already, the perception of two discrete types of authority that the pursuit of religious ideals outside the cloister seems to have fostered.

The tendency by male hagiographers in the late Middle Ages to focus upon elements of women's lives that were lacking in their own—and not necessarily the elements to which women themselves gave expression in their own writings—has been pointed out by many scholars. The use of bridal imagery itself, so common in vitae of women but generally considerably sparser in women's own writing, provides a case in point. Karen Glente, for instance, has examined such imagery in her analysis of the early-thirteenth-century vitae of Margaret of Ypres and Lutgard of Aywières by James of Vitry's admirer the Dominican friar Thomas of Cantimpré.[6] She shows that Thomas built the drama of each woman's early life around a supposed competition for her attentions between a human suitor and a divine one, namely Christ, whose representative on earth is her confessor. Christ of course wins the competition and thereby her confessor attracts the woman's interest to himself, distancing her emotionally from her own immediate environment and bringing her romantic life into his own sphere of concerns, otherwise significantly limited by his own celibacy. Thus, Glente would suggest, Thomas shows that male clerics could have a distinct personal investment in thinking about holy women as brides.

Amy Hollywood has also considered the distinctiveness of male interest in holy women, in several essays comparing the vita of the Cistercian nun Beatrice of Nazareth (1200–1260), by an anonymous and presumably male hagiographer, with Beatrice's own mystical treatise *Seven Manners of Loving*, which the hagiographer used as a source.[7] She finds that the hagiographer tended to transform experiences that in Beatrice's own recounting were clearly internal, presenting them instead in physical manifestations, thus externalizing those experiences and making them into a spectacle—as, for instance, when he converts Beatrice's apparently metaphorical account of the melting of her heart and overflowing of her soul into a concrete description of the "flood of tears from her melted heart." In her most recent work, Hollywood has characterized this "somatizing" tendency of male hagiographers as a tendency to make the woman into a "fetishistic site" on which to project their own desires or unresolved conflicts, in this case concerning the human body and their connection to it: "Men's desire for the salvation of the body, a desire perhaps partially repressed by the claim that men are closer to reason and the higher faculties of the soul, reemerges in the suffering and ecstatic bodies of women through which men's bodies are redeemed."[8]

It is often evident that the men's interest in drawing such contrasts between themselves and the women arises from concerns peculiar to themselves as male clerics. This is especially clear in James of Vitry and Peter of Dacia. James's presentation of Mary of Oignies as the person who knows his own heart better than he himself knows it, and who supplies the essential animating spirit of ministry through her prayers, suggests a sense of anxiety over something he feels to be lacking in himself in spite of—or perhaps because of—his own considerable success as a preacher: a true devotion, or vital connection to the divine, which his priestly calling evidently demands of him but does not give him. James imagines Mary in such a way that she embodies for him what he both lacks and needs, and thus the stark difference between her and himself is of the essence of his portrayal.[9] A similar dynamic appears, and in considerably more detail, in Peter's writings about Christine of Stommeln. Here is the self-portrait of a young Dominican scholar who, in the process of absorbing a scholastic education that does not keep him from being "dry" and "cold" in devotion, becomes fixated on a troubled Beguine. What draws him to her are her bizarre behaviors that, as he doggedly believes, are her responses to the work of demons who attack her because of the ecstasies that mark her as a bride of Christ. The spectacle of these, he finds, produces in him pious emotions that he cannot find apart from her. Although Angela's friar, by contrast, reveals little of himself, still the sudden reversal that moves him from the stance of a confessor sternly judging Angela to that of her unquestioning devotee on the basis of "a new and special grace of God that I had never experienced before" suggests that his perceptions of her have direct implications for the exercise of his office. In Giunta, it is true, we find less evidence of a such a personal sense of connection between the woman's powers and his own perception of his office, although he makes reference to the use he made of her oracles to guide him in his ministry. Henry of Nördlingen, for his part, is constantly addressing Margaret Ebner in terms that accent her chosenness and his own abasement, and he employs the conceit reminiscent of James that Margaret, because of the efficacy of her prayers, can take more credit for his pastoral work than he himself. We also find the conceit of contrast in Raymond of Capua's reflections on Catherine of Siena, though, as I have suggested, he exhibits a certain restraint about exposing his own putative needs and desires. John Marienwerder also exhibits such restraint, though he hints at his personal feelings when he tells the reader his fantasy of being free of his religious vows, in which case he would choose to be continually by her side.

The men's tendency to emphasize the women's otherness appears particularly clearly when the men's writings about their relationship with women are compared to the few available texts written by those women themselves. It is true that these are not, strictly speaking, hagiographical texts—even though Margaret Ebner's imagining of Henry has a certain hagiographical tone to it— and so they generally lack evidence of the hagiographical motivation to place one's subject on a pedestal that is at work in all the men's writing and that by itself would not necessarily tell us much about gender. Even so, it is worth noting that in two of the three cases in which we have been able to compare the woman's writing about her relationship with the man to his own account of that relationship, there is a striking tendency to resist the effects of the man's effort at distancing her from himself. It is true that Hildegard is at pains to distinguish herself as prophet from Guibert as priest, when she writes to him about his collaborations with her, and thus, as I have remarked, she presages the distinction between spheres of authority that James and his successors will later assume and build upon. But she knows nothing of the sort of moral contrast that James will introduce between woman and collaborator as a fundamental element of the relationship. Margaret Ebner, in her *Revelations*, imagines Henry as receiving favor from God in a way parallel to her own experience, and she neither acknowledges nor imitates his self-abasing way of thinking about their relationship. And Catherine of Siena, in her letters to Raymond of Capua, pushes relentlessly to identify Raymond with herself in a common task that she conceives in a way that obscures the very moral and functional differences between them that Raymond highlights in the *Legenda maior*.

It would seem, then, that male hagiographers typically gave expression to a felt deficiency or lack in their own psyche as they constructed their portraits of women. Catherine Mooney has suggested that in this and other ways such authors "altered and misrepresented the self-understandings of the many women whose voices are lost to us."[10] That is surely true. But it is also true that male-authored hagiographical texts about women, or anyway those of the present study, are no mere fantasy portraits. For in each case the author's very emphasis on the woman's otherness functions to help him explore the implications of what to him are her real powers and the relationship of these to his own powers.

Our authors' self-inclusion in their texts gives depth and nuance to their reflection on the distinction between the woman's powers and their own, by presenting themselves as parties to the women's relationship to God or Christ. Like other hagiographers of women in the later Middle Ages, they drew both implicitly and explicitly upon the imagery of the Song of Songs to picture the woman and Christ as a couple. But by incorporating themselves as characters in their narratives, they are more likely to expand the couple into the threesome or triad—woman/Christ/cleric—that we have observed repeatedly. This triad appears in a variety of ways. Christ and the woman may appear talking about the man, as when Christ and Dorothy of Montau conspire to influence John Marienwerder's understanding of her visions. Or Christ may communicate through the woman to the man about himself or others, as when he gives

Margaret of Cortona messages for Giunta Bevegnati. Or Christ may explain to the woman the authority or responsibilities of the man, as when he lectures Dorothy or Margaret on their obligations to their collaborators. Or the man may speak of himself as a servant or subordinate to both the woman and Christ, as when Henry of Nördlingen pictures himself as a kitchen boy attending the banquet table of the royal couple Christ and Margaret Ebner, or when Peter of Dacia imagines himself as the inferior sister of Christ's bride Christine, making himself useful to her so as to hear about the secrets of the marriage bed. Or the woman and the man may develop a shared strategy for approaching the divinity, as in the case of Angela of Foligno and her Franciscan collaborator. In these various triadic scenes or images, knowledge and experience of God are inseparable from human interaction, and the human figures' respective claims to spiritual authority, distinct as they are, appear also as inseparable in their various forms of interaction. All of this makes for a thoughtful exploration of the encounter between formal and informal powers that I have been recalling, with all its resonance for the concerns about religious authority so important at the time.

In situating the woman and her powers in the context of issues about religious authority, the authors here typically, in effect, construed *partnership*—the partnership between holy women and clerics—as an element fundamental to female sanctity. I conclude by recalling the features of that imagined partnership.

Most often in these texts the partnership finds expression in stories of the women's exercise of their powers of prophecy or revelation, in which the men appear as having some involvement. Partnership is an important theme already in Ekbert of Schönau, who enlisted his visionary sister's supernatural aid in answering questions that his own scholastic training had taught him to ask. Guibert of Gembloux too aspired, if not entirely successfully, to a collaborative relationship with Hildegard in putting her visions of divine mysteries into words. In those instances it was desire to discern the "ways of God" (in the phrase of a title of one of Elisabeth's collections)—that is, hitherto-obscured particulars of God's will and action, or even of God's being—that focused the man's and woman's collaboration. In the subsequent texts that desire never entirely disappears and sometimes comes to the fore again, as in the *Memorial* of Angela of Foligno. But for the most part, while the men's sense of partnership with the women remains a central feature of their narratives and letters, we find the supernatural focus of that partnership shifting away from such matters of arcane and potentially dangerous speculative knowledge to the safer and more pastorally useful subject of the state of souls. Mary of Oignies, by her extraordinary powers, both causes James's hearers to open themselves to his preaching and makes him aware of the spiritual shortcomings he himself needs to address to make it more effective. Margaret of Cortona alerts Giunta Bevegnati to the unconfessed sins of his penitents, which he then ferrets out of them in the confessional. Dorothy of Montau, on the basis of her expertise on the ways of the soul, becomes her own confessor's tutor for the hearing of confessions. Such partnership finds its grandest, if also perhaps most self-conscious, expression in Raymond of Capua's vita of Catherine of Siena, in which he as priest and she as prophet pair their energies in pursuing the welfare not only of individual souls but also of Christendom itself.

Such learned and pastoral functions were not all that these partnerships were about, however, in the men's accounts; there was also a function of mutual supervision and restraint. It is true that—in part no doubt because of the nature of the hagiographical genre, if not also because of the experience they write from—the men are not particularly intent on portraying themselves as watchdogs for the women's orthodoxy or propriety. But even so, Ekbert occasionally challenges Elisabeth's revelatory angel, James of Vitry downplays Mary of Oignies' doctrinal pronouncements, Angela of Foligno's friar alerts her when she approaches the limits of orthodoxy, and John Marienwerder keeps watch on Dorothy of Montau's revelations for consistency. The women for their part often take a critical view of the men, this being indeed a function of that conceit of role reversal to which so many of the men were drawn: Mary confronts James with his pride, Margaret of Cortona's revelations criticize Giunta's techniques in the confessional, Dorothy alerts John Marienwerder to the limits of his spiritual progress. Especially in the works of John and Giunta, such a reciprocal sense of limitation makes in turn for nuanced reflection on the inadequacy of any human knowledge of God, all in the context of the representation of partnership between the man and the woman.

The basis of the partnerships in these texts also, at times, involves more than the joint exercise of institutional and informal powers. Angela and the friar-writer of the *Memorial* move from collaboration based on Angela's powers to another kind of collegiality based on a common intellectual task. Margaret Ebner and Henry of Nördlingen appear in Henry's letters as friends who share gifts and gossip when he is not depicting her as a bride of Christ. And we can glimpse in Raymond's vita of Catherine (though with greater clarity in Catherine's own letters) the contours of the grand shared project of a mission for the peace of Italy and the return of the papacy to Rome that relied on the persuasive gifts and zeal of both of them rather than on the saint's prophetic powers per se.

On the man's part, fascination with the woman for her gifts and powers not infrequently leads to deeper, or at any rate different, commitments and modes of collegiality.

To speak, therefore, of an idea of female sanctity in the male-authored literature examined in these pages is to speak not simply of the women's virtues but also of an economy of powers in which both the women and their male collaborators have a part. The texts propose a picture of cooperation or partnership between monks or clerics on one hand and holy women on the other, and thus a productive interaction between the institutional and informal powers that were their respective domains. It is, no doubt, an idealized picture, one that emphasizes the possibilities of such interaction and that, as many clues suggest, deliberately downplays the suspicion in which charismatic women could indeed be held—the suspicion, that is, that they would turn out to be possessed by the demonic rather than the divine.[11] But I have been examining, after all, the views and intentions of the authors of hagiographical texts, who by the nature of their task aimed to chronicle the fulfillment of divine purposes in the world rather than their obstruction or defeat. These are glimpses of how, in the authors' views, clerics and charismatic women *ought* to be in partnership with each other. The fact that they wrote first-hand, and were willing to position themselves as figures in their own narratives in witness to their vision of these relationships, speaks both to their own conviction that they had glimpsed something true and their confidence that there were well-disposed readers who would share their view.

NOTES

INTRODUCTION. "YOU DRAW US AFTER YOU"

1. "Vere enim ubera tua meliora nobis uino, flagrantia unguentis optimis [cf. Cant. 1.1–2], dum e contemplationum cellariis, in que rex eternus te ut sponsam sepe introducit [cf. Cant. 1.3], ad exteriora regrediens uisionum sanctarum, quas reuelata facie [2 Cor. 3.18] inter amplexus sponsi tui specularis, participes nos ex scriptis faciendo, in odore unguentorum tuorum alacriter [cf. Cant. 1.3] currentes, post te nos trahis" (*GGE* 16.11–17:217).

2. Peter Dinzelbacher, "Nascità e funzione della santità mistica alla fine del medioevo centrale," in *Les fonctions des saints dans le monde occidental, IIIe-XIIIe s.* (Rome: École française, 1991), 489–506. I discuss the changing notions of sanctity in the period in greater detail in chapter 1.

3. A convenient survey is Peter Dinzelbacher, "Europäische Frauenmystik des Mittelalters: Ein Überblick," in *Frauenmystik im Mittelalter*, ed. Peter Dinzelbacher and Dieter Bauer (Ostfildern bei Stuttgart: Schwaben, 1985), 11–23, reprinted in Dinzelbacher, *Mittelalterliche Frauenmystik* (Paderborn: Ferdinand Schöningh, 1993), 16–26.

4. Peter Dronke, *Women Writers of the Middle Ages* (Cambridge: Cambridge University Press, 1984), 202.

5. Caroline Walker Bynum, *Holy Feast and Holy Fast: The Religious Significance of Food to Medieval Women* (Berkeley: University of California Press, 1987), 13–30; Bynum, "Women Mystics and Eucharistic Devotion in the Thirteenth Century," *Women's Studies* 11 (1984): 179–214, reprinted in Bynum, *Fragmentation and Redemption: Essays on Gender and the Human Body in Medieval Religion* (New York: Zone, 1991), 119–50; Barbara Newman, "On the Threshold of the Dead: Purgatory, Hell, and Religious Women," in *From Virile Woman to WomanChrist: Studies in Medieval Religion and Literature* (Philadelphia: University of Pennsylvania Press, 1995), 108–136; Elizabeth A. Petroff, *Medieval Women's Visionary Literature* (New York: Oxford University Press, 1986), 3–59.

6. Herbert Grundmann, *Religious Movements in the Middle Ages*, trans. Steven Rowan (Notre Dame, Ind.: University of Notre Dame Press, 1995), 89–137; John B. Freed, "Urban Development and the 'Cura Monialium' in Thirteenth-Century Germany," *Viator*

3 (1972): 311–27; Kaspar Elm, "*Vita regularis sine regula.* Bedeutung, Rechtsstellung und Selbstverständnis des mittelalterlichen und frühneuzeitlichen Semireligiosentums," in *Häresie und Vorzeitige Reformation Im Spätmittelalter,* ed. Frantisek Smahel and Elisabeth Müller-Luckner (Munich: R. Oldenbourg Verlag, 1998), 239–73.

7. Ute Stargardt, "Male Clerical Authority in the Spiritual (Auto)Biographies of Medieval Holy Women," in *Women as Protagonists and Poets in the German Middle Ages: An Anthology of Feminist Approaches to Middle High German Literature,* ed. Albrecht Classen (Göppingen: Kümmerle Verlag, 1991), 209–38; Jo Ann McNamara, "The Rhetoric of Orthodoxy: Clerical Authority and Female Innovation in the Struggle with Heresy," in *Maps of Flesh and Light: The Religious Experience of Medieval Women Mystics,* ed. Ulrike Wiethaus (Syracuse, N.Y.: Syracuse University Press, 1992), 9–27; Janette Dillon, "Holy Women and Their Confessors or Confessors and Their Holy Women? Margery Kempe and Continental Tradition," in *Prophets Abroad: The Reception of Continental Holy Women in Late-Medieval England,* ed. Rosalynn Voaden (Cambridge: D. S. Brewer, 1996), 115–40; Grace Jantzen, *Power, Gender, and Christian Mysticism* (Cambridge: Cambridge University Press, 1995), 157–92.

8. Brian Patrick McGuire, "Holy Women and Monks in the Thirteenth Century: Friendship or Exploitation?" *Vox Benedictina* 6 (1989): 343–74; Elizabeth Alvilda Petroff, *Body and Soul: Essays on Medieval Women and Mysticism* (New York: Oxford University Press, 1994), 139–57; John Coakley, "Friars as Confidants of Holy Women in Medieval Dominican Hagiography," in *Images of Sainthood in Medieval Europe,* ed. Renate Blumenfeld-Kosinski and Timea Szell (Ithaca, N.Y.: Cornell University Press, 1991), 222–46; Kimberley M. Benedict, *Empowering Collaborations: Writing Partnerships Between Religious Women and Scribes in the Middle Ages* (New York: Routledge, 2004).

9. Hildegard's biographer Theoderic also used the phrase of her, *VSH* 2.1.20, 2.17.45; see Barbara Newman, "Hildegard and Her Hagiographers: The Remaking of Female Sainthood," in *Gendered Voices: Medieval Saints and Their Interpreters,* ed. Catherine M. Mooney (Philadelphia: University of Pennsylvania Press, 1999), 26. Guibert himself also places the phrase in Hildegard's mouth in his vita of the saint, *GGE* 38.126–27:370. In chapter 8, below, I discuss Henry of Nördlingen's use of this passage in his letters to Margaret Ebner.

10. Dyan Elliott, *Fallen Bodies: Pollution, Sexuality, and Demonology in the Middle Ages* (Philadelphia: University. of Pennsylvania Press, 1999), 80–156; Jo Ann McNamara, "The Herrenfrage: Restructuring the Gender System, 1050–1150," in *Medieval Masculinities: Regarding Men in the Middle Ages,* ed. Clare A. Lees (Minneapolis: University of Minnesota Press, 1994), 3–29.

11. On discerning the gender-specific aspects of perceptions of late-medieval saints and roles of gender in hagiographical portraits, see especially the essays in Catherine Mooney, ed., *Gendered Voices: Medieval Saints and Their Interpreters* (Philadelphia: University of Pennsylvania Press, 1999), to which I shall make frequent reference in the present study. On constructions of maleness in the Middle Ages, see Clare A. Lees, ed., *Medieval Masculinities: Regarding Men in the Middle Ages* (Minneapolis: University of Minnesota Press, 1994); Jeffrey Jerome Cohen and Bonnie Wheeler, eds., *Becom-*

ing Male in the Middle Ages (New York: Garland, 1997); and Ruth Mazo Karras, *From Boys to Men: Formulations of Masculinity in Medieval Europe* (Philadelphia: University of Pennsylvania Press, 2003).

12. It is true that the first two female saints to be considered, namely Elisabeth of Schönau and Hildegard of Bingen, do not yet fully exemplify these new ideals; most notably they do not display the affective and Passion-centered spirituality that would typify female saints of the thirteenth century and later, though they have in common the important role of revelations in their lives (see chapter 1 below).

13. Aviad M. Kleinberg, *Prophets in Their Own Country: Living Saints and the Making of Sainthood in the Later Middle Ages* (Chicago: University of Chicago Press, 1992).

14. Jean-Claude Poulin, *L'Idéal de sainteté dans l'Aquitaine carolingienne, 750–950* (Quebec: Université Laval, 1975), 33; Pierre Delooz, *Sociologie et canonisations* (Liège: Faculté de Droit, 1969).

15. Siegfried Ringler, *Viten- und Offenbarungsliteratur in Frauenklöstern des Mittelalters. Quellen und Studien* (Munich: Artemis, 1980); Ursula Peters, *Religiöse Erfahrung als literarisches Faktum. Zur Vorgeschichte und Genese frauenmystischer Texte des 13. und 14. Jahrhunderts* (Tübingen: Max Niemeyer, 1988). Such skepticism about hagiographical and visionary texts as records of religious experience has been challenged by Peter Dinzelbacher, "Zur Interpretation erlebnismystischer Texte des Mittelalters," in *Zeitschrift für deutsches Altertum* 117 (1988): 1–23, reprinted in Dinzelbacher, *Mittelalterliche Frauenmystik* (Paderborn: Ferdinand Schöningh, 1993), 304–31. On the debate between Ringler and Dinzelbacher, with further bibliography, see Frank Tobin, "Henry Suso and Elsbeth Stagel: Was the *Vita* a Cooperative Effort?" in *Gendered Voices: Medieval Saints and Their Interpreters*, ed. Catherine Mooney (Philadelphia: University of Pennsylvania Press, 1999), 126–27, 236–37n. See also the judicious remarks on this issue by Bernard McGinn, *The Flowering of Mysticism: Men and Women in the New Mysticism, 1200–1350* (New York: Crossroad, 1998), 27–30. On the differences between hagiographers' notion of truth and that of modern historians, see Thomas Heffernan, *Sacred Biography: Saints and Their Biographers in the Middle Ages* (New York: Oxford University Press, 1988), 38–71.

16. Heffernan, *Sacred Biography*; Alison Goddard Elliott, *Roads to Paradise: Reading the Lives of the Early Saints* (Hanover, N.H.: University Press of New England, 1987); Gail Ashton, *The Generation of Identity in Late Medieval Hagiography* (London: Routledge, 2000).

1. THE POWERS OF HOLY WOMEN

1. The classic study is Hans von Campenhausen, *Ecclesiastical Authority and Spiritual Power in the Church of the First Three Centuries*, trans. J. A. Baker (Stanford, Calif.: Stanford University Press, 1969). See also John Todd, ed., *Problems of Authority* (London: Darton Longman and Todd, 1962).

2. Hippolyte Delehaye, *Sanctus: Essai sur le culte des saints dans l'antiquité* (Brussels: Société des Bollandistes, 1927), 240. As Pierre Delooz has written, "Etre saint, c'est être

saint *pour les autres*, c'est-à-dire être réputé saint par les autres et jouer un rôle de saint pour les autres" (Delooz, *Sociologie et canonisations*, 7). Kleinberg, *Prophets in Their Own Country*, 1–16; John Coakley, "Friars, Sanctity, and Gender: Mendicant Encounters with Saints, 1250–1325," in *Medieval Masculinities: Regarding Men in the Middle Ages*, ed. Clare Lees (Minneapolis: University of Minnesota Press, 1994), 91–92.

3. André Vauchez, *Sainthood in the Later Middle Ages*, trans. Jean Birrell (Cambridge: Cambridge University Press, 1997), 22–84.

4. Vauchez, *Sainthood*, 106; Thomas Head, *Hagiography and the Cult of Saints: The Diocese of Orléans, 800–1200* (Cambridge: Cambridge University Press, 1990), 1–19.

5. Vauchez, *Sainthood*, 85–103.

6. Vauchez, *Sainthood*, 183–87; Donald Weinstein and Rudolph Bell, *Saints and Society: The Two Worlds of Western Christendom 1000–1700* (Chicago: University of Chicago Press, 1982), 194–219.

7. André Vauchez, "Lay People's Sanctity in Western Europe: Evolution of a Pattern (Twelfth and Thirteenth Centuries)," in *Images of Sainthood in Medieval Europe*, ed. Renate Blumenfeld-Kosinski and Timea Szell (Ithaca, N.Y.: Cornell University Press, 1991), 21–32.

8. Vauchez, *Sainthood*, 207–18.

9. Grundmann, *Religious Movements*, 8.

10. According to Jane Tibbetts Schulenburg's statistical study of early medieval saints, women accounted for 40 percent of French saints between 650 and 750, 39 percent of German saints between 700 and 799, and 40 percent of British saints between 700 and 799. Jane Tibbetts Schulenberg, *Forgetful of Their Sex: Female Sanctity and Society, Ca. 500–1100* (Chicago: University of Chicago Press, 1998), 77.

11. Of the thirteenth-, fourteenth- and fifteenth-century saints in Weinstein and Bell's large sample, 22.6, 23.4, and 27.7 percent, respectively, were female, as distinct from 11.8 percent of twelfth-century saints and 18.1 of sixteenth-century saints. (Note that these figures, based on much wider geographical distribution, are not strictly comparable to Schulenburg's figures for earlier periods, cited in note 10.) Weinstein and Bell, *Saints and Society*, 224, 220.

12. Grundmann, *Religious Movements*, 89–137; Micheline de Fontette, *Les religieuses à l'âge classique du droit canon: Recherches sur les structures juridiques des branches féminines des ordres* (Paris: J. Vrin, 1967).

13. Simone Roisin, *L'Hagiographie cistercienne dans le diocèse de Liège au XIIIe siècle* (Louvain: Bibliothèque de l'Université, 1947); Brenda M. Bolton, "*Vitae Matrum*: A Further Aspect of the *Frauenfrage*," in *Medieval Women*, ed. Derek T. Baker (Oxford: Blackwell, 1978), 253–73; Juliette Dor, Lesley Johnson, and Jocelyn Wogan-Browne, eds., *New Trends in Feminine Spirituality: The Holy Women of Liège and Their Impact* (Turnhout: Brepols, 1999); Walter Simons, *Cities of Ladies: Beguine Communities in the Medieval Low Countries, 1200–1565* (Philadelphia: University of Pennsylvania Press, 2001), 77–79.

14. Società Internazionale di Studi Francescani, *Movimento religioso femminile e francescanesimo nel secolo XII* (Assisi: Società Internazionale di Studi Francescani,

1980); Roberto Rusconi, ed., *Il movimento religioso femminile in Umbria nei secoli XII–XIV* (Perugia: "La Nuova Italia" Editrice, 1984); Anna Benvenuti Papi, *In castro poenitentiae. Santità e società femminile nell'Italia medievale* (Rome: Herder, 1990); Jacques Dalarun, "Hors des sentiers battus. Saintes femmes d'Italie aux XIIIe–XIVe siècles," in *Femmes-Mariage-Lignages, XIIe-XIVe siècles. Mélanges offerts à Georges Duby* (Brussels: De Boeck Université, 1992), 79–102.

15. Vauchez, *Sainthood*, 207–18; Coakley, "Friars, Sanctity, and Gender," 91–105.

16. Vauchez, *Sainthood*, 208–9; Richard Kieckhefer, "Holiness and the Culture of Devotion: Remarks on Some Late Medieval Male Saints," in *Images of Sainthood in Medieval Europe*, ed. Renate Blumenfeld-Kosinski and Timea Szell (Ithaca, N.Y.: Cornell University Press, 1991), 292.

17. F. Vernet, "Biographies spirituelles. IV. Le moyen age," *Dictionnaire de spiritualité, d'ascétique et de mystique*, vol. 1 (Paris: Beauchesne, 1936), cols. 1646–79; Maiju Lehmijoki-Gardner, *Worldly Saints: Social Interaction of Dominican Penitent Women in Italy, 1200–1500* (Helsinki: Suomen Historiallinen Seura, 1999); Michael Goodich, *Vita Perfecta: The Ideal of Sainthood in the Thirteenth Century* (Stuttgart: Anton Hiersemann, 1982), 48–68.

18. Hagiographers' emphasis shifted, as Richard Kieckhefer has observed (using a phrase suggested by Barbara Newman), from what God did "through" the saint to what God did "for" the saint. Kieckhefer, *Unquiet Souls: Fourteenth-Century Saints and Their Religious Milieu* (Chicago: University of Chicago Press, 1984), 10. Peter Brown has written that in the twelfth century, "the supernatural, which had tended to be treated as the main source of the objectified values of the group, came to be regarded as the preserve *par excellence* of the exact opposite; it became the preserve of intensely personal feeling": Peter Brown, "Society and the Supernatural: A Medieval Change," *Daedalus* 104 (1975): 143–44.

19. Sulpicius Severus, *Vie de saint Martin*, ed. Jacques Fontaine, 3 vols. (Paris: Éditions du Cerf, 1967–69); Thomas of Celano, *Vita prima s. Francisci Assisiensis* (Quaracchi: Collegium S. Bonaventurae, 1926); on the points of commonality between the hagiographical portraits of the two saints, see Kenneth Wolf, *The Poverty of Riches: St. Francis of Assisi Reconsidered* (New York: Oxford University Press, 2003), 55–57, 66–67.

20. Vauchez, *Saints, prophètes et visionnaires: Le Pouvoir surnaturel au moyen age* (Paris: Albin Michel, 1999), 56–78; Vauchez, *Sainthood*, 527–34.

21. Alain Boureau has pointed out that human imagination itself came to be a perceived locus of the miraculous in some late-medieval discourse about saints. Boureau, "Miracle, volonté et imagination: La Mutation scolastique (1270–1320)," in *Miracles, prodiges et merveilles au Moyen Age* (Paris: Publications de la Sorbonne, 1995), 159–72.

22. Caroline Walker Bynum, *Fragmentation and Redemption: Essays on Gender and the Human Body in Medieval Religion* (New York: Zone Books, 1991), 181–238.

23. Caroline Walker Bynum, *Holy Feast and Holy Fast*, 13–30; Weinstein and Bell, *Saints and Society*, 220–38; Dyan Elliott, "The Physiology of Rapture and Female Spirituality," in

Medieval Theology and the Natural Body, ed. Peter Biller and A. J. Minnis (Woodbridge, Suffolk: York Medieval Press, 1997), 141–73.

24. Bynum, *Fragmentation and Redemption*, 119–79.

25. Nancy Caciola, *Discerning Spirits: Divine and Demonic Possession in the Middle Ages* (Ithaca, N.Y.: Cornell University Press, 2003), 31–78, 129–75; Elliott, "Physiology of Rapture," 157–73; Catherine Mooney, "Women's Visions, Men's Words: The Portrayal of Holy Women and Men in Fourteenth-Century Italian Hagiography" (PhD diss., Yale University, 1991), 174–223.

26. On the characteristic combination of such themes of Christ-centered and extreme asceticism with those of voluntary poverty and the *vita apostolica* in works both about and by women beginning in the early thirteenth century ("the new mysticism"): McGinn, *The Flowering of Mysticism*, 2–69.

27. Vauchez, *Saints*, 57–66.

28. *VLA* 1.1.10:238; 1.1.11:238–39; 1.2.16:240; 1.1.17:240; 1.1.12–13:239; 1.2.14–15, 18–19:240–41. Alfred Deboutte, "The *Vita Lutgardis* of Thomas of Cantimpré," in *Hidden Springs: Cistercian Monastic Women*, ed. John A. Nichols and Lillian Thomas Shank (N.p.: Cistercian Publications, 1995), 255–81.

29. *VLA* 2.1.3–15:244–47; 2.2.25–6:249–50; 3.1.8:257–58; 3.2.15:260.

30. *VLA* 2.2.24, 27, 31:249–50.

31. *VLA* 3.2.15–16:260.

32. *VLA* 2.1.10–11:245–46.

33. *VLA* 2.2.33:250; 2.3.34:251.

34. *VLA* 2.3.35–36:251; 3.1.6:257; cf. 3.1.4–5:246–47.

35. Mooney, "Women's Visions," 135–73; *VLA* 2.2.27:250.

36. Thomas Aquinas, *Summa Theologiae* 2a2ae, quaest. 177, art. 2 ("whether the charism of wisdom in speech and knowledge pertains to women also"), in Blackfriars edition, vol. 45, ed. and tr. Roland Potter (New York: McGraw Hill; and London: Eyre & Spottiswoode, 1970), 132–35; Rosalynn Voaden, *God's Words, Women's Voices: The Discernment of Spirits in the Writing of Late-Medieval Women Visionaries* (York: York Medieval Press, 1999), 34–40; A. J. Minnis, "*De impedimento sexus*: Women's Bodies and Medieval Impediments to Ordination," in *Medieval Theology and the Natural Body*, ed. Peter Biller and A. J. Minnis (Woodbridge: York Medieval Press, 1997), 117–18, 128; Alcuin Blamires, "Women and Preaching in Medieval Orthodoxy, Heresy, and Saints' Lives," *Viator* 26 (1995): 145–46; Anneke B. Mulder-Bakker, "The Prime of Their Lives: Women and Age, Wisdom, and Religious Careers in Northern Europe," in *New Trends in Feminine Spirituality: The Holy Women of Liège and Their Impact*, ed. Juliette Dor, Lesley Johnson, and Jocelyn Wogan-Browne (Turnhout: Brepols, 1999), 223–27; Bernard McGinn, "Donne mistiche ed autorità esoterica nel XIV secolo," in *Poteri carismatici e informali: Chiesa e società medioevali*, ed. Agostino Bagliani and André Vauchez (Palermo: Sellerio, 1992), 154–56; Alcuin Blamires and C. W. Marx, "Woman Not to Preach: A Disputation in British Library MS Harley 31," *Journal of Medieval Latin* 3 (1993): 34–63; Francine Cardman, "The Medieval Question of Women and Orders," *The Thomist* 42 (1978): 582–99.

37. Peter Dinzelbacher, 'Revelationes' (Turnhout: Brepols, 1991), 31–34.

38. VH 24:392. On Humiliana see Anna Benvenuti Papi, "Umiliana dei Cerchi. Nascità di un culto nella Firenze del Dugento," Studi Francescani 77 (1980): 87–117.

39. Thomas of Cantimpré, Vita Christinae Mirabilis 26–28, AA SS, July, 5:655. Robert Sweetman, "Christine of Saint-Trond's Preaching Apostolate: Thomas of Cantimpré's Hagiographical Method Revisited," Vox Benedictina 9 (1992): 68–77.

40. Peter of St. Mary of Alvastra and Peter of Skänninge, Vita sanctae Birgittae auctoribus... confessoribus Birgittae, in Scriptores rerum suecicarum medii aevi, ed. Claudius Annerstedt, vol. 3 part 2 (Uppsala, 1876), 203; LM 2.4.153.

41. Vita Humilitatis 14, AA SS, May, 5:216.

42. Peter of St. Mary of Alvastra and Peter of Skänninge, Vita sanctae Birgittae, 196–97.

43. Conrad of Castellerio, Vita Benevenutae de Bojanis 48, in AA SS, October, 13:162.

44. On devout women as intercessors for souls in purgatory, see Newman, From Virile Woman to WomanChrist, 108–36.

45. Henry of Rheims, Vita Coletae 108–09, AA SS, March, 1:563–64; Bynum, Holy Feast and Holy Fast, 227–37.

46. André Vauchez, The Laity in the Middle Ages: Religious Beliefs and Devotional Practices, ed. Daniel E. Bornstein, trans. Margery J. Schneider (Notre Dame, Ind.: University of Notre Dame Press, 1993) 255–64.

47. Thomas of Cantimpré, Vita Christinae Mirabilis 44, 5:657.

48. Kathryn Kerby-Fulton, "Prophet and Reformer," in Voice of the Living Light: Hildegard of Bingen and Her World, ed. Barbara Newman (Berkeley: University of California Press, 1998), 70–90.

49. Vauchez, The Laity in the Middle Ages, 235.

50. HBE 90R:104; GGE 19.121–22, 173–74 (questions 6 and 20): 239–40. She also received, at the request of the monks of Disibodenberg, revelations about the otherwise obscure life of their patron saint St. Disibod. HBE 74R:161–62.

51. LV 3.16:68–69.

52. Blamires, "Women and Preaching," 149–52; Minnis, "De Impedimento Sexus," 134–39; and see Beverly Mayne Kienzle and Pamela J. Walker, eds., Women Preachers and Prophets Through Two Millennia of Christianity (Berkeley: University of California Press, 1998).

53. John Hilary Martin, "The Ordination of Women and the Theologians in the Middle Ages," in A History of Women and Ordination, vol. 1, ed. Bernard Cooke and Gary Macy (Lanham, Md.: Scarecrow, 2002), 31–109; McNamara, "The Herrenfrage," 7, 22. See also Elliott, Fallen Bodies, 81–126; Jacques Dalarun, "The Clerical Gaze," in Silences of the Middle Ages, ed. C. Klapisch-Zuber, vol. 2 of A History of Women in the West, ed. George Duby and Michelle Perrot (Cambridge, Mass.: Harvard University Press, 1992), 15–42; Coakley, "Friars, Sanctity and Gender," 93–94.

54. Peter Dinzelbacher, Mittelalterliche Frauenmystik, 31–35; Jeffrey Hamburger, "The Liber Miraculorum of Unterlinden: An Icon in Its Convent Setting," in The

Sacred Image East and West, ed. Robert Ousterhout and Leslie Brubaker (Urbana: University of Illinois Press, 1995), 167, 188n.

55. "Sa parole est prophétie; / S'ele rit, c'est compaignie; / S'ele pleure, dévocion; / s'ele dort, ele est ravie; / S'el songe, c'est vision; / S'ele ment, non créeiz mie": Rutebeuf, *Oeuvres complètes*, tome 1, ed. Michel Zink (Paris: Bordas, 1989), 240; Ernest W. McDonnell, *The Beguines and Beghards in Medieval Culture with Special Emphasis on the Belgian Scene* (New Brunswick, N.J.: Rutgers University Press, 1954), 472; Renate Blumenfeld-Kosinski, "Satirical Views of the Beguines in Northern French Literature," in *New Trends in Feminine Spirituality: The Holy Women of Liège and Their Impact*, ed. Juliette Dor, Lesley Johnson, and Jocelyn Wogan-Browne (Turnhout: Brepols, 1999), 237–49.

56. Robert Lerner, *The Heresy of the Free Spirit in the Later Middle Ages* (Notre Dame, Ind.: Notre Dame University Press, 1972), 68–78.

57. Elliott, "Physiology of Rapture," 163.

58. Dyan Elliott, *Proving Woman: Female Spirituality and Inquisitional Culture in the Later Middle Ages* (Princeton, N.J.: Princeton University Press, 2004), 233–303; Caciola, *Discerning Spirits*, 274–319; Peter Dinzelbacher, *Heilige oder Hexen? Schicksale auffälliger Frauen in Mittelalter und Früneuzeit* (Zürich: Artemis & Winkler, 1995), 114–15, 153–47; Richard Kieckhefer, "The Holy and the Unholy: Sainthood, Witchcraft, and Magic in Late Medieval Europe," in *Christendom and Its Discontents: Exclusion, Persecution, and Rebellion, 1000–1500*, ed. Scott Waugh and Peter Diehl (Cambridge: Cambridge University Press, 1996), 310–37.

59. See for example, Claire Sahlin, *Birgitta of Sweden and the Voice of Prophecy* (Woodbridge: Boydell, 2001), 113–20.

60. Elliott, *Proving Woman*, 85–116.

61. *VH* 1–8:387–88; 8:388. See note 38.

62. *VH* 18:391; 21:391–92.

63. *VH* 24:392.

64. "Fratre Michaele quadam die praesente ipsa, et non habente devotionem, quasi motus intrinsecus dixit ei: Filia mea, roga pro me, quia ego sum totus siccus. Cui obediens obedientiae filia, levatis oculis in coelum oravit ad Dominum. Cui statim tanta infusa est gratia, quod evidentissime appareret quod, recipere non posset infusae gratiae plenitudinem." *VH* 24:392. In the same passage, Vito cites an instance in which she similarly procured an experience of devotion for a matron.

65. C. H. Talbot, introduction to *VCM* 14–15, 6. See Thomas Head, "The Marriages of Christina of Markyate," *Viator* 21 (1990): 71–95; Christopher J. Holdsworth, "Christina of Markyate," in *Medieval Women*, ed. Derek T. Baker (Oxford: Blackwell, 1978), ed., 185–204; Sharon K. Elkins, *Holy Women of Twelfth-Century England* (Chapel Hill: University of North Carolina Press, 1988), 27–38; Samuel Fanous and Henrietta Leyser, eds., *Christina of Markyate: A Twelfth-Century Holy Woman* (New York: Routledge, 2004).

66. "In camino tamen paupertatis tribulabatur adhuc Christi virgo illarum egens rerum quarum egestas virtutes non minuit sed accumulat.... Cum vero secretorum

ille conscius oportunum censuit ut illi et in hiis subveniret: hoc modo disposuit."
VCM 54:132. The extent of Geoffrey's material aid of Christine apparently engen-
dered opposition at St. Albans: Rachel Koopmans, "The Conclusion of Christina of
Markyate's Vita," *Journal of Ecclesiastical History* 51 (2000): 663–98.

67. "Erat amor mutuus. sed cuiusque pro modo sanctitatis. Illam ipse in exterioribus sustentabat. ipsum illa suis sanctis precibus attencius Deo commendabat. Nec
minus immo amplius de ipso quam de se sollicita. tanto studio eius invigilabat sa-
luti ut quod dictu mirum est v[ix vel propius] vel remocius degens facto aut verbis
Deum offendisset. quin illa per spiritum idem in instanti sciret. Nec dissimulabat cum
terro[re] presentem arguere. quando senciebat absentem gravius deliquisse. meliora
reputans amici vulnera. quam inimici blandimenta." *VCM* 58:138–40.

68. *VCM* 56:134–36.

69. "Quo viso cultrix Dei roborata non destitit a precibus donec m[emo]ratum
virum. vel possidere columbam. vel possessum cerneret a columba." *VCM* 69:156.

70. *VCM* 63:146.

71. *VCM* 71–74:160–70.

72. "Cumque respiceret ad altare vidit benignum Ihesum cum habitu et vultu
quo propiciatur peccatoribus altario assistere. Giransque oculos vidit illum pro quo
laborabat familiarem suum ad dexteram suam que sinistra erat Domini consistere.
Cumque ad orandum decumberent. quoniam sinistra virginis ad dexteram erat
dominiut pote versis vultibus: timens ne ad sinistram esset divinam. estuare cepit.
quomodo ad dexteram transferri valeret. intollerabile ferens [remotiorem] dilectum
suum. Dei dextere se esse coniunctiorem. Dexteram enim Dei digniorem ipsius cer-
nebat partem. Nec tamen dilecto suo in oracione decumbenti. superferri volebat. sed
quovis alio modo transferri. Hoc ita permota desiderio. intellexit protinus illam se
comprehendisse dexteram quam in cunctis et pre cunctis sibi querebat clementem
unde inter cetera que sepius conferebant edificantia colloquia. illi suo familiari rep-
licare solebat. solam esse Dei dileccionem in qua nullus alium sibimet preferre iuste
liceat." *VCM* 79:181–82.

73. "Multa mea gloriacio si in presenti mei oblita sibi me presentes. ob cuius presencie dulcedinem hic me presenetem sentire non prevales." *VCM* 68:154.

74. John Coakley, "Gender and the Authority of Friars: The Significance of Holy
Women for Thirteenth-Century Franciscans and Dominicans," *Church History* 60
(1991): 445–60.

75. On the scope of late-medieval prophecy, male and female: Vauchez, *Saints*,
114–48; Vauchez, ed., "Les Textes prophétiques et la prophétie en occident (Xiie–Xvie
s.)," *Mélanges de l'École Française de Rome*, 102 (1990): 287–685. The conditions for
the exercise of informal powers could indeed be established in terms other than those
of gender. Recent work by Martha Newman implies that in thirteenth-century Cistercian hagiography, it was not only women but also institutionally powerless lay
brothers—whose difference from monks was a matter of status and literacy rather
than gender—who became potential figures of informal power. Martha G. Newman,
"Crucified by the Virtues: Monks, Lay Brothers, and Women in Thirteenth-Century

Cistercian Saints' Lives," in *Gender and Difference in the Middle Ages*, ed. Sharon Farmer and Carol Braun Pasternak (Minneapolis: University of Minnesota Press, 2003), 182–201.

76. André Vauchez, "Les Pouvoirs informels dans l'église aux derniers siècles du moyen âge: Visionnaires, prophètes et mystiques," *Mélanges de l'Ecole Française de Rome—Moyen Age, Temps Modernes* 96 (1984): 281. See also Vauchez, introduction to *Poteri carismatici e informali: Chiesa e società medioevali*, ed. Agostino Bagliani and André Vauchez (Palermo: Sellerio, 1992), 9–14; Vauchez, *Saints*, 221–29.

77. Max Weber, *Economy and Society*, ed. Guenther Roth and Klaus Wittig, 2 vols. (Berkeley: University of California Press, 1978), 1:241–54. Weber's distinction between institutions and charisma may itself however be implicitly more fluid than his definitions suggest: see S. N. Eisenstadt, ed., *Max Weber on Charisma and Institution Building* (Chicago: University of Chicago Press), 1968), esp. xix–xxii. See also the comments of Vauchez, introduction to *Poteri carismatici*, 9–12, and *Saints*, 223.

78. On the powers of bishops, see James L. Ash Jr., "The Decline of Ecstatic Prophecy in the Early Church," *Theological Studies* 37 (1976): 227–53; František Graus, *Volk, Herrscher und Heiliger im Reich der Merowinger* (Prague: Nakladatlství Československé akademie věd, 1965); Vauchez, *Saints*, 223–25.

79. Elliott, *Proving Woman*.

80. Yves Congar, "The Historical Development of Authority in the Church: Points for Christian Reflection," in *Problems of Authority*, ed. John Todd (London: Darton Longman and Todd, 1962), 130.

81. Vauchez, *Saints*, 226.

2. REVELATION AND AUTHORITY IN EKBERT AND ELISABETH OF SCHÖNAU

1. *LV* 1.1:1.

2. Apparently in 1154, at a moment after her angel had rebuked her for not making her revelations known, she gave to her abbot "a part of the present book which you, brother, had left with me [partem libelli presentis, quam apud me frater reliqueras]," and which she previously had told him she wished to keep secret during her lifetime: *LV* 1.78:37–38. Other sisters in the monastery seem also to have had some role, in this early period, in writing the visions; Elisabeth says that earlier in that same year, after a receiving a prophecy from her angel, "I made a sign to the sisters that…they put these words in writing [Ego autem signum feci sororibus, ut…verba ista scripto exciperent]." *LV* 1.67:32–33. Cf. Emecho of Schönau, *Vita Eckeberti*, ed. S. Widmann, *Neues Archiv der Gesellschaft für ältere deutsche Geschichtskunde* 11 (1886): 448–50.

3. Anne Clark, *Elisabeth of Schönau: A Twelfth-Century Visionary* (Philadelphia: University of Pennsylvania Press, 1992), 129–35.

4. According to Ekbert she was twenty-three and had been eleven years in the monastery in 1152 when the visions began. *LV* prol.:1.

5. In his account of Elisabeth's death, Ekbert pictures her sisters asking her to recommend a replacement for herself: "Most beloved mistress, since already we can no longer have you for ourselves, we beg of you to name for us some person among us who could have direction over us with the will of God and we will joyfully receive her with all good will [Domina dilectissima, quando quidem iam amplius habere non possumus vos ipsam, rogamus, ut denominetis nobis aliquam personam inter nos, que magisterium super nos cum dei voluntate possit habere, et hanc cum omni benivolentia gratantissime suscipiemus]." *De obitu* 270.

6. Her death occurred either in 1164 or 1165, but the latter year is more likely. See the discussion in Clark, *Elisabeth*, 25–26.

7. Peter Dinzelbacher, *Mittelalterliche Frauenmystik*, 92–96; cf. Dinzelbacher, *Vision und Visionsliteratur im Mittelalter* (Stuttgart: Anton Hiersemann, 1981), 37–38.

8. Bishop Ekbert of Münster, who was great-uncle of Elisabeth and of our Ekbert and was also the latter's godfather, died in 1132. Kurt Köster, "Elisabeth von Schönau: Leben, Persönlichkeit und Visionäre Werk," in *Schönauer Elisabeth Jubiläum 1965. Festschrift anläßlich des achthundertjährigen Todestages der Heiligen Elisabeth von Schönau*, ed. Prämonstratenser-Chorherrenstift Tepl in Kloster Schönau (Limburg: Pallottiner Druckerei, 1965), 19.

9. Rainald of Dassel is known to have been a student in Paris between 1140 and 1146 (see note 10). Köster, "Leben, Persönlichkeit und visionäre Werk," 19.

10. In his surviving letter to Rainald of Dassel, Ekbert refers to their student days. *Epistola Ecberti ad Reinoldum Coloniensem electum*, in *Die Visionen der Hl. Elisabeth und die Schriften der Abte Ekbert und Emecho von Schönau*, ed. F. W. E. Roth (Brünn: Verlag der Studien aus dem Benedictiner- und Cisterciener Orden, 1884), 311–12. The *Sermones contra Catharos* (see note 52) is addressed to Rainald.

11. For a list of Ekbert's works, see Köster, "Ekbert von Schönau," *Die deutsche Literatur des Mittelalters: Verfasserlexikon* 2 (1980): 437–39.

12. Kurt Köster, "Das visionäre Werk Elisabeths von Schönau: Studien zu Entstehung, Überlieferung und Wirkung in der mittelalterlichen Welt," *Archiv für Mittelrheinische Kirchengeschichte* 4 (1952): 84–101; Köster, "Elisabeth von Schönau: Werk und Wirkung im Spiegel der mittelalterlichen handschriftlichen Überlieferung," *Archiv für Mittelrheinische Kirchengeschichte* 3 (1951): 243–315 (an inventory of the known manuscripts); Clark, *Elisabeth*, 137–45 (revising Köster's stemma).

13. This redaction, "Redaction E" in Köster's stemma, formed the basis of Roth's edition: F. W. E. Roth, ed., *Die Visionen der Hl. Elisabeth und die Schriften der Abte Ekbert und Emecho von Schönau* (Brünn: Verlag der Studien aus dem Benedictiner- und Cisterciener Orden, 1884). As Köster observes, within the copious manuscript witnesses to Elisabeth's work in the medieval centuries—including some 150 MSS, of which "nearly 50" include some redaction of the collection—this redaction is known only from three manuscripts, of which two were produced at Schönau (Wiesbaden, Nassauische Landesbibliothek 3 [now lost], and 4), such that only one (Vienna, Österr. Nationalbibliothek 488) shows it to have had any influence beyond Schönau (cf. Köster, "Werk und Wirkung," 274–76 [MSS 36–38]); indeed, in terms of influence,

as Köster notes, this redaction had the "least importance of any of the redactions" (Köster, "Entstehung, Überlieferung und Wirkung," 85, 93). Nonetheless it seems to represent Ekbert's summing-up of his work on the visions.

14. In Roth, *Die Visionen*, 1–87 (cited as *LV*); Köster, "Entstehung, Überlieferung und Wirkung," 83, calls these books "diaries" and is followed by Clark, *Elisabeth*, 31 and passim.

15. Elisabeth of Schönau, *Liber viarum dei*, in *Die Visionen der Hl. Elisabeth und die Schriften der Abte Ekbert und Emecho von Schönau*, ed. F. W. E. Roth (Brünn: Verlag der Studien aus dem Benedictiner- und Cisterciener Orden, 1884), 88–122 (cited as *LVD*).

16. In Roth's edition, the vision appears in *LV* 2.31:53–55.

17. Elisabeth of Schönau, *Liber revelationum Elisabeth de sacro exercitu virginum Coloniensium*, in *Die Visionen der Hl. Elisabeth und die Schriften der Abte Ekbert und Emecho von Schönau*, ed. F. W. E. Roth (Brünn: Verlag der Studien aus dem Benedictiner- und Cisterciener Orden, 1884), 123–38 (cited as *LR*)

18. Elisabeth of Schönau, *Epistole*, in *Die Visionen der Hl. Elisabeth und die Schriften der Abte Ekbert und Emecho von Schönau*, ed. F. W. E. Roth (Brünn: Verlag der Studien aus dem Benedictiner- und Cisterciener Orden, 1884), 139–153 (cited as *ESE*).

19. Ekbert of Schönau, *Epistola Eckeberti ad cognatas suas de obitu domine Elisabeth*, in *Die Visionen der Hl. Elisabeth und die Schriften der Abte Ekbert und Emecho von Schönau*, ed. F. W. E. Roth (Brünn: Verlag der Studien aus dem Benedictiner- und Cisterciener Orden, 1884), 263–78 (cited as *De obitu*)

20. *LV* 1.prol.:1; *LV* 1.1:1–2. *De obitu* 263–65 (on her influence), 265–66, 268, 270–71, 271–73 (on himself as eyewitness).

21. *LV* 3.21:79–86.

22. Clark, *Elisabeth*, 32–33, 55; Clark, "Repression or Collaboration? The Case of Elisabeth and Ekbert of Schönau," in *Christendom and Its Discontents: Exclusion, Persecution, and Rebellion, 1000–1500*, ed. Scott L. Waugh and Peter D. Diehl (Cambridge: Cambridge University Press, 1996), 58–59; Kurt Köster, "Leben, Persönlichkeit, und visionäres Werk," 26–27.

23. *LV* 1.1:2–3; *LV* 1.48:24–25; *LV* 1.50:25–26; *LV* 1.53:26–27.

24. *LV* 3.11:66, 2.22:50 (kinfolk and associates); e.g., *LV* 3.8:63–65; *LV* 3.17–18:69–70; *ESE* 14:17 (questions).

25. *LV* 3.5:62–63; similarly she is seen delaying, apparently for reflection, before reporting an answer to the question (prompted by an unspecified person) whether the Virgin was corporeally assumed into heaven (*LV* 2.31:53); Clark, *Elisabeth*, 57–59; Clark, "Repression or Collaboration?" 160–61; Joan M. Ferrante, *To the Glory of Her Sex: Women's Roles in the Composition of Medieval Texts* (Bloomington: Indiana University Press, 1997), 141–52. In another instance, in a letter to the abbot of Odenheim identifying the relics of the Ursuline martyr in that monastery's possession as one "Viventia," Ekbert's presence serves as a prop for her admission of an error: immediately after this martyr's appearance to her, she reported the name to Ekbert as "Convivia," and the martyr, who apparently listened to her conversations with her brother, ap-

peared soon afterward to correct her. Text in Philibert Schmitz, "'Visions' inédites de Sainte Elisabeth de Schönau," *Revue Bénédictine* 47 (1935): 182–83. See Dinzelbacher, *Mittelalterliche Frauenmystik*, 91.

26. *LV* 3.2:57–59; *LV* 3.16:69; *LR* 14:130; *LR* 27:137.

27. "Non potes intelligere, quid ista significent, sed dic doctoribus, qui legunt scripturas; ipsi sciunt" (*LV* 1.40:21). Dinzelbacher, *Mittelalterliche Frauenmystik*, 98–101, points out that the vision gives the traditional image of the wheel of fortune a new twist in its amalgamation of added biblical imagery.

28. "Nunc igitur, amantissime frater, hunc tibi queso laborem assume, ut scripturas divinas scruteris, et congruam ex eis interpretationem visionis huius coneris invenire. Tibi enim fortassis a domino reservata est" (*LV* 1.40:21). Cf. *LV* 3.39:79.

29. "Non sum doctor, non sum dispensator misteriorum dei, sed homo pusillus et exigui sensus, et minor ad intelligentiam secretorum dei" (*LV* 3.31:79).

30. *LV* 3.31:80–81.

31. The angel replies that they take on visible forms for the specific purpose of being perceived by humans, just as the trinity took on human form to appear to Abraham (Gen. 18:1–2) (*LV* 3.15:68). This is an analogy that Lombard had rejected, asserting instead that angels, though normally invisible are, unlike God, corporeal; cf. Peter Lombard, *Sententiae in IV libris distinctae* 2.8.3–4 (Grottaferrata [Rome]: Editiones Collegii S. Bonaventurae ad Claras Aquas, 1971–81), vol. 1, 368–70. On discussions of angels by Lombard and other scholastic theologians, see Marcia L. Colish, *Peter Lombard* (Leiden: Brill, 1994), 303–97, and Colish, "Early Scholastic Angelology," *Recherches de théologie ancienne et médiévale* 62 (1995): 80–109.

32. The answers are yes and no, respectively (*LV* 3.16:68–69). Lombard had held on the contrary that the angels' division into orders postdated the apostasy: Lombard, *Sententiae*, 2.9.5, cols. 670–71.

33. "Sicut a doctiori premonita fueram." The answer is affirmative (*LV* 3.16:68). The question is unaddressed in Lombard's *Sententiae*.

34. Elisabeth's angel says the chief is Michael. *LV* 3.16:69. Lombard had remained unresolved whether angels' names identified particular individuals or were interchangeable according to circumstance: Lombard, *Sententiae*, 2.10.2:378–793.

35. The angel's answers are that everyone has a good angel and a bad angel, assigned at baptism; after death the angels are sometimes reassigned, sometimes not. *LV* 3.18:70. Cf. Lombard, *Sententiae*, 2.11.1–2:379–83.

36. "Hec dices fratri tuo, et quod iterum interrogaverit, dicito mihi" (*LV* 3.17:69). Lombard held instead that the number of blessed souls who will join the angels will equal the number of *persevering* angels. Lombard, *Sententiae*, 2.9.7:376.

37. "Interrogavi igitur alia vice de superiori versu" (*LV* 3.17:69–70). A "more learned" prompter also appears at *LV* 3.8:63.

38. *LV* 3.18:70.

39. "Sicut premonita fueram a fratre meo, qui eadem hora divinum apud nos celebrabat officium." The Virgin's answer is that this is not to be revealed, though she does say that Origen's errors were committed not out of malice but out of excess

fervor, and that his soul currently received special grace at the Marian feasts (*LV* 3.5:62–63).

40. *LV* 3.9:65. Cf. letter 6 (to the abbot of Deutz): "I reminded [the angel] about you, as I had been directed by my brother [feci memoriam vestri apud eum [sc. angelum] sicut premonita fueram a fratre meo]" (*ESE* 6:142)

41. *LV* 2.28:52–53.

42. "Sicut ab uno ex senioribus nostris premonita fuera" (*LV* 2.31:53). Scholars have indeed tended to assume that the figure is Ekbert: thus Köster, "Leben, Persönlichkeit, und visionäres Werk," 30; and Clark, *Elisabeth*, 60. There are, in addition, questions that are not attributed to any prompter at all but also convey a sense of similar concerns on behalf of Ekbert or others around her, for instance Elisabeth's question whether the bodies of the saints whose tombs were opened at Christ's Passion arose then or rather at his resurrection, a matter that is ambiguous in Matthew 27:52–53. *LV* 3.14:68.

43. "Rogavit me germanus meus, ut sciscitarer ab angelo" (*LVD* 13:103).

44. "Sicut premonita fueram"; "ut tanto congruentius etiam ad significandam beatam matrem eius visio posset aptari" (*LV* 3.4:61, 62). Clark comments that "Elisabeth's further reflection on this image, coaxed by Ekbert, produced the more conventional interpretation" ("Repression or Collaboration?" 163). See also Clark, *Elisabeth*, 6; Clark, "Holy Woman or Unworthy Vessel? The Representations of Elisabeth of Schönau," in *Gendered Voices: Medieval Saints and Their Interpreters*, ed. Catherine M. Mooney (Philadelphia: University of Pennsylvania Press, 1999), 38–39; Elisabeth Gössmann, "Das Menschenbild der Hilegard von Bingen und Elisabeth von Schönau vor dem Hintergrund der Frühscholastischen Anthropologie," in *Frauenmystik im Mittelalter*, ed. Peter Dinzelbacher and Dieter R. Bauer (Ostfildern: Schwabenverlag, 1985), 24–47; Gertrud Jaron Lewis, "Christus als Frau: Eine Vision Elisabeths von Schönau," *Jahrbuch für internationale Germanistik* 15 (1983): 70–80.

45. *LV* 1.29:16; "collega fratris mei in Bunna," *LV* 2.22:50; Ekbert, *Epistola Ecberti ad Reinoldum*, 311–12. The identity of this Adam is unclear. See Raoul Manselli, "Ecberto di Schönau e l'eresia catara in Germania alla metà del secolo XII," in *Arte e storia: Studi in onore di Leonello Vincenti* (Turin: Giapichelli Editore, 1965), 314; and Clark, *Elisabeth*, 155 n. 32. *LV* 1.55:28–29.

46. Ekbert, *Ad beatam virginem deiparam sermo panegyricus*, PL 95:1514D–1519A; H. Barré, "Une prière d'Ekbert de Schönau au saint coeur de Marie," *Ephemerides mariologicae* 2 (1952): 409–23; Ekbert, *Stimulus dilectionis*, in *Die Visionen der Hl. Elisabeth und die Schriften der Abte Ekbert und Emecho von Schönau*, ed. F. W. E. Roth (Brünn: Verlag der Studien aus dem Benedictiner- und Cisterciener Orden, 1884), 293–311; P. F. O'Connell, "Eckbert of Schönau and the *Lignum Vitae* of St. Bonaventure," *Revue Bénédictine* 101 (1991): 341–82.; Thomas H. Bestul, *Texts of the Passion: Latin Devotional Literature and Medieval Society* (Philadelphia: University of Pennsylvania Press, 1996), 40–41. Other devotional treatises of Ekbert also display the immediacy of first-person narrative: *Salutacio ad sanctam crucem*, in *Die Visionen der Hl. Elisabeth und die Schriften der Abte Ekbert und Emecho von Schönau*, ed. F. W. E. Roth (Brünn: Verlag

der Studien aus dem Benedictiner- und Cisterciener Orden, 1884), 284–86. Ekbert's Mariological commentaries on the Annunciation and the Magnificat, "Et ait Maria ..." [Commentary on the Magnificat], in *Die Visionen der Hl. Elisabeth und die Schriften der Abte Ekbert und Emecho von Schönau*, ed. F. W. E. Roth (Brünn: Verlag der Studien aus dem Benedictiner- und Cisterciener Orden, 1884), 230–47 and 248–263, are thematically related to these works, though they lack first-person reflection.

47. Ekbert, *Stimulus dilectionis*, 293–94. "Ego homo perditus, totius contricionis, totius confusionis tue tibi causa extiti. Ego domine uvam acerbam comedi, et dentes tui obstupuerunt, quia, que non rapuisti, tunc exsolvebas" (298); ibid., 301–2.

48. Clark, "Holy Woman," 45–46.

49. "Que me peperit in lucem inexperte novitatis, que me traxit ad familiare ministerium Jesu domini mei, que ore mellifluo consolationes et instructiones dei de cele afferre solebat ad me, et gustare faciebat cor meum primicias dulcedinis abscondite sanctis in deo" (*De obitu* 263).

50. "Non ego nunc presumo ad similitudinem prophete: 'orate, ut fiat spiritus tuus duplex in me,' sed si simpliciter mihi dare spiritum tuum dominus vellet, sufficeret mihi" (*De obitu* 271).

51. "Posuit autem deus in ore duorum testium hoc verbum de nomine prefati martiris, quomodo et quod hoc esset nomen eius, et quod filius regis fuisset, eidem fratri, per quem allata fuerant corpora, in precedenti nocte per visionem fuerat revelatum" (*LR* 15:131). Ekbert also reported, at the end of the Ursuline revelations in redactions A and B (but omitted in later redactions) that he saw an extraordinary red flame appear three times above the altar at Deutz at which, on the same day, he consecrated one of the visions. But this appears to be only a sign rather than a substantive revelation on the order of the present example, pace Köster, "Enstehung, Überlieferung und Wirkung," 96.

52. Ekbert of Schönau, *Sermones contra Catharos*, PL 195:11–102; on Ekbert and Cathars at Bonn, see Ekbert, *Sermones contra Catharos*, preface, 11.8; Raoul Manselli, "Amicizia spirituale ed adzione pastorale nella Germania del sec. XII: Ildegarde di Bingen, Elisabetta ed Eckberto di Schönau contra l'eresia catara," *Studi e matierali di storia delle religioni* 38 (1967): 302–13; Elisabeth's prophecy: *LV* 3.25:76.

53. *LV*, 1.59:29.

54. Emecho, *Vita Eckeberti*, 449. See Clark, *Elisabeth*, 33.

55. *LV* 2.25–26:51–52. Clark, *Elisabeth*, 33.

56. "Satis mihi gloria mundi arridebat, satis plena manu rerum temporalium copias supernus provisor michi fundebat, dum adhuc essem canonicus in ecclesia Bunnensi. Si nunc, ex quo me totum conieci in gremium domini, et solo ipsius amore, nulla necessitate, nulla coactus infirmitate, monasticam vitam ab annis novem amplexatus sum, reciacula mendaciorum texo, pro captando michi ac sorori mee vento inanis glorie aut vili lucello temporalis subsidii, sim ego, quod absit, iudicio dei et hominum velut sal, quod evanuit": Ekbert, *Epistola ad eundem abbatem* [of Reinhusen], in *Die Visionen der Hl. Elisabeth und die Schriften der Abte Ekbert und Emecho von Schönau*, ed. F. W. E. Roth (Brünn: Verlag der Studien aus dem Benedictiner- und Cisterciener Orden, 1884), 318.

57. "Quia sciebat eum ab infancia delicate educatum"; "vidit in spiritu angelum Domini prope eum assistemtem et sexhortantem eum ad hanc ipsam abrenunciationem" (Emecho, *Vita Eckeberti*, 450).

58. In *LV* 2.5 she is shown receiving absolution from the abbot, to whom the angel refers as her "spiritual father," a title nowhere applied to Ekbert in these texts. She also confesses to the abbot on her deathbed (*De obitu* 268). Clark, *Elisabeth*, 55. Clark elsewhere calls attention to Ekbert's lack of interest in Elisabeth's "piety" ("Holy Woman," 45–46).

59. "Quoniam igitur omnia, que circa ipsam gesta sunt, ad gloriam dei et ad edificationem fidelium pertinere visa sunt, in presenti libello ex magna parte conscripta sunt iuxta narrationem ipsius, qua uni ex fratribus suis de ordine clericorum, quem pre ceteris familiarem habebat, singula exposuit. Cum enim ab inquirentibus multa occultaret, eo quod esset timorata valde et humillima spiritu, huic diligenter omnia investganti et memorie ea tradere cupienti germanitatis et dilectionis gratia, et abbatis iussione cuncta familiariter enarrare coacta est" (*LV* 1.1: 2).

60. See note 2.

61. "Ego autem Eckebertus, germanus ancille dei mirificentia dei ad cenobium Sconaugiense de Bunna attractus, et primum quidem monachus, deinde autem gratia dei ad abbatiam vocatus, conscripsi omnia hec, et alia, que de revelationibus eius leguntur, ita quidem, ut ubi erant latina verba angeli immutata relinquerem, ubi vero teutonica erant, in latinum transferrem, prout expressius, potui, nihil mea presumptione adiungens, nihil favoris humani, nihil terreni commodi querens, testis mihi est dus, cui nuda et aperta sunt omnia" (*LV* prologue:1). On the language of Elisabeth's visions, see Clark, "Repression or Collaboration?" 156.

62. "Fateor autem, quia multa magnifica ac valde miranda, et que multorum edificationi proficere possent, in negligentiam ire permisi, tum pro malicia detrahentium, que tedio et inercia me affecit, tum pre occupatione claustralis negotii, tum etiam pre penuria pergameni" (*Epistola ad eundem abbatem*, 318–19).

63. Emecho, *Vita Eckeberti*, 448–49. Clark, *Elisabeth of Schönau*, 51–53.

64. The vision appears in what Köster calls Redaction B (Köster, "Enstehung, Überlieferung und Wirkung," 95). Text: F. W. E. Roth, "Aus einer Handschrift der Schriften der Heiligen Elisabeth von Schönau," *Neues Archiv der Gesellschaft für ältere Deutsche Geschichtskunde* 36 (1911): 219–25. Clark, "Holy Woman," 37.

65. Köster, "Enstehung, Überlieferung und Wirkung," 96–97; Köster, "Leben, Persönlichkeit, und visionäres Werk," 34; Clark, "Repression or Collaboration?" 156–57.

66. The answer is that the Host was preserved by an angel and that masses should be offered in thanksgiving by the Deutz community for forty days (*ESE* 6:141–42).

67. The answer applies the qualities of cinnamon (sweet yet strong) and balsam (soothing) metaphorically to God. *ESE* 14:147–48.

68. On Gerlach's role in the Ursuline revelations: *LR* 1:123; 4:124; 15:131; *ESE* 5:141.

69. "Rogavi inquam immo multum et diu renitentem propter linguas detrahentium, magno instantia coegi, et qui absconditorum est cognitor, per eam michi, quod querebam aperuit" (*LR* 22:135).

70. *LR* 22:135–37.

71. "Hoc autem feci propter quendam cantum, quem ostenderatis mihi ante aliquot dies, cum essem apud vos, ex quo datur intelligi, quoniam sic fuisset" (*LR* 22:137).

72. "Stetit quasi cum indignatione avertens faciem ab ea…. 'Frater tuus me et fratres meos offendit. Sciebat enim per historias, quoniam Thebea legio ante tempus sancti Maximini fuerat, et quando hanc interrogationem tibi iniunxit, fecit quasi temptans, an forte dicturus essem contrarium sermoni meo, quem dixeram de tempore passionis martium predictorum. Et addidit dicens: Placatum me non habebitis nisi prium singulis ordinibus fratrum meorum singularem honorificentiam pro satisfactione exhibeatis" (*LR* 22:137).

73. "Dicent forte nonnulli, alicuius me sanctitatis esse, ac meis meritis gratiam dei attribuent, existimantes aliquid me esse, cum nihil sim. Alii vero cogitabunt, intra se dicentes: Hec si esset dei famula, sileret utique, et non sineret magnificari nomen suum in terra, nescientes, qualibus stimulis urgeri soleo ad dicendum. Non deerunt etiam, qui dicant muliebria figmenta ese omnia, que audierint de me, vel forsitan a sathana me illusam indicabunt. His et aliis modis karissime in ore hominum ventilari me oportebit. Et unde hoc mihi ut alicui hominum innotescam, que elegi esse in abscondito, et que certe nec dignam me arbitror, ut ad intuendum me quisquam oculos suos attollat? Illud quoque non parum angustias meas adauget, quod domino abbati conplacuit, ut scriptis verba mea commendentur. Ego enim, quid sum, ut memorie tradantur ea, que sunt de me? Nonne et hoc arrogantie poterit attribui?" (*LV* 1.1:2).

74. "Sed dicunt mihi quidam ex sapientibus, quia non propter me solam hec fecit mihi dominus, sed aliorum quoque edificationi per ista providit, eo quod ad fidei confirmationem aliquatenus attinere videantur, et ad consolationem eorum, qui tribulato sunt corde propter dominum. Et idcirco pro eiusmodi causis, que predicte sunt, opera dei silentio pretereunda non putant" (*LV* 1.1:2–3).

75. "Et ita quidem esse, ut dicunt, ex parte credo, propter quedam, que nunc tibi indicabo. Accidit aliquociens, cum in corde meo posuissem celare ea, que ostensa mihi erant a domino, tanta precordiorum tortura me arripi, ut morti proximam me existimarem. At ubi his, que erant circa me, quid vidissem, aperui, continuo alleviata sum" (*LV* 1.1:3).

76. "Petis a me frater, et ad hoc venisti, ut enarrem tibi misericordias domini, quas secundum beneplacitum gratie sue operari dignatus est in me. Promptum quidem est in me per omnia dilectioni tue satisfacere, nam et hoc ipsum diu desideravit anima mea, ut daretur mihi conferre tecum de omnibus his, ac tuum audire iudicium" (*LV* 1.1:2).

77. "Sed fateor, quia nec sic adhuc omnino certificata sum, quid potissimum agere debeam. Nam et tacere magnalia dei periculosum michi ese intelligo, et loqui periculosius fore pertimesco. Minus enim discretionis me habere cognosco, quam ut sufficiam discernere, quid ex his, que mihi revelantur, dici conveniat, quid vero silentio honorari oporteat. Et ecce inter hec omnia in periculo delinquendi posita sum. Propter hoc dilecte mi non cessant ab oculis meis lacrime, et anxiatur spiritus meus iugiter in me. Sed ecce ad introitum tuum consolari cepit anima mea, et facta est tranquillitas

magna in me… . Et nunc, quia domini voluntate ad me de longinquo directus es, non abscondam cor meum a te, sed ea, que sunt de me bona et mala, tibi aperiam. Deinde, quid fieri conveniat, in tua et domni abbatis siscretione positum sit" (*LV* 1.1:3).

78. On this letter, see Clark, *Elisabeth*, 14–15; and Lieven van Acker, "Der Brief-wechsel zwischen Elisabeth von Schönau und Hildegard von Bingen," in *Aevum inter utrumque: Mélanges offerts à Gabriel Sanders, professeur émérité à l'Université de Gand*, ed. Marc van Uytfanghe and Roland Demeulenaere (Steenbrugis: In Abbatia S. Petri; The Hague: Nijhoff, 1991), 409–17. On the vision, see note 64.

79. Van Acker, "Der Briefwechsel," 416.

80. *LV* 3.19:70–74.

81. Emecho, *Vita Eckeberti*, 448–49. Emecho however implies here that Ekbert assumed his discretionary role at the very beginning of her visionary career, while he was still at Bonn, rather than after his removal to Schönau as Elisabeth's introduction to *Liber visionum* would suggest.

82. See Clark, *Elisabeth*, 57–58; Clark, "Repression or Collaboration?" 161–62.

3. A Shared Endeavor? Guibert of Gembloux on Hildegard of Bingen

1. On Guibert: Hippolyte Delehaye, "Guibert, Abbé de Florennes et de Gembloux," *Revue des questions historiques* 46 (1889): 5–90 (still the fundamental study); Ildefons Herwegen, "Les collaborateurs de sainte Hildegarde," *Revue Bénédictine* 21 (1904): 192–203, 302–15, 381–403; Herwegen, *Alte Quellen neuer Kraft*, 2nd ed. (Düsseldorf: Schwann, 1922), 199–212; Marianna Schrader, "Wibert von Gembloux," *Erbe und Auftrag* 37 (1961): 381–92.

2. The most important of the three codices, denoted by Albert Derolez as *G* (Brussels, Royal Library, MS 5527–5534), contains fifty-six letters from or to Guibert and forms the basis of Derolez's edition: Derolez, introduction to *GGE*, xxiii–xxxi. A second manuscript (MS 5387–5396), which is probably the earliest of the three, contains Guibert's prose life of St. Martin as well as eighteen letters (all of which are witnessed in *G* as well) with some corrections probably in Guibert's own hand: *GGE* xiii–xxiii. The third (MS 5535–5537) contains fourteen long letters of Guibert on ascetical subjects, none of which has been published; see *GGE* xi, and Delehaye, "Guibert," 14–15.

3. Delehaye, "Guibert," 86–90, 9–12. Commentators on Guibert have not disagreed with Delehaye's dictum that his writing lacks "these essential qualities of epistolary style: simplicity and the natural. Even familiar subjects are treated in a style that smells of the school and the imitation of models" (Delehaye, "Guibert," 10).

4. The collection is what we have in MS *G* (see note 2). Guibert twice declared his intention to make a collection of his correspondence with Hildegard: in a letter to the Rupertsberg nuns, in which he speaks of bringing together "my writings to her as well as hers to me [tam nostra ad eam quam eius ad nos scripta]" (*GGE* 23.53–55:253) and in one of his letters to Hildegard, which concludes with his wish "to collect in one

writing everything that you have written to me and I to you [omnia, et tua ad me et mea ad te, sub uno scripta colligere]" (*GGE* 24.80–84:257). Derolez hypothesizes that *G* was Guibert's fulfillment of that intention, even though it contains more than simply his correspondence with Hildegard. Derolez, introduction, xxii.

5. Delehaye, "Guibert," 16–90.

6. *GGE* 14.28–32:208.

7. On the dating of Guibert's correspondence with Hildegard and his subsequent stay at the Rupertsberg, see Herwegen, "Les collaborateurs," 381–389.

8. *GGE* 16–17:217–24.

9. *HBE* 103R:258–65; *GGE* 18:226–34.

10. The letters in question are as follows: letter 19 from Guibert announces that he may be able to visit Hildegard, reports the reactions of the Cistercian monks at Villers to her letter, which he had shown to them, and attaches a list of thirty-eight questions for which those monks were requesting answers through her gifts. This is followed by letter 20, in which Guibert laments that plans for the visit have gone awry and urges her again to answer the questions. A reply from Hildegard (*HBE* 106R:265–68) informs him that she is asking the "living light" for answers to the Villers monks' questions. Guibert's letters 21 and 22 (*GGE* 246–50, written in his name by the Villers monks as he explains in the following letter) then urge her to answer the questions. In letter 23 (*GGE* 252–53), addressed to the nuns at Bingen, Guibert asks whether a rumor of Hildegard's death is to be believed and requests again her answers to the questions. In letter 24 he expresses thanksgiving for the news that she is alive—and urges her to answer the questions. Finally a letter from Hildegard (*HBE* 109R:269–71) reports that she has completed answers to fourteen of the questions. As for the answers, Guibert would later report that they could not be located; see note 66 below. A complete text of thirty-eight answers is to be found in *PL* 157 (cols. 1039–54), but its authenticity is open to serious question; see Delehaye, "Guibert," 34–35. Anne Clark Bartlett, "Commentary, Polemic, and Prophecy in Hildegard of Bingen's 'Solutiones Triginta Octo Quaestionum,'" *Viator* 23 (1992): 153–65, discusses the text of the answers, though not the question of authenticity. On Hildegard's teachings as an alternative to those of the schools, see *GGE* 18.139–57:229–30. The notion here that Hildegard's revelations offer a substitute for scholastic teaching also finds expression in Volmar of Disibodenberg's surviving letter to Hildegard, *HBE* 195.27–57:443–45. See Sabina Flanagan, *Hildegard of Bingen: A Visionary Life* (London: Routledge, 1989), 212–13.

11. *GGE* 26.240–252:277; *GGE* 22:395. Delehaye, "Guibert," 26; Herwegen, "Les collaborateurs," 386–87.

12. See note 61.

13. Lieven van Acker, "Der Briefwechsel der Heiligen Hildegard von Bingen: Vorbemerkungen zu einer kritischen Edition," *Revue Benedictine* 99 (1989):129–34.

14. *GGE* 26.307–329:279.

15. Flanagan, *Hildegard of Bingen*, 180–91.

16. On Volmar, see Herwegen, "Les collaborateurs," 197–203. On the dating of Volmar's death, see Mariana Schrader and Adelgundis Führkötter, *Die Echtheit des*

Schrifttums der Heiligen Hildegard von Bingen. Quellenkritisches Untersuchungen (Cologne/Graz: Böhlau, 1956), 142–44.

17. Guibert wrote to the monks of Gembloux in early 1180 agreeing to return after the coming Easter: *GGE* 29.128–29:325; Delehaye, "Guibert," 40–41; Herwegen, "Les collaborateurs," 388.

18. In his letter to the Rupertsberg nuns in Lent 1185, reminiscing about his sojourn there, he makes only three references to her, all incidental to his principal purpose, which was to recall and defend his own rectitude as a man living among women: *GGE* 32.58, 109, 202:335, 336, 339. His letters to individuals there—the abbess Ida (*GGE* 36:353–59) and the nun Gertrude (*GGE* 34 and 37:347–48, 361–65)—do not mention her at all. His correspondence after 1204 with Godfrey, abbot of St. Eucher in Trier (*GGE* 40–42:385–420), shows him at first interested in finishing the vita but then setting it aside again after reading Theoderic's *Vita sanctae Hildegardis* and finding it thoroughly satisfactory. See note 29. On his reworking of Theoderic, see Monica Klaes, "Einleitung," in *Vita S. Hildegardis*, ed. Klaes (Turhout: Brepols, 1993), 152*–56* (cited as *VSH*); and Anna Silvas, trans. and ed. *Jutta and Hildegard: The Biographical Sources* (Turnhout: Brepols, 1998), 220–37 (includes translated excerpts).

19. "Est istic miram uirtutum concertationem intueri" (*GGE* 38.47:368); "Ipsa ... ex caritate se omnibus impendens in dandis consiliis que exiguntur, in soluendis questionibus difficillimis que opponuntur, in scribendis libris, in erudiendis sororibus, in confortandis qui adueniunt peccatoribus, tota semper occupatur" (*GGE* 38.75–80:369).

20. There has been damage to the manuscript at this point and some of the vita has been lost; see Klaes, "Einleitung," 40*.

21. "Quomodo me habeam et que circa me sunt, et cuius uirtutis sit uenerabilis mater Hildegardis et sorores sub eius censura Domino seruientes" (*GGE* 38.9–12:367).

22. Here Guibert suggests that Hildegard received only a "reference [*mentio*]" in his preceding comments to Bovo, but in fact "he has spoken of almost nothing else!" (Herwegen, "Les collaborateurs," 396–97). See also Klaes, "Einleitung," 37*–38*.

23. *GGE* 15.159–66:215. Cf. *GGE* 26.330–87:279–81.

24. Klaes, "Einleitung," 40*–48*.

25. "Cumque quod stilus quo libellus ille scriptus erat humilis uideretur, a tot fere filiarum ejus choro ... rogarer, ut et ea quae in libello eodem continerentur, et si qua in voluminibus que ipsa ediderat, ad eam specialiter pertinentia inuenirem, in unum compingens, apposito transitu eius quo possem sermonis cultu meliorarem" (*GGE* 15.142–48:214).

26. *GGE* 15.166–73:215.

27. Herwegen, "Les collaborateurs," 203. See Klaes, "Einleitung," 28*. See note 30.

28. *GGE* 41.22–28:388; *VSH* prol.16–17:3. Theoderic himself probably supplied the last two chapters (8 and 9) and made stylistic changes: Klaes, "Einleitung," 91*–97*.

29. Klaes, "Einleitung," 44*–45*. Klaes acknowledges the problem raised by the fact that when Godfrey of St. Eucher, after 1204, sent Guibert a copy of the *Vita sanctae Hildegardis* (*GGE* 41.23–28:388), Guibert responded as though he had never seen it

before (*GGE* 42.106–30:394). She hypothesizes that Guibert may have added to letter 15 the apparent reference to the *Vita sanctae Hildegardis* at some point after receiving letter 41: Klaes, "Einleitung," 33*–36*.

30. If Guibert deliberately gave the *libellus* a false attribution, this would not be the only example of his willingness to rework his material. See Herwegen, "Les collaborateurs," 390–92. Indeed, he apparently altered information about Volmar elsewhere. Schrader and Führkötter, *Die Echtheit*, 148–50, conclude that since Volmar died in 1173, and since Guibert's removal to Bingen took place in 1177 (see Herwegen, "Les collaborateurs," 382), in the passages in which he presents the latter event as following directly upon Volmar's death (*GGE* 19.82:238; 26.289–90:278) he must have deliberately substituted the latter's name for that of the monk Godfrey, who had been Volmar's immediate successor as provost of the Rupertsberg monastery, as we know from Godfrey of St. Eucher's letter in Guibert's own collection (*GGE* 41.22–28:388). Schrader and Führkötter suggest the motive was his own vanity in wishing to cast himself as the successor of the better-known Volmar. But was the name Volmar indeed well known? Our ability to identify the name with Hildegard's first collaborator appears to derive from Guibert himself. See Klaes, "Einleitung," 26* n. 13.

31. Newman, "Hildegard and Her Hagiographers," 21–24; Klaes, "Einleitung," 97*–109*.

32. Klaes, "Einleitung," 44*–48*, 56*–59*, 112*–16*.

33. Barbara Newman, "Three-Part Invention: The *Vita S. Hildegardis* and Mystical Hagiography," in *Hildegard of Bingen: The Context of Her Thought and Art*, ed. Charles Burnett and Peter Dronke (London: Warburg Institute, 1998), 193–96; Newman, "Hildegard and her Hagiographers," 19–21.

34. Newman, "Hildegard and her Hagiographers," 25.

35. "Sapientia quoque in lumine karitatis docet et iubet me dicere, quomodo in hanc uisionem constituta sum" (*VSH* 2.2.34–35:22).

36. "Pre timore autem, quem ad homines habebam, quomodo uiderem, nulli dicere audebam; sed quedam nobilis femina, cui in disciplina eram subdita, hec notauit et cuidam sibi noto monacho aperuit" (*VSH* 2.2.68–70:23).

37. *VSH* 1.1.15–35:6; cf. Hildegard of Bingen, *Scivias*, ed. Adelgundis Führkötter and Angela Carlevaris, Corpus Christianorum, continuatio medievalis 43–43A (Turnhout: Brepols, 1978), 3–4 ("protestificatio," 25–35).

38. *VSH* 1.2.17–20:7–8: "Cumque in sancto proposito multis annis succrescens *Deo soli* complacere satageret, iamque tempus instaret quo ad multorum profectum uita eius facta, ut de cetero, que uideret uel audiret, scribere non cunctaretur" (*VSH* 1.3.1–5:8).

39. "Quasi reliquerant in sola Dei misericordia sperantem et non modo cogitatum suum, sed et se totam in eo iactantem" (*GGE* 38.128–30:370).

40. *GGE* 38.136–85 ("ergastulum," 154; "carcer," 164, "mausoleum," 176):370–71. Klaes, "Einleitung," 39*.

41. *GGE* 38.201–43, 265–68:372–74.

42. *GGE* 38.297–333:375–76.

43. "Cum in loco sue conuersionis aduc versaretur, post aliquot annos dormitionis domne Iutte ad sancte prelationis officium, licet renitens, assumitur, Deo nimirum iam merita eius propalare et eam pro exemplo ad laudem nominis sui et ad correctionem multorum manifestare mundo et magnificare disponente, sermo Domini non in nocturna uisione, sed in aperta illustrationis sue offensione factus est ad eam, precipiens ut ea que ei diuinitus reuelarentur stili officio declararet et legenda ecclesia traderet" (*GGE* 38.334–42:376).

44. "Tunc in eadem uisione magna pressura dolorum coacta sum palam manifestare, que uideram et audieram, sed ualde timui et erubui proferre, que tamdiu silueram. Vene autem et medulle mee tunc plene uirium erant, in quibus ab infantia et iuuentute mea defectum habebam. Ista cuidam monache magistro meo intimaui, qui bone conuersationis et diligentis intentionis ac ueluti peregrinus a sciscitacionibus morum multorum hominum erat, unde et eadem miracula libenter audiebat. Qui admirans michi iniunxit, ut ea absconse scriberem, donec uideret, que et unde essent. Intelligens autem, quod a Deo essent, abbati suo intimauit magnoque desiderio deinceps in his mecum laborauit" (*VSH* 2.2.77–87:24).

45. "Magnum est etiam illud et admiratione dignum, quod ea, que in spiritu audiuit vel uidit, eodem sensu et eisdem verbis circumspecta et pura mente manu propria scripsit et ore edidit, uno solo fideli uiro symmista contenta, qui ad euidentiam grammatice artis, quam ipsa nesciebat, casus, tempora et genera quidem disponere, sed ad sensum uel intellectum eorum nihil omnino addere presumebat uel demere" (*VSH* 2.1.24–30:20–21).

46. *GGE* 38.371–80 ("Indocta quippe quantum ad eruditionem artis grammatice erat," 375–76):377.

47. "Inter hec … insinuatur ei in eodem monasterio monachus sobrius, castus et eruditus corde et uerbo in sapientia, qui, protinus cum ista ei nota fierent, uotis eius libens consentiret et, censoris eius cautelam exhibens, uerba eius, quamlibet nuda et impolita decentiori sermonis cultu uestiret" (*GGE* 38.400–05:377).

48. *GGE* 38.406–22:377–78.

49. *GGE* 38.423–50:378–79.

50. *GGE* 16.34–45:218; cf. *GGE* 18.50–77:227–28.

51. *GGE* 18.182–214:230–31. This is all part of a speech placed in the mouth of an unnamed person ("alius quidem," transparently himself) attending the public reading of Hildegard's letter. Cf. *HBE* 103R.62–131:261–62.

52. *GGE* 18.158–81, 264–85:229–30, 232–33.

53. There is a strong hint here of the venerable notion of the "virile woman"—the woman of extraordinary virtue who transcends feminine weakness and thus ceases to be a woman—which, as Newman has shown, Hildegard herself avoided. See Barbara Newman, *Sister of Wisdom* (Berkeley: University of California Press, 1988), 254–55; Newman, *From Virile Woman to WomanChrist*, 6.

54. *GGE* 18.240–54:232; "non quorumlibet, sed summorum eminentie comparata uirorum, reuelata facie gloriam Domini speculans, in eandem transformatur imaginem, a claritate in claritatem, tamquam a Domini spiritu" (*GGE* 18.260–64:232). The

only woman to whom he is willing to liken her (in a rather complex comparison that in any case underscores her difference from other women) is the Virgin Mary: just as by becoming incarnate in Mary, Christ chose to restore life to humanity by means of the sex through which death had first arrived, so "in you, in salutary teachings, the same hand that inflicted the baleful drink of perdition on us now pours out the healing antidote [et de qua manu pestifer potus perditionis illatus nobis fuerat, de hac eadem manu in te salutaribus doctrinis antidotus recuperationis nobis refunditur]" (*GGE* 16.41–45:218; cf. *GGE* 18.62–69:227).

55. *GGE* 18.30–59 ("nam super uires meas erant que dicebantur, et magis uox spiritus uel lingua angelica quam hominis uidebatur," 52–54):226–27.

56. *GGE* 16.46–81:218–19.

57. *GGE* 18.316–333:234.

58. "Sed qui in ascensione anime sapientiam a Deo hauserunt et se pro nihilo computauerunt, hi columne celi facta sunt.... Ego quidem semper trementem timorem habeo, quoniam nullam securitatem ullius possibilitatis in me scio" (*HBE* 103R.47–48, 55–56:260). On the composition of this letter, see Klaes, "Einleitung," 49ˣ–54ˣ.

59. As demonstrated by Delehaye, the dating rests on letter 28, to "G," a monk at Gembloux. In that letter Guibert assumes Hildegard to be still living and also refers to the letter to Bovo as having been written about two years earlier (*GGE* 28.86:306). But Guibert, who arrived at the Rupertsberg in 1177, therefore only lived approximately two years with the saint before she died (29 September 1179), and so the letter to Bovo must have been written at the beginning of that time, hence in 1177, and the letter to "G" at the end of that time, in 1179. Delehaye, "Guibert," 37–39. "Quomodo me habeam et que circa me sunt, et cuius uirtutis sit uenerabilis mater Hildegardis et sorores sub eius censura Domino seruientes" (*GGE* 38.4–12:367).

60. *GGE* 38.75–80:369 (see note 19).

61. "Et nunc in pulchritudine pacis et totius iocunditatis et suauitatis cum ea habito. Consiliis eius dirigor, orationibus fulcior, nitor meritis, sustentor beneficiis, et cotidie recreor colloquiis. Nichil libentius ipsa ad presens, quantum ad exteriora spectat, uideret, quam ut in domo Domini, quam regit ipsa, omnibus diebus uite sue permanerem habitare, et ut interiorem curam ipsius et filiarum eius et considerandorum librorum, quos scripsit, susciperem" (*GGE* 38.33–40:367–68). Guibert goes on to say (lines 41–46) that it is because he fears to offend her that he has not yet responded to her desire, but he does not intend to stay indefinitely because there are "some who lean upon my counsel [qui consilio meo innituntur]."

62. Thus the letter dates from well after the letter to Bovo, although Hildegard was still alive when he wrote, and therefore it antedates 27 September 1179. It is important to note, though, that the reference to the deaths of Hildegard's kinsman and sometime collaborator Wescelin and of Wescelin's nephew Gilbert, both of which occurred in 1185, shows that the text must have received later reworking: *GGE* 26.832–835:293. See Herwegen, "Les collaborateurs," 390; Derolez, in *GGE*, 270. See also note 66.

63. Radulphus, *GGE* 25.50–209:265–69. See note 10.

64. Guibert, Ep. 26.765–74:291–92. See note 102.

65. "Quis a tali instrumento, et scarie senectutis et egritudinis terebratione demolito, doctrine suauitatem et non potius gemituum eruptionem expectet?" (*GGE* 26.785–90:292).

66. He explains that Wescelin (on whom see Herwegen, "Les collaborateurs," 310–12) took Hildegard's answers to the monastery of St. Andrew at Cologne with him before he died, and his nephew who succeeded him there could not determine anything about them when Guibert asked, nor could anyone else in the house. Guibert thinks they have been stolen (*GGE* 26.822–43:293–94).

67. *GGE* 26.843–49:294. The pathos is unmistakable in view of Guibert's hopes for Hildegard as an alternative to the schools. See note 10.

68. *GGE* 25.3–5, 26.142–148. There were other critics as well. In a letter written at about the same time to his friend "G," Guibert defends himself against detractors at Gembloux who had said that he had defamed that monastery in the passage the letter to Bovo in which he had said that in leaving Gembloux for Bingen he had left Leah for Rachel (*GGE* 38.13–29:367): he explains, perhaps disingenuously, that it was his own mode of life at Gembloux that he had been criticizing (*GGE* 28.94–160:306–8). It is clear at any rate that he had been unhappy with what he saw as the lack of observance at Gembloux, which had been beset with divisions and which he later criticized implicitly with his description of the high level of observance at the monastery of Marmoutiers at Tours, where he spent eight months after leaving Bingen (*GGE* 8:113–27). See Delehaye, "Guibert," 16–24.

69. *GGE* 26.149–201:275–76.

70. *GGE* 26.202–22:276–77.

71. *GGE* 26.223–39, 253–80:277–78.

72. *GGE* 26.289–306:278–79. The letter, to which Guibert makes other references in addition to this one (in *GGE* 38.30–34 [to Bovo], 32.108–9 [to Bingen nuns], 38.277–78 [to his friend "G"]; cf. 25.13:264) is apparently lost. "It is quite astonishing that a letter so honorable for the monk of Gembloux has not been conserved" (Herwegen, "Les collaborateurs," 384).

73. *GGE* 26.313–24:279.

74. *GGE* 26.326–29:279.

75. *GGE* 26.330–62:279–80.

76. *GGE* 26.5–14:271. Ralph begins his own letter to Guibert—in fact a thoroughly sympathetic letter—by saying that those (unlike himself) who did not understand the reason for Guibert's long sojourn in Bingen criticized him for it (*GGE* 25.3–5:264). This was the extent of Ralph's reference to detractors.

77. "Neque enim ego ... aut leuitate usus aut instabilitate actus locum meum deserens huc emigraui" (*GGE* 26.145–48:275).

78. "'Sed domum ... professionis sue, in qua uota sua reddere et pro cuius restructione laborare deberet, reliquit et in extranea, alienum panem gratis manducans [cf. 2 Thess. 3:8], cum mulierculis moratur et cum iuuenculis in secretis claustri lasciuiens et otiose uictitans iocatur'" (*GGE* 26.470–74:283).

79. Guibert presents a long defensive response, making essentially two points, on the basis of a wide array of examples from the New Testament and the ancient church:

(1) that it is possible for a man to live virtuously among women, if God has granted him the gift of chastity, and (2) that women need pastoral care from men. The whole argument is thus pursued on a theoretical level, without reference to the particular situation at Bingen (*GGE* 26.388–753:281–91).

80. Derolez, introduction, xvi.

81. "Quoniam ergo noui uos eam uehementer dilexisse, et de gestis eius non licuit michi uobis satisfacere, saltem de uerbis ipsius, que mitto uobis, aliquam consolationem accipite, et epistolam mirabili instructione plenam, sed et uisionem pulcherrimam de excellentia sancti Martini diuinitus illi ostensam, quas, suo quidem prolatas sensu, sed meo exaratas stilo, cuidam amico suo direxit, diligenter perlegite" (*GGE* 15.173–179:215). On Guibert as the addressee of the visions, see Herwegen, "Les collaborateurs," 393–96.

82. Hildegard of Bingen, "Visio S. Hildegardis ad Guibertum missa" (cited as *HVGM*), in *Analecta Sacra*, vol. 8, ed. Jean Baptiste Pitra (Paris: A. Jouby et Roger, 1882), 415–34.

83. Thus Herwegen, "Les collaborateurs," 392–96; Schrader and Führkötter, *Die Echtheit*, 182–83; Newman, *Sister of Wisdom*, 23–4.

84. *GGE* 15.176:215.

85. "Ostende mihi faciem tuam; sonet vox tua in auribus meis; vox enim tua dulcis, et facies tua decora" (HVGM 2:416).

86. "Quaesisti, et subtiliter considerasti, qualiter sancti et electi Dei … ad eum pervenerint" (HVGM 3:416).

87. "Cavendum, inquam, ne cum indecenti, hoc est communi, descisso, vel aliquibus maculis infecto habitu … introire audeas" (HVGM 18:426).

88. "Qui si inter constipationem nuptias tam celebres frequentantium latere non potuit, tu quomodo qui inter sponsum et sponsam medius ex ministerio consistere debes, et a sponso manibus tuis traditum panem et calicem, et eum panem et calicem quos sola fides credentium vehementer ab aliis victualibus secernendos intelligit, sponsae habes porrigere?" (HVGM 18:426.)

89. "Sedit populus manducare et bibere, et surrexerunt ludere. Paulo post subjunctum est: Quia viderat Moyses populum quod eset nudum" (HVGM 19:427).

90. HVGM 6:418.

91. HVGM 7–12:419–23. She connects the Song of Songs text to the Lukan one (the substance of which she alters) by suggesting that *after* the slaying of the calf, the father permitted the "shepherds" to preach far and wide and that in the process they found that "*miser filius*" who then repented and returned (HVGM 7:419). Her advice in concluding the section on the parable: "take care in this perilous journey to show yourself cautious rather than confident, and moderate, not exceeding the limits placed by the fathers, that is, show yourself to be a traveler who turns neither to the right nor the left. And beware of not knowing, lest you not be known; fear to be extolled, lest you be reproved [satage ut in hac tam periculosa via cautum, non securum, mediocrem, non terminos a patribus positos excedentem, id est neque ad dexteram, neque ad sinistram declinantem viatorem te exhibeas. Et cave ignorare, ne ignoreris; et pertimesce extolli, ne reproberis]" (HVGM 12:422).

92. "Considera diligenter, et dignitatem conditionis, et infidelitatem dejectionis, et sublimitatem reparationis humanae" (HVGM 12:423). These three subjects occupy her through paragraph 15:424.

93. "Ut eisdem vestimentis gloriae suae infirmitatem naturae tuae dignetur obtegere" (HVGM 20:427).

94. "Et Dominus sine dubio replebit illud eodem Spiritu sapientiae, ad annuntiandum laudem ejus in medio Ecclesiae, et narrandum nomen ipsius fratribus tuis" (HVGM 22:428; 23–24:429–31).

95. "In hac epistola praeter morem concessi, totam visionis seriem, observata omnibus sensuum veritate, decentiori sermonis cultu vestire non negligas, quoniam sicut quilibet cibi quatenus ex se utiles, nisi aliunde conditi, non appetuntur, sic et quaevis scripta, salutaribus licet referta monitis, si non aliquo eloquii colore commendantur, auribus urbani styli assuefactis fastidiuntur" (HVGM 25:432).

96. Thus in Jerome's work, "word is not rendered for word, but rather meaning for meaning [non verbum a verbo, sed sensus reddatur ex sensu]." So it is clear that in arguing for a place in the communication of her visions, Guibert has cast himself as a Jerome, a translator, and Hildegard has acquiesced (HVGM 26:432). Guibert also used the example of Jerome to justify his presence among women (*GGE* 32.114–22:337); cf. Ferrante, *To the Glory of Her Sex*, 26.

97. "Non solum praedicta, sed et caetera, quae vel hactenus ad te scripsi, seu deinceps scriptura sum" (HVGM 26:432). Herwegen, "Les collaborateurs," 393–4.

98. "Thus I want to restrain you, that you (as is said) fashion each step in the same way, and moreover do not stray from my path [Ita volo te coercere, ut passum, sicut dicitur, passu resculpas, sed tamen ut a vestigiis itineris mei non recedas]" (HVGM 26:432).

99. "Nam in caeteris sive anterioribus scriptis meis, istud nec puellis quae ex ore meo excipiunt, nec ipsi unice dilecto piae memoriae filio meo Vulmaro, qui ante te in his corrigendis sedulus mihi astitit, unquam concessi" (HVGM 27:432).

100. On this theme see Newman, "Three Part Invention," 199–202; Newman, *Sister of Wisdom*, 255–57.

101. "Nec vero te, seu quempiam mea legentium, iste latini eloquii quem patior defectus, scandalizet, quod ad ea quae mihi revelantur vel per me manifestari divinitus imperantur proferenda, simul etiam mihi facultas aut competens latine proferendi non datur modus cum intimus confabulator Dei ineloquentem et impeditae seu tardioris linguae se profitens, Aaron fratrem suum pro supplemento suae inopiae ad expicanda quae per se non sufficeret, ab ipso Deo interpretem acceperit; et jeremias, sanctus antequam natus, se nescire loqui testetur; et egregius praedicator, non quidem scientia, sed sermone imperitum se esse, non solum sua voce asserat, sed etiam, ut audio dici, parum culto dictandi genere ostendat" (HVGM 27:433).

102. "Agat angelus idem quod agit, nec parcat; intrepide cedo ei carnem meam cribrandam, ut spiritus salvus sit in die Domini" (HVGM 28:433).

103. "Si per easdem virtutes, quarum in principio et formas vidisse, et voces audivisse me dixi, tu quoque et vincere cupis, et coronari humilia te nunc sub potenti

manu Dei... imitans quoque eum qui non venit facere voluntatem suam, sed factus est obediens usque ad mortem" (HVGM 29:433).

104. Hildegard's apparent understanding of why priests should be male suggests a parallel to her understanding of priest and prophet here, in the sense of construing their relationship in terms of functional distinction rather than subordination: priests are male because the church is female, not in the sense of exercising a putative masculine domination but rather in the sense of a distinction in roles understood in terms of sex distinction, whereby the church "conceives and is fruitful through his ministry": Augustine Thompson, "Hildegard of Bingen on Gender and the Priesthood," *Church History* 63 (1994): 364.

105. E.g., "Unlike most visionary women of the later Middle Ages, Hildegard wrote not to relate her subjective experience of God, but rather to teach faith and morals on the authority of this experience which her works presuppose but seldom elaborate": Barbara Newman, "Hildegard of Bingen: Visions and Validation," *Church History* 54 (1985): 163–64. See also Peter Dinzelbacher, *Mittelalterliche Frauenmystik*, 9.

106. *GGE* 15.6–24:211.

107. "Postpositis magistris ad hoc idoneis, quorum circa uos plurimi uersantur, id operis michi, homini utique indocto et nullius momenti, imponendum putastis" (*GGE* 15.39–43:212).

108. "Opus rude et impolitum curiosis et saeculari eloquentiae assuefactis auribus": Guibert of Gembloux, "De Laudibus B. Martini Turonensis," prologue, in *Analecta Sacra*, vol. 8, ed. Jean Baptiste Pitra (Paris: A. Jouby et Roger, 1882), 582.

109. Guibert often singled out Philip and the bishop of Liège as acting on Hildegard's behalf to cause him to stay at Bingen: *GGE* 32.110:336; 26.346–75:280; 28.328–339:313; 52.74–79:521–22.

4. James of Vitry and the Other World of Mary of Oignies

1. The recent monograph by Simons, *Cities of Ladies*, despite the geographical limits of its title, provides a lucid introduction to the Beguine movement in its complexity. The older comprehensive study by McDonnell, *Beguines and Beghards*, is dated but still useful. A brief but well-informed account of the movement, with particular reference to Mary, is Dennis Devlin, "Feminine Lay Piety in the High Middle Ages: The Beguines," in *Medieval Women*, ed. J. Nichols and L. Shank (Kalamazoo, Mich.: Cistercian Publications, 1984), 183–96. On the Beguines within the broader context of "semireligious" life in the period, see Kaspar Elm, "*Vita regularis sine regula*," 239–73, and Elm, "Die Stellung der Frau in Ordenswesen, Semireligiosentum und Häresie zur Zeit der Hl. Elisabeth," in *Sankt Elisabeth: Fürstin, Dienerin, Heilige* (Sigmaringen: Jan Thorbecke Verlag, 1981), 7–28, esp. 14–17; Grundmann, *Religious Movements*, 139–52. On the limitations of the *Vita Mariae* as a historical source for the Beguinal movement, see Michel Lauwers, "Expérience béguinale et récit hagiographique: à propos de la *Vita Mariae Oigniacensis* de Jacques de Vitry (vers 1215)," *Journal des savants* (1989):

61–103. On monastic, specifically Cistercian, influences on Beguines, see Simone Roisin, "L'efflorescence Cistercienne et le courant féminin de piété au XIIIe siècle," *Revue d'histoire ecclésiastique* 39 (1943): 342–78, and Thomas Renna, "Hagiography and
Feminine Spirituality in the Low Countries," *Cîteaux* 39 (1988): 285–96.

2. *VMO* 1.2.13–1.3.15:640.

3. Iris Geyer, *Maria von Oignies. Eine hochmittelalterliche Mystikerin zwischen
Ketzerei und Rechtgläubigkeit* (Frankfurt: Lang, 1992), 13–17; McDonnell, *Beguines and
Beghards*, 59–62. "As long as she was able, she worked with her own hands, so that
she might afflict her body through penance, and provide necessities to the poor, and
acquire food and clothing for herself, inasmuch as she had given up everything for
Christ [Unde manibus propriis, quamdiu potuit, laboravit; ut corpus per poeniten-
tiam affligeret, ut indigentibus necessaria ministraret, ut sibi etiam victum & vestitum
[utpote quae omnia pro Christo reliquerat] acquireret]" (*VMO* 1.12.38:646).

4. James is listed as a witness in a document of the Duke of Brabant concerning
the Cistercian house at Aywieres, dated 1211. This at least places him in the region, if
not precisely in Oignies. Phillip Funk, *Jakob von Vitry, Leben und Werke*, Beiträge zur
Kulturgeschichte des Mittelalters und der Renaissance 3 (Leipzig: Teubner, 1909), 23,
28. Funk's work remains the most comprehensive study of James. A recent shorter
account is that of Jean Longère, "Jacques de Vitry: La vie et les oeuvres," in James of
Vitry, *Histoire Occidentale*, trans. Gaston Duchet-Suchaux (Paris: Cerf, 1997), 7–49.
On James at Paris, see John W. Baldwin, *Masters, Princes, and Merchants: The Social
Views of Peter the Chanter and His Circle* (Princeton, N.J.: Princeton University Press,
1970), 1:38–39.

5. It was the mid-thirteenth-century Dominican historian Vincent of Beauvais who
reported that James had been a priest at Argenteuil before coming to Oignies: Vincent
of Beauvais, "Ex Vincentii speculo historiali," ed. O. Holder-Egger, in *Monumenta
Germaniae Historica* Scriptores 24 (1879): 166; the report however fits awkwardly with
Thomas of Cantimpré's assertion (*SVMO* 1.2:667) that James returned to Paris to be
ordained after coming to Oignies. Funk, *Jakob von Vitry*, 8–15; Longère, "Jacques de
Vitry," 9–10.

6. *SVMO* 1.2:667. Funk, *Jacobus von Vitry*, 15–24, considers the appeal of the recently founded St. Nicholas of Oignies a more likely motivation for James than the (otherwise undocumented) reputation of Mary, given James's well-witnessed attraction to
strict ascetic life and his stinging comments in chapter 7 of his *Historia Occidentalis*
(James of Vitry, *The Historia Occidentalis of Jacques de Vitry: A Critical Edition*, ed.
John Frederick Hinnebusch [Fribourg: University Press, 1972], 90–93) on the vanity
of university life in Paris; perhaps both factors were at work. On the founding of St.
Nicholas, see McDonnell, *Beguines and Beghards*, 8–19. A late-thirteenth-century history of the priory shows that James and Mary, along with the prior Giles who was their
contemporary, were later remembered as its shining stars. *Supplement to the Life of
Marie d'Oignies by Thomas of Cantimpré [and] Anonymous History of the Foundation
of the Venerable Church of Blessed Nicholas of Oignies…*, tr. Hugh Fiess (Saskatoon:
Peregrina, 1987), 37–41.

7. Funk, *Jakob von Vitry*, 31–68.

8. The Bollandist editor of the *AA SS* edition (Daniel Papenbroek) had access to four manuscripts (*Commentarius praevius* 3.18:634). The work's popularity is suggested by a manuscript tradition now known to have extended well beyond the diocese of Liège, as witnessed in more than two dozen manuscripts, by its use in thirteenth-century exemplum collections of Caesarius of Heisterbach, Thomas of Cantimpré, Stephen of Bourbon, and Arnold of Liège, and by its appearance in only slightly abridged form in the *Speculum historiale* of Vincent of Beauvais (see note 5). Michel Lauwers, "Expérience béguinale," 83; Lauwers, "Entre béguinisme et mysticisme. La Vie de Marie d'Oignies (+1213) de Jacques de Vitry ou la définition d'une sainteté féminine," *Ons Geestelijk Erf* 66 (1992): 46 n. 3; Geyer, *Maria von Oignies*, 45 n.97.

9. James of Vitry, *Lettres de Jacques de Vitry, 1160/1170–1240, évêque de St.-Jean d'Acre*, ed. R. B. C. Huygens (Leiden: Brill, 1960), ep. 1.76–83:74.

10. Detractors "make up new names against them, as the Jews called Christ a Samaritan and the Christians Galileans [nova nomina contra eos fingebant, sicut Judaei Christum Samaritanum & Christianos Galilaeos appellabant]" (*VMO* prol. 4:636). Elsewhere he made the point explicitly. "When a girl has purposed to retain her virginity and her parents have offered her a rich husband, let her treat him with contempt and reject him…. But the wise men of Egypt, that is the wise men of this world, namely secular prelates and other malicious men, want to destroy her and divert her from her good resolve, saying: 'she wants to be a "Beguine" (as they say in Flanders and Brabant) or a "Papelard" (in France) or a "Humiliata" (in Lombardy) or a "Bizoke" (in Italy) or a Coquennunne (in Germany), and by deriding and shaming them make them draw back from their holy purpose [Quando autem puella virginitatem suam custodire proposuit et parentes offerunt ei maritum cum diviciis, conculcet et respuat…. Sapientes autem Egypti, id est sapientes huius seculi, prelati scilicet seculares et alii maliciosi homines, volunt eam interficere et a bono proposito retrahere dicentes: 'Hec vult esse Beguina—sic enim nominantur in Flandria et Brabancia—, vel Papelarda—sic enim appellantur in Francia—, vel Humiliata—sicut dicitur in Lumbardia—vel Bizoke—secundum quod dicitur in Ytalia—vel Coquennunne—ut dicitur in Theotonia; et ita deridendo et quasi infamando nituntur eas a sancto proposito]": James of Vitry, "Secundus sermo ad virgines," in Joseph Greven, "Der Ursprung des Beginenwesens," *Historisches Jahrbuch* 35 (1914): 44–45.

11. Grundmann, *Religious Movements*, 81–82; Lauwers, "Experience béguinale," 62–63, 75–76; McDonnell, *Beguines and Beghards*, 20–39; R. W. Southern, *Western Society and the Church in the Middle Ages* (Hammondsworth: Penguin, 1970), 328–31.

12. Lauwers, "Expérience béguinale," 84–89. On her continence: *VMO* 1.3.13–14:640. On support for priests, see notes 45, 46, and 47, below.

13. He had begun this preaching tour at the time she died: *VMO* 2.10.96:661. On its circumstances and scope, see Funk, *Jakob von Vitry*, 32–34.

14. *VMO* prol. 9:638; *VMO* 1.13.41:647. André Vauchez, "Prosélitisme et action antihérétique en milieu féminin au XIIIe s.: La vie de Marie d'Oignies (+1213)," in

Problèmes d'histoire du Christianisme. Fasc. 17: Propagande et contrepropagande religieuses, ed. J. Marx (Brussels: Éditions de l'Université, 1987), 95–110; Geyer, *Maria von Oignies*, 151–224; Amy Hollywood, *Sensible Ecstasy: Mysticism, Sexual Difference, and the Demands of History* (Chicago: University of Chicago Press, 2002), 254–55; Elliott, *Proving Woman*, 47–84.

15. *VMO* prol. 2:636; *VMO* prol. 7:637–38. He declines to write about the other women because they are still alive: *VMO* prol. 9:638.

16. "Eam quandoque reprehendebamus," (*VMO* 1.6.20:641); "quaereremus ab ea, utrum ejus infirmitatis dolor in taedium aliquo modo veniret" (*VMO* 2.5.74:656); see also *VMO* 2.2.49:649; 2.4.65:654; 2.5.74:656; 2.7.82:658; 2.8.87:659.

17. "Deum testem invoco, numquam in tota ejus vita seu conversatione vel unum percipere potui peccatum mortale" (*VMO* 1.6.19:641); *VMO* 2.6.79:657; 2.9.94:661; "auro & argento mihi cariora" (*VMO* 2.10.96:661). Cf. *VMO* 1.5.18:641; 2.4.66:654.

18. *VMO* 2.4.69:654–55 (cf. 2.12.101:663); "quidam amicus sibi carissimus" (*VMO* 2.7.86:659). Thomas of Cantimpré assumes that the former passage refers to James and says that she urged him to be ordained (*SVMO* 1.2:667).

19. *VMO* prol. 7–8:637–38.

20. *VMO* 1.8.25:642. On the importance of fasting for Mary and other holy women of her time and region and the importance of the body in their spirituality, see Bynum, *Holy Feast and Holy Fast*, 115–29; Maria Grazia Calza, *Dem Weiblichen ist das Verstehen des Göttlichen "auf der Leib" geschrieben: Die Begine Maria von Oignies ([gest.] 1213) in der hagiographischen Darstellung Jakobs von Vitry ([gest.] 1240)* (Würzburg: Ergon, 2000).

21. "Dum volaret sublimius per diem integrum … solem justitiae velut aquila intuebatur. Hujus solis radiis, ab omni sensibilium humore desiccata, ab omni corporalium imaginum nube purgata, absque omni phantasia seu imaginatione, formas simplices & divinas quasi in puro speculo suscipiebat in anima" (*VMO* 2.7.81:658).

22. *VMO* 2.8.88:659–60. Her vision at the Feast of Purification, and its pairing with the visionary's experience of holding the Christ child (instances of which James reports in the same paragraph), were to be influential in subsequent visionary literature. Carolyn Larrington, "The Candlemas Vision and Marie d'Oignies's Role in Its Dissemination," in *New Trends in Feminine Spirituality: The Holy Women of Liège and Their Impact*, ed. Juliette Dor, Lesley Johnson, and Jocelyn Wogan-Browne (Turnhout: Brepols, 1999), 195–214.

23. *VMO* 2.8.89:660; 2.8.81:658.

24. *VMO* 1.8.24:642; 2.8.90:660.

25. "For she had to obey a familiar angel who had been deputed to guard her, as though he were her own abbot, and thus sometimes, when she was much distressed by vigils, he directed her to rest, and when she had rested awhile, he got her up and led her back to the church [Familiari enim Angelo, sibique ad custodiam deputato, velut Abbati proprio, eam oportebat obedire: quia quandoque, dum nimiis esset afflicta vigiliis, ut quiesceret admonebat: cum autem paululum quievisset, ad ecclesiam excitando eam reducebat]" (*VMO* 1.10.35:645).

26. "Vix aliqua dies vel nox praeterierit, quin aliquam à Deo aut ejus Angelis, vel Sanctis caelestibus... habuerit visitationem" (*VMO* prol. 11:638). Cf. *VMO* 2.9.97:662.

27. "Numquid non aliquando, cum introduceret te Rex in cellam vinariam, prae ebrietate clamabas, Cur te Domine abscondis, cur te qualis es non ostendis?... Nam cum jam ferventis spiritus aestuante musto, nisi respiraculum haberes; rumpereris; cum jam ignis incendium sine evaporatione aliqua ferre non posses; tunc demum à [corde] puro & ebrio extorquebatur veritas; tunc mira & inaudita de plenitudine eructans de libro Vitae, si possemus capere, multas & mirabiles lectiones, de discipula in magistram subito conversa, nobis legebas. Cum autem, tamquam potens crapulata à vino, post somnum expergefacta ad te redires, tunc vel oblita quae dilexisses silebas; vel si forte aliqua ad memoriam reduceres, tunc prae verecundia confusa, te garrulam & fatuam judicabas; & quid tibi accidisset admirans, a Domino veniam postulabas" (*VMO* 2.2.48:649).

28. "Antiphonam suam inchoavit à sancta scilicet Trinitate, Trinitatem in Unitate, & Unitatem in Trinitate diutissimè laudans, & mirabilia quasi ineffabilia cantilenae suae interserens. Quaedam etiam de divinis Scripturis, novo & mirabili modo exponens; de Euangelio, de Psalmis, de novo & veteri Testamento quae numquam audierat, multa & subtiliter edisserens" (*VMO* 2.10.99:663). On Mary's song as an example of the high-medieval association of music with a spirituality centered on the body, see Bruce Holsinger, *Music, Body, and Desire in Medieval Culture: Hildegard of Bingen to Chaucer* (Stanford, Calif.: Stanford University Press, 2001), 216–18.

29. *VMO* 2.10.100:663.

30. "Ii multa de arcanis caeliestibus, quae illa dicebat, intelligere non poterant" (*VMO* 2.12.99:663).

31. "Ex abundanti autem humilitate semper quantum in ipsa erat latere appetebat. Unde cum ex cordis jubilo, & ex plenitudine gratiae intra se occultari non posset; quandoque ad vicina rura vel dumeta fugiebat, ut humanos devitans oculos, secretum suum sibi & in arca purae conscientiae conservaret. Quandoque tamen precibus amicorum compulsa, vel a Domino ad aliquem specialiter missa, vel affectu compassionis ut consolaretur pusillanimes incitata; ex multis, quae sentiebat, pauca cum humilitate & verecundia referebat. O quoties amicis dicebat: Quid me interrogatis? Non sum digna talia sentire, qualia quaeritis. Quoties Domino quasi cum murmure respondebat; Quid ad me, Domine? mitte quem missurus es. Non sum digna ut eam, & consilia tua aliis nuntiem. Nec tamen Spiritu sancto instigante poterat resistere, quin aliorum utilitati aliqua nuntiando deserviret. Quot enim familiarium suorum in periculis praemunivit? Occultos malignorum spirituum laqueos quotiens amicis suis detexit? Quoties pusillanimes & in fide vacillantes, divinae revelationis miraculis roboravit? Quoties quae sola mente homines cogitaverant, ne perficerent admonuit? Quoties jam corruentes, & fere desperantes, divinis consolationibus relevavit?" (*VMO* 2.2.47:649).

32. "Defunctorum animae, quae torquentur in purgatorio, orationum suarum suffragia postularent; quibus quasi pretioso unguento dolores earum mulcebantur" (*VMO* 1.9.27:143).

33. *VMO* 2.3.52:650; 2.3.53:650–51. On the perception of Mary and other female visionaries as expeditors of purgatorial pains and thus softeners of divine justice, see Elliott, *Proving Women*, 74–82; Newman, *From Virile Woman to WomanChrist*, 108–36. On John of Dinant, see McDonnell, *Beguines and Beghards*, 11 n. 28, 45.

34. *VMO* 2.7.82:658.

35. *VMO* 2.7.83:658.

36. *VMO* 2.6.79:657; 2.3.58–60:652.

37. *VMO* 2.6.77:656.

38. *VMO* 2.6.78:656–57.

39. *VMO* 2.3.61:653–53 Barbara Newman, in "Possessed by the Spirit: Devout Women, Demoniacs, and the Apostolic Life in the Thirteenth Century," *Speculum* 73 (1998): 732–70, esp. 741–42, has suggested that Mary's "vicarious suffering" (as in these cases through fasting) is a prime example of the empathetic or "therapeutic" approach to demon-possessed persons that was new in the thirteenth century, and typical of women.

40. "Obstinatio desperationis & nigredo tristitiae & doloris," *VMO* 2.3.63:653.

41. *VMO* 1.9.30:643.

42. *VMO* 1.9.31–32:644.

43. *VMO* 2.3.50–51:650.

44. *VMO* 2.7.85:658–59.

45. "Licet autem unctione Spiritus sancti, & divinis revelationibus doceretur interius; testimonia tamen Scripturarum, quae Spiritui sancto penitus concordabant, libenter audiebat exterius. Nam quamvis Dominus discipulos interius illuminans, sine voce posset instruere, exterius tamen vocis officio docens, Scripturas etiam eis exponebat, quibus ipse dixit: Jam vos mundi estis propter sermonem quem locutus sum vobis. Ipsa igitur de die in diem divinae Scripturae sermonibus amplius lavabatur ad munditiam, aedificabatur ad morum exornationem, illuminabatur ad fidem; si tamen fides in ea proprie dici valeat, quia Domino revelante invisibilia, quasi visibiliter fide oculata percipiebat" (*VMO* 2.4.71, . 655).

46. *VMO* 2.4.71:655.

47. *VMO* 2.7.86:659; 2.8.91:660–61; 2.4.72:655.

48. *SVMO* 1.2:667.

49. *VMO* 1.6.19–20:641.

50. "Cum in ultima aegritudine, jam fere penitus morte vicina deficeret, & aliquis in ecclesia ad populum sermonem faceret; tunc spiritu ejus ad verbum Dei reviviscente, aures invita morti erigebat, cor praeparabat, circumstantibus etiam de sermone aliqua verba referebat. Adeo autem Praedicatores & fideles animarum Pastores diligebat, quod pedes eorum post praedicationis laborem mira affectione constringens, etiam ipsis invitis vel diu osculari oportebat, vel prae anxietate cum se subtraherent, clamabat" (*VMO* 2.4.68:654).

51. *VMO* 1.13.40:647.

52. *VMO* 2.8.91:660–61.

53. For instance, she often saw the Christ child between the priest's hands when he elevated the Host (*VMO* 2.4.72:655); she saw a dove on the shoulder of a devout priest

saying mass (*VMO* 2.8.91:660) and in the mouth of Fulk of Toulouse when he partook of the Eucharist while celebrating mass (*VMO* 2.12.104:664); she saw angels helping worthy priests (*VMO* 2.7.86:659).

54. *VMO* 1.6.19–20:641.

55. Lauwers, "Entre béguinisme et mysticisme," 59–61; Lauwers, "Expérience béguinale," 100–102.

56. See note 18 above.

57. "Multis autem lacrymosis suspiriis, multis orationibus & jejuniis a Domino instantissime postulando obtinuit, ut meritum & officium praedicationis quod in se actualiter exercere non poterat, in aliqua alia persona Dominus ei recompensaret: & quod sibi Dominus pro magno munere unum Praedicatorem daret. Quo dato, licet per eum dominus, tamquam per instrumentum verba praedicationis emitteret; sanctae mulieris precibus cor praeparabat, virtutem corporis in labore conferebat, verbum ministrabat, gressus dirigebat, gratiam & fructum in auditoribus meritis ancillae suae praeparabat. Nam pro ipso singulis diebus, dum esset in labore praedicandi, Domino & beatae Virgini dicendo Ave Maria centies supplicabat, sicut praedicante Hilario Martinus orabat. Suum vero Praedicatorem, quem in morte praesentialiter reliquit, Domino devotissime commendavit. Cum enim dilexisset suos in finem dilexit eos" (*VMO* 2.4.69:654–55). That Martin of Tours prayed for Hilary of Poitiers's preaching is a tradition witnessed in the *Verbum abbreviatum* of James's teacher Peter the Chanter, *PL* 205, col. 319.

58. She is shown assisting a woman too, the young recluse Heldewid of Willambroux, whose mind she read to expose her temptations and whose future difficulties she predicted—but her role here is more that of helpful colleague than of catalyst or indispensable patroness of Heldewid's salvation (*VMO* 2.6.80:657).

59. "Divinitus inspiratus, & Sanctae mulieris admonitionibus & orationibus adjutus, relicto seculo converteretur ad Dominum" (*VMO* 2.3.58:652).

60. "'Maximum damnum per te nuper recepi: unum enim de specialibus ministris meis mihi abstulisti'" (*VMO* 2.3.58:652).

61. "Cum autem reverteretur ad propria, tamquam ovis de luporum faucibus evulsa, ad Matris spiritualis post tantum naufragium recurrebat solatium" (*VMO*, 2.3.60:652).

62. *VMO* 2.3.58–59:652; "Non enim de facili poterat ab ejus familiaritate separari, cui adhuc debitis adstrictus erat" (2.3.58).

63. Cf., two paragraphs later, the summary description of the efficacy of her prayers for individual friends at Willambroux: the Lord would reveal to her afterward "the extent of the pit of sin in which her close friend would have fallen if the enemy had not been suppressed by her fasts and prayers [in quantam foveam peccati, nisi jejuiis & orationibus ejus oppressus fuisset inimicus, familiaris ejus amicus corruisset]" (*VMO* 2.2.61:652).

64. "Ad se reversus [cf. Luke 15.17, the prodigal son], ex tantae revelationis miraculo salubriter compunctus" (*VMO* 2.2.59:652).

65. "Quidam autem ex sociis ejus, qui nondum forte per experientiam cognoverat, quantum piis mentibus visitatio bonorum familiaritasque conferat... Cumque forte

in vultum ancillae Christi oculos figeret, subito & mirabiliter mutatus animo, in tantam lacrymarum copiam resolutus est, quod vix longo tempore post a loco & ab ejus
praesentia potuit amoveri. Tunc Cantor, licet ille prae verecundia latere vellet, attendens & cognoscens rei eventum, gaudens, & socium suum vice versa irridens, ait:
Eamus, quid hic stamus? Forte papiliones fugare vultis. Ille vero, post multa suspiria
& lacrymas, vix tandem inde avelli potuit, dicens: Ignoscite mihi, quia prius quid
dicerem penitus ignorabam: nunc autem in hac sancta muliere virtutem Dei per experientiam percepi" (*VMO* 1.13.39:646–47). Thomas of Cantimpré tells a similar story
of Lutgard (*VLA* 2.2.27).

66. "Quidam autem ex amicorum suorum praecipuis, à daemonio meridiano
perambulante in tenebris . . . ; tentabatur . . . promittens antidotum, ut latentius subin-
ferret venenum" (*VMO* 1.10.30:643). On the tradition of the "noontide demon," see
Jeffrey B. Russell, *Satan* (Ithaca, N.Y.: Cornell University Press, 1981), 183–84 and the
bibliography there. Also see Geyer, *Maria von Oignies*, 198–203.

67. "Tunc illa ad solita orationum arma confugiens, pedes Domini fletibus rigavit,
caelum precibus instanter pulsavit" (*VMO* 1.10.30:644). The echo of Luke 7:38 suggests the identification of Mary of Oignies with Mary Magdalene. See Michel Lauwers,
" 'Noli Me Tangere.' Marie Madeleine, Marie d'Oignies et les pénitentes Du XIIIe s,"
Mélanges de l'École Française de Rome—Moyen Age 104 (1992): 209–68: James never
explicitly refers to the Magdalene in the *VMO*, but "all that she incarnated for medieval
people can be found in the saint of Oignies" (213). And through the influence of the
vita Mary in a certain sense took over from her, at least as an example for late medieval
preachers: "already at the outset of the fourteenth century, in collections of exempla,
the woman of tears is no longer Mary Magdalene, but Mary of Oignies" (258).

68. See note 45.

69. "Licet autem familiari Spiritus sancti consilio interius uteretur, licet divinis
Scripturis sufficienter instrueretur; prae nimia tamen humilitatis abundantia, ne sapiens in oculis suis videretur, aliorum consiliis, propriae voluntati abrenuntiando,
seipsam libenter & devote subjicere non dedignabatur" (*VMO* 2.6.76:656).

70. "Impetravitque a Domino cum lacrymis, ut praedicto Sacerdoti ostenderet,
quia non est in homine lacrymarum impetum retinere, quando flante spiritu vehe-
menti fluunt aquae. . . . Nunc, inquit, per experientiam didicisti, quod non est in homine impetum spiritus Austro flante retinere" (*VMO* 1.5.17:640).

71. See note 27.

72. See note 57. Cf. Thomas of Cantimpré's story of Lutgard protecting himself by
her prayers from "stirrings of temptation" when he hears confessions of sexual sins
(*VLA* 2.3.38:251).

73. "Ut autem sine personarum acceptione magnalia sanctae mulieris referam,
mihi etiam non parcam, scilicet infelicitatis meae referam historiam. Dum verbum
Dei licet indignus laicis simplicibus praedicare inciperem, & necdum exercitium seu
consuetudinem faciendi sermonem ad populum haberem, semper mihi metuens, ne
forte sermone imperfecto deficerem; multa mihi undecumque colligebam, multis vero
congregatis quidquid in mente habebam in medium proferre volebam. . . . Cumque

tanta prodigalitate meipsum confunderem, ad me post sermonem revertens [cf. Luke 15:17], quasi quoddam mentis taedium, eo quod inordinate & incomposite multa mihi dixisse videbar, incurrebam" (*VMO* 2.6.79:657).

74. "Quibus te laudibus, ô sancta mulier efferam nescio, quae secretorum Dei [eras] conscia. Hominum cogitationes non frustra tibi Dominus aperiebat, sed orationibus tuis virtutem medendi languoribus conferebat" (*VMO* 2.6.79:657).

75. *VMO* 2.2.101:663.

76. Born in 1200 or 1201, Thomas served as a regular canon at Cantimpré, near Cambrai, from 1217 until 1232. He then became a Dominican friar, later studied at Paris, served at some time as subprior of the house of his order at Louvain, and died around 1270. On Thomas as hagiographer, see Simone Roisin, "La méthode hagiographique de Thomas de Cantimpré," in *Miscellanea Historica in Honorem Alberti de Meyer* (Louvain, 1946), 1:546–57; and John Coakley, "Thomas of Cantimpré and Female Sanctity," in *In the Comic Mode*, ed. Rachel Fulton and Bruce Holsinger (New York: Columbia University Press, forthcoming). At the end of the *Supplement* he makes reference to his longtime admiration of James: "I was not yet fifteen years of age and you were not yet a bishop, when I heard you preaching in the region of Lorraine, and loved you with such veneration that the sound of your name alone made me happy: from which time my love for you has endured [Nondum enim annorum quindecim aetatem attigeram, cum vos necdum Praesulem in Lotharingiae partibus praedicantem audiens, tanta veneratione dilexi, ut me solius nominis vestri laetificaret auditus: ex tunc mecum vestri amor individuus perseverat]" (*SVMO* 4.27:676). But see also note 81.

77. The story of the merchant is in *SVMO* 1.4–7:668–69. Miracles: prayer to keep herself and others dry traveling during a rainstorm, *SVMO* 2.8:669–670; two miraculous crossings of the Sambre, *SVMO* 2.9:670; foreknowledge of the arrival of the prior of Oignies from a journey, *SVMO* 2.10:670; appearance of her deceased mother from hell, to say that her prayers will not aid her, *SVMO* 2.12:670–71 (on this, see Alexandra Barratt, "Undutiful Daughters and Metaphorical Mothers among the Beguines" in *New Trends in Feminine Spirituality: The Holy Women of Liège and Their Impact*, ed. Juliette Dor, Lesley Johnson, and Jocelyn Wogan-Browne [Turnhout: Brepols, 1999], 90–93); prophecy of the replacement, in ten years (by James, in the event), of vestments destroyed by fire at priory of Oignies, *SVMO* 2.13:671; prophecy that she will not let Prior Giles take her teeth from her body after death, *SVMO* 3.14:672 .

78. "Compulit ergo ancilla Christi dictum venerabilem virum praedicare populis ... precibus & meritis beatissimae feminae in brevi tempore ad tantam eminentiam praedicationis attingeret, ut in exponendis Scripturis & destructione peccaminum vix ei quisquam inter mortales posset aequari.... elegit eum Deus inter mortales gloriosius sublimandum, ut per eum in salutem animarum mirabiliter operetur.... Vere, inquit illa ... quia virum hunc, in transmarinis partibus Terrae sanctae Episcopali Cathedra sublimabit" (*SVMO* 1.2–3:667).

79. *SVMO* 3.20:674.

80. "Famula Dei ... exegit ab eo precum instantia, ut cum Fratribus de Oignies derelicta Gallia permaneret. Hic est de quo tacito nomine suo in libro Vitae ejusdem

ipse venerabilis Jacobus refert, quia praedicatorem quemdam ancillae suae Dominus dederat, quem in morte sua Domino multis precibus commendabat" (*SVMO* 1.2:667). In his vita of Lutgard of Aywieres, Thomas mentions that Mary prayed insistently for James of Vitry to be liberated from an inappropriate love for a certain religious woman, who was taking him from his preaching; Thomas, perhaps on good knowledge, may be taking Mary's dream about James and the prostitute (see above at note 74) to have a less purely symbolic reference that James himself attached to it (*VLA* 2.1.3:244).

81. "Sed tu, homo voluntatis tuae, consiliis meis & eorum qui spiritualiter amabant te, numquam acquiescere voluisti; semperque tuis, & non alienis judiciis ambulasti" (*SVMO* 4.21:674). Thomas likes to point out the flaws of the otherwise admirable James; in his vita of Lutgard, Thomas reports that Lutgard had a revelation that James was making it difficult for her intercessions on his behalf to be answered (*VLA* 2.1.3:244) and that after his death he appeared to Lutgard, telling her that he had spent three nights and two days in purgatory (*VLA* 3.1.5:257). Ursula Peters has pointed out Thomas's interest in James's ambivalence about his own ambitions (*Religiöse Erfahrung*, 112–13).

82. Like Hildegard, Mary in James's portrait understands weakness in a Pauline sense as the *sine qua non* of her power: after a serious illness "she gave thanks to God who scourges every child whom he has received, with such joy that in her that saying of the apostle is manifestly fulfilled, 'when I am weak, then am I strong' [cf. 2 Cor. 12.10] [cum tanto gaudio Domino gratias agebat, qui flagellat omnem filium quem recepit, quod in ea illud Apostoli manifeste impletum est: Cum infirmor, tunc fortior sum]" (*VMO* 1.13.40:647). Flanagan, *Hildegard of Bingen*, 15.

5. SELF AND SAINT: PETER OF DACIA ON CHRISTINE OF STOMMELN

1. Christine did receive visions, but she appears not to have claimed prophetic knowledge of impending events, the identity of relics, the meaning of obscurities in scripture, or the spiritual state of living persons, and only once of the state of a dead person (a revelation of the parish priest's place in purgatory, *VCS* 187.15–26, letter 26).

2. *VCS* 109–13, quaternus.

3. Christine Ruhrberg, *Der literarische Körper der Heiligen: Leben und Viten der Christina von Stommeln (1242–1312)* (Tübingen and Basel: Francke Verlag, 1995), 110–14 and (on her status as Beguine), 58–60.

4. *VCS* 205.4–16, letter 29; Ruhrberg, *Der literarische Körper*, 114.

5. *Vita … auctore anonymo*, *AA SS* June, 4:454, par. 108. This vita is known from a fifteenth-century manuscript at Vienna of the *Novale sanctorum* of Johan Gielemans, *De codicibus hagiographicis Iohannis Gielemans* (Brussels: Société des Bollandistes, 1895), 62. Although it mainly relies on the sources we know from the *Codex Iuliacensis* (see note 13), this vita appears also to witness to some other early traditions. See Ruhrberg, *Der literarische Körper*, 16–17.

6. On the date, see Peter Nieveler, *Codex Iuliacensis: Christina von Stommeln und Petrus von Dacien, ihr Leben und Nachleben in Geschichte, Kunst und Literatur* (Mönchengladbach: Kuhlen, 1975), 90–91.

7. *VCS* 2–10.

8. M. Michèle Mulcahey, *"First the Bow Is Bent in Study—": Dominican Education Before 1350* (Toronto: Pontifical Institute of Medieval Studies, 1998), 350–84.

9. On the chronology of Peter's life and correspondence, from the evidence of the *Codex Iuliacensis* (see note 13): Jarl Gallén, *La Province de Dacie de l'ordre des frères prècheurs* (Helsingfors: Soderstrom, 1946), 225–44. Here and elsewhere in this chapter I follow Gallén's dating of letters and events.

10. *VCS* 254.9–15, letter 59, 222.11–223.11, letter 37 (possibly referring to Ingrid); see Jarl Gallén, "Les causes de Sainte Ingrid et des saints suédois au temps de la Réforme," *Archivum Fratrum Praedicatorum* 7 (1937): 9–12; Gallén, *La province de Dacie*, 126–27.

11. *VCS* 151–59 (seventeenth, eighteenth, and nineteenth visits in 1279); 218.8–219.7, letter 35 (anticipating an imminent visit in 1287); 244.3–22, letter 52 (apparently thanking her for her hospitality in 1287); Gallén, *La province de Dacie*, 238.

12. Ruhrberg, *Der Literarische Körper.*

13. On the *Codex Iuliacensis* and its history, see Monika Asztalos, introduction to *GND*, 16–27; Ruhrberg, *Der literarische Körper*, 15–16, 136–46; Nieveler, *Codex Iuliacensis*, 13–28; Nieveler, "Christina von Stommeln—historische Bemerkungen zu einem erstaunlichen Leben," *Pulheimer Beitrage zur Geschichte und Heimatkund* 4 (1980): 18–21.

14. Ruhrberg, *Der literarische Körper*, 142–43.

15. *GND* 83–189. *VCS* 182.5–12, letter 24 (13 Jan. 1280); *VCS* 233.28–31, letter 43 (Spring 1282); Ruhrberg, *Der literarische Körper*, 10.

16. It is Asztalos who definitively established the distinction between Peter's compilation and the unedited letters that follow it in the second part of the *Codex Iuliacensis*. Monika Asztalos, "Les lettres de direction et les sermons épistolaires de Pierre de Dacie," in *The Editing of Theological and Philosophical Texts from the Middle Ages*, ed. Monika Asztalos (Stockholm: Almquist & Wiksell International, 1986), 161–84. Johannes Paulson gave the title *Vita Christinae Stumbelensis* to his 1896 edition of the whole of the second part (i.e., *VCS*), which supersedes the seventeenth-century edition of Daniel Papenbroek in *AA SS*, June, vol. 5.

17. In the account of his first visit (1267) as having occurred eleven years before (*VCS* 4.18–19); the latest of the letters is 30, *VCS* 210.

18. Gallén, *La province de Dacie*, 235–40. His death: *VCS* 256, letter 52.

19. *AA SS*, June, 5:294–348, completed by Johannes Paulson, *In Tertiam Partem Libri Juliacensis Annotationes* (Göteborg: Wettergren & Kerber, 1896); Ruhrberg, *Der literarische Körper*, 291–316.

20. The texts identify the scribes of seven of the fourteen letters of Christine: the parish priest in the case of letters 16, 17, 18, and 19 (*VCS* 134.19–20; 142.9–11); he is also identified as the writer of her "notebook" (*quaternus*; 131.17–18); Lawrence for letter 21 (148.26); and John the schoolmaster for letters 25 (165.16–17) and 26 (182.23–4). An

aside addressed by the writer to Peter in letter 29 (198.16–24; see note 22) strongly suggests the schoolmaster. On the question of the possible extent of the role of the collaborators in the persona of Christine as presented in these texts, see John Coakley, "A Marriage and Its Observer: Christine of Stommeln, the Heavenly Bridegroom, and Friar Peter of Dacia," in *Gendered Voices: Medieval Saints and Their Interpreters*, ed. Catherine Mooney (Philadelphia: University of Pennsylvania Press, 1999), 99–101, 115–17. The formation of the persona of Christine under clerical influence suggests a possible parallel to the case of Christine the Astonishing (vita by Thomas of Cantimpré) who may have been, as Barbara Newman has hypothesized an "*obsessa*" taught by "a priest and his circle ... to model her behavior, insofar as she could control it, on the devotions of the lay *mulieres sanctae*": Newman, "Possessed by the Spirit: Devout Women, Demoniacs, and the Apostolic Life in the Thirteenth Century," *Speculum* 73 (1998): 766–67.

21. The three letters of Christine for which the schoolmaster was the evident scribe (25, 26, and 29) refer to her almost entirely in the third person; so do the "notebook" (109.17–131.20) and portions of two other letters, 17 (136.1–138.24) and 19 (141.10–34, 142.6–8), all penned by the parish priest. On the variation of styles—that of the parish priest, in particular, showing more evidence of Germanic syntax than the others—see Ruhrberg, *Der literarische Körper*, 267–70.

22. The first passage: "I make these secrets known to your charity, which are manifested to me not by a human being, but by divine inspiration. Nor is this surprising, for when it is said generally of the servants of God 'for you are not the one who speaks but the spirit of your father, who speaks in you [Matt. 10.20],' how much more truly is this to be understood of the bride, and especially at that moment when she comes forth from the bridechamber, and forgets all things including even herself. I write you this, so that you may know that Christine, your daughter, told me nothing of those things that are written here while in control of herself, except a little about her sufferings, which she certainly would not have done, if she had not understood me as a kind of accomplice when I asked it of her [haec secreta uestre caritati notifico, que michi non ab homine, sed diuinitus sunt manifestata. nec mirum; cum enim de ministris dei generaliter dicatur: 'non enim uos estis, qui loquimini, sed spiritus patris uestri, qui loquitur in uobis,' multo uerius de sponsa hoc intelligendum est, et maxime illo tempore, cum recenter de thalamo sponsi proficiscitur, et non solum omnium rerum. uerum eciam sui ipsius obliuiscitur. Hoc uobis scribo, ut sciatis, quia christina, uestra filia, sui conpos, nichil horum, que scripta sunt, preter pauca de passionibus michi retulit; quod tamen omnino non fecisset, si non me quasi conscium pro huiusmodi requirere audiuisset]" (*VCS* 181.13–25, letter 25). See also Ruhrberg, *Der literarische Körper*, 294–96. There is, however, another version of the narrative of this letter in the third part of the *Codex Iuliacensis*—which was not edited by Peter—in which the passage in question is missing. Paulson, *In Tertiam Partem*, 55 (see note 13). See Ruhrberg, *Der literarische Körper*, 294–96. The second passage: "I have proposed to declare to you certain of the sufferings of your daughter, along with her consolations, which, however, I could not do were it not for the fact that the blessed alienation of your

daughter after Communion, to a greater extent than anything she consciously told me, showed me what I ought to write [quedam uobis de passionibus filie uestre simul et consolacionibus proposui declarare. Quod tamen omnino facere non possem, si non magis filie uestre post conmunionem felix alienacio, quam ipsius conscie relacio michi ea, que scribere uobis debeo, ostendisset]" (*VCS* 198.19–21, letter 29).

23. For a careful description of the demonic vexations, see Anna J. Martin, "Christina von Stommeln." *Mediaevistik* 4 (1991): 227–40.

24. "You asked certain things of me," she wrote in her first letter after his departure for Paris, "which I did not reveal to you, for which reason I was sorry afterward; and I know that it would have been a good thing for me to tell you these things and many others [Quedam requisiuistis a me, que uobis non reuelaui, unde postea dolui; et scio michi bonum fuisse illa et alia plura uobis recitasse]" (*VCS* 67.10–12, letter 2).

25. Letter 9 (*VCS* 88–92) is a commentary on phrases from letter 7; see note 83. In letter 5 (78.25–79.11), he asks for more details of her raptures.

26. "Nullus est, quem in meis libencius tribulacionibus haberem, quia semper paratus fuistis, cum tribularer, ad me uenire" (*VCS* 70.14–16, letter 4.

27. *VCS* 69–75, letter 4, and *VCS* 82–88, letter 7.

28. "Rogo uos … ut michi scribi faciatis de statu uestro, quantum colligere potestis in unumquaternum" (*VCS* 100.1–4, letter 10).

29. "Preterea ea que michi scripsistis nuper, qualiter iam dudum scire dedideratis scire de statu meo et notari in quaternum: scire debetis, quod hoc propono, quantum possum, et in hoc habetis prerog atiuam, quia nemini sub celo facere hoc bene possem" (*VCS* 101.10–15, letter 13). He replies that he was "comforted (*consolatur*) by her promise" (*VCS* 103.9–12, letter 14).

30. "'Amicus tuus est et erit et multa pro te faciet; sed et tu pro eo facies ea, que pro nullo alio mortalium es factura. sed et scias, quod tecum commansurus est in uita eterna'" (*VCS* 107.23–26; fifteenth visit).

31. "Omnia in bonum convertistis, quasi amicus sciens faciliter meam intencionem" (*VCS* 133.26–27, letter 16; 134.14–16, letter 16).

32. On her family misfortunes: *VCS* 138.28–140.27, letter 18; 148.23–150.7, letter 21. On Sigwin: 195.24–198.6, letter 28; cf. 181.29–32, letter 25; 206.29–207.5, letter 29; 196.21–197.18, letter 28.

33. *VCS* 234.4–6, letter 43; 216.27–218.4, letter 34; "et quia nemo suis tependiis militat umquam, non miremini deinceps, si pauciores littere mee ad uos peruenerint, quem secretorum uestrorum, ut estimo, indigmum fore iudicastis" (215.6–9, letter 33).

34. *VCS* 239.18–30, letter 48; 234.8–13, letter 43.

35. *VCS* 165–82, letter 25; 182–89, letter 26; 198–207, letter 29.

36. Peter requested him to undertake this project: *VCS* 236.11–16, letter 45; Ruhrberg, *Der literarische Körper*, 291–99.

37. *VCS* 109.17–112.14, quaternus.

38. *VCS* 113.21–25, quaternus.

39. *VCS* 119.8–10, quaternus.

40. *VCS* 122.13–29, quaternus.

41. *VCS* 125.8–23, quaternus.

42. *VCS* 129.14–23, quaternus.

43. *VCS* 71.4–7, letter 4. In another letter to Peter in Paris she describes a demon substituting himself for the Host at mass and says that Communion subsequently was a source of bitterness for her in contrast to previous experience (*VCS* 83.8–10, 84.15–20, letter 7).

44. "Ille dulcissimus sponsus, beatam eius animam rapiens, in archanum sui dilectissimi cordis thalamum hanc transuexit; ubi secundum multitudinem dolorum precedencium diuine consolaciones eius animam ineffabiliter letificaverunt" (*VCS* 202.17–21, letter 29). Cf. *VCS* 172.25–27, letter 25; (175.2–18, letter 25).

45. It is important to distinguish the picture of Christine as the text itself presents her—which is my concern here—from inferences about the supposed actual experience of Christine, as, for instance, in Aviad Kleinberg's discussion of Christine in *Prophets in Their Own Country*, 84–98. I am understanding "mysticism" here as, in Bernard McGinn's helpfully broad characterization, "a direct consciousness of the presence of God" (McGinn, *The Foundations of Mysticism: Origins to the Fifth Century* [New York: Crossroad, 1991], xix).

46. "Uerum eciam sui sponsi desiderabilem uisionem et intimam cordis exultacionem" (*VCS* 181.2–3, letter 25).

47. *VCS* 202.19–21, letter 29. See note 44.

48. "'Dearest daughter, behold, I am Jesus Christ; promise me your allegiance, such that you will always serve me. If anyone else asks some other allegiance of you, say that because you have promised it to Jesus Christ in his hands'—in which therefore she promised—'[and] you will stay with the Beguines' [karissima filia, ecce ihesus cristus sum; promitte michi fidem tuam, ita quod semper michi seruias. Siquis de cetero te de altera fide requisierit, dicas: quia ihesu cristo eam promisisti in suas manus—in quas igitur promisit—cum beginis manebis]" (*VCS* 109.21–110.1, quaternus).

49. *VCS* 110.4–9, quaternus.

50. *VCS* 111.23–112.2, quaternus.

51. *VCS* 70.18–71.8, letter 4; 85.2–8, letter 7.

52. *VCS* 83.5–6, letter 7; 84.5–6, 20–24, letter 7.

53. E.g., most spectacularly, a repeated visit by a demon in the form of a man who made sexual advances on her and who, when she resisted, appeared to kill her father (*VCS* 126.23–130.8, quaternus).

54. *VCS* 112.15–113.17, quaternus.

55. *VCS* 122.2–13; 123.22–125.8, quaternus.

56. *VCS* 114.1–19, quaternus.

57. *VCS* 120.6–17, quaternus.

58. *VCS* 134.23–135.1, letter 17.

59. *VCS* 135.29–136.1; 136.13–24; 137.18–138.24, letter 17. Her apparent epilepsy did not go unremarked: *VCS* 111.28–112.1, quaternus.

60. *VCS* 167.12–23; 170.23–31; 168.29–169.10, letter 25.

61. *VCS* 170.11–15, letter 25.

62. *VCS* 199.24–27; 199.33–200.1; 203.24–204.20, letter 29.

63. According to Gallén's dating, the first through the thirteenth visits (*VCS* 2–65) occurred from 20 December 1267 through 14 April 1269, the fourteenth through sixteenth visits (*VCS* 105–109) in late spring 1270, and the seventeenth, eighteenth, and nineteenth visits (*VCS* 151–59) between 15 September and 25 October 1279: Gallén, *La province de Dacie*, 227–229, 233.

64. Nonetheless, Paulson did not innovate in denominating the contents of the second part of the *Codex Iuliacensis*, a vita (see note 16); the fourteenth-century rubricator of the codex already entitled it "liber secundus de vita benedicte virginis Christi Cristine" (the other sections being entitled "liber primus de virtitubus sponse Cristi Christine" and "liber tercius de passionibus.. virginis Christi Cristine"): Asztalos, introduction, 16.

65. To be sure, in conveying autobiographical information Peter is not concerned to stake out his own individuality as a person—his particular uniqueness or the distinction between himself and other people—in the manner of modern autobiographers. See Ruhrberg, *Der literarische Körper*, 208–13.

66. *VCS* 1.7–21, prologue.

67. *VCS* 2–65.

68. *VCS* 65–105: seven are addressed by Peter to Christine (letters 1, 5, 8, 9, 10, 14, 15), four by Christine to Peter (letters 2, 4, 7, 13), and four by others in their circle, respectively the friars Gerard (letter 3) and Maurice (letters 6, 11) and the parish priest (letter 12).

69. *VCS* 105–9.

70. *VCS* 109–31.

71. *VCS* 131–50: five addressed by Christine to Peter (letters 16, 17, 18, 19, 21), one addressed by Peter to Christine (letter 20), and one addressed by Friar Lawrence to Peter (letter 22).

72. *VCS* 151–59.

73. *VCS* 159–213: four addressed by Peter to Christine (letters 23, 24, 37, 42), five addressed by Christine to Peter (letters 25, 26, 28, 29, 30), and one by Friar Lawrence to Peter (letter 31).

74. *VCS* 67.6–7; 68.29–33; 75.1–4; 81.17–20; 82.17–18; 87.28–88.2; 100.5–6, 14, 25; 102.6–7; 109.4–11; 131.15–24; 134.20–22; 138.25–27; 140.28–9; 142.9–14; 148.16–22; 150.8–9; 159.6–8; 162.3; 165.18–21; 182.22–24; 189.26–29; 198.3–6; 207.27–208.17; 210.9–12.

75. *VCS* 70.20–26, letter 4; 73.29–31, letter 4; 129.4–8, 23–24, quaternus; cf. 72.11–14, letter 4; 73.31–74.4, letter 4; 85.7–9,21–23, letter 5; 110.4–9,20–27, quaternus; 111.23–112.2, quaternus; 115.16–20, quaternus; 120.19–121.29, quaternus; 123.7–10, quaternus; 130.4–8, quaternus; 138.3–10, letter 17; 139.6–8, letter 18; 187.21–6, letter 26; 210.20–33, letter 31.

76. "Numquam tamen intendi, quod affectionem uestram circa me occuparem, uel saltem ad me inclinarem: quin pocius, quantum sciui, laboraui uerbis, ostendi signis, ut in cristi tota ferremini affectum, transferremini amplexum; quem tociens non solum non formidando, sed et iubilando sponsum nominatis, ipsoque intimo gaudio

non solum nomen, sed et ipsam rem uobis uendicatis" (*VCS* 75.15–21, letter 5). Christine had written that no one else comforted her as he did (*VCS* 70.5–11, letter 4).

77. "Sed hoc solum uolo, ut frequenter cogitetis, intime ametis, feruenter desideretis quidquid illud sit, quod est tam uictoriosum, ut naturalia triumphet; tam intimum, ut omnes sensus exteriores in interiora introducat; tam iocundum, ut sui ipsius obliuiosum uel pocius omnino insensibilem faciat; Tam gaudiosum, ut se in se continere non ualeat, quin in uerbis et in gestibus prodat inuitus, quod uult omnibus esse occultum; quod utique gaudium non solum uos letificauit, cui se non solum exhibebat, sed et medullitus infundebat, immo quam et implebat et inebriabat sed et eructare faciebat, sed et me quoque indignum et in longinquo regionis dissimilitudinis positum non modice nec semel, sed multociens letificabat" (*VCS* 76.1–14, letter 5).

78. *VCS* 76.21–27, letter 5.

79. *VCS* 77.20–32, letter 5.

80. *VCS* 78.20–79.21, letter 5.

81. *VCS* 79.20–80.8, letter 5.

82. His comment that "from the words or responses of the bride, of which I have heard many, I have inferred his sayings or promises [ex uerbis tamen uel responsis sponse, que pluries audiui, dicta eius uel promissa conieci]" (*VCS* 80.18–20 letter 5), stands without supporting examples of such "words or responses."

83. "Quid sibi uolunt uerba, que in litteris uestris legi: 'uobis, sicut michi est in corde, non possum scribere', et iterum: 'conqueror uobis de absencia dilecti,' et post pauca: 'Tamen nunc aliquantulum clara dies effulsit'?" (*VCS* 89.14–18 letter 9). The phrases are taken from her letter 7: "when I remember how how kind and compassionate and useful a helper you were for me, I mourn again the absence of my beloved, knowing no one, who would believe the bitterness I feel to the extent that you do; nonetheless now a little light shines forth.... I cannot write to you of what is in my heart because of the modesty that, as you know, is in me [cum recorder, quam propicius, quam misericors, quam utilis coadiutor michi fuistis, iterum conqueror uobis de absencia mei dilecti, cum nullum scio, qui de tanta acerbitate michi sit adeo credibilis, sicut uos; tamen nunc aliquantulum dies clara effulsit.... Vobis, sicut michi est in corde, non possum propter erubescenciam, quam scitis in me esse, scribere]" (*VCS* 87.5–10, 15–17, letter 7).

84. E.g., *VCS* 75–81, letter 5; 162–165, letter 24; 189–95, letter 27. The thought occurs to every reader that Christine and Peter must have experienced what we would construe as romantic attraction. See for instance Friedrich Ochsner, *Petrus de Dacia Gothensis: Mystiker der Freundschaft* (Visby: Barry Press, 1975), 89–97; Volker Schmidt-Kohl, "Petrus de Dacia, ein Skandinavischer Mystiker des 13. Jahrhunderts," *Zeitschrift für Religions- und Geistesgeschichte* 18 (1966): 258–59; Martin, "Christina von Stommeln," 213–15. This is certainly believable, on the basis of these texts, but it is important to note that the texts do not suggest any tension or contradiction between their affection for each other and the divine love of which Peter speaks, or accordingly any sense that they had feelings that needed to be checked. On this point see the helpful discussion by Ruhrberg, *Der literarische Körper*, 122–36.

85. *VCS* 159.19–21, letter 23).

86. *VCS* 160.1–161.8, letter 23).

87. *VCS* 163.26–165.16, letter 24).

88. *VCS* 3.18–27, 5.21–6.3, 7.9–32 (first visit).

89. *VCS* 11.9–14.31 (second visit). On late-medieval understandings of such raptures, see Elliott, "The Physiology of Rapture," 141–73, esp. 142–48; Caciola, *Discerning Spirits*, 54–78.

90. *VCS* 16.15–30 (third visit); 18.27–20.21 (fourth visit).

91. *VCS* 25.19–26.6 (fifth visit); 26.8–27.34 (sixth visit); 34.9–36.26 (seventh visit); 37.30–38.23 (eighth visit).

92. *VCS* 41.15–48.27 (ninth visit); triplication of the cross: *VCS* 48.17–20 (ninth visit); 48.5–55.31 (tenth visit).

93. *VCS* 56.1–57.6 (eleventh visit); 58.26–62.19 (twelfth visit).

94. "Ut aliquem seruorum suorum michi ostenderet, in quo conuersacionem sanctorum suorum non solum uerbis sed factis et exemplis secure et plane addiscerem; cui caritate ex corde coniungerer et consociarer; cuius moribus informarer; cuius deuocione inflammarer et ab accidia, que me a puericia depresserat, excitarer; cuius collocucione illuminarer; cuius familiaritate consolarer; cuius exemplis de omnibus certificarer dubiis, maxime que ad conuersacionem pertinent sanctorum" (*VCS* 2.11–19 [first visit]).

95. "Ex inopinato michi personam quandam hoc modo ostendit, cuius aspectu simul et affatu me multipliciter letificauit non solum per presencie exhibicionem, sed memorie recordacionem" (*VCS* 2.32–3.2 [first visit]).

96. "Solus ego gaudio quodam inusitato perfundebar intimeque consolabar et in stuporem mentis suspendebar" (*VCS* 4.2–4 [first visit]).

97. "Hanc crucem oculis uidi, sed uirtutem eius corde meo intrinsecus percepi. Nam ab illa hora familiarius michi fuit de cruce et crucifixo meditari" (*VCS* 16.29–31 [third visit]).

98. "Ad hanc uisionem secundo iteratam erat stupor quidam in oculis meis et admiracio et mira ad cristum passum in corde nascebatur compassio; et nescio, si ad illud tempus de uisis uel auditis, lectis uel scriptis, usque ad illam horam aliquid cor meum sic penetrauit et cristi passionem in eo sic profundauit" (*VCS* 19.27–20.5 [fourth visit]).

99. "Gaudium speciale … facile enim erat probare, quod uisu aparuit" (*VCS* 28.18, 20–1 [fifth visit]).

100. "Insuper et in corde gaudio magno et prius inconperto sum perfusus et ideo a risu me non possum continere" (*VCS* 46.3–4 [seventh visit]).

101. *VCS* 46.7–19 (ninth visit).

102. "Nichil enim talium sensibus forinsecus offerebatur, quod cordi tantum intrinsecus gaudium posset causare. Quin pocius, ut predictum est, demonis adesse senciebatur presencia, timebatur seuicia, familie audiebatur mesticia, puelle prememorate facile aduerti poterat tristicia; et inter hec, queso: unde oriri poterat leticia et inmutacio tam insolita?" (*VCS* 4.6–12 [first visit]).

103. "Ad hec cepi admirari, quod inter tot ictus et tam graues nullos audiui puellam emittere gemitus uel singultus, sed et quod nec alicuius alterius, non dico inpaciencie, sed nec doloris signa in uerbis uel factis depromebat, sed inmobilis permansit, non murmur nec queremoniam resonans" (*VCS* 5.3–8 [first visit]).

104. "Audiui dictam puellam suspirantem, quasi ex inopinato aliquid doloris ei euenisset" (*VCS* 5.15–16 [first visit]).

105. "Et ideo desideraui mirabilibus dei intendere et interesse, que in persona predicta lucide et multifarie ostendebantur, cui iam in spiritu ueritatis et dilectione sinceritatis anima mea erat conglutinata in tantum, ut uix dei potuerim recordari sine illius recordacione" (*VCS* 9.28–10.2 [first visit]).

106. "'Uere tota illa conpressio non fuit naturalis…. hoc credo fuisse supernaturale'" (*VCS* 36.21, 25–26 [seventh visit]).

107. "Et rapta est predicta puella in tantum mentis excessum, ut in omnibus sensibus inmobilis facta et toto corpore indurata nullum uite sensibilis preferret indicium, et—quod plus addidit stuporis—nec perpendi poterat, quod attraheret spiritum. fateor: dum hec fierent, pre gaudio flebam et pro miraculo stupebam et pro tanto diuine influencie dono gracias largitori referebam; nichil enim de hiis nature uel humane industrie attribuebam, sed diuinam presenciam in hoc facto sum ueneratus … cum ergo talem disposicionem in homine mortali numquam uidissem, putabam hoc esse, quod in apostolo legi: 'siue mente excedimus,' nulli enim alii rei michi, quod uidi, uidebatur esse similius cepique tanto solicicius cuncta considerare facta, ascultare uerba, motus et gestus ponderare et memorie alcius recommendare, quia priuilegio gracie singularis omnia esse iudicaui attribuenda" (*VCS* 11.17–12.1 [second visit]). Peter later likens other raptures to this one: *VCS* 25.28–26.4 (fifth visit); 26.17–24 (sixth visit).

108. See notes 92 and 93.

109. In the poem (*GND* 1,83–85), which he presents as an exhibition of the "flowers of [Christine's] virtues" (vv. 1–8; "virtutum colligo flores," v. 1), Peter treats, in sequence, her likeness to Christ and to both Mary and Martha (vv. 9–16), the devotion of her friends and the ignorance of her enemies (vv. 17–18), her union with Christ (vv. 19–24), her virtues per se (vv. 25–32), the devil's trials (vv. 33–38), and her effect on others including himself (vv. 39–43). The commentary, which consists for the most part of quotations and paraphrases of various other authors, begins with an exposition of vv. 1–8 (*GND* 2, 85–88) and then, following a large lacuna (22 folios of the manuscript), proceeds in the bulk of what remains (*GND* 3–11, 89–151) to present what Asztalos calls an "exposition of the dogmatic system comprised in" vv. 27–28, which expresses "the rapports between nature, grace and glory" (introduction, 42) with expositions of various categories of grace (see note 112), before presenting an exposition of v. 29 and the notion of a "privileged grace" (see note 111 below) as implied in v. 29 (*GND* 12, 151–69) and finally a line-by-line exposition of vv. 29–43 (*GND* 13, 169–88).

110. Thomas Aquinas offered a course of lectures at Paris in the winter of 1269–70. Gallén, *La province de Dacie*, 228–29. Two works by Thomas are among Peter's sources in *GND*: *Scriptum super libros Sententiarum*, which is his single most cited source in the discussions of categories of grace in chaps. 3 through 11, and *Quaestiones disputatae*

de veritate, which is his major source in the discussion of privileged grace in chap. 12. Asztalos, introduction, 56–58, 43.

111. "Et licet ad perfectam beatitudinem in hac vita nullus possit pervenire, datur tamen aliquibus per graciam privilegiatam ut per raptum de ea aliquid presenciant" (*GND* 11.26, 151). Asztalos, introduction, 49–50.

112. *GND* 3, 89–110 (gracia condicionis); *GND* 4, 111–119 (gracia assumptionis); *GND* 5, 120–131, 6, 132, 8, 139–40 (gracia iustificacionis); *GND* 7, 133–38, 9, 141 (gracia glorificacionis). Asztalos, introduction, 43–49.

113. Asztalos, introduction, 50–52.

114. *GND* 1, 84, vv. 25–28.

115. *GND* 1, 84, vv. 29–32.

116. Asztalos, introduction, 50; Asztalos, "La conception de l'homme dans les écrits de Pierre de Dacie," in *L'Homme et son univers au Moyen Age. Actes du Septième Congrès International de Philosophie Médiévale 30.8–4.9.1982*, vol. 1, ed. Christian Wenin (Louvain-la-Neuve, Institut Supérieur de Philosophie, 1986), 262–65.

117. "'Non' ait; 'sed uolo hac arte corpus, cuius sensus in malum ab adolescencia sua proni sunt, per spiritum sic affectum ad me conuertere et attrahere, ut meo degustato spiritu desipiat omnis caro'" (*VCS* 95.1–4, letter 10).

118. "Tali enim arte ad me traham spiritum, mea ymagine insignitum, et per eum lucrabor limum ex omni elementorum genere conpositum, ut, sicut a me creata sunt corporalia et spiritualia, sic utraque secundum modum sibi possibilem pro me et in me beatificentur et a se quodammodo alienentur, ut in me transformentur" (*VCS* 95.9–14, letter 10). He proceeds to quote John the Scot that "'just as the air, illuminated by the sun, appears to be nothing except light, not because it loses its own nature but because the light prevails over it so that it would be taken to be of the light; thus human nature, joined to God, is said to be God in every way, not because it ceases to be nature, but because it receives the participation of God in such a way that only God might be seen to be in it [sicut aer, a sole illuminatus, nichil aliud uidetur esse nisi lux, non quia sui naturam perdat, sed quia lux in eo preualeat, ut id ipsum lucis esse estimetur; sic humana natura, deo adiuncta, deus per omnia dicitur esse, non quod desinat esse natura, sed quod deitatis participacionem accipiat, ut solus in ea deus esse uideatur'" (*VCS* 95.16–21, letter 10).

119. "Quis michi det, ut desiderium meum audiat omnipotens, ut tali possim uiuere uiuendi modo uel, ut uerius dicam, diuino dono, sicut uiuitis, quando abscondimini in diuine faciei abscondito et protegimini in tabernaculo ab hominum conturbacione et linguarum contradictione" (*VCS* 95.28–96.1, letter 10).

120. "Si, inquam, huiusmodi uite aliqua uel extrema participacio daretur michi, quam pacienter et diligenter ascultarem!" (*VCS* 96.1–3, letter 10).

121. "Thalamum cum obsequio et reuerencia introire, epithalamium intente et deuote audire" (*VCS* 76.29–31, letter 5); 80.14–20, letter 5. Coakley, "A Marriage and Its Observer," 105–7.

122. "Quam affectuose congratularer de uestro et uestri dilecti concursu et conuictu, coniunctione et coniocundacione duorum michi tam dilectorum et desideratorum, sibi inuicem karissimorum, cum ex parte uestra audirem uota deuocionis, uerba dilectionis, sonos obedicionis, preces expectacionis, gaudia suscepcionis, exultacionis,

perfruicionis, desideria remansionis, suspiria separacionis et fletus desolacionis!" (*VCS* 96.4–11, letter 10).

123. Ruhrberg discusses the passage but, without noting the allusion to Rachel and Leah, suggests an allusion to the brother of the bride in Cant. 8:8 (*Der literarische Körper*, 246). There is no clear verbal reminiscence of that verse, however, and Peter is making himself out as sister, not brother.

124. "Quia omnino pauper et inops sum, nec habeo, unde hanc mercedem soluam, puritatem dico et caritatem, deuocionem simul et honestam conuersacionem, iugem et feruentem oracionem, sublimem et affectuosam contemplacionem" (*VCS* 96.28–32, letter 10).

125. *VCS* 96.34–97.5, letter 10.

126. "Quid igitur michi restat, qui annis antiquior, nupciis iam factus inepcior—quia corde frigidior, facie rugosior, mercede pauperior, fetu sterilior, superductione iunioris sororis despectior—nisi ut, qui in me placere non merui, saltem caueam displicere? Scio, quid faciam. exhibebo me sorori mee familiarem et sponso eius deuotum et obsequiosum, ut et hec michi saltem de effluencia gaudiorum et sciencia secretorum aliquid communicet, et ille eo libencius, frequencius, festiuius et familiarius ueniat, dum in una sororum paratum inueniat thalamum cordis et in alia promtum reperiat obsequium corporis, in utraque autem desiderium deuote expectacionis. sic igitur placabo sponsum precibus, placabo muneribus, placabo obsequiosis operibus; et dicam, ut facilius alliciam, efficacius suadeam et forcius traham: habeo sororem iuniorem, uenustiorem; ad illam ingredere, illi coniungere, illam amplectere, ut uel sic memoria mei ab affectu eius non deleatur" (*VCS* 97.9–25, letter 10).

127. "In tanta et tantorum deuocione aridus, tam multorum feruenti dilectione frigidus, tam strennua convuersacione remissus, tam rigida religione dissolutus conuersari non formido" (*VCS* 104.13–15, letter 15).

128. "Rogate autem dominum, karissima et per amorem diuinum deo et anime mee desponsata, ut huius desponsacionis fidem seruemus intemeratam et arram amoris senciamus incontaminatam" (*VCS* 228.7–10, letter 39, a letter not in Peter's own compilation), 12 November 1279 (Gallén, *La province de Dacie*, 242).

129. "Similitudinem quandam in nobis video eternis societatis et intime sanctorum caritatis" (*VCS* 190.8–10, letter 27, November–December 1280; Gallén, *La province de Dacie*, 243).

130. "Ipse eciam nos, distantes loco, dispares merito et dissimiles cotidiano exercicio, in unum fedus amicicie adunauit" (*VCS* 247.1–3, letter 55, not in Peter's compilation, of uncertain date between 1280 and 1286); Gallén, *La province de Dacie*, 244.

131. *VCS* 159.23–26, letter 33, 24 November 1279; Gallén, *La province de Dacie*, 242.

6. HAGIOGRAPHY AND THEOLOGY IN THE *MEMORIAL* OF ANGELA OF FOLIGNO

1. On the manuscript witnesses, see Angela of Foligno, *Il Libro della beata Angela da Foligno*, ed. Ludger Thier and Abele Calufetti (Rome: Collegii S. Bonaventurae

Ad Claras Aquas, 1985), 51–73. I shall work from the so-called major (longer) recension which is witnessed in, among others, the Assisi manuscript (see note 5), as distinct from the minor recension that is witnessed in five MSS of Belgian provenance, in which much of the friar's self-referential comment is lacking. Thier and Calufetti present both versions in their edition (cited as *Mem.*), italicizing text that is unique to the major recension. Emore Paoli, "Le due redazioni del *Liber*: Il perché di una riscritta," in *Angèle de Foligno: Le Dossier*, ed. Giulia Barone and Jacques Dalarun (Rome: École française de Rome, 1999), 29–70, has now confirmed the hypothesis of Enrico Menestò, "Problemi critico-testuali nel 'Liber' della Beata Angela," in *Angela da Foligno Terziaria Francescana. Atti del Convegno storico nel VII centenario cell'ingresso della beata Angela da Foligno nell'Ordine Francescano Secolare (1291–1991)*, ed. Enrico Menestò (Spoleto: Centro Italiano du Studi sull'Alto Medioevo, 1992), 161–79, that the minor recension represents a condensation of the major recension by a different redactor (likely from the circles of the fifteenth-century Devotio Moderna [see note 25]) over against Thier and Calufetti who considered both recensions to be the work of the friar-writer, with the shorter preceding the longer (*Il libro*, 108–13). Dominique Poirel, "Le *Liber* d'Angèle de Foligno: Enquête sur un *exemplar* disparu," *Revue d'histoire des textes* 32 (2002): 225–63, has now compellingly argued the bold thesis that the exemplar not only of the Assisi manuscript but also of the other fourteenth-century manuscript witnesses of the major recension, was the friar-writer's own annotated copy of the work and that the textual variants reflect, in part, the variety of copyists' attempts to incorporate his annotations into the text, thus explaining the "chaotic" character of the variants, which appears to resist explanation by the various stemmata that have been proposed.

2. On the content of the Book, see Angela of Foligno, *Il Libro*, 41–42. The *Instructions* include letters, brief narratives, and discourses, apparently produced by various redactors and in different combinations and order depending upon the manuscript: Angela of Foligno, *Il Libro*, 112–15; Angela of Foligno, *Complete Works*, ed. and trans. Paul Lachance (New York: Paulist Press, 1993), 81–84.

3. The sixth supplementary step "began...a little while before the pontificate of pope Celestine [5 July to 13 December 1294] and lasted for more than two years [incoepit...aliquo tempore ante pontificatum papae Coelestini, et duravit plus quam per duos annos]" (*Mem.* 7.181–3:352); "antequam cum summo pontifice in scandalum incideret" (*Mem.*, Test.5–6:12). Maria Pia Alberzoni, "L''approbatio': Curia romana, Ordine Minoritico e *Liber*," in *Angèle de Foligno: Le Dossier*, ed. Giulia Barone and Jacques Dalarun (Rome: École française de Rome, 1999), 293 (on the manuscript witnesses to the *Testificatio*), 306–7 (on the logic of the dating).

4. "In the twenty-fifth year of my religious life, it came about—I will not go into detail—that I encountered the reverend and most holy mother, Angela of Foligno, a veritable angel, to whom Jesus revealed my heart's defects and his secret kindness in such a manner that I was convinced he spoke through her. She restored a thousand-fold all those spiritual gifts I had lost through my sins; so that from that moment I have not been the same man I was before [Vigesimoquinto autem anno etatis mee

et modo quem pretereo ad reverende matris et sanctissime Angele de Fulgineo vere angelice vite in terris me adduxit noticiam. Cui sic cordis mei defectus & sua secreta beneficia revelavit Iesus ut dubitare non possem ipsum esse qui loquebatur in illa & sic omnia dona propria per meam malitiam perdita in immensum multiplicata restituit ut iam ex tunc non fuerim ille qui fui]": Ubertino of Casale, *Arbor vitae crucifixae Jesu*, ed. Charles T. Davis (reprint, Turin: Bottega d'Erasmo, 1961), 5A–B; translation by Paul Lachance, Angela of Foligno, *Complete Works*, 110.

5. "The venerable bride of Christ A. of F. departed the shipwreck of this world … on the day before the nones of January in the year of the Lord 1309 [Transiit autem venerabilis sponsa Christi A. de F. ex hoc mundi naufragio … anno dominice incarnationis. m.ccc.ix., pridie nonas ianuarii]" The appearance of this note on a page of the *Instructions* (f. 48v.) that otherwise does not prompt it suggests its insertion as a piece of breaking news: Attilio Bartoli Langeli, "Il codice di Assisi, ovvero il *Liber sororis Lelle*," in *Angèle de Foligno: Le Dossier*, ed. Giulia Barone and Jacques Dalarun (Rome: École française de Rome, 1999), 14–15. On the name "Angela" see note 13.

6. Much work remains to be done on the *Instructions* (see note 2) before their value as historical sources is clear.

7. On the penitential movement, see especially Gilles Meersseman, *Dossier de l'ordre de la pénitence au XIIIe siècle* (Fribourg: Editions universitaires, 1961), 1–38; on the relation of the Italian penitents to the Beguines of the north, see Alcantara Mens, *De l'Ombrie italienne et l'Ombrie brabançonne* (Paris: Etudes Franciscaines, 1967); Martina Wehrli-Johns, "Vorraussetzungen und Perspektiven mittelalterlicher Laienfrömmigkeit seit Innocenz III. Eine Auseinandersetzung mit Herbert Grundmanns 'Religiöse Bewegungen,'" in *Mitteilungen des Instituts für Österreichische Geschichtsforschung* 104 (1996): 299–303; on Italian penitent women, see Silvestro Nessi, "Spiritualità femminile penitenziale in Umbria nel secolo XIII," in *Vita e spiritualità della beata Angela da Foligno. Atti del convegno di studi per il VII centenario della conversione della beata Angela da Foligno (1285–1985)*, ed. Clément Schmitt (Perugia: Serafica provincia di san Francesco OFM Conv., 1987), 129–42; Lehmijoki-Gardner, *Worldly Saints*, 26–55; Mario Sensi, "Anchoresses and Penitents in Thirteenth- and Fourteenth-Century Umbria," in *Women and Religion in Medieval and Renaissance Italy*, ed. Daniel Bornstein and Roberto Rusconi, trans. Margery J. Schneider (Chicago: University of Chicago Press, 1996), 56–83; Mario Sensi, "La B. Angela nel contesto religioso folignate," in *Vita e spiritualità della beata Angela da Foligno. Atti del convegno di studi per il VII centenario della conversione della beata Angela da Foligno (1285–1985)*, ed. Clément Schmitt (Perugia: Serafica provincia di san Francesco OFM Conv., 1987), 53–56. Mariano D'Alatri, *Aetas poenitentialis. L'Antico ordine francescano della penitenza* (Rome: Istituto storico dei Cappucini, 1993).

8. *Mem.* 1.87–95:138.

9. *Mem.* 1.120–37:140–42, 1.256–64:152, 3.17–21:178. Mario Sensi, "Foligno all'incrocio delle strade," in *Angèle de Foligno: Le Dossier*, ed. Giulia Barone and Jacques Dalarun (Rome: École française de Rome, 1999), 279. In embracing poverty, Angela was in fact going beyond what the Franciscan Order of Penance required of her; see Giovanna

Casagrande, "Il terz'ordine e la beata Angela. La povertà nell'ordine della non-povertà," in *Angela da Foligno Terziaria Francescana. Atti del Convegno storico nel VII centenario dell'ingresso della beata Angela da Foligno nell'Ordine Francescano Secolare (1291–1991)*, ed. Enrico Menestò (Spoleto: Centro Italiano du Studi sull'Alto Medioevo, 1992), 7–38.

    10. E.g., *Mem.* 1.138–43:142; 9.200–86:372–78; 6.90–96:264.

    11. *Mem.* 5.122–41:242.

    12. *Mem.* 3.17–21:176–78; 2.115–31:170. On the friars' exercise of the pastoral care of women, see Grundmann, *Religious Movements*, 89–137; Freed, "Urban Develoment," 311–27; Raoul Manselli, "La Chiesa e il Francescanesimo femminile," in *Movimento religioso femminile e Francescanesimo nel secolo XIII. Atti del VII Convegno Internazionale, Assisi, 11–13 ottobre 1979*, ed. Roberto Rusconi (Assisi: Società internazionale di studi francescani, 1980), 239–61; Anna Benvenuti Papi, "Mendicant Friars and Female Pinzochere in Tuscany: From Social Marginality to Models of Sanctity," in *Women and Religion in Medieval and Renaissance Italy*, ed. Daniel Bornstein and Roberto Rusconi, trans. Margery J. Schneider (Chicago: University of Chicago Press, 1996), 84–103; Coakley, "Gender and the Authority of Friars," 445–60.

    13. Jacques Dalarun, "Angèle de Foligno a-t-elle existé?" in *Alla Signorina: Mélanges offerts à Noëlle de la Blanchardière* (Rome: École Française, 1995), 72–73. "The Holy Spirit is within L [Spiritus Sanctus est intus in L]" (*Mem.* 3.167:188). Though the Assisi manuscript (see note 5) appears in the catalogue of the library of the Sacro Convento of Assisi after 1381 as "Liber sororis Lelle de Fulgineo" and the binding has been marked accordingly, an apparently earlier note on the first leaf of the Assisi manuscript witnesses to the anonymity of the text itself: "this book was given to me as something unknown and I have not yet been able to inquire as to what it might be [iste liber fuit mihi datus pro incognito et ego nondum potui perquirere quid sit]" (Bartoli Langeli, "Il codice di Assisi," 22–26).

    14. Dalarun, "Angèle de Foligno," 73. Thus anonymously a "Friar E. of the Marches" is said to have asked for revelations (*Mem.* 5.249:252), and "a certain friar [quidam frater]" is said to have himself received a revelation of the extent of Angela's sufferings (*Mem.* 8.27:338; cf. *Mem.* 5.203:248; 6.90:264; 6.132:266; 7.10:288; 9.243:374; 5.28:400). Only four individuals are mentioned by name: "Petrucius" (*Mem.* 1.260:152, i.e., the saintly Franciscan penitent Peter Crisci, her contemporary in Foligno), "Giliola" (5.126:242, a servant at a leper hospital, unnamed but apparently that of San Lazzaro, where her name survives in archival documents: Sensi, "Foligno all'incrocio delle strade," 279), a friar "Apicus" (*Mem.* 9.240:374), and a friar "Dominicus de Marchia" (5.234:250). See also Sensi, "La B. Angela nel contesto religioso Folignate," 39–95.

    15. Martin-Jean Ferré, "Les principales dates de la vie d'Angèle de Foligno," *Revue d'histoire Franciscaine* 2 (1925): 21–35.

    16. Dalarun, "Angèle de Foligno," 60–67.

    17. I have avoided translating "*scriptor*" as "scribe," a word that in its meaning as "copyist" may prejudice the question, addressed below, of the extent of the friar's role in composing the work. "Friar A.": *Mem.* 3.188:190 (see note 74); cf. also "instruction" 26, which concerns prophecies of assurance she made to "Friar A.," (26.45,

59:628, 630). The convention of naming the friar "Arnold" appears not to antedate the fifteenth century. Dalarun, "Angèle de Foligno," 76; Mario Sensi, "Fra Bernardo Arnolti il 'Frater Scriptor' del Memoriale di Angela?" in *Angela da Foligno Terziaria Francescana. Atti del Convegno storico nel VII centenario dell'ingresso della beata Angela da Foligno nell'Ordine Francescano Secolare (1291–1991)*, ed. Enrico Menestò (Spoleto: Centro Italiano du Studi sull'Alto Medioevo, 1992), 136–41.

18. "Eram suus confessor et consanguineus et etiam consiliarius praecipuus et singularis" (*Mem.* 2.100–101:168).

19. *Mem.* 1.17–19:132. Dalarun, "Angèle de Foligno," 75–6; Sensi, "Fra Bernardo Arnolti," 134–36.

20. Dalarun, "Angèle de Foligno," 75.

21. Alberzoni, "L' 'approbatio,' " 293–318.

22. Alfonso Marini, "Ubertino e Angela: L'*Arbor vitae* e il *Liber*," in *Angèle de Foligno: Le Dossier*, ed. Giulia Barone and Jacques Dalarun (Rome: École française de Rome, 1999), 319–44; cf. Stefano Brufani, "Angela da Foligno e gli Spirituali," in *Angela da Foligno Terziaria Francescana. Atti del Convegno storico nel VII centenario dell'ingresso della beata Angela da Foligno nell'Ordine Francescano Secolare (1291–1991)*, ed. Enrico Menestò (Spoleto: Centro Italiano du Studi sull'Alto Medioevo, 1992), 83–104; and Giacinto D'Urso, "La B. Angela e Ubertino da Casale," in *Vita e spiritualità della beata Angela da Foligno. Atti del convegno distudi per il VII centenario della conversione della beata Angela da Foligno (1285–1985)*, ed. Clément Schmitt (Perugia: Serafica provincia di san Francesco OFM Conv., 1987), 155–70. Romana Guarnieri has pointed out that the epilogue to the *Memorial* (*Mem.* 9.495–532:398–400), present in only some manuscripts, displays a much more confrontational, Ubertino-like tone: "Santa Angela? Angela, Ubertino e lo spiritualismo francescano. Prime ipotesi sulla *Peroratio*," in *Angèle de Foligno: Le Dossier*, ed. Giulia Barone and Jacques Dalarun (Rome: École française de Rome, 1999), 203–65.

23. David Burr, *The Spiritual Franciscans: From Protest to Persecution in the Century After Saint Francis* (University Park: Pennsylvania State University Press, 2001), 339–44. See note 91.

24. "The experience of truly faithful persons demonstrates, examines and appropriates what the incarnate Word of life says in the Gospel.... This experience, and the doctrine of that same experience, God himself causes his faithful ones to demonstrate very fully. And here, very recently, he displayed through one of his faithful ones, for their devotion, the aforesaid experience and doctrine, which … are described in the words to follow [Vere fidelium experientia probat, perspicit et contrectat de Verbo Vitae Incarnato quemadmodum ipse in Evangelio dicit.... Quam experientiam et ipsius experientiae doctrinam ipse Deus suos fideles facit probare plenissime. Et hic etiam nuper per aliquam suorum fidelium ad devotionem suorum praedictam experientiam et doctrinam fecit aliqualiter indicare … in verbis sequentibus describuntur]" (*Mem.* Prol.15–16, 20–24:128–30).

25. Thus the minor recension (see note 1) omits, in addition to most other references to interactions between the two figures (4.61–70:204–6; 4.112–19:208–10;

4.317–28:226–28; 6.203–26:274; 7.354–56:318–20; 7.403–11:322–24; 9.19–65:356–60; 9.107–23:362–64; 9.145–50:366), the long section of text between the account of the twentieth step and its continuation in the first supplementary step (*Mem.* 2.1–3.206:158–92), in which the friar gives his account of the origins of the *Memorial* in the Assisi episode and its aftermath. As Paoli shows, this recension also omits passages that affirm Angela's "certainty of her understanding of the truth" through her experience, e.g., 3.263–4:198; 6.84–7:262; 6.247–9:276. See Paoli, "Le due redazione," 49. The result is a narrative that, in comparison to that of the major recension, focuses on Angela's ascetic program as distinct from her radical, if paradoxical, claims to mystical knowledge. This is a focus that would have been congenial to the ideals of the Modern Devotion (as expressed for example in the *Imitation of Christ* by Thomas à Kempis); moreover, at least four of the five MSS of the minor recension (B1, B2, B4, B5; cf. Angela of Foligno, *Il Libro*, 51–55), all from the fifteenth century, originated in monastic or canonical houses with some connection to the Modern Devotion. See Paoli, "Le due redazione," 64–70.

26. The first level is, in Gennette's terminology, "extradiegetic," the second "intradiegetic," according to whether the addressee is to be found outside the narrative or within it. The divine locutions addressed to Angela can be said to constitute a third level of narrative, contained within the second and designated "metadiegetic" in Gennette's scheme. Beatrice Coppini, *La Scrittura e il percorso mistico. Il "liber" di Angela da Foligno* (Rome: Ianua, 1986), 67–77; cf. Gérard Gennette, *Narrative Discourse: An Essay in Method*, trans. Jane E. Lewin (Ithaca, N.Y.: Cornell University Press, 1980), 227–37.

27. "Assignaverat triginta passus vel mutationes quas facit anima, quae profiscitur per viam paenitentiae, quas inveniebat in se" (*Mem.* 1.4–6:132). First twenty steps: 1.7–310:132–156.

28. *Mem.* 2.7–173:158–74.

29. *Mem.* 2.123–26:170. See note 67.

30. The autobiographical narratives of Hildegard (see chap. 3) provide another example, as do the *Seven Spiritual Arms* of Catherine of Bologna, the *Life of the Servant* of Henry Suso, and the *Book* of Margery Kempe. Barbara Newman, "Three-Part Invention," 190–92; Kate Greenspan, "Autohagiography and Medieval Women's Spiritual Autobiography," in *Gender and Text in the Later Middle Ages*, ed. Jane Chance (Gainesville: University Press of Florida, 1996), 216–36.

31. *Mem.* 1.1–310:132–56.

32. Divine locutions during the Assisi episode: *Mem.* 3.30–3.128:176–86; physical sensations of the presence of God: 4.9–18:200, 4.324–28:228.

33. *Mem.* 3.52–54:180; 3.72–74:182; 4.44–46, 61–64:204; 5.154–55:244; 6.21–23:258; 6.44–52:260; 6.148–53:268–70; 6.266–68:278.

34. *Mem.* 3.45–46:180; 4.31–32:202; 6.122–25:266; 9.280–83:378.

35. *Mem.* 9.11–15:354.

36. *Mem.* 5.1–41:230–32; 6.55–66:234–36.

37. *Mem.* 6.232–38:276; 6.263–65:278; 7.98–111:296–98.

38. *Mem.* 7.23–56:290–92.

39. E.g., *Mem.* 9.7–38:354–56; 9.289–314:378–80. For Angela, unlike some other late-medieval speculative mystical writers such as Eckhart, the human subject remains unquestionably discrete from the divine object of contemplation. See Carole Slade, "Alterity in Union: The Mystical Experience of Angela of Foligno and Margery Kempe," *Religion and Literature* 23 (1991): 114–15.

40. She received a response in the form of an exemplum of a "great and most noble man [*magnus et nobilissimus homo*]" who benefited his subordinates both indirectly through his actions and directly through personal kindnesses, though the latter benefits were greater: *Mem.* 5.202–18:248.

41. Answer: by a divine power that is incomprehensible to us in the present life: *Mem.* 5.224–30:250.

42. *Mem.* 6.90–96:264.

43. *Mem.* 6.166–79:244–46.

44. "Et videtur mihi quod haec omnia dicamus modo quasi pro truffis, quia aliter erat quam posset dici; et ego ipsa verecundor dicere magis efficaciter" (*Mem.* 4.11–18:200); cf. 4.125–28:210; 5.53–54:234; 5.101–5:238–40.

45. E.g. *Mem.* 5.13–34:230–32; 5.45–54:234.

46. *Mem.* 6.60–78:260–62.

47. *Mem.* 7.273–435:312–26.

48. *Mem.* 7.438–94:326–30.

49. *Mem.* 9.50–65:358–60; 90–103:362.

50. *Mem.* 9.316–440:382–92.

51. "It is by means of vision that Angela becomes involved in theology as a theologian": Alain de Libera, "Angèle de Foligno et la mystique 'féminine': Eléments pour une typologie," in *Angèle de Foligno: Le Dossier*, ed. Giulia Barone and Jacques Dalarun (Rome: École française de Rome, 1999), 367; cf. Claudio Leonardi, "Angela da Foligno tra teologia e mistica," in *Angela da Foligno Terziaria Francescana. Atti del Convegno storico nel VII centenario dell'ingresso della beata Angela da Foligno nell'Ordine Francescano Secolare (1291–1991)*, ed. Enrico Menestò (Spoleto: Centro Italiano du Studi sull'Alto Medioevo, 1992), 257–59. Theological treatments of the *Memorial* include: Paul Lachance, *The Spiritual Journey of the Blessed Angela of Foligno According to the Memorial of Frater A.* (Rome: Pontificium Athenaeum Antonianum, 1984), 123–406; Giovanni Benedetti, "Elementi per una teologia spirituale nel 'Libro della Beata Angela,'" in *Vita e spiritualità della beata Angela da Foligno. Atti del convegno di studi per il VII centenario della conversione della beata Angela da Foligno (1285–1985)*, ed. Clément Schmitt (Perugia: Serafica provincia di san Francesco OFM Conv., 1987), 15–38; Leonardi, "Angela da Foligno tra teologia e mistica," 251–59.

52. *Mem.* 4.197–99:216.

53. *Mem.* 5.63–65:234–36. Cf. 8.13–15:336; 9.243–48:374.

54. *Mem.* 7.18–95:290–96; "Behold it was meagerly and badly written.... But... I translated it into Latin as I found it, not adding anything, like someone making a painting, because I did not understand [Ideo valde diminute et male scripta fuit....

Sed … rescripsi eam latine sicut reperi, nihil addens, immo sicut pictor pingens, quia non intelligebam eam]" (*Mem.* 7.11–12, 14–17:288). On painting as a metaphor for communicating without comprehension (cf. 8.13–15:336) and on the relation of the friar's Latin to the Umbrian vernacular that not only the "boy" but also Angela herself must have used, see Pascale Bourgain, "Angèle de Foligno: Le Latin du *Liber*," in *Angèle de Foligno: Le Dossier*, ed. Giulia Barone and Jacques Dalarun (Rome: École française de Rome, 1999), 145–67. The friar, however, does not specifically mention the necessity of translation from the vernacular as a factor in the difficulties he experienced in conveying what he heard directly from her.

55. "Et hic potest aliqualiter patere quod ego non poteram capere de verbis divinis nisi magis grossa, quia aliquando, dum ego scribebam recte sicut a suo ore capere poteram, relegenti sibi illa quae scripseram ut ipsa alia diceret ad scribendum, dixit mihi admirando quod non recognoscebat illa. Et alia vice quando ego relegebam ei ut ipsa videret si ego bene scripseram, et ipsa respondit, quod ego sicce et sine omni sapore loquebar; et admirabatur de hoc. Et alia vice exposuit ita dicens: Per ista verba recordor illorum quae dixi tibi, sed est obscurissima scriptura, quia haec verba quae legis mihi non explicant illa quae portant, ideo est obscura scriptura. Item alia vice dixit ita: Illud quod deterius est et quod nihil est scripsisti, sed de pretioso quod sentit anima nihil scripsisti" (*Mem.* 2.143–52:172).

56. *Mem.* 4.210–18:215 (see note 94), a revelation echoed at 2.6–10:158–60; 3.25–29:178.

57. See the thorough inventory of evidence by Catherine Mooney, "The Authorial Role of Brother A. in the Composition of Angela of Foligno's Revelations," in *Creative Women in Medieval and Early Modern Italy: A Religious and Artistic Renaissance*, ed. E. Ann Matter and John Coakley (Philadelphia: University of Pennsylvania Press, 1994), 34–63.

58. "Cum magna reverentia et timore scribens ut nihil possem addere de meo nec unam dictionem tantummodo nisi recte sicut ab ipso ore referentis poteram capere, nolebam aliquid scribere postquam recedebam ab ea. Sed et quando scribens sedebam cum ea, faciebam mihi verbum quod debebam scribere ab ea pluries iterari" (*Mem.* 2.136–39:172). Similarly, at the end of the *Memorial* he claims "I have tried to set down such of her own statements (*verba*) as I could grasp, not wishing to write after I had gone away from her and then find myself fearfully and sincerely unable to write them lest it might happen that I would set down something, even one statement, that she had not herself said [Sed et ego conabar, et propria verba sua ponebam quae ego poteram capere, nolens ea scribere postquam recedebam ab ea et nesciens ea postea scribere pro timore et zelo, ne forte accideret quod ego aliquid vel unum tantum verbum ponerem quod ipsa proprie non dixisset]" (*Mem.* 9.522–25:400).

59. See note 55.

60. "Haec supradicta ipsa fidelis Christi dicebat mihi fratri scriptori aliis verbis, scilicet pluribus et magis efficacibus et lumine plenis" (*Mem.* 4.257–58:222).

61. "But she was not able to explain, such that though she did cause me to understand something through what she said, still I was not able to grasp it so as to

write it down [Sed nec ipsa poterat explicare, quamvis daret mihi intelligere aliquid per illa quae dicebat, nec ego etiam illa capere poteram ad scribendum]" (Mem. 9.171–73:368).

62. Here I disagree with Catherine Mooney, who sees the friar's self-presentation as at odds with the evidence contained in his own narrative of his role in producing the work, as though that evidence were given inadvertently. In Mooney's view, "Brother A. is, in his own mind, a simple secretary...a mere conduit putting to page another's dictation. Scattered throughout his lengthy report of what he claims to have heard Angela say, however, are myriad clues about his own relationship with Angela and his involvement in committing her story to page" ("Authorial Role," 40).

63. "Et ipsa dicebat quod ego vere scribebam, sed detruncate et diminute.... Et revelatum fuit ei et dictum quod ego omnia vere scripseram et sine omni mendacio, sed erant scripta cum multo defectu" (Mem. 2.154–55, 160–61:172). Cf. also 4.197–99:216; and 4.210–19:218.

64. "Ipsa dixit quod ego non actatum sed e contrario siccum et deactatum scripseram illud, quamvis confirmaverit quod verum scripseram" (Mem. 4.259–60:222).

65. "Totum illud quod scriptum est, totum scriptum est secundum voluntatem meam et a me venit, idest a me processit" (Mem. 9.506–8:398).

66. "Illud quod deterius est et quod nihil est scripsisti, sed de pretioso quod sentit anima nihil scripsisti" (Mem. 2.151–52:172).

67. "Et consului et coegi eam quod totum diceret mihi et quod ego volebam illud scribere omnino, ut possem consulere super illo aliquem sapientem et spiritualem virum qui nunquam eam cognosceret. Et hoc dicebam me velle facere ut ipsa nullo modo posset ab aliquo malo spiritu esse decepta. Et conabar incutere sibi timorem et dicere sibi exempla quomodo multae personae iam exstiterunt deceptae, unde et ipsa similiter poterat esse decepta" (Mem. 2.123–28:170).

68. Mem. 2.132–38:170–72. See note 58.

69. Mem. 7.269–70:310; 4.206–9:216; 6.166–73, 168–82:244–46.

70. Mem. 7.208–20:306; on his curiosity regarding her graces during Communion, see also 3.233–36:194–96; 9.217–20:372; 8.73–75:342.

71. When she says she saw God, he presses her for a description: Mem. 3.233–35:194–96; in reference to her desire for martyrdom, given to her by God as a sign of the genuineness of her experience, he asks if she desires the shame: 4.112:208; when she has had revelations at the moment of the elevation of the Host at Mass, he asks her whether she saw anything in the Host and how she could feel Christ's presence: 4.317–20:226; he asks her "how God can be known in creatures," 5.201–5:248; he asks how the body of Christ can be on many altars simultaneously: 5.224–5:250; he asks her to pray that one Friar Dominic of the Marches would not be deceived: 5.233–4:250; he asks her to pray for illumination regarding a "doubt" she had expressed about the benefit of tribulation: 6.203–4:274; he asks an unspecified question that, from the answer, can be inferred (cf. 6.341–45:286) as being concerned with the issue why God created humans and afterward permitted them to sin: 275–78:278–80.

72. A direct reply to the question how Christ can be simultaneously on all altars: Mem. 5.226–30:250; a direct reply regarding the request for information on Fr. Dominic

of the Marches: 5.235–9; a reply to his request for illumination about the benefits of tribulation: "'Dicas illi fratri,'" 6.204–12:274; her answer to an unspecified question that turns out to be about God's reason for allowing sin, 6.279–339:280–84.

73. *Mem.* 3.33–178:178–90; "'Ego diligo te plus quam aliquam quae sit in valle Spoletina,'" 3.46:180; "Ego sum qui fui crucifixus pro te," 3.65–66:182.

74. *Mem.* 3.184–206:190–92. "Quaere ab eo, scilicet fratre A., quia illud quod fuit tibi dictum iam venit in te, scilicet Trinitas," 3.188–89:190.

75. Having asked why God had permitted sin, she says that she was given the answer that thereby God's goodness could be better shown but that she professed herself unsatisfied with the answer until she was given a vision that gave her certitude: *Mem.* 6.275–345:278–84; "et videbat Dei potentiam inenarrabilem et videbat Dei voluntatem," 6.302–3:282. Similarly, when the friar asks her "how God can be known in creatures [*cognosci in creaturis*]," she describes how she had already had occasion to ask this question on her own and had received a revelation in the form of an exemplum about a great man whose kindness was best experienced by those with direct knowledge of him: 5.202–18:248.

76. *Mem.* 5.109–40:240–42.

77. *Mem.* 6.294–345:280–86.

78. *Mem.* 7.140–48:300; 7.220–41:306–8; 9.179–82:370.

79. *Mem.* 9.200–26:272–74.

80. In this vision, she kissed him and he, pressing her cheek against his own, said, "before I lay in the tomb I held you tightly thus [antequam iacerem in sepulcro tenui te ita astrictam]" (*Mem.* 7.98–111:296–98, quot. 107–8). On the image as suggesting a possible Byzantine influence, see Sensi, "Foligno all'incroce," 289–90; on the same image as reflecting the image of the Pietà that was commonly found on "little icons and personal altars" at the time in Italy, see Chiara Frugoni, "Female Mystics, Visions, and Iconography," in *Women and Religion in Medieval and Renaissance Italy*, ed. Daniel Bornstein and Roberto Rusconi, trans. Margery J. Schneider (Chicago: University of Chicago Press, 1996), 149, 163 n. 76.

81. *Mem.* 7.34–95:290–96.

82. *Mem.* 7.115–30:298.

83. *Mem.* 7.273–415:312–24; 7.438–94:326–330.

84. *Mem.* 8.89–110:344–46.

85. Thus she compares this vision of God in darkness with previous visions of God filling all creation and of God's power and of God's wisdom (exactly which previous visions she has in mind is not clear, see Angela of Foligno, *Il Libro*, 358n.5): Mem. 9.39–65:358–60; see note 89; she also compares this vision of darkness with her visions of Christ, which, though delightful, are less compelling (9.89–103:362).

86. E.g., "if all the spiritual joys and all the divine consolations and all the divine delights which all the saints who have been from the beginning of the world until the present moment have explained themselves to have from God, and even all the things—which were many—which they could explain and did not explain, were given to me ... I would not give or change or exchange this inexpressible good for the space of one opening or closing of an eye [Si omnes laetitiae spirituales et omnes

consolationes divinae et omnia delectamenta divina quae omnes sancti qui fuerunt a principio mundi usque modo explicaverunt se habuisse de Deo, et etiam omnia—quae fuerunt multa—quae potuerunt explicare et non explicaverunt, darentur mihi … ego non darem et non commutarem vel non cambiarem tantum de illo omnino inenarrabili bono quantum est unum solum levare vel claudere oculorum]" (*Mem.* 9.381–85, 389–91:386–88).

87. "Dicas illi fratri, 'Quid est quod in tota tribulatione ipsa non dilexit minus sed plus quando videbatur sibi quod esset derelicta'?" (*Mem.* 6.204–6).

88. "The soul in no way sees anything that can be narrated with the mouth or the heart afterward; and sees nothing, and yet sees everything [Et nihil omnino videt anima quod narrari possit ore nec cum corde postea; et nihil videt, et videt omnia omnino]" (*Mem.* 9.34–35:356).

89. "Et cum ego frater resisterem ei de praedicta tenebra et non intelligerem" (*Mem.* 9.39–40:358); "because that good that I see in the darkness is the whole, and all other things are [only] part [quia illud bonum quod video cum tenebra est totum, illa vero omnia alia sunt pars]" (*Mem.* 9.48–49:358).

90. "Amor est in mensura et quod spiritus datur in mensura" (*Mem.* 9.145–46:366); "Et verum est quod dicit ille, quod Deus non dat spiritum ad mensuram; sed anima mea natat et delectatur, quod Deus etiam Filio suo et omnibus sanctis dat ad mensuram" (*Mem.* 9.147–50:366). Thier and Calufetti note that Angela also has some Scripture on her side, viz. Rom. 12:3 and Eph. 4:7, and—perhaps more to the point—that, even if open to scriptural challenge, Angela's position here distances her from the implicit danger of "falling into a form of heterodox mysticism" that would assert the possibility of an unmeasured, i.e., unlimited, experience of God (Angela of Foligno, *Il Libro*, 266–67 n. 19).

91. *Mem.* 9.357–60:384; 9.301–302:380; "et tamen [homo] aliquid balbutit [de scripturis]. Sed de illis ineffabilibus operationibus divinis … nihilomnino loqui vel balbutire potest" (9.370–72:386); cf. 7.162–166:302; 7.303–7:314; 7.412–15:324; and Giuseppe Betori, "La Scrittura nell'esperienza spirituale della B. Angela da Foligno. Annotazioni preliminari," in *Vita e spiritualità della beata Angela da Foligno. Atti del convegno di studi per il VII centenario della conversione della beata Angela da Foligno (1285–1985),* ed. Clément Schmitt (Perugia: Serafica provincia di san Francesco OFM Conv., 1987), 171–98.

92. "Et cum ego frater resisterem ei hic de credulitate, ipsa fidelis Christi respondit: Posset forsitan credere aliquid, sed non illo modo" (*Mem.* 7.354–56:318–20).

93. *Mem.* 7.400–401:322; "Ite cum Deo, quia de Deo nihil vobis possum dicere" (7.410–11:324).

94. "Hodie … dum fieret mihi conscientia ne forte totum esset verum quod ego de me dixi et quod tu scripsisti, … defectuose est dictum et quod scriptor scripserat diminute vel cum defectu" (*Mem.* 4.210–18:218).

95. Edith Pasztor, "Le visione di Angela da Foligno nella religiosità femminile italiana del suo tempo," in *Vita e spiritualità della beata Angela da Foligno. Atti del convegno di studi per il VII centenario della conversione della beata Angela da Foligno*

(1285–1985), ed. Clément Schmitt (Perugia: Serafica provincia di san Francesco OFM Conv., 1987), 290, is surely right that words about indescribability "call up the unimaginable" for the friar whereas for Angela they signify the "incapacity to transmit faithfully the images of the spiritual experience she has had." Even so, communication is the essential task for both.

96. "Nulla persona poterit habere excusationem salutis, quia non oportet eas plus facere nisi sicut facit infirmus medico, qui ostendit ei infirmitatem et disponit se ad faciendum quae dicit sibi" (*Mem.* 4.230–33:218–20).

97. "Ego vocavi omnes ad vitam aeternam et invitavi; qui volunt venire veniant, quia nullus potest excusari quod non sit vocatus" (*Mem.* 5.20–22:232). Cf. 4.176–81:214.

7. THE LIMITS OF RELIGIOUS AUTHORITY: MARGARET OF CORTONA AND GIUNTA BEVEGNATI

1. *LMC* 1.17–19:181; 4.18–19:217. The date of 1247 often given for her birth is, as Iozzelli points out, "purely hypothetical": Iozzelli, "Introduzione," in Giunta Bevegnati, *Legenda de vita et miraculis beatae Margaritae de Cortona*, ed. Iozzelli (Rome: Editiones Collegii S. Bonaventurae ad Claras Aquas, 1997), 51.

2. *LMC* 1.64–66:183 (Christ recalls to her that she lived for nine years with her "deceiver [*deceptor*]"); 2.556–62:204 (account of her later return as a penitent to the territory of Montepulciano); 2.81–83:187 (she forbade her son to speak of his father).

3. *LMC* 1.17–21:181.

4. *LMC* 1.83–85:183; 2.38–40:186. On Margaret's social status as "illegitmate widow," see Anna Benvenuti Papi, "'Margherita Filia Ierusalem.' Una visione mistica della terrasanta nella spiritualità femminile Francescana," in *Toscana e terrasanta nel medioevo*, ed. F. Cardini (Florence: Alinea, 1982), 120.

5. Meersseman, *Dossier*; Lehmijoki-Gardner, *Worldly Saints*, 26–55.

6. Giunta states the year explicitly, "anno a natiuitate Christi millesimo cc° lxxvii°" (*LMC* 1.2:181). Giunta's eighteenth-century editor da Pelago considered 1275 a more likely date, inferring from Giunta's report that Margaret prophesied the peace between Cortona and its bishop that occurred in July of that year, and that not only in that prophecy but also in previous revelations Christ called her "daughter [*filia*]," which in turn implies that she had already received the habit. Giunta Bevegnati, *Antica leggenda della vita e de'miracoli di s. Margherita di Cortona scritta dal di lei confessore Fr. Giunta Bevegnati dell'ordine de'Minori colla traduzione italiana di detta leggenda posta dicontro al testo originale latino e con annotazioni e dissertazioni diverse ad illustrazione del medesimo testo*, ed. Ludovico Bargigli da Pelago, 2 vols. (Lucca: Francesco Bonsignori, 1793), 1:17–19. Most other scholars have followed da Pelago, but one wonders if Giunta reported the revelations so carefully as to allow them to bear the weight of such reasoning, especially when it contradicts his explicit statement of the date of 1277. See Iozzelli, "Introduzione," 60.

7. On her respective moves to the two cells, see *LMC* 2.24–28:186; 2.403–44:199–200.

8. On individual actions, Iozelli, "Introduzione," 73 n. 78, cites *LMC* 2.86–109:188; 2.133–61:189–90; 3.77–91:211–12; 6.555–65:307–8. On the hospice: 2.65–78:187. A fifteenth-century document declares her the founder, in 1286, of the Fraternitas Sanctae Mariae de Misericordia, a confraternity that "met at the Church of Sant'Andrea and initially had as its prior the priest Ser Badia who was to be the saint's last spiritual director" (see note 30). Anyway she "must certainly have had close links with the Fraternitas, which was later associated with the cult accorded to her in the sanctuary of San Basilio": André Vauchez, "Margherita and Cortona," in *Margherita of Cortona and the Lorenzetti: Sienese Art and the Cult of a Holy Woman in Medieval Tuscany*, ed. Joanna Cannon and André Vauchez (University Park: Pennsylvania State University Press, 1999), 24. See also Iozzelli, "Introduzione," 75–76.

9. *LMC* 8.52–55:351; 8.291–307:358; 8.320–54:359; 8.371–403:361, all noted by Iozzelli, "Introduzione," 77.

10. Giunta pictures Ubertino accompanying Margaret's son (who had become a Franciscan) on a visit to her (*LMC* 9.467–81), and also says, in the "Testimony," that Ubertino "preached" from the *Legenda* (*LMC* appendix 9–10:477) and was present to hear Cardinal Orsini approve the work at the Casali palace in Cortona (*LMC* appendix 19–20:477). Ubertino, however, says nothing about Margaret in his *Arbor Vitae*, where he acknowledges a profound debt to Angela, who was apparently "much closer to the antiestablishment currents" (Vauchez, "Margherita and Cortona," 26). Arguments for a close association between Margaret and the spirituals include Maria Caterina Jacobelli, *Una donna senza volto: Lineamenti anthropologio culturale della santità di Margherita da Cortona* (Rome: Borla, 1992), 190–91; and Mario Sensi, "Margherita da Cortona nel contesto storico-sociale cortonese," *Collectanea Franciscana* 69 (1999): 251–58. For a balanced critical evaluation of these arguments see Burr, *The Spiritual Franciscans*, 325–33. See also note 27.

11. Giunta, *Antica leggenda*, ed. Da Pelago, 2:54.

12. In addition to his many references to Margaret's confessions to himself, Giunta refers to a revelation from Christ exhorting him to be more zealous in hearing confessions (*LMC* 6.190–95:294) and to incidents in which Margaret gave him details of sins of his other penitents (8.35–40:350; 9.117–27:376–77). As for preaching, he describes her interrupting a sermon (5.143–45:246) and receiving a revelation advising him how to preach (8.119–123:353). As for peacemaking, he refers to this practice himself (8.306–7:358), and she receives a revelation about his peacemaking (8.371–87:361–62).

13. His absence was for seven years (*LMC* 10.610–11:450); he was present with her at her death (5.1158–59:281). See Iozzelli, "Introduzione," 5.

14. Iozzelli, "Introduzione," 7.

15. Text: *LMC* appendix:477–78. On the "Testimony": Iozzelli, "Introduzione," 7–15; Giunta, *Antica leggenda*, ed. Da Pelago, 349–50. The manuscript in question is: *A*, Cortona, Archivio del Convento di S. Margherita 61, on which Iozzelli bases his edition except for portions of the miracle collection (chap. 11), which the MS lacks. The latter derive from *Rc*, Rome, Biblioteca Corsiniana, Cors 1532), a seventeenth-century MS that apparently stands otherwise in the same text tradition as *A*. On the priority

of *A* over the other two medieval MSS of the *Legenda*, both likewise conserved at Cortona, see Iozzelli, "Introduzione," 149–69. On the miracles, see Fortunato Iozzelli, "I miracoli nella 'Legenda' di santa Margherita da Cortona," *Archivum franciscanum historicum* 86 (1993): 217–76.

16. "Frater I. compiled this legend at the command of Friar Iohannes de Castillione, inquisitor into heretical error, who was the confessor and father of the blessed Margaret [Hanc legendam compilauit frater I. de mandato fratris Iohannis de Castillione, inquisitoris heretice prauitatis, qui erat confessor beate Margarite et pater]" (*LMC* appendix 2–4:477). Castiglione is identified as "guardian [*custos*]" in 9.1277–80:416; inquisitor in 9.167–68:378. On Castiglione, see Iozzelli, "Introduzione," 66–69.

17. The dating of Castiglione's death rests on the inference that Giunta's assumption of the role of the saint's confessor (*LMC* 7.254–57:328) can hardly have occurred after his transferal to Siena, which was in 1290, for he was absent from her for seven years, he says (10.609–11:450) and yet had returned from Siena by the time of her death (5.1158–59:281). Iozzelli, "Introduzione," 5.

18. "Item the venerable lord Napoleon, legate of the apostolic see and cardinal... directed... that [the *Legenda*] be kept always whole [*intesa*], and be made available to all who want to copy it, or to have it copied, and that, notwithstanding any past or future directive, preaching be done from it [Item uenerabilis dominus Neapoleo, apostolice sedis legatus et cardinalis... precepit... quod custodiretur semper intesa, et accomodaretur omnibus uolentibus eam scribere, uel facere scribi, et non obstante aliquo precepto preterito, uel futuro, de ipsa predicaretur]." This occurred "in the cloister of the palace of Lord Huguccio of Casali... on 15 Feb. 1308 [in claustro palatii domini Hugucii de Casali... anno Domini m° ccc° viii°, indictione viᵃ, die xᵃ februarii]" (*LMC* appendix 11–2, 13–15, 19–20, 21–22:477). On Margaret's saintly patronage in the context of the (Ghibelline) Casali family's ascendancy in the city, see Benvenuti Papi, "'Margherita Filia Ierusalem,'" 117–23; Roberto Rusconi, "Margherita da Cortona: Peccatrice redenta e patrona cittadina," in *Umbria: Sacra e Civile* (Turin: Nuova Eri Edizioni Rai, 1989), 89–104; Vauchez, "Margherita and Cortona," 11–36; Franco Cardini, "Agiografia e politica: Margherita da Cortona e le vicende di una città inqueta," *Studi Francescani* 76 (1979): 127–36.

19. "Flores quosdam eligere de uita mirabili Deo deuotissime Margarite, agentis austeram penitentiam in Cortona" (*LMC* Prol.5–6:179).

20. Iozzelli, "Introduzione," 26.

21. E.g., *LMC* 4.40–64:218–19; 4.141–75:222–23; 4.383–434:230–32; 4.480–507:234–35; 4.508–35:235–36; 4.591–626:238–39; 5.727–66:267–68; 5.945–94:274–75; 6.820–39:316–17.

22. "Tu es stella mundo concessa.... Tu es uexillum nouum" (*LMC* 7.551–53:337).

23. *LMC* 3.134–63:214–15; 3.164–93:215–16.

24. *LMC* 5.706–26:266–67; 5.1054–68:277–78; 8.153–290:354–58 (state of souls); 7.187–94:325–26 (unworthy priests); 8.291–331:358–59 (peacemaking).

25. Benvenuti Papi, "'Margherita Filia Ierusalem,'" 119. See also Jacobelli, *Una donna,* 153–83.

26. Joanna Cannon, "'Fama Laudabilis Beate Sororis Margherite': Art in the Service of the Cult of Margherita," in *Margherita of Cortona and the Lorenzetti: Sienese*

Art and the Cult of a Holy Woman in Medieval Tuscany, ed. Joanna Cannon and André Vauchez (University Park: Pennsylvania State University Press, 1999), 212–13.

27. The example suggests, moreover, a moderating position with respect to the Franciscan spirituals: "in a time when groups of spiritual friars, extremists, and many lay people, men as well as women, proposed the life of the desert as antidote to the corruption of the church and the Franciscan Order, the *Legenda Margaritae* tends to demonstrate that all the values found in the desert can be better and more usefully lived in the city": Jérôme Poulenc, "Presenza dei movimenti spirituali nella 'Leggenda' di Santa Margherita da Cortona," In *Celestino V e i suoi tempi: Realtà spirituale e realtà politica. Atti del Convegno Storico Internazionale, L'Aquila, 26–27 Agosto 1989*, ed. W. Cappelli (L'Aquila: Centro Celestiniano, sezione storica, 1990), 101. Benvenuti Papi, "Margherita filia Ierusalem," 117–22.

28. " 'Tu es tertia lux in ordine dilecti mei Francisci concessa: nam in ordine fratrum minorum ipse est prima lux, in ordine monialium beata Clara secunda, et tu in ordine penitentium tertia' " (*LMC* 10.287–90:439).

29. Declaration of favor toward the friars: *LMC* 5.19–21:241; revelations for or about the friars: e.g., 5.751–53:267; 8.73–78:351; 9.61–77:375; 9.274–320:382–84; 9.303–20 (the characteristics of the "true friar"); 9.321–357:384–85; 9.425–28:387; 9.514–21:390–91; 9.918–47:404–5; her intercessions: e.g., 4.188–94:223–24; 4.202–9:224; 6.259–60:296, 9.918–47:404–5; Christ's admonitions to speak only to friars: 2.389–91:198–99; 2.640–43:207; 5.946–48:274, 5.1295–97:286.

30. Iozzelli, "Introduzione," 81–86. On the location of her body, see *LMC* 2.409–11:199; cf. Daniel Bornstein, "The Uses of the Body: The Church and the Cult of Santa Margherita da Cortona." *Church History* 62 (1993): 163–177.

31. Mariano D'Alatri, "L'Ordine della Penitenza nella Leggenda di Margherita da Cortona," *Analecta Tertii Ordinis Regularis (Rome)* 15 (1982): 72. The crucial passages are *LMC* 2.403–44:199–200, in which Christ tells her to remain under the friars' care but also commands her to make the move against their wishes; 5.853–91:271–72, in which Christ directs her to tell Giunta both that he should not impede the move himself and that he should tell Giovanni Castiglione not to let it cause him to "subtract his solicitude" from her; and 5.220–266:380–82, in which the chapter's limitation of Giunta's visits is reported, first as a prophecy from Christ and then as an established fact. See Iozzelli, "Introduzione," 67–69.

32. Bornstein, "Uses of the Body," 167; Rusconi, "Margherita da Cortona," 103. Along similar lines, Nancy Caciola has drawn a contrast between Margaret's self-fashioning as a penitent and Giunta's attempt to make of her a specifically Franciscan saint (Caciola, *Discerning Spirits*, 98–113). On the bull, see Edith Pasztor, "La 'supra montem' e la cancelleria pontificia al tempo di Niccolò IV," in *La 'supra montem' di Niccolò IV (1289): Genesi e diffusione di una regola*, ed. R. Pazzelli and L. Temperini (Rome, 1988), 65–92; and Robert M. Stewart, *"De illis qui faciunt penitentiam": The Rule of the Secular Franciscan Order: Origins, Development, Interpretation* (Rome: Istituto Storico dei Cappuccini, 1991), 206–16.

33. Margaret receives revelations for Giunta regarding Castiglione: e.g., a revelation directing Castiglione to pray for her (*LMC* 5.551–54:261) and another directing Giunta

himself to confer with Castiglione about her visions (9.1277–80:416). Giunta, *Antica leggenda*, ed. Da Pelago, "Dissertazione" 4.55.

34. " 'Et ego tibi dico quod desideria tua, que habes de me, michi accepta sunt. Tamen uenialiter me offendis, quia in uisis et auditis distractionem mentis recipis ex timore, cum deberes solum cogitare de me' " (*LMC* 7.593–97:339). Cf. 8.641–44:371; 5.1085–89:278–79.

35. *LMC* 7.725–27:344; 9.1567–72:426; 9.8–12:373. Cf. 5.1251–53:284 (the inadequacy of her response to Christ).

36. *LMC* 6.641–45:310; 4.50–53:218; 4.180–84:223 (cf. *Mem.* 3.45–46:180).

37. " 'Recordare quod possum cui uolo mea dona largiri.' " (*LMC* 4.513–14:235). Cf. 5.630–36:263–64; 4.54–64:218–19.

38. " 'Et dico tibi quod, si tota puritas angelorum sanctorumque omnium qui in celo terraque sunt poneretur simul, si non condescenderem eis, nil esset respectu mee clarissime puritatis. Non descendi ego, filia, ad sumendam carnem de uirgine Maria...? Ita feci, o simplex mea. Numquid non descendi ad permictendum me tangi a peccatoribus et ad morandum et comedendum cum eis?' " (*LMC* 4.607–13:238). Cf. 4.419–21:231.

39. *LMC* 4.103–140:220–21; 4.383–409:230–31; 11.299–309:463; 11.630–36:473–74.

40. "Ille... diligentibus se non dixit: Discite a me mortuos suscitare, [non] super aquas siccis pedibus ambulare, aut leprosos mundare et cecos illuminare, set: *Discite a me, quia mitis sum et humilis corde*" (*LMC* 4.312–15:228).

41. "Quando credebat Dei famula Margarita recipere noue consolationis signum a Domino, dicebat prius intra se: 'Quid michi dabit Dominus nunc?' De qua meditatione redarguit eam saluator, dicens: 'Cur niteris extimare sapientiam infinitam? Numquam imponere audeas operibus meis finem; in nulla sui parte, mea tangas opera perscruptando. Si autem uis pertingere ad id quod optas, curre per viam crucis et inde secure uenire poteris ad dona maxima que expectas' " (*LMC* 9.687–93:396).

42. *LMC* 6.35–37:288; 10.167–69:435.

43. *LMC* 5.306–13:251–52.

44. *LMC* 7.432–42:333–34.

45. *LMC* 6.91–94:290; 6.791–93:315–16; 10.169–71:435.

46. *LMC* 5.27–42:242; 10.33–46:430. Cf. 5.347–88:253–54: her reception of special graces is linked to her devotion to the Passion.

47. " 'Quemadmodum subtraxi et abscondi potentiam in ligno crucis, ita me tibi abscondi in augmentum corone tue et ut cognoscas qualis es per te sine me' " (*LMC* 5.1133–35:280).

48. *LMC* 5.685–99:265–66. Cf. 5.935–37:273 (in the tribulations to come she will be "abandoned [*derelicta*]"); 5.909–21:273 (Christ links her pains with his own).

49. " 'Numquam post redemptionem factam tot ierunt ad inferni supplicia, quot uadunt modo' " (*LMC* 5.1056–57:277). Cf. 5.707–65:266–68; 5.1263–1304:285–86; 7.187–94:325–26 (on unworthy priests); 9.623–48:394–95; 9.750–802:398–400; 9.1286–88:417; 10.262–75:438.

50. " 'In die illa iocundabuntur omnes qui ad uocem fame et presentie tue fecerunt penitentiam de laboribus tuis et penis, quas modo pateris' " (*LMC* 9.819–20:401).

51. *LMC* 2.344–46:197; 2.355–366:197–98; 5.945–54:274; 9.1180–82:413.

52. "'Plora inobedientiam tuam, quia non obedisti michi de piscatione animarum, que indigent me, summo et vero bono, non ego eis'" (*LMC* 8.131–33:353).

53. "Dixit quod uolebat plenius gaudium de Christi gustare presentia…'Tuus gustus infirmatus est, quia gratias, quas tibi donare dignatus sum, non tibi concessi propter te tantum, set etiam propter amorem illorum, qui me quantum in eis est in cruce reponere non desistunt. Et tamen eis paterna pietate, ut ad me redeant, in omni re misericorditer condescendo'" (*LMC* 7.627–28, 631–35:340). "'Tu non curas, Margarita, nisi de te'" (7.29.685:342).

54. "'Ego eram delectabilis in conspectu discipulorum et tu es in conspectu creaturarum, quia te faciam lucem quantum ad tenebrarum cognoscendam subtilitatem'" (*LMC* 5.1101–1103:279).

55. "'Dico tibi quod tu es noua lux, quam huic mundo donaui, illuminata per me…. Nonne, filia, cunctis mundi delectationibus te amore meo priuasti? Nonne mei amore nominis optas cunta ferre supplicia? Nonne propter me uniuersos pauperes in tuo corde recludis?'" (*LMC* 9.1419–20, 1423–26:421).

56. "'Filia, tu dixisti quod amor uestri ad patiendum me compulit et quod uestrarum zelo animarum feci quicquid feci. Et scias quod quemadmodum ego cum maxima ueni angustia ad requirendum te, ita uenies tu cum multis amaritudinibus et afflictionibus ad requirendum me. Para igitur te ad tribulationes maximas: sicut enim uita tua uana olim contra me per linguas murmuratorum clamauit in castris, siluis agris, pratis et uillis, ita tu clamare non cesses meam per ordinem passionem et quod semper in hac uita pro amore humani generis uixi in laboribus et in penis. Qui autem super hoc presumpserit murmurare, offendet me grauiter et tu michi placebis. Clama igitur, filia, quod uestri amore captus, ego de sinu Patris descendi in uterum Virginis matris quando celorum Domina se dixit ancillam. Clama circumcisionis cauterium, adorationem magorum, oblationem in templo in manu senis mei Symeonis, persecutionem Herodis et fugam in Egiptum…. Volo autem ut ad quodlibet opus tante dignationis mee dicas quod solus amor animarum me inclinauit ad omnia hec agenda'" (*LMC* 5.392–406, 453–54:254–57). Cf. 4.336–37:228–29; 4.371–79:230.

57. *LMC* 5.43–155:242–246.

58. "Quia deuote domine circumdabant eam…et sepe suis uerbis impediebant orantem" (*LMC* 2.337–39:197).

59. "'Cur ergo me non recipis omni die, cum in te locum odoris et quietis reperiam?' Et quia timere cepit ne feruor de donis et consolationibus promissis conceptus pateret astantibus, rogauit omnes qui aderant, pre deuotione plorantes, ut sine mora exirent de cella. Verum lux uera sui comunicatiua nobis equaliter, dixit ei: 'Non loquar tecum, si emiseris assistentes, cum fecerim te speculum peccatorum'" (*LMC* 7.236–42:327).

60. *LMC* 2.355–73:197–98.

61. "'Filia, ideo te non ponunt, quia tu es stella mundo concessa nouiter ad cecos illuminandum, deuios reducendum ad uiam rectam et erigendum lapsos de sarcina

delictorum. Tu es uexillum nouum, quo reducentur peccatores ad me, sub quo etiam penitentes deuote fundent lacrimas suas largiter et suspiria'" (*LMC* 7.550–55:337–38).

62. "'Dabo autem tibi [inquit Dominus] meos apostolos fratres minores, qui predicabunt que in te fient sicut apostoli predicauerunt gentibus euangelium meum.... Et ego dico quod, licet augeri uel minui nequeam in me, per exempla tamen uite tue et dona mea, que operabuntur in te, exaltabor ab illis per immitationem uite, qui modo tamquam paruulum me uilipendunt et debilem, sua reiterando uitia, nec me diligunt neque laudant set ore ac opere me blasphemant'" (*LMC* 4.216–23:224).

63. For instance, Hadewijch, *Letter 6*, in *Hadewijch: The Complete Works*, trans. Columba Ward (New York: Paulist Press, 1983), 56–63. Cf. the comments of Amy Hollywood, *The Soul as Virgin Wife* (Notre Dame, Ind.: University of Notre Dame Press, 1995), 44–50 and (specifically on Mechthild of Magdeburg) 73–78.

64. *LMC* 2.229–58:193–94.

65. *LMC* 2.573–79:205. Apparently it is Dinah's sortie to "visit the women of the land" (Gen. 34:1) that Giunta has in mind, for its disastrous aftermath in the revenge of Jacob's sons on her new in-laws; he worries, anyway, about possible scandal.

66. He also tells her that if she goes through with her plan, he will not hear her confession anymore and he and the other friars will abandon their pastoral care of her (*LMC* 2.580–607:205–6).

67. *LMC* 5.194–204:248.

68. *LMC* 9.337–39:384.

69. *LMC* 9.527–38:391; 3.164–76:215; 9.1332–40:418.

70. *LMC* 5.563–73:261.

71. *LMC* 9.1075–83:409–10; 9.1094–1106:410; 5.337–46:252–53; "cepi legere quedam ei de diuinis promissionibus sibi factis" (5.679–80:265).

72. *LMC* 5.43–155:242–46. "Tum ad ingerendam cordi eius fiduciam de reinueniendo magistrum; tum ne praedicatio uerbi Dei impedimentum reciperet, alta uoce respondi" (5.150–52:246).

73. "'Adhuc tale taleque peccatum, talis et talis, propter ignorantiam pariter et ruborem, in confessione minime sunt confessi.' Propter que ab illorum conscientiis expellenda, obstetricando sollicite interrogatione cauta, inueniebam que numquam confitentes ausi, propter verecundiam, fuerant confiteri" (*LMC* 8.36–40:350). Cf. 9.667–76:395–96: the story of a seriously ill young man who would not confess his sins until Margaret prevailed upon him to confess to Giunta.

74. "Contra Domini voluntatem et proximi commodum" (*LMC* 4.80:219). Cf. 9.39–45:374 (on her reluctance to inform).

75. *LMC* 8.153–290:354–58.

76. *LMC* 8.291–305:358; 8.306–15:358–59; 8.340–54:360. There are also passages of peacemaking advice to an unnamed friar who may be Giunta: 9.140–60:377–78; 9.437–50:388. Iozzelli, "Introduzione," 77–80.

77. *LMC* 9.1057–58:409.

78. *LMC* 8.404–16:362–63.

79. *LMC* 9.61–77:375; 9.2.13–22:373. Cf. 9.28.482–503:389–90: a friar who wanted to communicate once a week is told by Christ only to do so once every fortnight, so that his desire for him might increase, until—as eventually happened, says Giunta—he might become ready for daily communication.

80. *LMC* 9.358–73:385–86 (including a report of a vision Conrad had of Margaret, in which an angel declared that she wanted nothing but Christ); 9.132–39:377.

81. *LMC* 9.161–204:378–80.

82. *LMC* 7.271–75:328; "'Et dicas confessori tuo, qui... dixit tibi quod nolebat purgare stabula tot in die, dic quod non purgat stabula set preparat in animabus confitentium michi sedem, dum audit confitentes'" (6.190–95:294).

83. *LMC* 6.833–35:317; 8.79–89:351–52; 8.599–611:393–94; 9.437–50:388 (if the friar in question is Giunta); 9.504–21:390–91; 9.891–901:403. Cf. 9.140–60:377–78: the unnamed friar who is advised here to preach fervently and boldly may be Giunta, since he seems to have been involved in the peacemaking activities that were Giunta's specialty.

84. "Quare doceo te, sicut pater filium, ut cum populo praedicaueris, prebeas te peccatoribus tractabilem et humanum, et in comminationibus quas contra peccata facies, peccatoribus meam clementiam, quam libenter largior peccatori redeunti, misceas uerbis illis" (*LMC* 8.119–23:353); cf. also 8.144–52:353–54 (encouragement to Giunta to persevere in his preaching at Siena).

85. "Tum quia magis coram predicto confessore uerecundabatur, tum quia plus aliis confessoribus redarguebat eandem" (*LMC* 7.57–60:321).

86. *LMC* 9.624–25:394.

87. "'Tibi mando ut quoties a confessore tuo quicquam tibi fuerit imperatum, obedias ei, quia largiturus sum menti eius, in omnibus dispositionibus uitae tue, lumen gratie specialis'" (*LMC* 4.455–57:233).

88. *LMC* 4.240–43:225.

89. *LMC* 7.378–87:332; 7.425–26:333; cf. 7.429–31:333.

90. *LMC* 7.460–61:334; 7.472–73:335; 7.479–82:335.

91. "'Filia, fratres dicunt quod ualde laborauerunt in te et uerum est; set ego cariori pretio te redemi et in maioribus laboribus pro te steti. Et quamuis eos fecerim tuos magistros exteriores, ego tamen tuus magister interior sum et fui. Ego tui dux itineris factus, misericorditer dignatus sum educere te de abysso profundissima huius mundi et tuarum miseriarum. Meum namque fuit tue conuersionis initium meaque omnis tue conuersationis regula et ero medium et finis salutis tue. Ego te duxi ad cellam istam, in qua minus offendor et magis a te seruior'" (*LMC* 2.433–40:200). Cf. also 5.877–81:271–72: Christ approves her move to the last cell, telling her that she did it properly for love of him, and again instructs her to tell Giunta that he should not try to impede her and that he should write to Castiglione to sustain the friars' pastoral concern for her. Cf. also 9.744–49:398: Christ tells her to tell Giunta not to doubt her decision to move.

92. On at least one other occasion Christ corrects Giunta's direction, namely when he upholds Margaret's habit of addressing him as "father," over Giunta's objection on Trinitarian grounds, 7.111–30:323.

8. HAGIOGRAPHY IN PROCESS: HENRY OF NÖRDLINGEN AND MARGARET EBNER

1. Gertrude Jaron Lewis, *For Women, By Women, About Women: The Sister-Books of Fourteenth-Century Germany* (Toronto: Pontifical Institute, 1996); Leonard P. Hindsley, *The Mystics of Engelthal: Writings from a Medieval Monastery* (New York: St. Martin's Press, 1998), 3–23.

2. Debra Lynn Stoudt, "The Vernacular Letters of Heinrich von Nördlingen and Heinrich Seuse" (Ph.D. diss., University of North Carolina, 1986), 258–59. The text used here is Henry of Nördlingen et al., *Briefe an Margaretha Ebner*, in *Margaretha Ebner und Heinrich von Nördlingen. Ein Beitrag zur Geschichte der deutschen Mystik*, ed. Philipp Strauch (Tübingen: J. C. B. Mohr, 1882; reprint, Amsterdam: P. Schippers, 1966), 164–284, 320–403 (cited as *BME*). Selections of the letters in modern German translation include: Maria Windstosser, ed. and trans., *Frauenmystik im Mittelalter* (Kempten and Munich: Verlag Josef Kösel & Friedrich Pustet, 1919), 167–94; Hieronymus Wilms, ed. and trans. *Der seligen Margareta Ebner Offenbarungen und Briefe* (Vechta: Albertus Magnus Verlag, 1928), 243–79; Wilhelm Oehl, ed. and trans.. *Deutsche Mystikerbriefe des Mittelalters 100–1550* (Munich: Georg Müller, 1931), 297–343; Louise Gnädinger, ed. and trans., *Deutsche Mystik* (Zürich: Manesse, 1989), 337–63.

3. See Lucia Corsini, "Notizie introduttive," in *Heinrich von Nördlingen e Margaretha Ebner: Le Lettere (1332–1350)*, ed. and trans. L. Corsini (Pisa: Edizioni ETS, 2001), 23n, for authorities.

4. "Die brieff hat ir gesant ir gaistlicher geträwer vatter Meister Hainrich von nerlingen gehaissen, ain andechtiger selliger man und besunderer fründ gottes, der ir und andern gottes kindern von got ward geben v. zugesand und dem sie in götlicher lieb und ausz dem einsprechē gottes ir leben und wesen und das got mit ir wircket geoffenbart hatt und von ym ratt und und hilff entpfangen etc.": quoted in Philipp Strauch, "Einleitung," in *Margaretha Ebner und Heinrich von Nördlingen. Ein Beitrag zur Geschichte der deutschen Mystik*, ed. Strauch (Tübingen: J. C. B. Mohr, 1882; reprint, Amsterdam: P. Schippers, 1966), xxi.

5. Peters, *Religiöse Erfahrung*, 153.

6. Peters, *Religiöse Erfahrung*, 154. It would be a mistake however to doubt (as Peters at points seems close to doing) that these sources can tell us anything about the relations between the two figures. As Stoudt has argued, adducing in addition to Henry's letters the evidence of the affectionate letter from Margaret to Henry that is included in the collection in the London manuscript (*BME* 63:281–83), it can hardly be questioned that there was a real friendship there. Debra Stoudt, "Production and Preservation of Letters by Fourteenth-Century Dominican Nuns," *Medieval Studies* 53 (1991): 320–21. Nonetheless, the great value of Peters' analysis is its careful consideration of the nature of the sources and accordingly the questions that they are capable of answering. See note 67.

7. There is one exception, a letter dated "the Saturday of Quinquagesima," though not specifying the year (*BME* 21.44:205, 342n). Stoudt, "Vernacular Letters," 125–26.

8. Stoudt, "Vernacular Letters," 360. Although Peters is in principle suspicious of the historical reliability of the letters, on the grounds of Henry's "stylized self-presentation" and the fact that they are witnessed only in a single late manuscript source clearly connected with Margaret's cult, she makes no attempt to challenge Strauch's arguments for dating. Peters, *Religiöse Erfahrung*, 153.

9. Stoudt, "Vernacular Letters," 86–128.; Corsini, "Notizie introduttive," 59–61, considers the personal news to be part of the *conclusio* rather than the *narratio*. See also Kirsten M. Christensen, "The Conciliatory Rhetoric of Mysticism in the Correspondence of Heinrich von Nördlingen and Margaretha Ebner," in *Peace and Negotiation: Strategies for Coexistence in the Middle Ages and Renaissance*, ed. Diane Wolfthal (Turnhout: Brepols, 2000), 129–32.

10. *BME* 7:179–80. Stoudt, "Vernacular Letters," 90–92.

11. *BME* 21.11–17:204. Stoudt, "Vernacular Letters," 96.

12. Stoudt, "Vernacular Letters," 98–121. Stoudt refers to the two parts of the *narratio* as "religious" and "personal," respectively. "From time to time Henry adapts the style to the content, using a more involved and emotional style for his more profound thoughts and a more informal and colloquial style for information of a more personal and 'mundane' type" (Corsini, "Notizie introduttive," 67–68).

13. Stoudt, "Vernacular Letters," 121–28.

14. Margaret mentions Henry's trip to Avignon in *MEO* 42.17–19; he himself mentions it, *BME* 29.30:214, cf. 342–43n. On gifts: *BME* 4.70:175; 9.53:182; 12.18–19:187–88. More than half of Henry's letters allude to a gift. Stoudt, "Vernacular Letters," 113–24.

15. Jeffrey Hamburger has shown that the practice of exchanging gifts as "tokens of spiritual affection" was a common part of the pastoral care of nuns at the time: Jeffrey Hamburger, "The *Liber Miraculorum* of Unterlinden: An Icon in Its Convent Setting," in *The Sacred Image East and West*, ed. Robert Ousterhout and Leslie Brubaker (Urbana: University of Illinois Press, 1995), 147–90.

16. *BME* 11.63–64:186; 14.43:192.

17. Euphemia Frick is mentioned at *BME* 2.22:171; 6.40:178; and 8.11:180, and then later, in the Basel correspondence, at 42.43:242; 47.67:255; 51.98:264. Irmel is mentioned at 3.37:172; 6.39:178; 8.11:180; 13.79:190; 14.44:192; 16.80:196; 33.30:220; 34.70:225. Cf. 322–23n: it appears that though he wanted her to come to Basel she never did. On both women, see Angelus Walz, "Gottesfreunde um Margarete Ebner," *Historisches Jahrbuch der Görresgesellschaft* 72 (1953): 254.

18. *BME* 13.50:189.

19. *BME* 16.63:196.

20. The punishment for noncompliance was outlaw status and confiscation of goods. *BME*, 352n.

21. *BME* 26.19–27. Cf. 27:210–11, and 28:212–13.

22. He reports to Margaret in a letter written sometime before 8 July of that year that the abbot of the Cistercian abbey of Kaisheim has summoned him about a church (*BME* 23.9:206). In a letter written later that month he reports having been obliged to

canvass support for himself for "my church of Fessenheim" at Niedershönenfeld from two sisters who were of the von Graisbach family, which had originally endowed Fessenheim (25.22–23:208–9). Strauch, "Einleitung," xliii. Much later, in early 1345, Henry reports from Basel that the rival came to him and renounced his claim to the church at Fessenheim (40.97–100:239).

23. *BME* 29.32–36:214; 30.9–11:215.

24. He was briefly at Constance, 21 December through 6 January (*BME* 31.5–9:216) and then, apparently sometime during January, at Kloster Königsfelden in Aargau, where he had hoped for help from "Queen" Agnes (widow of Andreas III of Hungary), resident there (32.7–9:217).

25. "und da kumt das best volck, das in Basel ist von armen gotzkindern und von reichen, von manen und von frawen, von pfefen, münchen, prudern, burgern, chorheren, edlen und gemainen luten… wunderlich gnad git got dem volck zu mir und mir zu in" (*BME* 32.18–21, 33–34:217). Cf. 33.101–102:222.

26. "I accuse myself to you before God," he says, "that by great constant work of preaching and hearing confession, I am drawn out of myself, so that I cannot attain inward devotion [so klag ich dir vor got ab mir selber, das ich von groszer stetter arbeit predigens und picht hörens usz mir selbe verfüret wirt, das ich ze inwendiger andacht nit komen kan]" (*BME* 35.67–69:228).

27. "I am offered parishes, chaplaincies, benefices, orders, and many things that many others would be glad to have, so that I do not know what I should take [man buit mich an pfar, capeln, pfründ und orden und vil dinges, des vil ander fro werint, also das ich nit waisz, was ich nemen sol]" (32.34–36:217).

28. "Although the people are in general favorable to me, from the clerics I suffer many malicious blows, because I preach often and the people favor me: help me bear this [das volck gemaincklichen ist mir günstig, aber von den geistlichen personen leid ich vil giftiger stösz umb das, das ich dick predigen und die leut mein gnad hand: das hilf mir tragen]" (*BME* 34.85–88:225).

29. On this informal movement, which included Tauler, Suso, and Rulman Merswin, see M. Gerwing, "Gottesfreund(e)," in *Lexikon des Mittelalters* (Munich: Artemis Verlag, 1987), 4:1586–87; Richard Egenter, "Die Idee der Gottesfreundschaft im vierzehnten Jahrhundert," in *Aus der Geisteswelt des Mittelalters: Studien und Texte Martin Grabmann zur Vollendung des 60. Lebensjahres von Freunden und Schülern gewidmet,* ed. Albert Lang, Joseph Lehner, and Michael Schmaus (Münster: Aschendorffschen Verlagsbuchhandlung, 1935), 1021–35; Rufus Jones, *The Flowering of Mysticism: The Friends of God in the Fourteenth Century* (New York: Macmillan, 1939); Anna Groh Seesholtz, *Friends of God: Practical Mystics of the Fourteenth Century* (New York: Columbia University Press, 1934).

30. "My heart does not attach to Suso as it once did [mein hertz haltet nit mer zu dem Süsen, als es etwan tet]" (*BME* 51.86–87:263); cf. *BME* 388n: Henry may have been one of those whom Suso accused in the *Exemplar,* chap. 38, of being fair-weather friends in his time of tribulation. Henry Suso, *The Exemplar, with Two German Sermons.,* ed. and trans. Frank Tobin (New York: Paulist Press, 1989), 152.

31. *BME* 34.91–93:225–26; 35.53–56:228; 50.29:260. On the friendship group, see Walz, "Gottesfreunde," 256–58.

32. "sie all dem nach dringen, des nam dir so gar in gedruckt is, in dem allein funden wirt als das ie in dem vatter in warhait gestanden ist" (*BME* 34.47–49:224).

33. *BME* 32.69–73:219

34. "und dar umb so getorst ich in dir noch in kainem gotzfründ sollich bedachte, kreftig und bewert begird in got und zu got nit hindertreiben" (*BME* 33.26–29:220). On the use of the Esther story here and elsewhere in the literature of German mysticism, see Louise Gnädinger, "Esther. Eine Skizze," *Zeitschrift für deutsche Philologie* 113 (1994): 31–62.

35. Margaret of the Golden Ring: *BME* 40.101:239; 42.47–48:242; 45.6:249; 50.24:260; her letter to Margaret Ebner is 63:275–76. Her confessor Henry of Rumerschein (mentioned by her, though not by name, at 63.38:276) also figures in the letters as a close associate of Henry of Nördlingen: 40.101:239; 44.65–66:249; 42.46:242; 46.88:253; 51.81:263; cf. 370–71n. Walz, "Gottesfreunde," 260.

36. *BME* 40.43–46:237; 48.57–60:258; 49.25:259 (on burden of work); 48.24–56:257–58 (on the action of grace through him).

37. "ich beger auch, als ich dich gebeten han, das du mir in dem willen gotz die wandlung, die got mit dir gethan hat, ordenlichen schribest" (*BME* 40.57–60: 237–38).

38. "was sol ich dir scheiben? dein got redender munt machet mich redenlosz" (*BME* 42.5–6:240), trans. Margot Schmidt in "An Example of Spiritual Friendship: The Correspondence Between Heinrich of Nördlingen and Margaretha Ebner," trans. Susan Johnson, in *Maps of Flesh and Light: The Religious Experience of Medieval Women Mystics*, ed. Ulrike Wiethaus (Syracuse, N.Y.: Syracuse University Press, 1993), 84.

39. *BME* 43.35–38:243; cf. 42.38–41:242.

40. On the trip to Cologne and Aachen, see Strauch, "Einleitung," liii–liv; cf. *BME* 46.71:253; and 48.62–63:258. On the trip to Bamberg, see Strauch, "Einleitung," liv–lv. In letter 44 he sends relics to her from Cologne and Aachen, asks her to pray to identify them, and speaks of the finger of St. Agnes that has come into his possession (44.34–38 and 40–45:248). He mentions Agnes's finger repeatedly afterward: 46.68–70:252; 47.75–76:256; 48.70–71:258. In letter 50, he again requests her to pray to identify a relic (50.25–29:260).

41. *BME* 47.61–64:255, and 50.18–20:260 (contributions from Queen Agnes; see note 24); 49.26–27:259 (a guilder from himself).

42. *BME* 40.74–82:238; 43.49–68:244; cf. 65.19–21:280 (Henry to Elisabeth Schepach).

43. *BME* 43.117–41:246–47; cf. 44.52–54:248–49: he asks for the book to be returned so that he can send it to Engelthal, where, as we know from the *Revelations* of Christine Ebner, Christine had it in hand by the summer. Strauch, 375–76. Since no copy of Mechthild's original Middle Low German text of *The Flowing Light* survives, the Middle High German translation to which Henry refers here, which he apparently produced in conjunction with other Friends of God at Basel and which is preserved

in the so-called "Einsiedler MS" (Einsiedeln, Stiftsbibliothek, Msc 277), is in fact the most important surviving witness to the work: Hans Neumann, "Beiträge zur Textgeschichte des 'Fliessenden Lichts der Gottheit' und zur Lebensgeschichte Mechthilds von Magdeburg," in *Altdeutsche und Altniederländische Mystik*, ed. Kurt Ruh (Darmstadt: Wissenschaftliche Buchgesellschaft, 1964), 175–241. On Henry's translation and its audience, see Sara Poor, *Mechthild of Magdeburg and Her Book* (Philadelphia: University of Pennsylvania Press, 2004), 89–98.

44. *BME* 52.54:266; her death has occurred by the time of letter 54, no later than the spring of 1350: 54.10–11:268.

45. *BME* 52.60–63:266.

46. *BME* 52.55–58:266.

47. "das meiner arwait anderswa basser bedorft dan zu Basel" (*BME* 52.18–19:265).

48. *BME* 52.12–15:265; "da mit traibt er mich mit sinen lemern under die wolf, der mich maniger grimiglich an zanet und veintlichen an hönet und schlaglichen verspottet" (52.44–47:266).

49. *BME* 53.3–26, 27–28 ("und keinen niderlasz han in keinem convent"): 267–68; on the sojourn at Engelthal, Strauch, "Einleitung," lix–lx.

50. *BME* 54.8:268.

51. *BME* 62.12–13:274; Strauch, "Einleitung," lx.

52. A document in the city archives of Nuremberg records that "Heinrich von Nordelingen" celebrated a commemorative mass there on 1 September 1379, but whether this is our Henry is not certain: Heinrich Gürsching, "Neue urkundliche Nachrichten über den Mystiker Heinrich von Nördlingen," in *Festgabe Aus Anlaß Des 75. Geburtstages von D. Dr. Karl Schornbaum am 7. März 1950.*, ed. Heinrich Gürsching (Neustadt: P. C. W. Schmidt, 1950), 42–57.

53. On the extravagance of his imagery, see Strauch, "Einleitung," lxxiii–lxxiv. See also Stoudt, "Vernacular Letters," 186–215.

54. "und sich in dein hertz schiesz, das du da von wider in in gangist, und das du da bekennist als du bekant bist, und du da minist als du gemint bist, das du da enphahist durch die geeder Jhesu Cristi des aller besten gutz, das usz dem mark der suszen minne gotz in keinen minbrinenden geist ie gefloszen ist" (*BME* 4.24–30:174). Cf. 5.22–26:176; 37.1–7:232, etc. Grete Lüers, *Die Sprache der deutschen Mystik des Mittelalters im Werke der Mechthild von Magdeburg* (Munich: Ernst Reinhardt, 1926), 140–43 and 278–84, s.v. "vliezen," and "brunnen."

55. "ich beger über dich, das dich got erlucht in deinem innern menschen und dich in seinem liecht weisz in sich selben, in das abgrund seiner ewiger klarheit" (*BME* 5.13–15:176); "in dem inglast des ewigen liechz, das usz brechend ist usz dem claren antlutz gotz in dich und dich erheben sol in sich" (13.58–60:190). Cf. 3.17–26:172; 4.48–53:174. For other examples see Lüers, *Die Sprache*, 212–18, s.v. "lieht," and 262–65, s.v. "sunne."

56. "mit der die wol geleuttert is in dem miniglichen blut ires gemacheln, die so wol gehauszet hat in ires liebes wunden, die in ires herren trautbette das ist in der

298   8. Hagiography in Process

sichern kamer sines hertzen rawend ist, die umbstond die sechzig starcken" (*BME* 35.2–6:226. Cf. 4.15–24:173–74; 25.13–21:208. For other examples, see Lüers, *Die Sprache*, s.v. "connubium spirituale," 160–67.

57. "[Ich] beger dir der freud in dein minendes hertz, die Maria enpfing in dem ersten anplick, den si tet an ir kind in dem ewigen leben" (*BME* 50.4–6:260); "in die crippe deins andechtigen hertzens" (9.35:182); cf. 16.41–47:195; 36.55–64:231; 50.4–10:260; 29.1–20:202. These passages make explicit the "imitation of Mary" that is implicit in the *Revelations* when Margaret describes nursing and playing with the Christ child, as pointed out by Rosemary Hale, "*Imitatio Mariae:* Motherhood Motifs in Devotional Memoirs," *Mystics Quarterly* 16 (1991): 196–97. See also Hale, "Rocking the Cradle: Margaretha Ebner (Be)Holds the Divine," in *Performance and Transformation: New Approaches to Late Medieval Spirituality*, ed. Mary A. Suydam and Joanna E. Ziegler (New York: St. Martin's, 1999), 211–39. Lüers, *Die Sprache*, s.v. "berhaftigkeit," 152–54.

58. "in der waggusze der vetterlichen barmhertzigkeit" (*BME* 4.30–31:174). Lüers, *Die Sprache*, 20, and 224–26, s.v. "mer."

59. "ze einer uberwesenlicher stille werd, die alle geschaffen sinne ubertreffe in dem frid gotz und in dem inglast des ewigen liechz, … denne waistu nit als sant Pauls, wa du bist oder wie dir beschehen ist, so du dir selber und uns wider geben wirst" (*BME* 13.56–58, 69–71:190). Cf. 21.17–27:204, where he again waxes eloquent on her silence and associates it with the beatific vision.

60. "Dem us erwelten kint gotz … enbuit ich, ir und iren truwen gar ain unglicher friund, waz ich bin und han in got" (*BME* 14.1–3:190–91). "Der diemüttig dirnengotts enbütt ir unwirdiger frünt ze Basel Jhesum Christum" (*BME* 41.1–2:239–40). Stoudt notes that "in thirty-seven out of the fifty-six letters," the salutation has "three characteristic features": (1) the addressing of Margaret in the dative, (2) the use of the "verb *enbieten* 'offer, send' or occasionally the verb *grüezen*," (3) the introduction of the writer "in self-abasing terms" (*armer unwurdiger frünt, ain unglicher friund, armes wirmlin*, etc.): Stoudt, "Vernacular Letters," 88–89. Christenson, "Conciliatory Rhetoric," 134–38, notes that in his salutations Henry diverges from "commonly accepted salutory rules" (136) whereby the salutation served to establish the respective social rank or status of sender and recipient.

61. "das du in deiner inwendigkeit mein gebresten nit clagen mugist" (*BME* 7.39–40:180).

62. *BME* 10.12–31:183–84.

63. *BME* 11.8–9:185.

64. "There is truly one thing however in all your letters, my faithful one in God, to which I can [reply] nothing, since I am nothing: namely the high words, which you write about me. Where nothing in them corresponds to me, as I truly believe, so may your loving bridegroom, Jesus Christ, realize them through his goodness and also your faithful prayers [eins ist aber an deinen briffen allen werlich mein träwe in got, dar zu ich nichtz kan noch bin: das ist die groszen wort, die du von mir schribest. wa die an mir nit sient, als ich ir auch in warhait werlich nit bekennen kan, so müsze

si dein liebst lieb Christus Jhesus durch sein güti war machen und auch durch deins getruwen gebetz willen]" (*BME* 13.31–37:189). 26.14–16:211; 36.28–29:230

65. "Ain armes kuchenbueblin" (*BME* 35.9:226). The image of the little kitchen boy is also to be found in Suso, who uses it as an image for the soul who has forgotten its divine origin. Lüers, *Die Sprache*, 64.

66. *BME* 43.9–15:243; 47.14–19:254.

67. Richard Schultz, "Heinrich von Nördlingen: Seine Zeit, sein Leben und seine Stellung innerhalb der Deutschen Mystik," *Jahrbuch des Vereins für Augsburger Bistumsgeschichte* 10 (1976): 155. Wilhelm Preger, the pioneering nineteenth-century scholar of German mysticism, wrote that "Henry displays in his letters a very soft, sentimental nature. He is full of feeling, rapturous, and controlled by his feelings to the point of unmanliness": Preger, *Geschichte der Deutschen Mystik im Mittelalter* (Leipzig: Dörfling und Franke, 1874–1893; reprint, Aalen: Zeller, 1962), 2:279. For Walter Muschg, he is "a windbag, who has wandered into the worn pathways of mystical piety": Muschg, *Die Mystik in der Schweiz 1200–1500* (Frauenfeld: Huber, 1935), 292. Manfred Weitlauff, mildly countering such views, maintains that Henry's writing has literary merit in spite of his personal shortcomings: Weitlauff, " 'Dein Got redender Munt machet mich redenlosz': Margareta Ebner und Heinrich von Nördlingen," in *Religiöse Frauenbewegung und Mystische Frömmigkeit in Mittelalter*, ed. Peter Dinzelbacher and Dieter R. Bauer (Cologne: Böhlau Verlag, 1988), 328–32. Margot Schmidt argues sharply with the negative views of Henry, contending that his contrasting estimations of himself and Margaret rested on a careful evaluation of Margaret: Schmidt, "An Example," 79. All of these views, however, tend to assume that the texts are transparent witnesses to the personalities of Henry and Margaret and to their actual interactions—an assumption that Peters has rightly thrown into question. See note 6.

68. "ich bin geweszen vor den fursten diszer welt. die durchechten mich, also das ich ze land sicher stat nit mer han, ich welle auch den singen.... bit dein gewaltigz lieb Jhesu Christum, das er sich über mich erbarm aller ding, als er mein armut bekennt, und das er dich bewisz, was ich ton söll und was ich beleiben sül. grusz mir unszer getrüwen. bit got auch für alle meine feind. schreib mir ausz got was mir not sei" (*BME* 28.27–30, 36–40:212–13). Cf. letter 30, written shortly afterward, in which he commends himself and his "business [gescheft]" to her (30.22–23:215).

69. "so klag ich dir vor got ab mir selber, das ich von groszer stetter arbeit predigens und picht hörens usz mir selber verfüret wirt, das ich ze inwendiger andacht nit komen kan.... ich leg uf dich den schwerer tail als mins lidens, wann so vil du mer minnen hast, so vil magtu mer tragen den ich ... also wirstu billicher niessen die frucht meiner arbeit, so vil du si mincklicher und warlicher pflantzend bist den ich" (*BME* 35.67–69, 72–74, 80–81:228).

70. E.g., *BME* 34.32–35:224; 39.10–13:235; 47.24–32:254; 52.31–36:265.

71. "es begert auch unszer liber vatter der Tauler und ander gotzfründ, das du uns in der gemein etwas schribest, was dir dein lieb Jhesus geb und sunderlichen von dem weszen der cristenhait und seiner fruind, die dar under vil lident" (*BME* 32.69–73:219).

72. See note 94.

73. "und dar umb bitt ich dich in gott, als ich vor geton hab, was dir got ze spre-chen geb, das du vileicht vor vergeszen habest oder on das noch nit gescriben habest" (*BME* 41.10–12:240).

74. See note 40.

75. "frolich maht du sprechen: 'der künig hat mich ein geleit in seinen weinkeller' und da versuchest du und schowest wie susz der kunig ist, da trinckest du den lustli-chen most des hailigen geistes in reicher genuglicheit baide dir selber und auch den andern, das du uns usz deinen mutterlichen vollen megdlichen brusten weiszlich und freintlich gesögen kanst, uns armen durstigen, die vor der cellen deiner widerkunft mit groszem jamer wartent seint" (*BME* 42.21–28:241–42). On the final image, cf. Song of Songs 1:3.

76. *BME* 46.31–36:251; 51.11–21:261; cf. 54.1–7:268.

77. Lüers, *Die Sprache*, 259–60; Schmidt, "An Example," 88.

78. "was ich gewinen und erjag in Christo, das bring ich zu dir als einer genemen wol gevelliger gemaheln des ewigen kaisers sun, die sie durch irs liebs willen seinen eren uf tragi met träwen. eia! hertzlichs lieb gotz, nit enlasz ab deinem seil dein und sein arms und rüdigs jagdhündlin, bis du es mit dir ze hoff bringist" (*BME* 45.15–25:250).

79. See also Strauch's comments, *BME* 379n., on the use of the image of the dog in other German mysticism of the time as a figure for the faithful soul who will not be parted from God.

80. Peters, *Religiöse Erfahrung*, 153.

81. *MEO* 1.1–3.10 (*H* 85–86). Although the year 1312 is the only year named, Mar-garet afterwards appears to relate events in meticulous chronological order and refers throughout to the liturgical feasts and seasons. With the help of the few externally datable events as points of reference Strauch inferred dates for much of what the nar-rative describes.

82. On crucifixes: *MEO* 20.18–21.24 (*H* 96). On souls in purgatory: *MEO* 5.27–7.3 (*H* 87–88); 38.1–40.13 (*H* 105–6); 155.12–15 (*H* 169), 158.24–159.15 (*H* 170–71).

83. *MEO* 27.13–14, 17–21 (*H* 99–100).

84. Beginning of the binding silence: *MEO* 47.20–48.11 (*H* 110–11). Ludwig Zoepf, *Die Mystikerin Margaretha Ebner (ca. 1291–1351)* (Leipzig: B. G. Teubner, 1914), 48–51.

85. Beginning of the cries: *MEO* 54.6–55.3 (*H* 114). Zoepf, *Die Mystikerin*, 64.

86. *MEO* 119.24–121.16 (*H* 150–51).

87. *MEO* 87.3–90.21 (*H* 132–34). Hale, "*Imitatio Mariae*," 193–203; Ulinka Rublack, "Female Spirituality and the Infant Jesus in Late Medieval Dominican Convents," *Gender and History* 6 (1994): 37–57.

88. *MEO* 99.10–105.15 (*H* 139–42).

89. *MEO* 148.1–150.3 (*H* 165–66); cf. 158.1–161.6 (*H* 170–72) (prophecies not specifi-cally attributed to Christ child).

90. *MEO* 16.3–18 (*H* 93) (29 October 1332); 24.3–25.6 (*H* 98) (31 October until after 1 November 1334); 29.26–31.5 (*H* 101) (a Tuesday in Lent, 1335); 33.8–11 (*H* 103) (Easter, 1335); 60.2–25 (*H* 117–18) (before 1 November until 4 November 1341); 72.16–24 (*H* 124)

(before 9 October until 9 October 1344); 138.22–142.5 (*H* 160–62) (16 to 28 July 1347); 148.13–16 (*H* 165) (11 October 1347); cf. *MEO* 290n.

91. *MEO* 83.27–84.24 (*H* 130–31). On the topos of the command to write (*Schreibbefehl*), see Corsini, "Notizie introduttive," 39–40; Peters, *Religiöse Erfahrung*, 7, 108–10.

92. *MEO* 29.4–7 (*H* 100); 42.17–19 (*H* 108); 45.11–26 (*H* 109).

93. *MEO* 76.6–77.2 (*H* 126); 90.8–10 (*H* 134); 103.16–22 (*H* 141).

94. "I send you back your letter, finished [Ich send dir deinen brief beraiten]" (*BME* 4.66:175). Cf. 3.37–38:172; 6.33–38:178; 7.17–37:179–80 (referring to four seals, which appear also in a vision in the *Revelations*, *MEO* 18.22–19.9; *H* 95); 13.48–49:189 (dream of Henry; cf. *MEO* 26.21; *H* 99); 24.8–9:207 (John the Evangelist as her scribe; cf. *MEO* 84.5–8; *H* 130). Zoepf, *Die Mystikerin*, 28–29.

95. "Ich getar auch weder dar zu oder dar von gelegen weder in latein noch in tüchtz bis das ich es mit dir überlesz und es ausz dinem mund und ausz dinem hertzen in newer warhait verstand" (*BME* 41.15–18:240).

96. Zoepf, *Die Mystikerin*, 43–45.

97. Zoepf, *Die Mystikerin*, 125–27; Margot Schmidt, "An Example," 87–88. See note 43. On Mechthild's influence on Margaret, see Jeanne Ancelet-Hustache, *Mechtilde de Magdebourg: Étude de psychologie religieuse* (Paris: Champion, 1926), 352–58.

98. Hindsley's translation, *H* 99 ("daz ich in het in miner triwe … 'hab kain betrüebt umb in, wan ist kain mensch uf erderiche, daz in der zwelf botten leben ist, daz ist auch er'": *MEO* 26.21, 27.4–5).

99. *H* 126 ("ich wil in ziehen in daz wild ain miner hailigen gothet, in der er sich selber von minnen in mir verliesen sol": *MEO* 76.18–20). In another revelation Christ tells her "'I have chosen him for myself and I will bring to perfection my delight in him [wan ich in mir han usserwelt, daz ich minen lust an im volbringe]'" (*H* 141; *MEO* 103.21–22).

100. *H* 162 ("'er ist daz war sicher leben, daz min ere behüet'": *MEO* 143.9–10).

101. "Gradually I learned by experience of the world's ways: those who had once been close to me now kept their distance saying they could not bear to see me suffer so. Then I understood that God alone remains faithful. He would never abandon me [dar zuo ward mich manend der lauf diser welt, so ich sach, daz die von mir giengen, den vor wol mit mir was. sunderlich so mir aller wirst was, so giengen sie von mir und sprachen: sie möhten es an mir niht geliden. so gedaht ich, daz got allain diu war triwe wer, der mich nimmer verliesse]" (*H* 85–86; *MEO* 2.21–26).

102. *H* 109 ("nu het ich in allen minen unkunden wegen, die mir an laugen, nieman denn die warhaften triu, die mir got geben het an sinem lieben friunt, von des worten und leben ich alle zit creftigen trost enphieng, daz mich dik dar ab wundert in mir selber": *MEO* 45.12–16). "Yet I had no courage to dare tell anyone except the Friend of our Lord who was given me by God [nu het ich kainen geturst, daz ich ez kainem menschen immer gesagen törst denn dem friunde unsers herren, der mir von got geben ist]" (*H* 134; *MEO* 90.8–10). In fact, she must have told Elisabeth Schepach, her scribe for the *Revelations*, who was by then prioress of the convent; Henry's letters, with their frequent reference to Schepach and other sisters of the monastery, leave the

impression that Margaret was rather less detached from the convent's life than we would otherwise guess. Zoepf, *Die Mystikerin*, 133–67.

103. She "listened gladly to his true teaching [hort ich sin warhft ler gar gern]" (*H* 93; *MEO* 16.6–7), and calls him a "powerful teacher (creftelichen lerer)" (*H* 98; *MEO* 25.12). To the correspondence itself, remarkably, Margaret makes only one oblique reference: "I heard nothing from him for a very long time [nu was ich lang, daz ich von im nit hort]" (*H* 109; *MEO* 45.20–21).

104. *MEO* 16.4–18 (*H* 93).

105. *H* 98 ("do ich do zuo im kom, do luht mir uz im ain umessigiu gnaude und ain inder lust rehter süezkait in sinen worten in den mir gegenwertig wart mit im ze reden in begirden alle die sach, die mir an legen…. so wart mir so gegenwertig diu genaud gotes in begirden mit im ze reden … und wart mir ze der selben zit grozzin gab geben uz dem milten richtum gotes … ain so unkundiu geringkait des libes, da von ich niht gereden kan": *MEO* 24.7–11, 19–20, 22–23). In the following Lent, in the days when the "speaking" was first coming upon her, he visited again and "recognized the merciful works of God in me. I revealed all my cares to him as my trusted physician sent to me by God," and afterward "I felt nothing in me but the grace of our merciful God with great joy [(er) mir von got geben was und sach diu barmherczigen werk gottes an mir. dem gab ich ze erkennen alles daz mir an lag als ainem getriwen arczat, der mir von got gesent war…. und enphant nihtz an mir dan der barmherczigen gnaud gotes mit vil fräuden]" (*H* 101; *MEO* 29.27–30.6).

106. *H* 103 ("do kom der friunt gotes, mit dem mir alle zit diu genade unsers herren gemert wart": *MEO* 33.8–9). Indeed, she speaks of such "grace" throughout the *Revelations*, in a way that is doubtless consistent with scholastic theologians' notion of an extraordinary indwelling presence of God. See Wolf-Dieter Hauschild, "Gnade IV," *Theologische Realenzycolpädie* 13:485.52–486.19. But she construes it rather in terms that suggest sensation, as something immediately experienced, for example after a revelatory dream, or after partaking of the Eucharist, or as either a concomitant or aftermath to episodes of physical suffering. E.g., *MEO* 68.17–19, *H* 122 (after dream); 18.20–21, *H* 94 (after Eucharist); 61.5–10, *H* 118 (after suffering); 61.5–10, *H* 118 (during suffering) Cf. 85.1 (*H* 131); 105.16–21 (*H* 142); 126.15–19 (*H* 153–54).

107. "[Er] begert von mir, daz ich in het in miner triwe. do sprach ich: 'ich wil ez gern tuon, ist daz ir die ere gottes dar inne mainent.' er antwurt, daz er ez niht anders mainte, als ich ez sider in der warhait funden han, wan ich ain unschuldiges warhaftz leben an im bekant" (*MEO* 26.19–25; cf. *H* 99).

108. *BME*, 406–7.

109. The letters appear in the collection in the following sequence: 41, 52, 47, 25, 1, 33, 19, 35, 42, 65, 34, 44, 38, 2, 17, 5, 3, 37, 24, 50, 31, 32, 16, 20, 30, 36, 54, 18, 22, 45, 12, 55, 39, 57, 8, 60, 61, 62, 69, 58, 66, 36, 6, 9, 40, 4, 27, 28, 49, 21, 11, 43, 15, 46, 10, 29, 48, 51, 7, 32, 13, 14, 53, 63, 68, 67, 44, 56. Strauch, in *BME* 407.

110. On the variety of principles of compilation of medieval letter collections and the lack of "general rules" for the practice, see Giles Constable, *Letters and Letter Collections* (Turnhout: Brepols, 1976), 58–59.

111. Peters, Religiöse Erfahrung, 151–53.

9. Managing Holiness: Raymond of Capua and Catherine of Siena

1. Gabriella Zarri, *Le sante vive. Cultura e religiosità femminile nella prima età moderna* (Turin: Rosenberg and Sellier, 1990); and now Jodi Bilinkoff, *Related Lives: Confessors, Female Penitents, and Catholic Culture, 1450–1750* (Ithaca, N.Y.: Cornell University Press, 2005).

2. Robert Fawtier, *Sainte Catherine de Sienne: Essai de critique des sources* (Paris: A. de Boccard, 1921–30), 1:162. Cf. *LM* 2.12.317:941.

3. The bull is dated 17 August 1376. M. Hyacinth Laurent, ed., *Documenti*, Fontes vitae S. Catharinae Sensis historici 1 (Siena: R. Università di Siena, 1936), 38. We know of Catherine's presence at the chapter meeting from the *Miracoli*, the oldest hagiographical text about Catherine, written by an anonymous Florentine shortly after her sojourn in Florence: M. Hyacinth Laurent and Francesco Valli, eds., *I Miracoli di Caterina da Iacopo da Siena di Anonimo Fiorentino*, Fontes vitae S. Catherinae historici 4 (Florence: Sansoni, 1936), 1–2 . Fawtier, *Sainte Catherine*, 1:159–62.

4. *AA SS* April, vol. 2 (Antwerp, 1675): 792–812. Raymond also probably wrote the vita of Benedict XI that Cormier included in his collection of Raymond's writings: Raymond of Capua, *Opuscula et Litterae*, ed. Hyacinthe-Marie Cormier. (Rome: Ex Typographia Polyglotta, 1895), 19–24.

5. A. W. Van Ree, "Raymond de Capoue: Éléments biographiques," *Archivum Fratrrum Praedicatorum* 33 (1963):163–69. The only full-scale biography of Raymond, by the early-twentieth-century Dominican master general Hyacinthe-Marie Cormier, *La bienheureux Raymond de Capoue. Sa vie, ses vertus, son action dans l'église et dans l'ordre de saint Dominique* (Rome: Imprimerie Vaticane, 1899), is largely a work of edification.

6. Robert Fawtier and Louis Canet, *La Double expérience de Catherine Benincasa* (Paris: Gallimard, 1948), 61–76.

7. Fawtier and Canet, *La Double expérience*, 83–85 (on her correspondence with the cardinal Pierre d'Estaing and the abbot Bérenger of Lezat, both papal legates to Italy); 92–93 (on her reference in letter 127, 26 March 1374, to a previous letter to Gregory XI, which has not survived).

8. Letter 127. Fawtier and Canet, *La Double expérience*, 93–94; Francis Thomas Luongo, "The Politics of Marginality: Catherine of Siena in the War of Eight Saints, 1374–1378" (Ph.D. diss., University of Notre Dame, 1997), 102–4.

9. "Sane petitio pro parte tua nobis exhibita continebat quod olim dilectus filius Helias dicti ordinis magister attendens quod … Caterina … se valde fructuose circa animarum salutem et ultramarini passagii, et alia sancte Romane ecclesie negocia occupabat … prefatus magister, ne animarum fructus a quoquam inpediri posset, curam Caterine predicte et sociarum ipsius … tibi … deputavit, tibique omnem potestatum quam prefatus ordo super eas habet eadem auctoritate commisit, ut eas videlicet regeres et corrigeres" (Laurent, ed., *Documenti*, 38).

10. "[Catherine] entered public affairs at the instigation of high church leaders and with an already established network of politically aware and active clerical supporters/promoters" (Luongo, "The Politics of Marginality," 115). Fawtier, both in *Sainte*

Catherine, 1:161–64, and *La double expérience*, 94–96, emphasizes the motive of establishing and supervising her orthodoxy.

11. Karen Scott, " 'Io Catarina': Ecclesiastical Politics and Oral Culture in the Letters of Catherine of Siena," in *Dear Sister: Medieval Women and the Epistolary Genre*, ed. Karen Cherewatuk and Ulrike Wiethaus (Philadelphia: University of Pennsylvania Press, 1993), 87–121. Cf. Fawtier and Canet, *La Double experience*, 148–49.

12. Fawtier, who saw Catherine as profoundly naïve in political matters, doubted the extent of her actual influence or even celebrity; see, for instance, his eloquent conclusion in *La Double expérience*, 234–36. Karen Scott, "Not Only with Words, but with Deeds: The Role of Speech in Catherine of Siena's Understanding of Her Mission" (Ph.D. diss., University of California, Berkeley, 1989), 76–98, and Luongo, in "The Politics of Marginality," have argued that Catherine exerted more influence than Fawtier recognizes.

13. The episode is known from a report of Sienese ambassadors to the Sienese signoria, 27 June 1375 (Laurent, ed., *Documenti*, 34–35).

14. Van Ree, "Raymond de Capoue," 174–180; Fawtier and Canet, *La Double Experience*, 159–70.

15. Raymond reports the meeting in *LM* 3.1.336:946; Fawtier, however, argues that Raymond had probably departed on his embassy to Charles V, and therefore did not actually meet her, his report being the result of poor memory or a desire to enhance his reader's impression of the extent of his contact with the saint (*La Double expérience*, 196–201).

16. *Vita Catherinae Senensis [Legenda maior]*, in *AA SS*, third ed. April 3 (Paris: V. Palmé, 1866): 863–97 (cited as *LM*). (In this instance I use the third edition of *AA SS* because of the extensive errors of pagination in the first edition.) At one point in part 2 of *LM*, recalling an outbreak of plague, Raymond indicates that he was at work on that part of the work in 1390: "[The outbreak] happened seventeen years or thereabouts before the present year 1390 [Accidit decimo septimo anno, vel circiter, ante annum hunc nonagesimum qui nunc currit]" (*LM* 2.8.245:923). Elsewhere in part 2 he says that he began the work at the urging of the saint's followers while he was taking a rest cure at the baths near Siena five years earlier: "ante annos hos quinque" (2.11.304:937). In a letter to Neri di Landoccio (another member of Catherine's *famiglia*), 13 March 1392, Thomas of Siena wrote, "although the reverend Master of the order is very busy, I bothered him every day with my offering to be of whatever help possible in expediting the legend, so that at last we began to correct that second part, which is not yet perfect, and after that to write the last one, with him dictating and me writing [licet reverendus Magister ordinis esset multum occupatus, attamen continue quotidie ipsum molestabam offerendo me ad omne adiutorium michi possibile pro expeditione illius legende, propter quod tandem cepimus illam secundam partem nondum perfectam corrigere; deinde ulterius scribere, ipse dictando et ego scribendo]": F. Grottanelli, *Leggenda minore di S. Caterina da Siena e lettere dei suoi discepoli* (Bologna: Presso Gaetano Romagnoli, 1868), 328. Raymond himself wrote to two of Catherine's Sienese admirers, on 18 June 1392, that he had finished the first two parts, and he promised to use his access to the pope to promote her canonization (Ray-

mond of Capua, *Opuscula et litterae*, 74–75; Van Ree, "Raymond de Capoue," 213). It is Thomas of Siena, in his *Supplementum* to the *Legenda maior*, who says that Raymond finished the work in 1395: Thomas of Siena, *Libellus de supplemento*, ed. Iuliana Cavallini and Imelda Foralosso (Rome: Edizioni cateriniane, 1974), 380–81.

17. Fawtier, *Sainte Catherine*, 1:121–24.

18. On the subject of Raymond's interest in Catherine's apostolate, see Antonio Volpato, "Tra sante profetesse e santi dottori: Caterina da Siena," in *Women and Men in Spiritual Culture, Fourteenth–Seventeenth Centuries: A Meeting of South and North.*, ed. E. Schulte van Kessel (The Hague: Netherlands Government Publishing Office, 1986), 149–61; and Scott, "Not Only with Words," 99–181. Scott revises and nuances the analysis of Sofia Boesch Gajano and Odile Redon, "La *Legenda maior* di Raimundo da Capua, costruzione di una santa," in *Atti del Simposio Internazionale Cateriniano-Bernardiniano, Siena 17–20 Aprile 1980*, ed. Domenico Mafei and Paolo Nardi (Siena: Accademia Senese degli Intronati, 1982), 15–35, who decide from Raymond's emphasis on Catherine's inner life that he places her apostolate "on a second plane": "One might conclude," Scott writes, "that Raymond had had to discuss and defend her public endeavors with a great deal of tact and discretion because otherwise he felt that he would have failed in his goal of furthering her canonization. But in fact, Raymond did say a great deal about Catherine the activist" (180). See also Luongo, "The Politics of Marginality," 36–87, who characterizes Raymond's defense of Catherine as based on her "marginality" in the sense of finding her authority in her supposed charisms and prophecies as distinct from real political influence.

19. Lehmijoki-Gardner, *Worldly Saints*, 73, 115.

20. *LM* prol.21:867; cf. 3.1.330–31:944–45.

21. Karen Scott, "Mystical Death, Bodily Death: Catherine of Siena and Raymond of Capua on the Mystic's Encounter with God," in *Gendered Voices: Medieval Saints and Their Interpreters*, ed. Catherine M. Mooney (Philadelphia: University of Pennsylvania Press, 1999), 156, 162.

22. Karen Scott, "St. Catherine of Siena, 'Apostola,'" *Church History* 61 (1992): 34–46; Scott, "Not Only with Words," 161–81; Scott, "Mystical Death," 136–40, 147–51.

23. Scott, "Mystical Death," 152–67. The letters are 371 (*LCS* 5:273–78 [on Raymond as addressee, see 6:142n]) and 373 (5:284–92). *LM* 2.6.180:907 (exchange of hearts), 2.6.214–16:915 ("first death").

24. *LM* 1.2.28–29,31:869–70; 1.3.35:871.

25. *LM*, 1.5.53–54:875–76; 1.10.93–101:885–87; "'vel per suam inspirationem, vel per claram apparitionem loquens mihi, sicut ego modo loquor vobiscum'" (1.9.84:883); "vix duo possunt homines reperiri, qui tam assiduam conversationem haberent ad invicem, quam continuam habebat haec sacra virgo cum Sponso suo" (1.9.86:883).

26. *LM* 1.12.112–13:890.

27. *LM*, 1.12.115:890–91.

28. "Ut … virtutis fidei largiretur perfectionem" (*LM* 1.12.114:890); "non auferendo ei tamen divinam, imo quantum ad mensuram perfectionis, potius accrescendo" (1.12.120:892).

29. *LM* 1.2.126–27:893–94; "Mox namque ut sacri Sponsi memoria paulisper recentificabatur in anima illa sancta, a sensibus se corporis quantum poterat retrahebat, et extremitates corporis, scilicet manus et pedes, contrahebantur" (1.2.126:893).

30. *LM*, 2.4.142–49, 154–64:898–99, 900–903; 2.4.163:903.

31. *LM*, 2.6.179–180, 181–87, 188–95, 206–12, 214–16:907–15.

32. *LM* 2.4.164:903 (*mens*); 2.5.165:903 (*anima*); 2.5.167:904 (*mens*); 2.6.178:907. (*spiritus*).

33. Rudolph Bell, *Holy Anorexia* (Chicago: University of Chicago Press, 1985), 26–51; Bynum, *Holy Feast and Holy Fast*, 194–207. For a comparison of these two scholars' approaches to the food-related asceticism of late-medieval holy women, see John Coakley, "Introduction: Women's Creativity in Religious Context," in *Creative Women in Medieval and Early Modern Italy*, ed. E. Ann Matter and John Coakley (Philadelphia: University of Pennsylvania Press, 1994), 3–6.

34. "Numquam post illam horam cibum sumpsit eo modo quo prius, nec sumere potuit" (*LM* 2.4.164:903); for Raymond's replies to her detractors on this point, 2.5.167–77:904–7.

35. "Insuper erga salutem proximorum tam vehementer accendetur cor tuum, quod proprii sexus oblita, quasi ex toto conversationem praeteritam omnino immutabis, hominumque et feminarum consortium, prout assoles, non vitabis, imo pro salute animarum ipsorum et ipsarum, te ipsam exponere pro viribus ad omnes labores" (*LM* 2.5.165:903).

36. "Coepit enim Dominus ex tunc non tantum in locis secretis, ut prius consueverat, sed etiam in patentibus, palam et familiariter se ostendere sponsae suae, tam eunti quam stanti" (*LM* 2.6.178:907).

37. John Coakley, "Friars, Sanctity, and Gender," 94–98. Richard Kieckhefer has noted the central importance of patience as a virtue in fourteenth-century hagiography generally, as indicating precisely the difficulties of living an ascetic ideal in the secular world (*Unquiet Souls*, 85–88).

38. "Ut nullus a minimo usque ad magnum viam excusationis haberet, quod Deo servire non posset juxta possibilitatem suam in domo propria et habitu seculari" (Vito of Cortona, *Vita Humilianae*, 13:389). For other examples, see Coakley, "Friars, Sanctity, and Gender," 94–98.

39. *LMC* 7.550–55:337–38.

40. "Pro certo igitur teneatis, quod anima mea vidit divinam essentiam: et haec est causa, quare tam impatienter maneo in hoc ergastulo corporis" (*LM* 2.6.215:915).

41. "Multarum animarum salus requirit ut redeas, nec amplius modum vivendi tenebis, quem tenuisti huc usque, nec cellam pro habitaculo habebis de cetero; quin potius et urbem te propriam egredi oportebit pro animarum salute. Ego autem semper tecum ero, et ducam et reducam; portabisque nominis mei honorem et spiritalia documenta coram parvis et magnis, tam laicis quam clericis et religiosis: ego enim tibi dabo os et sapientiam, cui nullus resistere poterit. Adducam etiam te coram Pontificibus et Rectoribus Ecclesiarum ac populi Christiani, ut consueto meo modo, per infirma fortiorum confundam superbiam" (*LM* 2.6.216:915).

42. "Padre dell'anima mia" (letter 373, *LCS* 5:288).

43. Letter 226, *LCS* 3:299–300.

44. Letter 100, *LCS* 2:118–19; letter 102, *LCS* 2:127–30; letter 275, *LCS* 4:179–81. Fawtier, *Sainte Catherine*, 2:200–201.

45. Letters 104, 219, 226, 267, 272, 273, 371, 373.

46. The exception is letter 272, *LCS* 4:158–72, written late 1377 or early 1378, a letter not so much of admonition or exhortation as of instruction based on oracles, and which stands as a sort of first draft of Catherine's *Dialogue*.

47. Letter 219, *The Letters of St. Catherine of Siena*, trans. Suzanne Noffke (Binghamton: Medieval and Renaissance Texts and Studies, 1988), 1:206–9, *LCS* 3:266–70.

48. Letter 219, *The Letters of St. Catherine*, 208; *LCS*, 3:269.

49. Letter 104, *LCS* 2:136.

50. Letter 273, *LCS* 4:173–78. Curiously the incident is not mentioned in the *Legenda maior*. A. Dondaine, "Sainte Catherine de Sienne et Niccolò Toldo," *Archivum Fratrum Praedicatorum* 19 (1949): 168–207, established, over the doubts of Fawtier (*La Double expérience*, 122–32; *Sainte Catherine* 1:169–71) the likelihood that the traditional identification the man with Niccolò, which derives from Thomas of Siena's testimony in the canonization process, was correct: Marie-Hyacinthe Laurent, ed., *Il Processo Castellano*, Fontes vitae S. Catherinae historici 9 (Milan: Fratelli Bocca, 1942), 43. Thomas Luongo, "Catherine of Siena: Rewriting Female Holy Authority," in *Women, the Book, and the Godly*, ed. Lesley Smith and Jane H.M. Taylor (Oxford: D. S. Brewer, 1995), 92.

51. Letter 373, *LCS* 5:284–92.

52. Letter 344, *LCS* 5:148–56.

53. *LM* 3.1.336:946.

54. Letter 333, *LCS* 5:95–98.

55. Letter 344, Catherine of Siena, *I, Catherine: Selected Writings of Catherine of Siena*, trans. Kenelm Foster and Mary John Ronayne (London: Collins, 1980), 248 ("io insieme con voi ci anneghiamo nel sangue dell'umile Agnello"; "uno amore stretto particolare, il quale amore dimostra la fede. E tanta ne mostra, che non può credere nè immaginare che egli voglia altro che'l suo bene [*LCS* 5:149–50]). Scott, "Not Only with Words," 221–35, points out Catherine's customary guardedness in expressing affection.

56. Letter 354, *LCS* 5:150.

57. Letter 344, Catherine, *I, Catherine*, 249–52 ("E potreste voi mai credere ch'io volessi altro che la vita dell'anima vostra? ... E quando vi fussero mostrati i difetti vostri, godete, e ringraziate la divina bontà, che v'ha posto chi lavori sopra di voi, e veglia nel suo cospetto voi" [*LCS* 5:151,155]). Paul M. Conner, "Catherine of Siena and Raymond of Capua—Enduring Friends," *Studia Mystica* 12, no. 1 (1989): 24–25.

58. Letter 226, *LCS* 3:299–300.

59. Letter 273, *LCS* 4:177–78; *The Letters of St. Catherine*, 111–12 ("Poichè ebbe ricevuto il sangue e il desiderio suo, ed egli ricevette l'anima sua, la quale mise nella bottiga aperta del costato suo, pieno di misericordia.... Ma egli faceva uno atto dolce da trare

mille cuori. E non me ne maraviglio; perocchè già gustava la divina dolcezza. Volsesi come fa la sposa quando è giunta all'uscio dello sposo suo, che volge l'occhio e il capo a dietro, inchinando chi l'ha accompagnata, e con l'atto dimostra segni di ringraziamento" [LCS 4:177,178]).

60. Letter 273, LCS 4:175; The Letters of St. Catherine, 109, 110 ("Io allora sentiva uno giubilo e un odore del sangue suo; e non era senza l'odore del mio, ilquale io desidero di spandere per lo dolce sposo Gesù.... ma non vi venne, che io avessi pieno l'affetto di me. [LCS 4:175–76]).

61. LM 2.5.172–77:905–7.

62. LM 2.10.288–93:934–35.

63. LM 2.12.311–19:939–42.

64. LM 1.9.86:883; 2.11.309:939; 2.12.327:943; 3.4.365:953; 3.6.416:964.

65. LM prol. 21:867. The chapter within the first eighteen that contains no list of sources is 1.12, the chapter on her spiritual marriage (an episode that Catherine herself never mentions in her letters; see Scott, "Catherine of Siena, 'Apostola,'" 44.) After the first eighteen chapters he continues to cite witnesses throughout the text, but no longer at the beginnings of chapters.

66. "Concessum est ... per ipsam essem in Confessorem electus, ad participandum et sciendum quaecumque secreta sibi a Domino concessa vel revelata ... Vidi ego, Raymundus nomine usitato, ab ipsa tamen virgine vocatus ab eventu Joannes, propter secreta revelata mihi ab ea, ut aestimo" (LM prol. 5–6:863); cf. LM 1.4.49:874–75. Several scholars have speculated that Raymond is the "Giovanni singolare" whom Catherine saw among others entering the side of Christi in letter 219 (LCS 3:268): see the discussion in Scott, "Not Only with Words," 585–86.

67. LM 1.9.86–89:883–84.

68. "Eratque facies oblonga, aetatis mediae, non prolixam habens barbam coloris triticei" (LM 1.9.90:884).

69. LM 2.12.315–16:940–41 (rising of the Host); 2.12.317–22:941–42 (flight of the fragment).

70. LM 1.9.84:993 (Christ as teacher); 1.11.112:890 (Psalms); 1.2.31:870 (Spirit); 2.5.165:903 (consolation); 2.1.119:392 (pain).

71. LM 1.3.38:872 (Euphrosyne); 1.6.58:876–77 (smell); 3.4.365:953 (what others said); 3.6.417:964 (pain of Passion); 1.6.63:877 (discipline).

72. Other examples: LM Prol. 13, 1.2.28:869; 1.2.32:870; 1.4.45:874; 1.4.50:875; 1.4.51:875; 1.5.56:876; 1.11.108:889; 1.11.113:890; 2.6.195:910; 2.6.211:914; 2.6.214–17:915–16; 2.7.229:918; 2.8.257:926; 2.11.300:936–37.

73. LM 1.10.90:884.

74. "Forti sonitu excitabat me, dicens: Ut quid propter somnum perditis animae vestrae profectum? Numquid muro loquor verba Dei, an vobis?" (LM 1.6.62:868).

75. LM 2.5.177:906–7.

76. "Scio ego de me ipso, et ipsum fateor coram tota Christi Ecclesia militante, quod cum saepius me reprehenderet de quibusdam cogitationibus, quae tunc actualiter mea versabantur in mente, egoque (quod non erubesco fateri pro gloria ejus

declaranda) me vellem mendaciter excusare, ipsa mihi respondit: Quare mihi negatis illud, quod ego clarius video quam vos ipse qui cogitatis? Ac post hoc saluberrimam addebat doctrinam circa eamdem materiam, quam exemplo suo etiam demonstrabat" (*LM* 2.10.277:931).

77. See chapter 4, page 84.

78. "Respondebat, quod nimie excessive sororem suam dilexerat, et videbatur sibi quod plus quam Deum eam tunc dilexisset … 'Ha! domine Deus meus, qualem Patrem spiritualem ego nunbc habeo, qui excusat peccata mea?'" *LM* 1.4.43:873. "Tum coactus sum tacere" (*LM* 1.4.44:873).

79. Coakley, "Friars as Confidants," 237–38.

80. "Stabamus, tam ego quam socii, jejuni frequenter usque ad vesperas, nec sufficere poteramus audire confiteri volentes. Et ut meum fatear imperfectum, et virginis hujus sacrae profectum, tanta erat pressura volentium confiteri, quod pluries gravatus sum et attaediatus prae laboribus excessivis. Ipsa vero sine intermissione orabat, et sicut victrix capta praeda in domino exultabat uberius, jubens ceteris filiis et filiabus, ut ministrarent nobis qui habebamus rete, quod ipsa miserat in capturam" (*LM* 2.7.240:922); cf. *LM* 2.8.257:926.

81. Luongo, "Politics of Marginality," 242–51, argues that in fact "Nanni's notoriety derived more obviously from his activities against the [Sienese] regime than from personal *vendette*" (245) and that his politics were compatible with those of Catherine's circle.

82. *LM* 2.7.235–38:921–22.

83. "Disposui pro salute animarum periculo mortis corpus exponere, et nulllum vitare infirmum; … Verum considerans quod multo plus potest Christus quam Galenus, et plus gratia quam naatura; attendens etiam, quod ceteris fugientibus, animae transeuntes absque consilio et auxilio remanebant" (*LM* 2.8.254:925).

84. *LM* 2.8.254–55:925–26.

85. Van Ree, "Raymond de Capoue," 206.

86. D. A. Mortier, *Histoire des Maîtres Généraux de l'ordre des Frères Prêcheurs*, vol. 3 (Paris, Picard et fils, 1903).

87. "Considerans, quod Frater, qui iuvatur a Fratre, est quasi Civitas firma" (Raymond of Capua, *Opuscula et litterae*, 58).

88. Raymond of Capua, *Opuscula et litterae*, 65–66. Caroline Bynum has suggested that Raymond's interest in Catherine's fasting owes something to his "guilt" about his own inability to fast (*Holy Feast and Holy Fast*, 166, 338).

89. Raymond of Capua, *Opuscula et litterae*, 68–69.

90. Raymond of Capua, *Opuscula et litterae*, 104, 111–13.

91. He also recalls the parable of the talents (Matt. 25:14–30, Luke 19:12–28) in writing both of his obligations to speak of Catherine (*LM* Prol. 5:863; 2.12.329:944) and his obligation to work for the reform (*Opuscula et litterae*, 92–93): he must speak out, however meager his gifts.

92. "Noveris igitur, lector bone, quod antequam hujus sacrae virginis meruissem habere notitiam, vix poterat unum actum devotionis exercere in publice quin

pateretur calumnias, impedimenta, et persecutiones, ab his potissime, qui magis debuissent ei favere, ac etiam ad actus eosdem continue promovere. Nec mireris: quia ... nisi spiritualies personae perfecte proprium amorem extinxerint, acriorem incurrunt invidiae foveam, quam quicumque carnales" (*LM* 3.6.406:961–62).

93. Laurent, ed., *Il Processo Castellano* (see note 50).

94. *Sanctae Catharinae Senensis Legenda minor*, ed. E. Franceschini, Fontes Vitae S. Catharinae Senensis Historici 10 (Siena: R. Università di Siena and Milan: Bocca, 1942). The *Supplement* (see note 16) contains miracle stories and treatises on Catherine, organized according to the same three-part scheme as the *Legenda maior*. On Thomas's place in the development of the dossier of sources for canonization, see Fawtier, *Sainte Catherine* 1:21–52.

95. Thomas of [Caffarini] of Siena, *Legenda B. Mariae de Venetiis*, in *Ecclesiae Venetae antiquis monumentis nunc etiam primum editis illustratae ac in decades distributae*, ed. Flaminio Cornelio, vol. 11, part 1, 364–420 (Venice, 1749); Fernanda Sorelli, *La santità imitabile: "Leggenda di Maria da Venezia" di Tommaso da Siena* (Venice: Deputazione editrice, 1984), includes Italian text; Sorelli, "La production hagiographique du Dominicain T. Caffarini: Exemples de sainteté, sens et visée d'une propagande," in *Faire Croire: Modalités de la diffusion et de la réception des messages religieux du XIIe au XVe siècle* (Rome: École Française de Rome, 1981), 189–200; Daniel Bornstein, "Spiritual Kinship and Domestic Devotions," in *Gender and Society in Renaissance Italy*, ed. Judith C. Brown and Robert C. Davis, 173–92. (London: Longman, 1998), 179–82; Coakley, "Friars as Confidants," 238–40.

96. Volpato, "Tra sante profetesse," 154–58.

10. Revelation and Authority Revisited: John Marienwerder on Dorothy of Montau

1. Petra Hörner, *Dorothea von Montau* (Frankfurt: Lang, 1993), 21. On Dorothy's place in the history of spiritual movements in Prussia, see Philipp Funk, "Zur Geschichte der Frömmigkeit und Mystik im Ordenslande Preußen," ed. Leo Juhnke, *Zeitschrift für die Geschichte und Altertumskunde Ermlands* 30, no. 1 (1960): 1–37.

2. The sources are the works of John (see below) and the canonization process: Richard Stachnik, Anneliese Triller, and Hans Westpfahl, eds., *Die Akten Des Kanonisationsprozesses Dorotheae von Montau, von 1394–1521* (Cologne: Böhlau, 1978) (cited as *AKDM*). A convenient biographical summary is Hans Westpfahl and Anneliese Triller, "Zeittafel zum Leben der H. Dorothea von Montau," in *Dorothea von Montau: Eine preußische Heilige des 14. Jahrhunderts*, ed. Richard Stachnik and Anneliese Triller (Münster: Selbstverlag des Historischen Vereins für Ermland, 1976), 9–20; the authors' previous version of the timeline, in *VLDM*, 409–18, is still useful, as it includes citations of sources, absent from the revised version. See also Hörner, *Dorothea*; Elisabeth Schraut, "Dorothea von Montau: Wahrnehmungsweisen von Kindheit und Eheleben einer spätmittelalterlichen Heiligen," in *Religiöse Frauenbewegung und mystische Frömmigkeit in Mittelalter*, ed. Peter Dinzelbacher and Dieter R. Bauer (Co-

logne: Böhlau Verlag, 1988), 374–94 (especially on the disputed question of the location of the "Finsterwald" of Dorothy's first pilgrimage, 390 n. 57, and on Adalbert's and Dorothy's marital conflicts, 383–88 [cf. also *VLDM* 2.41.a–b:107]). There is a brief account in English of Dorothy's life in Kieckhefer, *Unquiet Souls*, 22–33.

3. Franz Hipler, "Johannes Marienwerder, der Beichtvater der seligen Dorothea von Montau," ed. Hans Westpfahl and Hans Schmauch, *Zeitschrift für Geschichte und Altertumskunde Ermlands* 29 (1956): 14–32; Arnold Schleiff, "Die Bedeutung Johann Marienwerders für Theologie und Frömmigkeit im Ordensstaat Preußen." *Zeitschrift für Kirchengeschichte* 60 (1941): 50–53; Heribert Rossmann, "Johannes Marienverder, ein ostdeutscher Theologe des Späten Mittelalters," *Archiv für Kirchengeschichte von Böhmen-Mähren-Schlesien* 3 (1973): 221–34.

4. Richard Stachnik, "Zum Schrifttum über die Heilige Dorothea v. Montau," in *Dorothea von Montau: Eine preußische Heilige des 14. Jahrhunderts*, ed. Stachnik and Anneliese Triller (Münster: Selbstverlag des historischen Vereins für Ermland, 1976), 59–105; on John's writings about Dorothy, 59–79. On the history of attempts to canonize Dorothy, medieval and modern, see Ute Stargardt, "The Political and Social Backgrounds of the Canonization of Dorothea of Montau," *Mystics Quarterly* 11 (1985): 107–22.

5. Texts of John's letters: *AKDM* 497–509. The September letters came, variously, from the four Prussian bishops, their cathedral chapters, the master and other officials of the Teutonic Order, John Marienwerder and John Reymann themselves (writing as her confessors), an array of other Prussian clerics, and the Prussian Cistercian abbots and Carthusian prior. Texts of the supporting letters: *AKDM* 509–39.

6. John Marienwerder, *Vita prima*, in *AA. SS.*, October (Paris: Victor Palmé, 1883), 13:493–98; and John Marienwerder, *Vita prima*, ed. A. Amore, in *Gedanen. Beatificationis et canonizationis servae Dei Dorotheae Montoviensis viduae et reclusae "beatae" seu "sanctae" nuncupatae (+1394). Positio super cultu et virtutibus servae Dei ex officio concinnata* (Vatican City, 1976), 21–36. (I have not been able to consult the latter edition.) *Vita Lindana* (so called for its eighteenth-century editor de Linda): *AA. SS.*, 13:499–560.

7. *VLDM*; John Marienwerder, *Liber de Festis Magistri Johannis Marienwerder*, ed. Anneliese Triller (Cologne: Böhlau, 1992) (cited as *LFDM*); John Marienwerder, "Septililium B. Dorotheae Montoviensis," ed. Franz Hipler, *Analecta Bollandiana* 2 (1883): 381–472; 3 (1884): 113–40 and 408–48; 4 (1884): 207–51 (cited as *SDM*).

8. John Marienwerder, *Das Leben der heiligen Dorothea*, ed. Max Toeppen, in *Scriptores Rerum Prussicarum—die Geschichtsquellen der preußischen Vorzeit*, vol. 2 (1863; reprint, Frankfurt: Minerva, 1965), 179–374. English translation: John Marienwerder, *The Life of Dorothea von Montau, a Fourteenth-Century Recluse*, trans. Ute Stargardt (Lewiston, N.Y.: Edwin Mellen Press, 1997).

9. *AKDM* 19. His testimony (254–327) includes in fact another written vita of the saint (297–327), which he had originally submitted when it became apparent that he would not testify during the first sitting of the commission, which concluded on 27 June 1404, against the possibility of his dying before it reconvened in October.

(Reymann also submitted a vita, which, however, he declined to have included with the documents of the process.) *AKDM* 87.

10. Dyan Elliott, "Authorizing a Life: The Collaboration of Dorothea of Montau and John Marienwerder," in *Gendered Voices*, ed. Catherine Mooney (Philadelphia: University of Pennsylvania Press, 1999), 168–91. Elliott is particularly concerned to show how this motive of "clerical self-authorization" worked to obscure, or even alter, the saint's own spirituality (169). Thus she argues that as Dorothy's confessor, John would have had the power to interrogate her and prompt her memory (172–81) and suggests the possibility that the "inchoate perceptions of her past, present, and even future experiences were reformatted" by John (191) so that her ostensible spirituality here becomes, in effect, his creation. With reference to the German vita, Ute Stargardt has argued in a similar vein that John's own agenda dominates the narrative and makes it difficult for the reader to discern the real voice of Dorothy. "Whose Life History Is This Anyway? Johannes von Marienwerder's Narrative Strategies in the German *Vita* of Dorothy of Montau," *Michigan Academician* 27 (1994): 39–40.

11. In the anchorage she does offer intercessory prayers for others: e.g., *VLDM* 4.4 a–b:156; *VLDM* 5.12 b–k:229–31; *VLDM* 4.29 a–d:194–95; *VLDM* 5.33 f:265.

12. There is some sense of spiritual development in Dorothy's life, in all John's versions of it. It is clearest in the German *Leben der heiligen Dorothea* (see note 8). Hörner has pointed out that though most of the content of its first three books is derived from the *Vita Latina*, the *Leben* is organized as a chronological narrative; whereas the *Vita* is organized around seven heads which serve as conceptual categories, the first three books of the *Leben* (the last being derived from the *Septililium*) are presented as a straightforward chronological narrative, in which some of the more bizarre or controversial aspects of Dorothy's life are omitted or minimized (e.g., the spiritual birth episodes, her lack of bodily wastes, and the woundings by Christ). Thus the *Leben* brings her "inner development" to the fore in a continuous narrative—and this, as Hörner suggests, is a different enterprise than that of the more discursive *Vita Latina*. Furthermore, in the *Leben* John reordered material from the *Vita Latina* in order to achieve this effect; thus Hörner rightly objects to previous scholars' characterization of the *Leben* simply as an abridgment of the *Vita Latina*. Nonetheless almost all the material in the *Leben* is in the *Vita Latina*, which has much more besides, and the *Vita Latina* does proceed more or less chronologically, for all its ostensibly conceptual ordering. And so the two works are consistent with each other in this respect (Hörner, *Dorothea*, 141–46).

13. "In toto illo tempore Dominus omnipotens, piissimus afflictorum consolator, gracia visitacionis prevenit illam benedictam, adeo sustollens illius afflicte puelle desiderium ad se, quod ab illa hora usque ad extremum vite sue nunquam suscepit detrimentum, sed virtutum continuum incrementum" (*VLDM* 2.13 a:76).

14. "Ipsa tandem post labores multos in matrimonio, afflictiones et agones permissa est a Domino quandoque quiescere.... Porro in huiusmodi sompno sensit spiritum suum dulciter delectari. Dominum cum anima sua susurrare et magnum habere

gaudium, quanquam nondum intelligeret, quid esset Domini susurrium" (*VLDM* 2.39 a–b:105). On the dating, John says (2.39 d) that these events began more than sixteen years before her death (25 June 1394).

15. "Sensit tunc Dorothea a sensibus exterioribus alienata et supra se elevata sibi cor extrahi, et in locum illius quandam massam carneam, totaliter ignitam, poni" (*VLDM* 3.1 b:112).

16. "Hec nominatur eciam caritas sacians, vivificans, bene ordinata, bene sapida, bene odorifera, fructuosa, inseperabilis, insuperabilis et immortalis" (*VLDM* 3.1 c:113); cf. *SDM* 1.1:400–408.

17. "In illa hora momentanea, … ipsa perfectius est de vita sanctorum instructa, quam a docto homine informata assidue per unum annum didicisset" (*VLDM* 3.1 f:113).

18. *VLDM* 3.2 e–i:114–15; "Que existens in matrimonio ex cura rei familiaris et occupacione cum seculo primo non perfecte Domino adhesit totaliter mundum derelinquens. Ideo Dominus tunc misit ei Spiritum Sanctum, qui ipsam arguit et perdocuit, in quibus Dominum offendit" (*VLDM* 6.7 c:298).

19. *VLDM* 3.2 m:115.

20. *VLDM* 3.3 c:116; cf. *LFDM* chaps. 12, 15, 16, 23, 60, where she is said to swaddle and to play with the Christ child.

21. "Nunc ad eius osculum, nunc ad amplexus, nunc ad suave susurrium, nunc ad eius interius cubiculum … admissa" (*VLDM* 3.6 a:118).

22. *VLDM* 3.2 b:114; 3.4:115–16; 3.7:119–20.

23. On "consolations," see *VLDM* 5.8 a:223; on the presence of crowds of saints in the anchorage, *VLDM* 5.13–14:231–32, 5.26:253–54, 7.12:344–46, 7.15–18:349–54 (the saintly processions preceding her death). Except in *de Festis*, in which he dates her experiences according to the feast and year in which they occurred, John does not distinguish (e.g., in his detailed relations in the *Septililium* of the sending of the Holy Spirit to her, and of her experiences concerning the Eucharist) between experiences before and after her entrance into the anchorage.

24. Most scholarship on Dorothy routinely notes her devotion to Bridget, but, as Hörner points out, no one has yet studied Bridget's influence on her (*Dorothea*, 38–39).

25. *VLDM* 5.1 b–c:211–12.

26. "Dic [ad confessarium] … quod nullum intromittat preter ministrum, ut possitis soli esse mecum, et de hoc simul regraciamini michi, quod sic valetis esse ab hominibus separati!" (*VLDM* 5.6 i:220).

27. *VLDM* 5.15:234–36; "'Quomodo audes te a me et a Matre mea avertere et ad creaturas convertere, cum possis die noctuque meam sine intermissione audire vocem, ammonicionem et inspiracionem?'" (5.15 f:235).

28. *VLDM* 5.9 b:225.

29. "Ego enim ibi volo auferre a te aliquas huius miserias vite… . Omnia quidem in mundo agenda bene agentur abs te absque cura tua et sollicitudine. Et iterum largiter flendo humiliter rogita me, ut disponam tibi locum ordinans habitaculum, in quo valeas me adorando perfecte laudare, vitam terminare tuam et michi placere" (*VLDM* 5.3 b:215).

30. "Ac si vellem iam dicere ad te: Ecce iam omnia sunt parata" (*VLDM* 5.7 f:221).

31. "Extraxit autem omnia supradicta non ex maximis, id est generalibus, regulis dyalecticorum aut a locis communibus rethorum aut ab amphorismis phisicorum aut ex principiis phisicorum et aliarum arcium liberalium, quarum spiritus vanitatis et presumpcionis [est]. Nonnunquam prefocant suos lectores et auditores, dum inflati non captivant intellectum suum in obsequium Christi [2 Cor. 10:5] et ei que est secundum pietatem doctrine [1 Tim. 6:3]. Sed sapiens hec mulier extraxit illa ab exemplari celesti et libro vite, que est virtus et Dei sapiencia, qui (inquam) liber intus scriptus est exemplari disposicione, foris mentali revelacione. Et si sapientis est scire omnia, et difficilia per certitudinem et causam ipsam scire propter se querens, ipsa tamen per altissimas causas sue philosophie non ignoravit principia, quibus studiose vacavit in illo, in quo sunt omnes thezauri sapiencie et sciencie absconditi [Col. 2:3], non propter se, sed illum solum scire querens" (*VLDM* Prol. 1.1 f:15).

32. What she learns to "read" is identified as three letters: the first, black in color, pertained to the *liber consciencie*, and in it she read her sins; the second and third, red and gold in color, respectively, pertained to the *liber vitae*, and in them she read of, respectively, Christ's Passion and the joys of heaven (*VLDM* 2.2:32–33).

33. "'Aliqui homines presumptuose audent dicere se a Deo solo didicisse, cum laborem notabilem non habuerint in studendo'… 'Quomodo talis predicator dicere audet, quod addiscens a Deo non laboret, cum nullus inmediate possit a Deo addiscere, nisi habeat caritatem eum ferventer inflamantem.'… 'Tu potes secure illi predicatori dicere, quod graviore labore a Domino addiscentes quam in libro studentes onerentur.'" (*VLDM* 1.1 b–c:30).

34. *VLDM* 1.2 h–l:33–34

35. *VLDM* 1.3 i:36. In *LFDM* she is pictured contemplating the Trinity on its feast day, and wanting to speak of it, but Christ will not allow her. Christ explains that he does not want such subtleties spoken of to common folk, which means, he says, that she is only to communicate a part of the instruction he has given her (*LFDM* 76:129).

36. *VLDM* 1.4 a:36.

37. "Sane, eius noticia extitit bene magna, nam in aliquibus excessit scienciam humanitus acquisitam" (*VLDM* 1.4 b:36); 1.4 h–k:38–39.

38. "Scivit vias rectas directo tramite ad vitam eternam tendentes ostendere et ambulare. Cognovit eciam, quales et quantos labores mundacionem anime oporteat precedere, et quid requiratur ad rectitudinem vite. Denique agnoscens, quid amandum aut odiendum sit in anima hominis, et quale fuerit medium inter ipsam et Dominum, hoc est, 'an odio aut amore fuerit digna' [Eccles. 9.1]" (*VLDM* 1.4 b:36).

39. *VLDM* 1.4 g:38.

40. "Quando circa te sedeo aliqua referens de Domino meo, non oportet te cogitare me illa relata ex me concepisse seu ex meo hausisse intellectu, sed habeo Dominum meum in me, in os meum verba directe ponentem et per me pronunciantem…Aliquociens te veniente ad scribendum nichil scio, quid protunc pronunciare debeo, et nisi tunc me Dominus instrueret et verba in os meum poneret, nichil exprimere valerem" (*VLDM* 1.7 h:51). Cf. 1.6 v:47.

41. Once the Lord revealed to her certain "ineffible things concerning his divine goodness [*ineffabilia divine sue bonitatis*]" and was obliged to repeat them to her when, after he directed her to tell her confessor, it became evident that she had forgotten what she had been told (*VLDM* 1.1 f:31). She would sometimes withhold things from her confessors out of humility, but then the Lord would refute her and oblige her to tell (*VLDM* 1.6 c:42). Often when she was telling John what he should write down, the Holy Spirit came and recalled forgotten things to memory (*VLDM* 1.6 e:42). She was told not to report anything to the confessors unless directed (*VLDM* 1.6 n:44).

42. "Scripserunt cum magna laboris difficultate.. affligentes siquidem se, diu non invenientes verba apta ad exprimendum revelata protunc exaranda" (*VLDM* 1.7 m:52). Elliott, "Authorizing a Life," 180, has interpreted a passage in the earlier *Vita Lindana* as suggesting that John, in writing her visions, would question her about matters with which he had difficulty and thus cause her to seek clarifying revelation. "And for the purpose of writing more clearly on the experience of the spiritual effects with which she was marvelously visited by God, the person writing (who sometimes had difficulty with the material) would instruct, with God counseling and she being traversed completely by the supernatural light very clearly, that the grace of the visiting Lord should illuminate more in her and narrate the things that were supposed to be written in more appropriate terms [Et ut scribentem clarius in experientia spiritualium effectuum, quibus mirabiliter a Domino visitabatur, instrueret, ipse scribens nonnunquam difficultavit materiam, quatenus consulto Domino, ac lumine supernaturali limpidius perlustrata gratia visitantis Domini in ea plus elucesceret, et scribenda aptioribus terminis enarraret]" (John Marienwerder, *Vita Lindana*, 59.86:538; trans. Elliott, 180). This would suggest that John may have affected her visions rather as Ekbert had affected Elizabeth's, that is, by suggesting paths for her to follow.

43. E.g., *VLDM* Prol. 1.1 f:15; 1.1 d:31; 1.5 b:40; 3.4 c:117.

44. *VLDM* 1.6 u:46–47; "quando non plene expressit, que Dominus iussit aut non debite pronunciavit" (46).

45. *VLDM* 4.36 d–e:204–205.

46. "In hiis beneficiis tibi factis solum grossiora dixisti, magis vero spiritualia pretiosa et utilia omisisti" (*LFDM* 52:86).

47. "Tu cum patre confessore non debes te occupare superflue, quod revelatio tibi a me facta non sit aliis revelationibus concors totaliter et consona. Nam sancti evangelistae, qui facta mea et dicta conscripsere, quibus aliqui eorum interfuerunt, non in toto concordaverunt" (*LFDM* 54:89).

48. *VLDM* 5.39 c:275 ("procus = *Werber*; procare = *umwerben*" [275 n]).

49. *VLDM* 2.15 a–b:77–78; Elliott, "Authorizing a Life," 172, 184, notes Dorothy's initial assent to the confessors but not the negative sequel.

50. *LFDM* 90:155.

51. *VLDM* 7.25 a–c:362–63.

52. *VLDM* 2.33 b:96. She then "immediately [*statim*]" remembered then an incident in her own childhood when a priest touched her familiarly, to her great indignation (2.33 c:96).

53. "Hominem quendam iam per XX annos sacerdotem" (*VLDM* 4.17 h:175).

54. *LFDM* 116:197.

55. *VLDM* 7.27 e:367.

56. "Nihil tam confessori tuo nocet ut hoc, quod non acute me vidit. Si enim oculis animae me bene videret, extunc bonitas mea sibi in me agnita ipsum ad me magnifice traheret" (*LFDM* 122:206).

57. *VLDM* 1.6 k:43. She could perceive how Marienwerder's love for her compared with Reymann's (the comparison varied) and how their respective love for her compared with their love of their blood siblings (they loved her more). *VLDM* 1.6 l:43–44.

58. *LFDM* 74:125–26.

59. "Nullus debet me multoties suscipere, nisi prius me magnifice cognoscat et ferventer ex desiderio ardeat" (*SDM* 3.5:415). On frequent partaking as a debated issue at Prague, see Hipler, "Johannes Marienwerder," 35–36.

60. *VLDM* 5.12:229–31.

61. *SDM* 7.4:248. The chapter also includes other general advice for the practice of confession.

62. *SDM* 7.5:249–50.

63. *LFDM* 82:139–40.

64. "'Ego ditioribus panniculis et verbis, vellem Dominum Iesum involvere quam tu.' ... 'Tibi provide, ne ex hoc aliqua tibi inanis gloria adveniat, aut ne ex aliqua propria complacentia hoc procedat. Solet enim vana gloria assidue bonis operibus insidiari'" (*LFDM* 4:10). Protestations against representing the Virgin and Christ as poor appear again later in the work: *LFDM* 22:43; 27:51; 34:63–64.

65. "Adhuc non ita proprie de ea loqui posses, quemadmodum faceres, si eam oculis proriis vidisses" (*LFDM*, 5:11).

66. "Cum tam magna caritate impatiente ac in caritate inebriante non contentiva" (*LFDM* 87:147; the adjectives modifying "*caritas*" identify particular modes of love). Cf. *LFDM*, 89:152; *SDM* 1.1:400–408.

67. "Qui nescirent de spirituali esurie, de gaudio spiritus et sapore, de dulcedine osculorum ac suavitate amplexuum, de spirituali partu, ac cordis iubilo loqui ita proprie et discrete sicut tu" (*VLDM* 1.4 h:38).

68. "Qualiter homo se debeat gerere, ut mei capax magnifice possit esse" (*LFDM* 44:75).

69. *VLDM* 7.2:329–30. Cf. also the following chapter, 7.3:330–32, in which she, as the mother of these "spiritual sons," is told to tell them to bear adversity.

70. *VLDM* 3.26 b:147.

71. Anneliese Triller, "Häresien in Altpreussen um 1390?" in *Studien Zur Geschichte Des Preussenlandes*, ed. Ernst Bahr (Marburg: N. G. Elwert Verlag, 1963), 400–402; Elliott, "Authorizing a Life," 187–88.

72. "Ex odore sanctitatis eius non vivificati, sed veneficati" (*VLDM* 3.26:147); John Marienwerder, *The Life of Dorothea von Montau*, trans. Stargardt, 2.26:123.

73. "Virum sapientem secundum Deum et homines ... cui secure posset revelare occulta cordis sui"; "quem reputaret bene posse suas dissolvere difficultates et dubias" (*VLDM* 3.26 b–c:147).

74. *VLDM* 3.29 e:149.

75. Cf. *LM* 1.9.80:882.

76. "Tunc enim me dignam ut tecum loquerer reputavi; nunc vero etiam ut videam non aestimo me dignam" (*SDM* 2.6:124).

77. *VLDM* 4.25 h:190.

78. Ute Stargardt has suggested that John's interest, or willingness, to convey Dorothy's shortcomings responds to his popular audience, who would not have been satisfied with "a one-dimensional, abstract portrayal of Dorothy's spirituality" (Stargardt, "Male Clerical Authority," 226). This is possible, but I am arguing here that fundamental theological issues concerning religious authority are also at stake.

79. Vow: *VLDM* 3.28:149–51; will: *VLDM* 1.6 m:44.

80. "Amplius infra eundem annum Dominus volens stabilire Sponse animum, qui interdum fluctuabat,an circa Confessarium permaneret an ab eo recederet, iussit eam votum emittere, quod in vita sua a Confessario numquam vellet recedere. Et hoc precipiens ostendit ei viam regiam ad vitam perducentem eternam, quasi diceret: Noli timere, quod hoc votum tibi sit inpedimentum, sed erit pocius promocio ad celum.... Et tunc apparuit sibi, prout eciam Dominus postea Sponse dixit, quod per hoc votum taliter eam ad commanendum Confessario astrinxisset, ac si eas matrimonialiter copulasset" (*VLDM* 3.28 h:151).

81. "Quia hanc rem fecisti propter me, michi confidens sis absque sollicitudine. Ego enim volo tuum Confessarium adiuvare ut tibi valeat salubriter preesse" (*VLDM* 3.28 i:151).

82. *LFDM* 10:21; 28:54; 31:58, 63:104, 83:140, 119:201.

83. *VLDM* 3.19:138–39. Elliott, "Authorizing a Life," 175, cites this as an example of Dorothy's excessive scrupulosity in confession.

84. *VLDM* 1.7 a–g:49–51.

85. *VLDM* 4.10 f:167.

86. *VLDM* 5.28 c:257–58.

87. *LFDM* 13:28.

88. *VLDM* 5.1 d–g:212.

89. "'Non oportet Prepositus et Confessarius putare, quod tu sis dicens illud, quod ipsi a te scribunt et a te de me percipiunt. Sed ego ipsemet dico, egomet operor, egomet facio illud'" (*VLDM* 1.5 v:47).

90. Gerson, *De probatione spirituum*, in *Oeuvres complètes*, ed. P. Glorieux, vol. 9 (Paris: Desclée, 1972), 179. See also chapter 11, page 211.

11. Authority and Female Sanctity: Conclusions

1. Andre Vauchez, "La nascità del sospetto," in *Finzione e santità tra medioevo ed età moderna*, ed. Gabriella Zarri (Turin: Rosenberg & Sellier, 1992), 39–49. French version in Vauchez, *Saints, prophètes et visionnaires* (Paris: Albin Michel, 1999) 208–19.

2. "Cave preterea quisquis eris auditor aut consultor, ut non applaudas tali personae.... Obsiste potius, increpa dure, sperne eam cujus sic exaltatum est cor et elevati sunt oculi ut ambulet in magnis et mirabilibus super se, ne digna sibi videatur quae

non humano aliorum more operetur salutem suam" (Gerson, *De probatione spirituum*, 181); Gerson, *De examinatione doctrinarum*, in *Oeuvres complètes*, ed. Palémon Glorieux (Paris: Desclée, 1972), 9:2.3.469 (in regard to Catherine); Dyan Elliott, "Seeing Double: Jean Gerson, the Discernment of Spirits, and Joan of Arc," *American Historical Review* 107 (2002): 26–54; Caciola, *Discerning Spirits*, 291–306; Voaden, *God's Words*, 41–72.

3. Caciola, *Discerning Spirits*, 274–319; Elliott, *Proving Woman*, 233–96.

4. Bilinkoff, *Related Lives*; Bilinkoff, "Confession, Gender, Life-Writing: Some Cases (Mainly) from Spain," in *Penitence in the Age of Reformations*, ed. Katharine Jackson Lualdi and Anne T. Thayer (Aldershot: Ashgate, 2000), 169–83; Patricia Ranft, "A Key to Counter-Reformation Women's Activism: The Confessor-Spiritual Director," *Journal of Feminist Studies in Religion* 10, no. 2 (1994): 7–26; Gabriella Zarri, "Living Saints: A Typology of Female Sanctity in the Early Sixteenth Century," in *Women and Religion in Medieval and Renaissance Italy*, ed. Daniel Bornstein and Roberto Rusconi (Chicago: University of Chicago Press, 1996), 233–48; Gillian T. W. Ahlgren, "Ecstasy, Prophecy and Reform: Catherine of Siena as a Model for Holy Women of Sixteenth-Century Spain," in *The Medieval Gesture: Essays on Medieval and Early Modern Spiritual Culture in Honor of Mary E. Giles*, ed. Robert Boenig (Aldershot: Ashgate, 2000), 53–65.

5. Elliott, *Fallen Bodies*, 81–156.

6. Karen Glente, "Mystikerinnenviten aus männlicher und weiblicher Sicht: Ein Vergleich zwischen Thomas von Cantimpré und Katherina von Unterlinden," in *Religiöse Frauenbewegung und Mystische Frömmigkeit im Mittelalter*, ed. Peter Dinzelbacher and Dieter R. Bauer (Cologne: Böhlau, 1988), 251–64. See also the comments by Catherine Mooney, "Voice, Gender, and the Portrayal of Sanctity," in *Gendered Voices: Medieval Saints and Their Interpreters*, ed. Mooney (Philadelphia: University of Pennsylvania Press, 1999), 11–12.

7. Hollywood, *The Soul as Virgin Wife*, 27–39; Hollywood, "Inside Out: Beatrice of Nazareth and Her Hagiographer," in *Gendered Voices: Medieval Saints and Their Interpreters*, ed. Catherine Mooney (Philadelphia: University of Pennsylvania Press, 1999), 78–98; Hollywood, *Sensible Ecstasy*, 247–73.

8. Hollywood, *Sensible Ecstasy*, 255–56.

9. He does this rather in the way that, as Caroline Bynum has pointed out, Cistercian abbots in the previous century had turned to feminine images to give expression to such virtues as "gentleness, compassion, tenderness, emotionality," of which they feared their exercise of authority deprived them: Bynum, *Jesus as Mother* (Berkeley: Univ. of California Press, 1982), 150. See also Coakley, "Gender and the Authority of Friars," 459.

10. Catherine Mooney, "*Imitatio Christi* or *Imitatio Mariae*? Clare of Assisi and Her Interpreters," in *Gendered Voices: Medieval Saints and Their Interpreters*, ed. Mooney (Philadelphia: University of Pennsylvania Press, 1999), 77.

11. Caciola has recently suggested the term "divinely possessed" as a characterization of late-medieval holy women, to emphasize the structural parallels between their perceived behaviors and those of women thought to be possessed by demons (Caciola, *Discerning Spirits*, 31–78).

ABBREVIATIONS

AA SS	*Acta Sanctorum*
AKDM	Stachnik et al., eds., *Die Akten des Kanonisationsprozesses Dorotheae von Montau*
BME	Henry of Nördlingen et al., *Briefe an Margaretha Ebner*
De obitu	Ekbert of Schönau, *Epistola Eckeberti ad cognatas suas de obitu domine Elisabeth*
ESE	Elisabeth of Schönau, *Epistole*
GGE	Guibert of Gembloux, *Epistolae*
GND	Peter of Dacia, *De gratia naturam ditante sive de virtutibus Christinae Stumbelensis*
H	*Margaret Ebner: Major Works,* trans. Hindsley
HBE	Hildegard of Bingen, *Epistolarium*
HVGM	Hildegard of Bingen, "Visio S. Hildegardis ad Guibertum missa"
LCS	Catherine of Siena, *Lettere*
LFDM	John Marienwerder, *Liber de Festis*
LM	Raymond of Capua, *Vita Catharina Senensis* [*Legenda maior*]
LMC	Giunta Bevegnati, *Legenda de vita et miraculis beatae Margaritae de Cortona*
LR	Elisabeth of Schönau, *Liber revelationum Elisabeth de sacro exercitu virginum Coloniensium*
LV	Elisabeth of Schönau, *Libri visionum*
LVD	Elisabeth of Schönau, *Liber viarum dei*
Mem.	Angela of Foligno, *Memoriale*
MEO	Margaret Ebner, *Offenbarungen*
PL	*Patrologia Latina*
SDM	John Marienwerder, *Septililium B. Dorotheae Montoviensis*
SVMO	Thomas of Cantimpré, *Supplementum ad vitam S. Mariae Oigniacensis*
VCM	*The Life of Christina of Markyate* [Latin text]
VCS	Peter of Dacia, *Vita Christinae Stumbelensis*
VH	Vito of Cortona, *Vita Humilianae*

VLA	Thomas of Cantimpré, *Vita Lutgardis Aquiriae*
VLDM	John Marienwerder, *Vita [Latina] Dorotheae Montoviensis Magistri Johannis Marienwerder*
VMO	James of Vitry, *Vita Mariae Oigniacensis*
VSH	*Vita S. Hildegardis*

BIBLIOGRAPHY

Sources

Acta Sanctorum. 68 vols. Antwerp, Brussels, and Paris: Socii Bollandiani, 1643–1940. Reprint: Turnhout: Brepols, 1966–71.

Angela of Foligno. *Il Libro della beata Angela da Foligno.* Ed. Ludger Thier and Abele Calufetti. Grottaferrata (Rome): Editiones Collegii S. Bonaventurae Ad Claras Aquas, 1985.

——. *Memoriale.* In Angela of Foligno, *Il Libro della beata Angela da Foligno,* ed. Ludger Thier and Abele Calufetti, 126–401. Grottaferrata (Rome): Editiones Collegii S. Bonaventurae Ad Claras Aquas, 1985.

Catherine of Siena. *Lettere.* Ed. Pero Misciatelli, with notes by Niccolò Tommasèo. 6 vols. Florence: Giunti, 1940.

Conrad of Castellerio. *Vita Benevenutae de Bojanis.* In *AA SS.* October. 13:152–85.

Ekbert of Schönau. *Ad beatam virginem deiparam sermo panegyricus. PL* 95:1514D–19A.

——. *Epistola ad eundem abbatem* [of Reinhusen]. In *Die Visionen der Hl. Elisabeth und die Schriften der Abte Ekbert und Emecho von Schönau,* ed. F. W. E. Roth, 318–19. Brünn: Verlag der Studien aus dem Benedictiner- und Cisterciener Orden, 1884.

——. *Epistola Ecberti ad Reinoldum Coloniensem electum.* In *Die Visionen der Hl. Elisabeth und die Schriften der Abte Ekbert und Emecho von Schönau,* ed. F. W. E. Roth, 311–17. Brünn: Verlag der Studien aus dem Benedictiner- und Cisterciener Orden, 1884.

——. *Epistola Eckeberti ad cognatas suas de obitu domine Elisabeth.* In *Die Visionen der Hl. Elisabeth und die Schriften der Abte Ekbert und Emecho von Schönau,* ed. F. W. E. Roth, 263–78. Brünn: Verlag der Studien aus dem Benedictiner- und Cisterciener Orden, 1884.

——. "Et ait Maria..." [Commentary on the Magnificat.] In *Die Visionen der Hl. Elisabeth und die Schriften der Abte Ekbert und Emecho von Schönau,* ed. F. W. E. Roth, 230–47. Brünn: Verlag der Studien aus dem Benedictiner- und Cisterciener Orden, 1884.

——. *Meditationes [seu Soliloquium] Eckeberti abbatis de Jesu et Maria.* In *Die Visionen der Hl. Elisabeth und die Schriften der Abte Ekbert und Emecho von Schönau,* ed. F. W. E. Roth, 278–84. Brünn: Verlag der Studien aus dem Benedictiner- und Cisterciener Orden, 1884.

——. *"Missus est angelus Gabriel …"* In *Die Visionen der Hl. Elisabeth und die Schriften der Abte Ekbert und Emecho von Schönau*, ed. F. W. E. Roth, 248–63. Brünn: Verlag der Studien aus dem Benedictiner- und Cisterciener Orden, 1884.

——. *Salutacio ad sanctam crucem.* In *Die Visionen der Hl. Elisabeth und die Schriften der Abte Ekbert und Emecho von Schönau*, ed. F. W. E. Roth, 284–86. Brünn: Verlag der Studien aus dem Benedictiner- und Cisterciener Orden, 1884.

——. *Sermones contra Catharos.* In *PL* 195:11–102.

——. *Stimulus dilectionis.* In *Die Visionen der Hl. Elisabeth und die Schriften der Abte Ekbert und Emecho von Schönau*, ed. F. W. E. Roth, 293–311. Brünn: Verlag der Studien aus dem Benedictiner- und Cisterciener Orden, 1884.

Elisabeth of Schönau. *Epistole.* In *Die Visionen der Hl. Elisabeth und die Schriften der Abte Ekbert und Emecho von Schönau*, ed. F. W. E. Roth, 139–53. Brünn: Verlag der Studien aus dem Benedictiner- und Cisterciener Orden, 1884.

——. *Liber revelationum Elisabeth de sacro exercitu virginum Coloniensium.* In *Die Visionen der Hl. Elisabeth und die Schriften der Abte Ekbert und Emecho von Schönau*, ed. F. W. E. Roth, 123–38. Brünn: Verlag der Studien aus dem Benedictiner- und Cisterciener Orden, 1884.

——. *Liber viarum dei.* In *Die Visionen der Hl. Elisabeth und die Schriften der Abte Ekbert und Emecho von Schönau*, ed. F. W. E. Roth, 88–122. Brünn: Verlag der Studien aus dem Benedictiner- und Cisterciener Orden, 1884.

——. *Libri visionum.* In *Die Visionen der Hl. Elisabeth und die Schriften der Abte Ekbert und Emecho von Schönau*, ed. F. W. E. Roth, 1–87. Brünn: Verlag der Studien aus dem Benedictiner- und Cisterciener Orden, 1884.

Emecho of Schönau. *Vita Eckeberti.* Ed. S. Widmann. *Neues Archiv der Gesellschaft für ältere deutsche Geschichtskunde* 11 (1886): 447–54.

Gielemans, Johan. *De codicibus hagiographicis Iohannis Gielemans, canonici regularis in Rubea Valle prope Bruxellas.* Brussels: Société des Bollandistes, 1895.

Giunta Bevegnati. *Antica leggenda della vita e de'miracoli di s. Margherita di Cortona scritta dal di lei confessore Fr. Giunta Bevegnati dell'ordine de'Minori colla traduzione italiana di detta leggenda posta dicontro al testo originale latino e con annotazioni e dissertazioni diverse ad illustrazione del medesimo testo.* Ed. Ludovico Bargigli da Pelago. 2 vols. Lucca: Francesco Bonsignori, 1793.

——. *Legenda de vita et miraculis beatae Margaritae de Cortona.* Ed. Fortunato Iozzelli. Rome: Editiones Collegii S. Bonaventurae ad Claras Aquas, 1997.

Gnädinger, Louise, ed. and trans. *Deutsche Mystik.* Zürich: Manesse, 1989.

Grottanelli, F., ed. *Leggenda minore di S. Caterina da Siena e lettere dei suoi discepoli.* Bologna: Presso Gaetano Romagnoli, 1868.

Guibert of Gembloux. "De laudibus B. Martini Turonensis." In *Analecta Sacra*, vol. 8, ed. Jean Baptiste Pitra, 584–91. Paris: A. Jouby et Roger, 1882.

——. *Guiberti Gemblacensis Epistolae.* Ed. Albert Derolez. Corpus Christianorum, continuatio mediaevalis, vols. 66 and 66A. Turnhout: Brepols, 1988–89.

Hadewijch of Brabant. *Letter 6.* In *Hadewijch: The Complete Works*, trans. Columba Ward, 56–63. New York: Paulist Press, 1983.

Henry of Nördlingen et al. *Briefe an Margaretha Ebner.* In *Margaretha Ebner und Heinrich von Nördlingen. Ein Beitrag zur Geschichte der deutschen Mystik*, ed. Philipp Strauch, 169–284, 320–403. Tübingen: J. C. B. Mohr, 1882; reprint, Amsterdam: P. Schippers, 1966.

Henry of Rheims. *Vita Coletae* [Life of Colette of Corbie]. In *AA SS*. March. 1:539–87.

Hildegard of Bingen. *Hildegardis Bingensis Epistolarium.* Ed. Lieven van Acker and Monika Klaes-Hachmüller. Corpus Christianorum, continuatio mediaevalis, vol. 91, parts 1–. Turnhout: Brepols, 1991–.

——. *Scivias.* Ed. Adelgundis Führktter and Angela Carlevaris. Corpus Christianorum, continuatio medievalis 43–43A. Turnhout: Brepols, 1978.

——. "Visio S. Hildegardis ad Guibertum missa." In *Analecta Sacra*, vol. 8, ed. Jean Baptiste Pitra, 415–34. Paris: A. Jouby et Roger, 1882.

James of Vitry. *The Historia Occidentalis of Jacques de Vitry: A Critical Edition.* Ed. John Frederick Hinnebusch. Fribourg: University Press, 1972.

——. *Lettres de Jacques de Vitry, 1160/1170–1240, évêque de St.-Jean d'Acre.* Ed. R. B. C. Huygens. Leiden: Brill, 1960.

——. *Vita Mariae Oigniacensis*, in *AA SS* June, 4:636–66.

——. "Secundus sermo ad virgines." In Joseph Greven, "Der Ursprung des Beginenwesens." *Historisches Jahrbuch* 35 (1914): 43–49.

John Gerson. *De examinatione doctrinarum* In *Oeuvres complètes*, 9:458–75.

——. *De probatione spirituum.* In *Oeuvres complètes*, 9:177–85.

——. *Oeuvres complètes.* Ed. Palémon Glorieux. 10 vols. Paris: Desclée, 1960–73.

John Marienwerder. *Das Leben der heiligen Dorothea.* Ed. Max Toeppen. In *Scriptores Rerum Prussicarum—die Geschichtsquellen der preußischen Vorzeit*, 2:179–374. 1863; reprint, Frankfurt: Minerva, 1965.

——. *Liber de Festis Magistri Johannis Marienwerder.* Ed. Anneliese Triller. Cologne: Böhlau, 1992.

——. "Septililium B. Dorotheae Montoviensis." Ed. Franz Hipler. *Analecta Bollandiana* 2 (1883): 381–472; 3 (1884): 113–40 and 408–48; 4 (1884): 207–51.

——. *Vita [Latina] Dorotheae Montoviensis Magistri Johannis Marienwerder.* Ed. Hans Westphal. Cologne: Böhlau, 1964.

——. *Vita Lindana* [of Dorothy of Montau]. In *AA SS*, October, 13:499–560.

——. *Vita prima* [of Dorothy of Montau]. In *AA SS*, October, 13:493–98.

——. *Vita prima* [of Dorothy of Montau]. Ed. A. Amore. In *Gedanen. Beatificationis et canonizationis servae Dei Dorotheae Montoviensis viduae et reclusae "beatae" seu "sanctae" nuncupatae (+1394). Positio super cultu et virtutibus servae Dei ex officio concinnata*, 21–36. Vatican City, 1976.

Klaes, Monica, ed. *Vita S. Hildegardis.* Corpus Christianorum, continuatio medievalis, vol. 126. Turhout: Brepols, 1993.

Laurent, Marie-Hyacinthe, ed. *Documenti.* Fontes vitae S. Catharinae Sensis historici 1. Siena: R. Università di Siena, 1936.

——, ed. *Il Processo Castellano*. Fontes vitae S. Catharinae historici 9. Milan: Fratelli Bocca, 1942.

Laurent, Marie-Hyacinth, and Francesco Valli, eds. *I Miracoli di Caterina da Iacopo da Siena di anonimo Fiorentino*. Fontes vitae S. Catharinae historici 4. Florence: Sansoni, 1936.

Margaret Ebner. *Major Works*. Ed. and trans. Leonard Hindsley. New York: Paulist Press, 1993.

——. *Offenbarungen der Margaretha Ebner*. In *Margaretha Ebner und Heinrich von Nördlingen. Ein Beitrag zur Geschichte der Deutschen Mystik*, ed. Philipp Strauch, 1–166, 287–319. Tübingen: J. C. B. Mohr, 1882; reprint, Amsterdam: P. Schippers, 1966.

Oehl, Wilhelm, ed. and trans. *Deutsche Mystikerbriefe des Mittelalters 100–1550*. Munich: Georg Müller, 1931.

Patrologiae cursus completus… series Latina. [Patrologia Latina.] Ed. J.-P. Migne. 221 vols. Paris: Garnier Fratres and J.-P. Migne, 1844–64.

Paulson, Johannes, ed. *In Tertiam Partem Libri Juliacensis Annotationes*. Göteborg: Wettergren & Kerber, 1896.

Peter Lombard. *Sententiae in IV libris distinctae*. Grottaferrata (Rome): Editiones Collegii S. Bonaventurae, 1971–1981.

Peter of Dacia. *De gratia naturam ditante sive de virtutibus Christinae Stumbelensis*. Ed. Monika Asztalos. Stockholm: Almqvist & Wiksell International, 1982.

——. *Vita Christinae Stumbelensis*. Ed. Johannes Paulson. Göteborg: Wettergren & Kerber, 1896.

Peter of St. Mary of Alvastra and Peter of Skänninge. *Vita sanctae Birgittae auctoribus… confessoribus Birgittae*. In *Scriptores rerum suecicarum medii aevi*. Vol. 3, part 2, ed. Claudius Annerstedt, 185–206. Uppsala, 1876.

Peter the Chanter. *Verbum Abbreviatum*. *PL* 205, cols. 21–370.

Raymond of Capua. *Legenda Agnetis de Montepulciano*. In *AA SS*, April, 2:792–812.

——. *Opuscula et Litterae*. Ed. Hyacinthe-Marie Cormier. Rome: Ex Typographia Polyglotta, 1895.

——. *Vita Catharina Senensis [Legenda maior]*. In *AA SS*, April. 3:863–967. Third ed. Paris: V. Palmé, 1866.

Roth, F. W. E., ed. *Die Visionen der Hl. Elisabeth und die Schriften der Abte Ekbert und Emecho von Schönau*. Brünn: Verlag der Studien aus dem Benedictiner- und Cisterciener Orden, 1884.

Rutebeuf. *Oeuvres complètes*. Vol. 1. Ed. and trans. Michel Zink. Paris: Bordas, 1989.

Stachnik, Richard, Anneliese Triller, and Hans Westpfahl, eds. *Die Akten des Kanonisationsprozesses Dorotheae von Montau, von 1394–1521*. Cologne: Böhlau, 1978.

Strauch, Philipp, ed. *Margaretha Ebner und Heinrich von Nördlingen. Ein Beitrag zur Geschichte der deutschen Mystik*. Tübingen: J. C. B. Mohr, 1882; reprint, Amsterdam: P. Schippers, 1966.

Sulpicius Severus. *Vie de saint Martin*. Latin text with French translation. Ed. Jacques Fontaine. 3 vols. Paris: Éditions du Cerf, 1967–69.

Talbot, C. H., ed. *The Life of Christina of Markyate: A Twelfth-Century Recluse*. Latin text with English translation. Oxford: Oxford University Press, 1959.

Thomas Aquinas. *Summa theologiae*. 60 vols. New York: McGraw Hill; and London: Eyre & Spottiswoode, 1964–73.

Thomas of Cantimpré. *Supplementum ad vitam S. Mariae Oigniacensis*. In *AA SS* June, 4:666–77.

——. *Supplement to the Life of Marie d'Oignies by Thomas of Cantimpré [and] Anonymous History of the Foundation of the Venerable Church of Blessed Nicholas of Oignies*. Trans. Hugh Fiess, 37–41. Saskatoon: Peregrina, 1987.

——. *Vita Christinae Mirabilis*. In *AA SS*. July. 5:650–60.

——. *Vita Lutgardis Aquiriae*. In *AA SS*. June. 3:231–63.

——. *Vita prima s. Francisci Assisiensis*. Quaracchi: Collegium S. Bonaventurae, 1926.

Thomas of Siena. *Legenda B. Mariae de Venetiis*. In *Ecclesiae Venetae antiquis monumentis nunc etiam primum editis illustratae ac in decades distributae, decadis undecimae pars prior*, edited by Flaminio Cornelio, vol. 11, part 1, 364–420. Venice, 1749.

——. *Libellus de supplemento*. Ed. Iuliana Cavallini and Imelda Foralosso. Rome: Edizioni cateriniane, 1974.

——. *Sanctae Catharinae Senensis Legenda minor*. Ed. Ezio Franceschini. Fontes Vitae S. Catharinae Senensis Historici 10. Siena: R. Università di Siena; Milan: Bocca, 1942.

Ubertino of Casale. *Arbor vitae crucifixae Jesu*. Reprint of the 1485 edition, presented by Charles T. Davis. Turin: Bottega d'Erasmo, 1961.

Vincent of Beauvais. "Ex Vincentii speculo historiali." Ed. O. Holder-Egger. *Monumenta Germaniae Historica*, Scriptores, 24:164–67. Hanover: Impensis Bibliopolii Hahniani 1879.

Vita ... auctore anonymo [Life of Christine of Stommeln]. *AA SS* June, 4:431–54.

Vita Humilitatis [Life of Humility of Faienza]. In *AA SS*. May. 5:205–22.

Vito of Cortona. *Vita Humilianae*. *AA SS*. May. 4:386–403.

Wilms, Hieronymus, ed. and trans. *Der seligen Margareta Ebner Offenbarungen und Briefe*. Vechta: Albertus Magnus Verlag, 1928.

Windstosser, Maria, ed. and trans. *Frauenmystik im Mittelalter*. Kempten and Munich: Verlag Josef Kösel & Friedrich Pustet, 1919.

English Translations of Sources

Angela of Foligno. *Complete Works*. Ed. and trans. Paul Lachance. New York: Paulist Press, 1993.

Catherine of Siena. *I, Catherine: Selected Writings of Catherine of Siena*. Ed. and trans. Kenelm Foster and Mary John Ronayne. London: Collins, 1980.

——. *The Letters of St. Catherine of Siena*. Trans. Suzanne Noffke. Vol. 1. Binghamton: Medieval and Renaissance Texts and Studies, 1988. 2nd ed.: Tempe: Arizona Center for Medieval and Renaissance Studies, 2000.

Elisabeth of Schönau. *Elisabeth of Schönau: The Complete Works*. Ed. and trans. Anne L. Clark. New York: Paulist Press, 2000.

Hildegard of Bingen. *The Letters of Hildegard of Bingen.* Trans. Joseph L. Baird and Radd K. Ehrman. Vols. 1–. New York: Oxford University Press, 1994–.

James of Vitry. *The Life of Marie d'Oignies by Jacques de Vitry.* Trans. Margot H. King. Saskatoon: Peregrina, 1986.

John Marienwerder. *The Life of Dorothea von Montau, a Fourteenth-Century Recluse.* Trans. Ute Stargardt. Lewiston, N.Y.: Edwin Mellen Press, 1997.

Raymond of Capua. *The Life of Catherine of Siena.* Trans, intro., and annot. Conleth Kearns. Wilmington, Del.: Glazier, 1980.

Silvas, Anna, trans. and ed. *Jutta and Hildegard: The Biographical Sources.* Turnhout: Brepols, 1998. Includes: Guibert of Gembloux, "Letter to Bovo," 99–117; and Theoderic of Echternach, *Vita sanctae Hildegardis,* 135–210.

Suso, Henry. *The Exemplar, with Two German Sermons.* Ed. and trans. Frank Tobin. New York: Paulist Press, 1989.

Talbot, C. H., ed. *The Life of Christina of Markyate: A Twelfth-Century Recluse.* Latin text with English translation. Oxford: Oxford University Press, 1959.

Thomas of Cantimpré. *The Life of Lutgard of Aywières by Thomas de Cantimpré.* Trans. Margot H. King. Saskatoon: Peregrina, 1987.

——. *Supplement ot the Life of Marie d'Oignies by Thomas of Cantimpré [and] Anonymous History of the Foundation of the Venerable Church of Blessed Nicholas of Oignies…* Trans. Hugh Feiss. Saskatoon: Peregrina, 1987.

STUDIES

Ahlgren, Gillian T.W. "Ecstasy, Prophecy and Reform: Catherine of Siena as a Model for Holy Women of Sixteenth-Century Spain." In *The Medieval Gesture: Essays on Medieval and Early Modern Spiritual Culture in Honor of Mary E. Giles,* ed. Robert Boenig, 53–65. Aldershot: Ashgate, 2000.

Alberzoni, Maria Pia. "L'*approbatio*': Curia romana, Ordine Minoritico e *Liber.*" In *Angèle de Foligno: Le Dossier,* ed. Giulia Barone and Jacques Dalarun, 293–318. Rome: École française de Rome, 1999.

Ancelet-Hustache. Jeanne. *Mechtilde de Magdebourg: Étude de psychologie religieuse.* Paris: Champion, 1926.

Ash, James L., Jr. "The Decline of Ecstatic Prophecy in the Early Church." *Theological Studies* 37 (1976): 227–53.

Ashton, Gail. *The Generation of Identity in Late Medieval Hagiography.* London: Routledge, 2000.

Asztalos, Monika. Introduction to *GND,* 16–27.

——. "La Conception de l'homme dans les écrits de Pierre de Dacie." In *L'Homme et son univers au moyen age. Actes du Septième Congrès International de Philosophie Médiévale 30.8–4.9.1982,* ed. C. Wenin, 1:260–66. Louvain-la-Neuve: Institut Supérieur de Philosophie, 1986.

——. "Les Lettres de direction et les sermons épistolaires de Pierre de Dacie." In *The Editing of Theological and Philosophical Texts from the Middle Ages,* ed. Monika Asztalos, 161–84. Stockholm: Almquist & Wiksell International, 1986.

Bagliani, Agostino, and André Vauchez, eds. *Poteri carismatici e informali: Chiesa e società medioevali*. Palermo: Sellerio, 1992.

Baker, Derek T., ed. *Medieval Women*. Oxford: Blackwell, 1978.

Baldwin, John W. *Masters, Princes, and Merchants: The Social Views of Peter the Chanter and His Circle*. 2 vols. Princeton, N.J.: Princeton University Press, 1970.

Barone, Giuilia, and Jacques Dalarun, eds. *Angèle de Foligno: Le Dossier*. Rome: École Française, 1999.

Barratt, Alexandra. "Undutiful Daughters and Metaphorical Mothers among the Beguines." In *New Trends in Feminine Spirituality: The Holy Women of Liège and Their Impact*, ed. Juliette Dor, Lesley Johnson, and Jocelyn Wogan-Browne, 90–93. Turnhout: Brepols, 1999.

Barré, H. "Une prière d'Ekbert de Schönau au saint coeur de Marie." *Ephemerides mariologicae* 2 (1952): 409–23.

Bartlett, Anne Clark. "Commentary, Polemic, and Prophecy in Hildegard of Bingen's 'Solutiones Triginta Octo Quaestionum.'" *Viator* 23 (1992): 153–65.

Bartoli Langeli, Attilio. "Il codice di Assisi, ovvero il *Liber sororis Lelle*." In *Angèle de Foligno: Le Dossier*, ed. Giulia Barone and Jacques Dalarun, 7–27. Rome: École française de Rome, 1999.

Bell, Rudolph. *Holy Anorexia*. Chicago: University of Chicago Press, 1985.

Benedict, Kimberley M. *Empowering Collaborations: Writing Partnerships between Religious Women and Scribes in the Middle Ages*. New York: Routledge, 2004.

Benedetti, Giovanni. "Elementi per una teologia spirituale nel 'Libro della Beata Angela.'" In *Vita e spiritualità della beata Angela da Foligno. Atti del convegno di studi per il VII centenario della conversione della beata Angela da Foligno (1285–1985)*, ed. Clément Schmitt, 15–38. Perugia: Serafica provincia di san Francesco OFM Conv., 1987.

Benvenuti Papi, Anna. *In castro poenitentiae. Santità e società femminile nell'Italia medievale*. Rome: Herder, 1990.

——. "'Margherita Filia Ierusalem.' Una visione mistica della terrasanta nella spiritualità femminile Francescana." In *Toscana e terrasanta nel medioevo*, ed. Franco Cardini, 117–37. Florence: Alinea, 1982.

——. "Mendicant Friars and Female Pinzochere in Tuscany: From Social Marginality to Models of Sanctity." In *Women and Religion in Medieval and Renaissance Italy*, ed. Daniel Bornstein and Roberto Rusconi, trans. Margery J. Schneider, 84–103. Chicago: University of Chicago Press, 1996.

——. "Umiliana dei Cerchi. Nascità di un culto nella Firenze del Dugento." *Studi Francescani* 77 (1980): 87–117.

Bestul, Thomas H. *Texts of the Passion: Latin Devotional Literature and Medieval Society*. Philadelphia: University of Pennsylvania Press, 1996.

Betori, Giuseppe. "La Scrittura nell'esperienza spirituale della B. Angela da Foligno. Annotazioni preliminari." In *Vita e spiritualità della beata Angela da Foligno. Atti del convegno di studi per il VII centenario della conversione della beata Angela da Foligno (1285–1985)*, ed. Clément Schmitt, 171–98. Perugia: Serafica provincia di san Francesco OFM Conv., 1987.

Bilinkoff, Jodi. "Confession, Gender, Life-Writing: Some Cases (Mainly) from Spain." In *Penitence in the Age of Reformations*, ed. Katharine Jackson Lualdi and Anne T. Thayer, 169–83. Aldershot: Ashgate, 2000.

——. *Related Lives: Confessors, Female Penitents, and Catholic Culture, 1450–1750*. Ithaca, N.Y.: Cornell University Press, 2005.

Biller, Peter, and A. J. Minnis. *Medieval Theology and the Natural Body*. Woodbridge: York Medieval Press, 1997.

Blamires, Alcuin. "Women and Preaching in Medieval Orthodoxy, Heresy, and Saints' Lives." *Viator* 26 (1995): 135–52.

Blamires, Alcuin, and C. W. Marx. "Woman Not to Preach: A Disputation in British Library MS Harley 31." *Journal of Medieval Latin* 3 (1993): 34–63.

Blumenfeld-Kosinski, Renate. "Satirical Views of the Beguines in Northern French Literature." In *New Trends in Feminine Spirituality: The Holy Women of Liège and Their Impact*, ed. Juliette Dor, Lesley Johnson, and Jocelyn Wogan-Browne, 237–49. Turnhout: Brepols, 1999.

Blumenfeld-Kosinski, Renate, and Timea Szell, eds. *Images of Sainthood in Medieval Europe*. Ithaca, N.Y.: Cornell University Press, 1991.

Boesch Gajano, Sofia, and Odile Redon. "La *Legenda maior* di Raimundo da Capua, costruzione di una santa." In *Atti del Simposio Internazionale Cateriniano-Bernardiniano, Siena 17–20 Aprile 1980*, ed. Domenico Maffei and Paolo Nardi, 15–35. Siena: Accademia Senese degli Intronati, 1982.

Bolton, Brenda M. "*Vitae Matrum*: A Further Aspect of the *Frauenfrage*." In *Medieval Women*, ed. Derek T. Baker, 253–73. Oxford: Blackwell, 1978.

Bornstein, Daniel. "Spiritual Kinship and Domestic Devotions." In *Gender and Society in Renaissance Italy*, ed. Judith C. Brown and Robert C. Davis, 173–92. London: Longman, 1998.

——. "The Uses of the Body: The Church and the Cult of Santa Margherita da Cortona." *Church History* 62 (1993): 163–77.

Bornstein, Daniel, and Roberto Rusconi, eds. *Women and Religion in Medieval and Renaissance Italy*, trans. Margery J. Schneider. Chicago: University of Chicago Press, 1996.

Boureau, Alain. "Miracle, volonté et imagination: La Mutation scolastique (1270–1320)." In *Miracles, prodiges et merveilles au Moyen Age*, 159–72. Paris: Publications de la Sorbonne, 1995.

Bourgain, Pascale. "Angèle de Foligno: Le Latin du *Liber*." In *Angèle de Foligno: Le Dossier*, ed. Giulia Barone and Jacques Dalarun, 145–67. Rome: École française de Rome, 1999.

Brown, Peter. "Society and the Supernatural: A Medieval Change." *Daedalus* 104 (1975): 133–51.

Brufani, Stefano. "Angela da Foligno e gli Spirituali." In *Angela da Foligno Terziaria Francescana. Atti del Convegno storico nel VII centenario dell'ingresso della beata Angela da Foligno nell'Ordine Francescano Secolare (1291–1991)*, ed. Enrico Menestò, 83–104. Spoleto: Centro Italiano du Studi sull'Alto Medioevo, 1992.

Burr, David. *The Spiritual Franciscans: From Protest to Persecution in the Century After Saint Francis*. University Park: Pennsylvania State University Press, 2001.

Bynum, Caroline Walker. *Fragmentation and Redemption: Essays on Gender and the Human Body in Medieval Religion.* New York: Zone, 1991.

———. *Holy Feast and Holy Fast: The Religious Significance of Food to Medieval Women.* Berkeley: University of California Press, 1986.

———. *Jesus as Mother.* Berkeley: University of California Press, 1982.

———. "Women Mystics and Eucharistic Devotion in the Thirteenth Century." *Women's Studies* 11 (1984): 179–214. Reprinted in Bynum, *Fragmentation and Redemption*, 119–50. New York: Zone, 1991.

Caciola, Nancy. *Discerning Spirits: Divine and Demonic Possession in the Middle Ages.* Ithaca, N.Y.: Cornell University Press, 2003.

Calza, Maria Grazia. *Dem Weiblichen ist das Verstehen des Göttlichen "auf der Leib" geschrieben: Die Begine Maria von Oignies ([gest.] 1213) in der hagiographischen Darstellung Jakobs von Vitry ([gest.] 1240).* Würzburg: Ergon, 2000.

Cannon, Joanna. "'Fama Laudabilis Beate Sororis Margherite': Art in the Service of the Cult of Margherita," in *Margherita of Cortona and the Lorenzetti: Sienese Art and the Cult of a Holy Woman in Medieval Tuscany,* ed. Cannon and André Vauchez, 159–220. University Park: Pennsylvania State University Press, 1999.

Cannon, Joanna, and André Vauchez, eds. *Margherita of Cortona and the Lorenzetti: Sienese Art and the Cult of a Holy Woman in Medieval Tuscany.* University Park: Pennsylvania State University Press, 1999.

Cardini, Franco. "Agiografia e politica: Margherita da Cortona e le vicende di una città inqueta." *Studi francescani* 76 (1979): 127–36.

Cardman, Francine. "The Medieval Question of Women and Orders," *The Thomist* 42 (1978): 582–99.

Casagrande, Giovanna. "Il terz'ordine e la beata Angela. La povertà nell'ordine della non-povertà." In *Angela da Foligno Terziaria Francescana. Atti del Convegno storico nel VII centenario dell'ingresso della beata Angela da Foligno nell'Ordine Francescano Secolare (1291–1991),* ed. Enrico Menestò, 7–38. Spoleto: Centro Italiano du Studi sull'Alto Medioevo, 1992.

Christensen, Kirsten M. "The Conciliatory Rhetoric of Mysticism in the Correspondence of Heinrich von Nördlingen and Margaretha Ebner." In *Peace and Negotiation: Strategies for Coexistence in the Middle Ages and Renaissance,* ed. Diane Wolfthal, 125–43. Turnhout: Brepols, 2000.

Clark, Anne. *Elisabeth of Schönau: A Twelfth-Century Visionary.* Philadelphia: University of Pennsylvania Press, 1992.

———. "Holy Woman or Unworthy Vessel? The Representations of Elisabeth of Schönau." In *Gendered Voices: Medieval Saints and Their Interpreters,* ed. Catherine M. Mooney, 35–51. Philadelphia: University of Pennsylvania Press, 1999.

Coakley, John. "Friars as Confidants of Holy Women in Medieval Dominican Hagiography." In *Images of Sainthood in Medieval Europe,* ed. Renate Blumenfeld-Kosinski and Timea Szell, 222–46. Ithaca, N.Y.: Cornell University Press, 1991.

———. "Friars, Sanctity, and Gender: Mendicant Encounters with Saints, 1250–1325." In *Medieval Masculinities: Regarding Men in the Middle Ages,* ed. Clare Lees, 91–110. Minneapolis: University of Minnesota Press, 1994.

———. "Gender and the Authority of Friars: The Significance of Holy Women for Thirteenth-Century Franciscans and Dominicans." *Church History* 60 (1991): 445–60.

———. "Introduction: Women's Creativity in Religious Context." In *Creative Women*, ed. E. Ann Matter and John Coakley, 1–16. Philadelphia: University of Pennsylvania Press

———. "A Marriage and Its Observer: Christine of Stommeln, the Heavenly Bridegroom, and Friar Peter of Dacia." In *Gendered Voices: Medieval Saints and Their Interpreters*, ed. Catherine Mooney, 99–117. Philadelphia: University of Pennsylvania Press, 1999.

———. "Thomas of Cantimpré and Female Sanctity." In *In the Comic Mode*, ed. Rachel Fulton and Bruce Holsinger. New York: Columbia University Press, forthcoming.

Cohen, Jeffrey Jerome, and Bonnie Wheeler, eds. *Becoming Male in the Middle Ages.* New York: Garland, 1997.

Colish, Marcia L. "Early Scholastic Angelology." *Recherches de théologie ancienne et médiévale* 62 (1995): 80–109.

———. *Peter Lombard.* 2 vols. Leiden: Brill, 1994.

Congar, Yves. "The Historical Development of Authority in the Church: Points for Christian Reflection." In *Problems of Authority*, ed. John Todd, 119–56. London: Darton Longman and Todd, 1962.

Conner, Paul M. "Catherine of Siena and Raymond of Capua—Enduring Friends." *Studia Mystica* 12, no. 1 (1989): 22–29.

Constable, Giles. *Letters and Letter Collections.* Turnhout: Brepols, 1976.

Coppini, Beatrice. *La Scrittura e il percorso mistico. Il "Liber" di Angela da Foligno.* Rome: Ianua, 1986.

Cormier, Hyacinthe-Marie. *La bienheureux Raymond de Capoue. Sa vie, ses vertus, son action dans l'église et dans l'ordre de saint Dominique.* Rome: Imprimerie Vaticane, 1899.

Corsini, Lucia. "Notizie introduttive." In *Heinrich von Nördlingen e Margaretha Ebner: Le Lettere (1332–1350)*, ed. and trans. Lucia Corsini, 25–53. Pisa: Edizioni ETS, 2001.

Dalarun, Jacques. "Angèle de Foligno a-t-elle existé?" In *Alla Signorina: Mélanges offerts à Noëlle de la Blanchardière*, 59–97. Rome: École Française, 1995.

———. "The Clerical Gaze." In *Silences of the Middle Ages*, ed. C. Klapisch-Zuber, 15–42. Vol. 2 of *A History of Women in the West*, ed. George Duby and Michelle Perrot. Cambridge, Mass.: Harvard University Press, 1992.

———. "Hors des sentiers battus. Saintes femmes d'Italie aux XIIIe–XIVe siècles." In *Femmes-Mariage-Lignages, XIIe-XIVe siècles. Mélanges offerts à Georges Duby*, 79–102. Brussels: De Boeck Université, 1992.

D'Alatri, Mariano. *Aetas poenitentialis. L'Antico Ordine Francescano de la Penitenza.* Rome: Istituto storico dei Cappucini, 1993.

———. "L'Ordine della Penitenza nella leggenda di Margherita da Cortona." *Analecta Tertii Ordinis Regularis (Rome)* 15 (1982): 67–80.

Deboutte, Alfred. "The *Vita Lutgardis* of Thomas of Cantimpré." In *Hidden Springs: Cistercian Monastic Women*, ed. John A. Nichols and Lillian Thomas Shank, 255–81. N.p.: Cistercian Publications, 1995.

de Fontette, Micheline. *Les religieuses à l'âge classique du droit canon: Rechereches sur les structures juridiques des branches féminines des ordres.* Paris: J. Vrin, 1967.

Delehaye, Hippolyte. "Guibert, Abbé de Florennes et de Gembloux." *Revue Des Questions Historiques* 46 (1889): 5–90.

——. *Sanctus: Essai sur le culte des saints dans l'antiquité.* Brussels: Société des Bollandistes, 1927.

De Libera, Alain. "Angèle de Foligno et la mystique 'féminine': éléments pour une typologie." In *Angèle de Foligno: Le Dossier,* ed. Giulia Barone and Jacques Dalarun, 345–71. Rome: École française de Rome, 1999.

Delooz, Pierre. *Sociologie et canonisations.* Liège: Faculté de Droit, 1969.

Derolez, Albert. Introduction to Guibert of Gembloux, *Guiberti Gemblacensis Epistolae,* Corpus Christianorum, continuatio mediaevalis, vols. 66 and 66A, vii–xxxviii. Turnhout: Brepols, 1988–89.

Devlin, Dennis. "Feminine Lay Piety in the High Middle Ages: The Beguines." In *Medieval Women,* ed. J. Nichols and L. Shank, 183–96. Kalamazoo, Mich.: Cistercian Publications, 1984.

Dillon, Janette. "Holy Women and Their Confessors or Confessors and Their Holy Women? Margery Kempe and Continental Tradition." In *Prophets Abroad: The Reception of Continental Holy Women in Late-Medieval England,* ed. Rosalynn Voaden, 115–40. Cambridge: D. S. Brewer, 1996.

Dinzelbacher, Peter. "Europäische Frauenmystik des Mittelalters: Ein Überblick." In *Frauenmystik im Mittelalter,* ed. Peter Dinzelbacher and Dieter Bauer, 11–23. Stuttgart: Schwaben, 1985. Reprinted in Dinzelbacher, *Mittelalterliche Frauenmystik,* 16–26. Paderborn: Ferdinand Schöningh, 1993.

——. *Heilige oder Hexen? Schicksale auffälliger Frauen in Mittelalter und Früneuzeit.* Zürich: Artemis & Winkler, 1995.

——. *Mittelalterliche Frauenmystik.* Paderborn: Ferdinand Schöningh, 1993.

——. "Nascità e funzione della sanctità mistica alla fine del medioevo centrale." In *Les fonctions des saints dans le monde occidental, IIIe-XIIIe s.,* 489–506. Rome: École Française, 1991.

——. *'Revelationes.'* Turnhout: Brepols, 1991.

——. *Vision und Visionsliteratur im Mittelalter.* Stuttgart: Anton Hiersemann, 1981.

——. "Zur Interpretation erlebnismystischer Texte des Mittelalters." *Zeitschrift für deutsches Altertum* 117 (1988):1–23. Reprinted in Dinzelbacher, *Mittelalterliche Frauenmystik,* 304–31. Paderborn: Ferdinand Schöningh, 1993.

Dinzelbacher, Peter, and Dieter Bauer, eds. *Frauenmystik im Mittelalter.* Stuttgart: Schwaben, 1985.

——, eds. *Religiöse Frauenbewegung und mystische Frömmigkeit in Mittelalter.* Cologne: Böhlau, 1988.

Dondaine, Antoine. "Sainte Catherine de Sienne et Niccolò Toldo." *Archivum Fratrum Praedicatorum* 19 (1949):168–207.

Dor, Juliette, Lesley Johnson, and Jocelyn Wogan-Browne, eds. *New Trends in Feminine Spirituality: The Holy Women of Liège and Their Impact.* Turnhout: Brepols, 1999.

Dronke, Peter. *Women Writers of the Middle Ages*. Cambridge: Cambridge University Press, 1984.

D'Urso, Giacinto. "La B. Angela e Ubertino da Casale." In *Vita e spiritualità della beata Angela da Foligno. Atti del convegno di studi per il VII centenario della conversione della beata Angela da Foligno (1285–1985)*, ed. Clément Schmitt, 155–70. Perugia: Serafica provincia di san Francesco OFM Conv., 1987.

Egenter, Richard. "Die Idee der Gottesfreundschaft im vierzehnten Jahrhundert." In *Aus der Geisteswelt des Mittelalters: Studien und Texte Martin Grabmann zur Vollendung des 60. Lebensjahres von Freunden und Schülern gewidmet*, ed. Albert Lang, Joseph Lehner, and Michael Schmaus, 1021–35. Münster: Aschendorffschen Verlagsbuchhandlung, 1935.

Eisenstadt, S. N., ed. *Max Weber on Charisma and Institution Building*. Chicago: University of Chicago Press, 1968.

Elkins, Sharon K. *Holy Women of Twelfth-Century England*. Chapel Hill: University of North Carolina Press, 1988.

Elliott, Alison Goddard. *Roads to Paradise: Reading the Lives of the Early Saints*. Hanover, N.H.: University Press of New England, 1987.

Elliott, Dyan. "Authorizing a Life: The Collaboration of Dorothea of Montau and John Marienwerder." In *Gendered Voices: Medieval Saints and Their Interpreters*, ed. Catherine Mooney, 168–91. Philadelphia: University of Pennsylvania Press, 1999.

——. *Fallen Bodies: Pollution, Sexuality, and Demonology in the Middle Ages*. Philadelphia: University of Pennsylvania Press, 1999.

——. "The Physiology of Rapture and Female Spirituality." In *Medieval Theology and the Natural Body*, ed. Peter Biller and A. J. Minnis, 141–73. Woodbridge: Boydell and Brewer, 1997.

——. *Proving Woman: Female Spirituality and Inquisitional Culture in the Later Middle Ages*. Princeton, N.J.: Princeton University Press, 2004.

——. "Seeing Double: Jean Gerson, the Discernment of Spirits, and Joan of Arc." *American Historical Review* 107 (2002): 26–54.

Elm, Kaspar. "Die Stellung der Frau in Ordenswesen, Semireligiosentum und Häresie zur Zeit der Hl. Elisabeth." In *Sankt Elisabeth: Fürstin, Dienterin, Heilige*. 7–38. Sigmaringen: Jan Thorbecke Verlag, 1981.

——. "*Vita regularis sine regula*. Bedeutung, Rechtsstellung und Selbstverständnis des Mittelalterlichen und Frühneuzeitlichen Semireligiosentums." In *Häresie und Vorzeitige Reformation Im Spätmittelalter*, ed. Frantisek Smahel and Elisabeth Müller-Luckner, 239–73. Munich: R. Oldenbourg Verlag, 1998.

Fanous, Samuel, and Henrietta Leyser, eds. *Christina of Markyate: A Twelfth-Century Holy Woman*. New York: Routledge, 2004.

Fawtier, Robert. *Sainte Catherine de Sienne: Essai de critique des sources*. 2 vols. Paris: A. de Boccard, 1921–30.

Fawtier, Robert, and Louis Canet. *La Double expérience de Catherine Benincasa*. Paris: Gallimard, 1948.

Ferrante, Joan M. *To the Glory of Her Sex: Women's Roles in the Composition of Medieval Texts*. Bloomington: Indiana University Press, 1997.

Ferré, Martin-Jean. "Les principales dates de la vie d'Angèle de Foligno." In *Revue d'histoire Franciscaine* 2 (1925): 21–35.

Flanagan, Sabina. *Hildegard of Bingen: A Visionary Life.* London: Routledge, 1989.

Freed, John B. "Urban Develoment and the 'Cura Monialium' in Thirteenth-Century Germany." *Viator* 3 (1972): 311–27.

Frugoni, Chiara. "Female Mystics, Visions, and Iconography." In *Women and Religion in Medieval and Renaissance Italy*, ed. Daniel Bornstein and Roberto Rusconi, trans. Margery J. Schneider, 130–64. Chicago: University of Chicago Press, 1996.

Funk, Phillip. *Jakob von Vitry, Leben und Werke.* Beiträge zur Kulturgeschichte des Mittelalters und der Renaissance 3 Leipzig: Teubner, 1909.

———. "Zur Geschichte der Frömmigkeit und Mystik im Ordenslande Preußen." Ed. Leo Juhnke. *Zeitschrift für die Geschichte und Altertumskunde Ermlands* 30, no. 1 (1960): 1–37.

Gallén, Jarl. *La Province de Dacie de l'ordre des frères prècheurs.* Helsingfors: Soderstrom, 1946.

———. "Les Causes de Sainte Ingrid et des saints suédois au temps de la Réforme." *Archivum Fratrum Praedicatorum* 7 (1937): 1–40.

Gennette, Gérard. *Narrative Discourse: An Essay in Method*, trans. Jane E. Lewin. Ithaca, N.Y.: Cornell University Press, 1980.

Gerwing, M. "Gottesfreund(e)." In *Lexikon des Mittelalters*, 4:1586–87. Munich: Artemis, 1987.

Geyer, Iris. *Maria von Oignies. Eine Hochmittelalterliche Mystikerin zwischen Ketzerei und Rechtgläubigkeit.* Frankfurt: Lang, 1992.

Glente, Karen. "Mystikerinnenviten aus männlicher und weiblicher Sicht: Ein Vergleich zwischen Thomas von Cantimpré und Katherina von Unterlinden." In *Religiöse Frauenbewegung und Mystische Frömmigkeit im Mittelalter*, ed. Peter Dinzelbacher and Dieter R. Bauer, 251–64. Cologne: Böhlau, 1988.

Gnädinger, Louise. "Esther. Eine Skizze." *Zeitschrift für deutsche Philologie* 113 (1994): 31–62.

Goodich, Michael. *Vita Perfecta: The Ideal of Sainthood in the Thireenth Century.* Stuttgart: Anton Hiersemann, 1982.

Gössmann, Elisabeth. "Das Menschenbild der Hilegard von Bingen und Elisabeth von Schönau vor dem Hintergrund der frühscholastischen Anthropologie." In *Frauenmystik im Mittelalter*, ed. Peter Dinzelbacher and Dieter R. Bauer, 24–47. Ostfildern: Schwabenverlag, 1985.

Graus, František. *Volk, Herrscher und Heiliger im Reich der Merowinger.* Prague: Nakladatlství československé akademie ved, 1965.

Greenspan, Kate. "Autohagiography and Medieval Women's Spiritual Autobiography." In *Gender and Text in the Later Middle Ages*, ed. Jane Chance, 216–36. Gainesville: University Press of Florida, 1996.

Grundmann, Herbert. *Religious Movements in the Middle Ages.* Trans. Steven Rowan. Notre Dame, Ind.: University of Notre Dame Press, 1995.

Guarnieri, Romana. "Santa Angela? Angela, Ubertino e lo spiritualismo Francescano. Prime ipotesi sulla *Peroratio*." In *Angèle de Foligno: Le Dossier*, ed. Giulia Barone and Jacques Dalarun, 203–65. Rome: École française de Rome, 1999.

Gürsching, Heinrich. "Neue urkundliche Nachrichten über den Mystiker Heinrich von Nördlingen." In *Festgabe aus Anlaß des 75. Geburtstages von D. Dr. Karl Schornbaum am 7. März 1950.*, ed. Heinrich Gürsching, 42–57. Neustadt: P. C. W. Schmidt, 1950.

Hale, Rosemary Drogue. "*Imitatio Mariae:* Motherhood Motifs in Devotional Memoirs." *Mystics Quarterly* 16 (1991): 193–203.

——. "Rocking the Cradle: Margaretha Ebner (Be)Holds the Divine." In *Performance and Transformation: New Approaches to Late Medieval Spirituality*, ed. Mary A. Suydam and Joanna E. Ziegler, 211–39. New York: St. Martin's, 1999.

Hamburger, Jeffrey. "The *Liber Miraculorum* of Unterlinden: An Icon in Its Convent Setting." In *The Sacred Image East and West*, ed. Robert Ousterhout and Leslie Brubaker, 147–90. Urbana: University of Illinois Press, 1995.

Hauschild, Wolf-Dieter. "Gnade IV." *Theologische Realenzycolpädie*, 13:485–486.

Head, Thomas. *Hagiography and the Cult of Saints: The Diocese of Orléans, 800–1200.* Cambridge: Cambridge University Press, 1990.

——. "The Marriages of Christina of Markyate." *Viator* 21 (1990): 71–95.

Heffernan, Thomas. *Sacred Biography: Saints and Their Biographers in the Middle Ages.* New York: Oxford University Press, 1988.

Herwegen, Ildefons. *Alte Quellen neuer Kraft.* 2nd ed. Düsseldorf: Schwann, 1922.

——. "Les collaborateurs de sainte Hildegarde," *Revue Bénédictine* 21 (1904): 192–203, 302–15, 381–403.

Hindsley, Leonard P. *The Mystics of Engelthal: Writings from a Medieval Monastery.* New York: St. Martin's Press, 1998.

Hipler, Franz. "Johannes Marienwerder, der Beichtvater der seligen Dorothea von Montau." Ed. Hans Westpfahl and Hans Schmauch. *Zeitschrift für Geschichte und Altertumskunde Ermlands* 29 (1956): 1–92.

Holdsworth, Christopher J. "Christina of Markyate." In *Medieval Women*, ed. Derek T. Baker, 185–204. Oxford: Blackwell, 1978.

Hollywood, Amy. "Inside Out: Beatrice of Nazareth and Her Hagiographer." In *Gendered Voices: Medieval Saints and Their Interpreters*, ed. Catherine Mooney, 78–98. Philadelphia: University of Pennsylvania Press, 1999.

——. *Sensible Ecstasy: Mysticism, Sexual Difference, and the Demands of History.* Chicago: University of Chicago Press, 2002.

——. *The Soul as Virgin Wife: Mechthild of Magdeburg, Marguerite Porete, and Meister Eckhart.* Notre Dame, Ind.: University of Notre Dame Press, 1995.

Holsinger, Bruce. *Music, Body, and Desire in Medieval Culture: Hildegard of Bingen to Chaucer.* Stanford, Calif.: Stanford University Press, 2001.

Hörner, Petra. *Dorothea von Montau.* Frankfurt: Lang, 1993.

Iozzelli, Fortunato. "I miracoli nella 'Legenda' di santa Margherita da Cortona." In *Archivum franciscanum historicum* 86 (1993): 217–76.

——. "Introduzione." In Giunta Bevegnati, *Legenda de vita et miraculis beatae Margaritae de Cortona*, ed. Iozzelli, 3–175. Rome: Editiones Collegii S. Bonaventurae ad Claras Aquas, 1997.

Jacobelli, Maria Caterina. *Una donna senza volto: Lineamenti anthropologio culturale della santità di Margherita da Cortona*. Rome: Borla, 1992.

Jantzen, Grace. *Power, Gender, and Christian Mysticism*. Cambridge: Cambridge University Press, 1995.

Jaron Lewis, Gertrude. "Christus als Frau: Eine Vision Elisabeths von Schönau," *Jahrbuch für internationale Germanistik* 15 (1983): 70–80.

———. *For Women, By Women, About Women: The Sister-Books of Fourteenth-Century Germany*. Toronto: Pontifical Institute for Medieval Studies, 1996.

Jones, Rufus. *The Flowering of Mysticism: The Friends of God in the Fourteenth Century*. New York: Macmillan, 1939.

Karras, Ruth Mazo. *From Boys to Men: Formulations of Masculinity in Medieval Europe*. Philadelphia: University of Pennsylvania Press, 2003.

Kerby-Fulton, Kathryn. "Prophet and Reformer." In *Voice of the Living Light: Hildegard of Bingen and Her World*, ed. Barbara Newman, 70–90. Berkeley: University of California Press, 1998.

Kieckhefer, Richard. "Holiness and the Culture of Devotion: Remarks on Some Late Medieval Male Saints." In *Images of Sainthood in Medieval Europe*, ed. Renate Blumenfeld-Kosinski and Timea Szell, 288–305. Ithaca, N.Y.: Cornell University Press, 1991.

———. "The Holy and the Unholy: Sainthood, Witchcraft, and Magic in Late Medieval Europe." In *Christendom and Its Discontents: Exclusion, Persecution, and Rebellion, 1000–1500*, ed. Scott Waugh and Peter Diehl, 310–37. Cambridge: Cambridge University Press, 1996.

———. *Unquiet Souls: Fourteenth-Century Saints and Their Religious Milieu*. Chicago: University of Chicago Press, 1984.

Kienzle, Beverly Mayne, and Pamela J. Walker, eds. *Women Preachers and Prophets Through Two Millennia of Christianity* Berkeley: University of California Press, 1998.

Klaes, Monica. "Einleitung." In *Vita S. Hildegardis*, 17*–194*. Corpus Christianorum, continuatio medievalis, Vol. 126. Turhout: Brepols, 1993.

Kleinberg, Aviad. *Prophets in Their Own Country: Living Saints and the Making of Sainthood in the Later Middle Ages*. Chicago University of Chicago Press, 1992.

Koopmans, Rachel. "The Conclusion of Christina of Markyate's Vita." *Journal of Ecclesiastical History* 51 (2000): 663–98.

Köster, Kurt. "Das visionäre Werk Elisabeths von Schönau: Studien zu Entstehung, Überlieferung und Wirkung in der Mittelalterlichen Welt." *Archiv für Mittelrheinische Kirchengeschichte* 4 (1952): 79–119.

———. "Ekbert von Schönau," *Die deutsche Literatur des Mittelalters: Verfasserlexikon* 2 (1980): 435–40.

———. "Elisabeth von Schönau: Leben, Persönlichkeit und visionäre Werk." In *Schönauer Elisabeth Jubiläum 1965. Festschrift Anläßlich des Achthundertjährigen Todestages der Heiligen Elisabeth von Schönau*, ed. Prämonstratenser-Chorherrenstift Tepl in Kloster Schönau, 17–43. Limburg: Pallottiner Druckerei, 1965.

——. "Elisabeth von Schönau: Werk und Wirkung im Spiegel der mittelalterlichen handscriftlichen Überlieferung." *Archiv für Mittelrheinische Kirchengeschichte* 3 (1951): 243–315.

Lachance, Paul. *The Spiritual Journey of the Blessed Angela of Foligno According to the Memorial of Frater A.* Rome: Pontificium Athenaeum Antonianum, 1984.

Larrington, Carolyn. "The Candlemas Vision and Marie d'Oignies's Role in Its Dissemination." In *New Trends in Feminine Spirituality: The Holy Women of Liège and Their Impact,* ed. Juliette Dor, Lesley Johnson, and Jocelyn Wogan-Browne, 195–214. Turnhout: Brepols, 1999.

Lauwers, Michel. "Expérience béguinale et récit hagiographique: à propos de la *Vita Mariae Oigniacensis* de Jacques de Vitry (vers 1215)." *Journal des savants* (1989): 61–103.

——. "Entre béguinisme et mysticisme. La Vie de Marie d'Oignies (+1213) de Jacques de Vitry ou la définition d'une sainteté féminine." *Ons Geestelijk Erf* 66 (1992): 46–70.

——. "'Noli Me Tangere.' Marie Madeleine, Marie d'Oignies et les pénitentes du XIIIe s." *Mélanges de l'École Française de Rome* 104 (1992): 209–68.

Lees, Clare A., ed. *Medieval Masculinities: Regarding Men in the Middle Ages.* Minneapolis: University of Minnesota Press, 1994.

Lehmijoki-Gardner, Maiju. *Worldly Saints: Social Interaction of Dominican Penitent Women in Italy, 1200–1500.* Helsinki: Suomen Historiallinen Seura, 1999.

Leonardi, Claudio. "Angela da Foligno tra teologia e mistica." In *Angela da Foligno Terziaria Francescana. Atti del Convegno storico nel VII centenario dell'ingresso della beata Angela da Foligno nell'Ordine Francescano Secolare (1291–1991),* ed. Enrico Menestò, 251–59. Spoleto: Centro Italiano du Studi sull'Alto Medioevo, 1992.

Lerner, Robert. *The Heresy of the Free Spirit in the Later Middle Ages.* Notre Dame, Ind.: University of Notre Dame Press, 1972.

Longère, Jean. "Jacques de Vitry: La vie et les oeuvres." In James of Vitry, *Histoire Occidentale,* trans. Gaston Duchet-Suchaux, 7–49. Paris: Editions du Cerf, 1997.

Lüers, Grete. *Die Sprache der deutschen Mystik des Mittelalters im Werke der Mechthild von Magdeburg.* Munich: Ernst Reinhardt, 1926.

Luongo, Francis Thomas. "Catherine of Siena: Rewriting Female Holy Authority." In *Women, the Book, and the Godly,* ed. Lesley Smith and Jane H.M. Taylor, 89–103. Oxford: D. S. Brewer, 1995.

——. "The Politics of Marginality: Catherine of Siena in the War of Eight Saints, 1374–1378." Ph.D. diss., University of Notre Dame, 1997.

Manselli, Raoul. "Amicizia spirituale ed adzione pastorale nella Germania del sec. XII: Ildegarde di Bingen, Elisabetta ed Eckberto di Schönau contra l'eresia catara." *Studi e matierali di storia delle religioni* 38 (1967): 302–13.

——. "Ecberto di Schönau e l'eresia catara in Germania alla metà del secolo XII." In *Arte e storia: Studi in onore di Leonello Vincenti,* 311–38. Turin: Giapichelli, 1965.

——. "La Chiesa e il Francescanesimo femminile." In *Movimento religioso femminile e Francescanesimo nel secolo XIII. Atti del VII Convegno Internazionale, Assisi, 11–13 ottobre 1979*, ed. Roberto Rusconi, 239–61. Assisi: Società internazionale di studi francescani, 1980.

Marini, Alfonso. "Ubertino e Angela: L'*Arbor vitae* e il *Liber*." In *Angèle de Foligno: Le Dossier*, ed. Giulia Barone and Jacques Dalarun, 319–44. Rome: École française de Rome, 1999.

Martin, Anna J. "Christina von Stommeln." *Mediaevistik* 4 (1991): 179–263.

Martin, John Hilary. "The Ordination of Women and the Theologians in the Middle Ages." In *A History of Women and Ordination*, vol. 1, ed. Bernard Cooke and Gary Macy, 31–109. Lanham, Md.: Scarecrow, 2002.

Matter, E. Ann, and John Coakley, eds. *Creative Women in Medieval and Early Modern Italy: A Religious and Artistic Renaissance*. Philadelphia: University of Pennsylvania Press, 1994.

McDonnell, Ernest W. *The Beguines and Beghards in Medieval Culture with Special Emphasis on the Belgian Scene*. New Brunswick, N.J.: Rutgers University Press, 1954.

McGinn, Bernard. "Donne mistiche ed autorità esoterica nel XIV secolo." In *Poteri carismatici e informali: Chiesa e società medioevali*, ed. Agostino Bagliani and André Vauchez, 153–74. Palermo: Sellerio, 1992.

———. *The Flowering of Mysticism: Men and Women in the New Mysticism, 1200–1350.* New York: Crossroad, 1998.

———. *The Foundations of Mysticism: Origins to the Fifth Century*. New York: Crossroad, 1991.

McGuire, Brian Patrick. "Holy Women and Monks in the Thirteenth Century: Friendship or Exploitation?" *Vox Benedictina* 6 (1989): 343–74.

McNamara, Jo Ann. "The Herrenfrage: Restructuring the Gender System, 1050–1150." In *Medieval Masculinities: Regarding Men in the Middle Ages*, ed. Clare A. Lees, 3–29. Minneapolis: University of Minnesota Press, 1994.

———. "The Rhetoric of Orthodoxy: Clerical Authority and Female Innovation in the Struggle with Heresy." In Wiethaus, *Maps of Flesh and Light*, 9–27. Syracuse, N.Y.: Syracuse University Press, 1992.

Meersseman, Gilles. *Dossier de l'ordre de la pénitence au XIIIe siècle*. Fribourg: Editions universitaires, 1961.

Menestò, Enrico, ed. *Angela da Foligno Terziaria Francescana. Atti del Convegno storico nel VII centenario dell'ingresso della beata Angela da Foligno nell'Ordine Francescano Secolare (1291–1991)*. Spoleto: Centro Italiano du Studi sull'Alto Medioevo, 1992.

———. "Problemi critico-testuali nel 'Liber' della Beata Angela." In *Angela da Foligno Terziaria Francescana. Atti del Convegno storico nel VII centenario dell'ingresso della beata Angela da Foligno nell'Ordine Francescano Secolare (1291–1991)*,ed. Menestò, 161–79. Spoleto: Centro Italiano du Studi sull'Alto Medioevo, 1992.

Mens, Alcantara. *De l'Ombrie italienne et l'Ombrie brabançonne*. Paris: Études Franciscaines, 1967.

Minnis, A.J. "*De impedimento sexus*: Women's Bodies and Medieval Impediments to Ordination." In *Medieval Theology and the Natural Body*, ed. Peter Biller and A. J. Minnis, 109–39. Woodbridge: York Medieval Press, 1997.

Mooney, Catherine. "The Authorial Role of Brother A. in the Composition of Angela of Foligno's Revelations." In *Creative Women in Medieval and Early Modern Italy: A Religious and Artistic Renaissance*, ed. E. Ann Matter and John Coakley, 34–63. Philadelphia: University of Pennsylvania Press, 1994.

——, ed. *Gendered Voices: Medieval Saints and Their Interpreters*. Philadelphia: University of Pennsylvania Press, 1999.

——. "*Imitatio Christi* or *Imitatio Mariae*? Clare of Assisi and Her Interpreters." In *Gendered Voices: Medieval Saints and Their Interpreters*, ed. Mooney, 52–77. Philadelphia: University of Pennsylvania Press, 1999.

——. "Voice, Gender, and the Portrayal of Sanctity." In *Gendered Voices: Medieval Saints and Their Interpreters*, ed. Mooney, 1–15. Philadelphia: University of Pennsylvania Press, 1999.

——. "Women's Visions, Men's Words: The Portrayal of Holy Women and Men in Fourteenth-Century Italian Hagiography." Ph.D. diss., Yale University, 1991.

Mortier, Daniel A. *Histoire des Maîtres Généraux de l'ordre des Frères Prêcheurs*. Vol. 3. Paris, Picard et fils, 1907.

Mulcahey, Marian Michèle. "*First the Bow Is Bent in Study*—": Dominican Education Before 1350. Toronto: Pontifical Institute of Medieval Studies, 1998.

Mulder-Bakker, Anneke B. "The Prime of Their Lives: Women and Age, Wisdom and Religious Careers in Northern Europe." In *New Trends in Feminine Spirituality: The Holy Women of Liège and Their Impact*, ed. Juliette Dor, Lesley Johnson, and Jocelyn Wogan-Browne, 215–36. Turnhout: Brepols, 1999.

Muschg, Walter. *Die Mystik in der Schweiz 1200–1500*. Frauenfeld: Huber, 1935.

Nessi, Silvestro. "Spiritualità femminile penitenziale in Umbria nel secolo XIII." In *Vita e spiritualità della beata Angela da Foligno. Atti del convegno di studi per il VII centenario della conversione della beata Angela da Foligno (1285–1985)*, ed. Clément Schmitt, 129–42. Perugia: Serafica provincia di san Francesco OFM Conv., 1987.

Neumann, Hans. "Beiträge zur Textgeschichte des 'Fliessenden Lichts der Gottheit' und zur Lebensgeschichte Mechthilds von Magdeburg." In *Altdeutsche und altniederländische Mystik*, ed. Kurt Ruh, 175–241. Darmstadt: Wissenschaftliche Buchgesellschaft, 1964.

Newman, Barbara. *From Virile Woman to WomanChrist: Studies in Medieval Religion and Literature*. Philadelphia: University of Pennsylvania Press, 1995.

——. "Hildegard and Her Hagiographers: The Remaking of Female Sainthood." In *Gendered Voices: Medieval Saints and Their Interpreters*, ed. Catherine M. Mooney, 16–34. Philadelphia: University of Pennsylvania Press, 1999.

——. "Hildegard of Bingen: Visions and Validation," *Church History* 54 (1985): 163–75.

——. "Possessed by the Spirit: Devout Women, Demoniacs, and the Apostolic Life in the Thirteenth Century." *Speculum* 73 (1998): 766–67.

——. *Sister of Wisdom: St. Hildegard's Theology of the Feminine*. Berkeley: University of California Press, 1988.

——. "Three-Part Invention: The *Vita S. Hildegardis* and Mystical Hagiography." In *Hildegard of Bingen: The Context of Her Thought and Art*, ed. Charles Burnett and Peter Dronke, 189–210. London: Warburg Institute, 1998.

Newman, Martha G. "Crucified by the Virtues: Monks, Lay Brothers, and Women in Thirteenth-Centuiry Cistercian Saints' Lives." In *Gender and Difference in the Middle Ages*, ed. Sharon Farmer and Carol Braun Pasternak, 182–201. Minneapolis: University of Minnesota Press, 2003.

Nieveler, Peter. "Christina von Stommeln—Historische Bemerkungen zu einem erstaunlichen Leben." *Pulheimer Beitrage zur Geschichte und Heimatkund* 4 (1980): 11–21.

———. *Codex Iuliacensis: Christina von Stommeln und Petrus von Dacien, ihr Leben und Nachleben in Geschichte, Kunst und Literatur*. Mönchengladbach: Kuhlen, 1975.

Ochsner, Friedrich. *Petrus de Dacia Gothensis: Mystiker der Freundschaft*. Visby: Barry Press, 1975.

O'Connell, Patrick F. "Eckbert of Schönau and the *Lignum Vitae* of St. Bonaventure." *Revue Bénédictine* 101 (1991): 341–82.

Paoli, Emore. "Le due redazioni del *Liber*: Il perché di una riscritta." In *Angèle de Foligno: Le Dossier*, ed. Giulia Barone and Jacques Dalarun, 29–70. Rome: École française de Rome, 1999.

Pasztor, Edith. "La 'supra montem' e la cancelleria pontificia al tempo di Niccolò IV." In *La 'supra montem' di Niccolò IV (1289): Genesi e diffusione di una regola*, ed. R. Pazzelli and L. Temperini, 65–92. Rome: Edizioni Analecta TOR, 1998.

———. "Le visione di Angela da Foligno nella religiosità femminile italiana del suo tempo." In *Vita e spiritualità della beata Angela da Foligno. Atti del convegno di studi per il VII centenario della conversione della beata Angela da Foligno (1285–1985)*, ed. Clément Schmitt, 287–311. Perugia: Serafica provincia di san Francesco OFM Conv., 1987.

Peters, Ursula. *Religiöse Erfahrung als literarisches Faktum. Zur Vorgeschichte und Genese frauenmystischer Texte des 13. und 14. Jahrhunderts*. Tübingen: Max Niemeyer, 1988.

Petroff, Elizabeth Alvilda. *Body and Soul: Essays on Medieval Women and Mysticism*. New York: Oxford University Press, 1994.

———. *Medieval Women's Visionary Literature*. New York: Oxford University Press, 1986.

Poirel, Dominique. "Le *Liber* d'Angèle de Foligno: Enquête sur un *exemplar* disparu." *Revue d'histoire des textes* 32 (2002): 225–63.

Poor, Sara. *Mechthild of Magdeburg and Her Book*. Philadelphia: University of Pennsylvania Press, 2004.

Poulenc, Jérôme. "Presenza dei movimenti spirituali nella 'Leggenda' di Santa Margherita da Cortona." In *Celestino V e i Suoi Tempi: Realtà spirituale e realtà politica. Atti del Convegno Storico Internazionale, L'Aquila, 26–27 Agosto 1989*, ed. Walter Capezzali, 97–106. L'Aquila: Centro Celestiniano, sezione storica, 1990.

Poulin, Jean-Claude. *L'Idéal de sainteté dans l'Aquitaine carolingienne, 750–950*. Quebec: Université Laval, 1975.

Preger, Wilhelm. *Geschichte der deutschen Mystik im Mittelalter*. 3 vols. Leipzig: Dörfling und Franke, 1874–1893; reprint, Aalen: Otto Zeller, 1962.

Ranft, Patricia. "A Key to Counter-Reformation Women's Activism: The Confessor-Spiritual Director." *Journal of Feminist Studies in Religion* 10, no. 2 (1994): 7–26.

Renna, Thomas. "Hagiography and Feminine Spirituality in the Low Countries." *Cîteaux* 39 (1988): 285–96.

Ringler, Siegfried. *Viten- und Offenbarungsliteratur in Frauenklöstern Des Mittelalters. Quellen und Studien.* Munich: Artemis Verlag, 1980.

Roisin, Simone. "La méthode hagiographique de Thomas de Cantimpré." In *Miscellanea Historica in Honorem Alberti de Meyer*, 1:546–57. Louvain, 1946.

——. "L'efflorescence cistercienne et le courant féminin de piété au XIIIe siècle." *Revue d'histoire ecclésiastique* 39 (1943): 342–78.

——. *L'hagiographie cistercienne dans le diocèse de Liège au XIIIe siècle.* Louvain: Bibliothèque de l'Univerisité, 1947.

Rossmann, Heribert. "Johannes Marienverder, ein ostdeutscher Theologe des Späten Mittelalters." *Archiv für Kirchengeschichte von Böhmen-Mähren-Schlesien* 3 (1973): 221–53.

Roth, F. W. E. "Aus einer Handschrift der Schriften der Heiligen Elisabeth von Schönau." *Neues Archiv der Gesellschaft für ältere Deutsche Geschichtskunde* 36 (1911): 219–25.

Rublack, Ulinka. "Female Spirituality and the Infant Jesus in Late Medieval Dominican Convents." *Gender and History* 6 (1994): 37–57.

Ruhrberg, Christine. *Der literarische Körper der Heiligen: Leben und Viten der Christina von Stommeln (1242–1312).* Tübingen and Basel: Francke Verlag, 1995.

Rusconi, Roberto, ed. *Il movimento religioso femminile in Umbria nei secoli XII–XIV.* Perugia: "La Nuova Italia," 1984.

——. "Margherita da Cortona: Peccatrice redenta e patrona cittadina." In *Umbria: Sacra e Civile*, 89–104. Turin: Nuova Eri Edizioni Rai, 1989.

Russell, Jeffrey B. *Satan.* Ithaca, N.Y.: Cornell University Press, 1981).

Sahlin, Claire. *Birgitta of Sweden and the Voice of Prophecy.* Woodbridge, U.K.: Boydell, 2001.

Schleiff, Arnold. "Die Bedeutung Johann Marienwerders für Theologie und Frömmigkeit im Ordensstaat Preußen." *Zeitschrift für Kirchengeschichte* 60 (1941):49–66.

Schmidt, Margot. "An Example of Spiritual Friendship: The Correspondence Between Heinrich of Nördlingen and Margaretha Ebner." Trans. Susan Johnson. In *Maps of Flesh and Light: The Religious Experience of Medieval Women Mystics*, ed. Ulrike Wiethaus, 74–92. Syracuse, N.Y.: Syracuse University Press, 1993.

Schmidt-Kohl, Volker. "Petrus de Dacia, ein Skandinavischer Mystiker des 13. Jahrhunderts." *Zeitschrift für Religions- und Geistesgeschichte* 18 (1966): 258–59.

Schmitt, Clément, ed. *Vita e spiritualità della beata Angela da Foligno. Atti del convegno di studi per il VII centenario della conversione della beata Angela da Foligno (1285–1985).* Perugia: Serafica Provincia di San Francesco OFM Conv., 1987.

Schmitz, Philibert. "'Visions' inédites de Sainte Elisabeth de Schönau." *Revue Bénédictine* 47 (1935): 181–83.

Schrader, Marianna. "Wibert von Gembloux." *Erbe und Auftrag* 37 (1961): 381–92.

Schrader, Marianna, and Adelgundis Führkötter. *Die Echtheit des Schrifttums der Heiligen Hildegard von Bingen. Quellenkritisches Untersuchungen.* Cologne/Graz: Böhlau, 1956.

Schraut, Elisabeth. "Dorothea von Montau: Wahrnehmungsweisen von Kindheit und Eheleben einer spätmittelalterlichen Heiligen." In *Religiöse Frauenbewegung und mystische Frömmigkeit in Mittelalter*, ed. Peter Dinzelbacher and Dieter R. Bauer, 374–94. Cologne: Böhlau Verlag, 1988.

Schulenberg, Jane Tibbetts. *Forgetful of Their Sex: Female Sanctity and Society, ca. 500–1100*. Chicago: University of Chicago Press, 1998.

Schultz, Richard. "Heinrich von Nördlingen: Seine Zeit, sein Leben und seine Stellung innerhalb der Deutschen Mystik." *Jahrbuch des Vereins für Augsburger Bistumsgeschichte* 10 (1976): 114–64.

Scott, Karen. "'Io Catarina': Ecclesiastical Politics and Oral Culture in the Letters of Catherine of Siena." In *Dear Sister: Medieval Women and the Epistolary Genre*, ed. Karen Cherewatuk and Ulrike Wiethaus, 87–121. Philadelphia: University of Pennsylvania Press, 1993.

——. "Mystical Death, Bodily Death: Catherine of Siena and Raymond of Capua on the Mystic's Encounter with God." In *Gendered Voices: Medieval Saints and Their Interpreters*, ed. Catherine M. Mooney, 136–167. Philadelphia: University of Pennsylvania Press, 1999.

——. "Not Only with Words, but with Deeds: The Role of Speech in Catherine of Siena's Understanding of Her Mission." Ph.D. diss., University of California, Berkeley, 1989.

——. "Saint Catherine of Siena, 'Apostola.'" *Church History* 61 (1992): 34–46.

Seesholtz, Anna Groh. *Friends of God: Practical Mystics of the Fourteenth Century*. New York: Columbia University Press, 1934.

Sensi, Mario. "Anchoresses and Penitents in Thirteenth- and Fourteenth-Century Umbria." In *Women and Religion in Medieval and Renaissance Italy*, ed. Daniel Bornstein and Roberto Rusconi, trans. Margery J. Schneider, 56–83. Chicago: University of Chicago Press, 1996.;

——. "Foligno all'incrocio delle strade." In *Angèle de Foligno: Le Dossier*, ed. Giulia Barone and Jacques Dalarun, 267–92. Rome: École française de Rome, 1999.

——. "Fra Bernardo Arnolti il 'frater scriptor' del *Memoriale* di Angela?" In *Angela da Foligno Terziaria Francescana. Atti del Convegno storico nel VII centenario dell'ingresso della beata Angela da Foligno nell'Ordine Francescano Secolare (1291–1991)*, ed. Enrico Menestò), 127–59. Spoleto: Centro Italiano du Studi sull'Alto Medioevo, 199.

——. "La B. Angela nel contesto religioso folignate." In *Vita e spiritualità della beata Angela da Foligno. Atti del convegno di studi per il VII centenario della conversione della beata Angela da Foligno (1285–1985)*, ed. Clément Schmitt, 39–95. Perugia: Serafica provincia di san Francesco OFM Conv., 1987.

——. "Margherita da Cortona nel contesto storico-sociale cortonese." *Collectanea Franciscana* 69 (1999): 223–62.

Simons, Walter. *Cities of Ladies: Beguine Communities in the Medieval Low Countries, 1200–1565*. Philadelphia: University of Pennsylvania Press, 2001.

Slade, Carole. "Alterity in Union: The Mystical Experience of Angela of Foligno and Margery Kempe." *Religion and Literature* 23 (1991): 109–26.

Società Internazionale di Studi Francescani. *Movimento religioso femminile e fran-cescanesimo nel secolo XII*. Assisi: Società Internazionale di Studi Francescani, 1980.

Sorelli, Fernanda. "La production hagiographique du Dominicain T. Caffarini: Ex-emples de sainteté, sens et visée d'une propagande." In *Faire Croire: Modalités de la diffusion et de la réception des messages religieux du XIIe au XVe siècle*, 189–200. Rome: École Française de Rome, 1981.

———. *La santità imitabile: "Leggenda di Maria da Venezia" di Tommaso da Siena*. Ven-ice: Deputazione editrice, 1984.

Southern, Richard W. *Western Society and the Church in the Middle Ages*. Hammond-sworth: Penguin, 1970.

Stachnik, Richard. "Zum Schrifttum über die heilige Dorothea v. Montau." In *Doro-thea von Montau: Eine preußische Heilige des 14. Jahrhunderts*, ed. Stachnik and An-neliese Triller, 59–105. Münster: Selbstverlag des historischen Vereins für Ermland, 1976.

Stachnik, Richard, and Anneliese Triller, eds. *Dorothea von Montau: Eine preußische Heilige des 14. Jahrhunderts*. Münster: Selbstverlag des historischen Vereins für Ermland, 1976.

Stargardt, Ute. "Male Clerical Authority in the Spiritual (Auto)Biographies of Me-dieval Holy Women." In *Women as Protagonists and Poets in the German Middle Ages: An Anthology of Feminist Approaches to Middle High German Literature*, ed. Albrecht Classen, 209–38. Göppingen: Kümmerle, 1991.

———. "The Political and Social Backgrounds of the Canonization of Dorothea of Montau." *Mystics Quarterly* 11 (1985): 107–22.

———. "Whose Life History Is This Anyway? Johannes von Marienwerder's Narrative Strategies in the German *Vita* of Dorothy of Montau." *Michigan Academician* 27 (1994): 39–56.

Stewart, Robert M. *"De illis qui faciunt penitentiam": The Rule of the Secular Franciscan Order: Origins, Development, Interpretation*. Rome: Istituto Storico dei Cappuccini, 1991.

Stoudt, Debra L. "The Production and Preservation of Letters by Fourteenth-century Dominican Nuns." *Medieval Studies* 53 (1991): 309–26.

———. "The Vernacular Letters of Heinrich von Nördlingen and Heinrich Seuse." Ph.D. diss., University of North Carolina, 1986.

Sweetman, Robert. "Christine of Saint-Trond's Preaching Apostolate: Thomas of Cantimpré's Hagiographical Method Revisited." *Vox Benedictina* 9 (1992): 67–97.

Strauch, Philipp. "Einleitung." In *Margaretha Ebner und Heinrich von Nördlingen. Ein Beitrag zur Geschichte der deutschen Mystik*, ed. Philipp Strauch, xiii–cvi. Tübingen: J. C. B. Mohr, 1882. Reprint, Amsterdam: P. Schippers, 1966.

Thompson, Augustine. "Hildegard of Bingen on Gender and the Priesthood." *Church History* 63 (1994): 349–64.

Tobin, Frank. "Henry Suso and Elsbeth Stagel: Was the *Vita* a Cooperative Effort?" in *Gendered Voices: Medieval Saints and Their Interpreters*, ed. Catherine Mooney, 118–35. Philadelphia: University of Pennsylvania Press, 1999.

Todd, John, ed. *Problems of Authority*. London: Darton, Longman and Todd, 1962.

Triller, Anneliese. "Häresien in Altpreussen um 1390?" In *Studien zur Geschichte des Preussenlandes*, ed. Ernst Bahr, 397–404. Marburg: N. G. Elwert Verlag, 1963.

van Acker, Lieven. "Der Briefwechsel der Heiligen Hildegard von Bingen: Vorbemerkungen zu einer Kritischen Edition." *Revue Benedictine* 98 (1988): 141–68 and 99 (1989): 118–54.

——. "Der Briefwechsel zwischen Elisabeth von Schönau und Hildegard von Bingen." In *Aevum inter utrumque: Mélanges offerts à Gabriel Sanders, professeur émérité à l'Université de Gand*, ed. Marc van Uytfanghe and Roland Demeulenaere, 409–17. Steenbrugis: Abbatia S. Petri; The Hague: Nijhoff, 1991.

Van Ree, A. W. "Raymond de Capoue: Éléments biographiques." *Archivum Fratrum Praedicatorum* 33 (1963): 159–241.

Vauchez, André. Introduction to *Poteri carismatici e informali: Chiesa e società medioevali*, ed. Agostino Bagliani and André Vauchez, 9–14. Palermo: Sellerio, 1992.

——. *The Laity in the Middle Ages: Religious Beliefs and Devotional Practices*. Ed. Daniel E. Bornstein. Trans. Margery J. Schneider. Notre Dame, Ind.: University of Notre Dame Press, 1993.

——. "La nascità del sospetto." In *Finzione e santità tra medioevo ed età moderna*, ed. Gabriella Zarri, 39–49. Turin: Rosenberg & Sellier, 1992. French version in Vauchez, *Saints, prophètes et visionnaires*, 208–19.

——. "Lay People's Sanctity in Western Europe: Evolution of a Pattern (Twelfth and Thirteenth Centuries)." In *Images of Sainthood in Medieval Europe*, ed. Renate Blumenfeld-Kosinski and Timea Szell, 21–32. Ithaca, N.Y.: Cornell University Press, 1991.

——. "Les Pouvoirs informels dans l'église aux derniers siècles du moyen âge: Visionnaires, prophètes et mystiques." *Mélanges de l'Ecole Française de Rome* 96 (1984): 281–93.

——, ed. "Les Textes prophétiques et la prophétie en occident (Xiie–Xvie s.)." *Mélanges de l'École Française de Rome* 102 (1990): 287–685.

——. "Margherita and Cortona," in *Margherita of Cortona and the Lorenzetti: Sienese Art and the Cult of a Holy Woman in Medieval Tuscany*, ed. Joanna Cannon and André Vauchez, 9–36. University Park: Pennsylvania State University Press, 1999.

——. "Prosélitisme et action antihérétique en milieu féminin au XIIIe s.: La vie de Marie d'Oignies (+1213)." In *Problèmes d'histoire du Christianisme. Fasc. 17: Propagande et contrepropagande religieuses*, ed. J. Marx, 95–110. Brussels: Éditions de l'Université, 1987.

——. *Sainthood in the Later Middle Ages*. Trans. Jean Birrell. Cambridge: Cambridge University Press, 1997.

——. *Saints, prophètes et visionnaires: Le Pouvoir surnaturel au moyen age*. Paris: Albin Michel, 1999.

Vernet, Félix. "Biographies spirituelles. IV. Le moyen age." In *Dictionnaire de spiritualité, d'ascétique et de mystique*. Vol. 1, cols. 1646–79. Paris: Beauchesne, 1936.

Voaden, Rosalynn. *God's Words, Women's Voices: The Discernment of Spirits in the Writing of Late-Medieval Women Visionaries*. York: York Medieval Press, 1999.

Volpato, Antonio. "Tra sante profetesse e santi dottori: Caterina da Siena," in *Women and Men in Spiritual Culture, Fourteenth–Seventeenth Centuries: A Meeting of South and North.*, ed. E. Schulte van Kessel, 141–61. The Hague: Netherlands Government Publishing Office, 1986.

von Campenhausen, Hans. *Ecclesiastical Authority and Spiritual Power in the Church of the First Three Centuries.* Trans. J. A. Baker. Stanford, Calif.: Stanford University Press, 1969.

Walz, Angelus. "Gottesfreunde um Margarete Ebner." *Historisches Jahrbuch der Görregesellschaft* 72 (1953): 254.

Weber, Max. *Economy and Society.* Ed. Guenther Roth and Klaus Wittig. 2 vols. Berkeley: University of California Press, 1978.

Wehrli-Johns, Martina. "Vorraussetzungen und Perspektiven mittelalterlicher Laienfrömmigkeit seit Innocenz III. Eine Auseinandersetzung mit Herbert Grundmanns 'Religiöse Bewegungen.'" *Mitteilungen des Instituts für Österreichische Geschichtsforschung* 104 (1996): 286–309.

Weinstein, Donald, and Rudolph Bell. *Saints and Society: The Two Worlds of Western Christendom 1000–1700.* Chicago: University of Chicago Press, 1982.

Weitlauff, Manfred. "'Dein Got redender Munt machet mich redenlosz': Margareta Ebner und Heinrich von Nördlingen." In *Religiöse Frauenbewegung und mystische Frömmigkeit in Mittelalter*, ed. Peter Dinzelbacher and Dieter R. Bauer, 303–52. Cologne: Böhlau Verlag, 1988.

Westpfahl, Hans, and Anneliese Triller. "Zeittafel zum Leben der H. Dorothea von Montau." In *Dorothea von Montau: Eine preußische Heilige des 14. Jahrhunderts*, ed. Richard Stachnik and Anneliese Triller, 9–20. Münster: Selbstverlag des Historischen Vereins für Ermland, 1976.

Wiethaus, Ulrike, ed. *Maps of Flesh and Light: The Religious Experience of Medieval Women Mystics.* Syracuse, N.Y.: Syracuse University Press, 1992.

Wolf, Kenneth. *The Poverty of Riches: St. Francis of Assisi Reconsidered.* New York: Oxford University Press, 2003.

Zarri, Gabriella. *Le sante vive. Cultura e religiosità femminile nella prima età moderna.* Turin: Rosenberg and Sellier, 1990.

——. "Living Saints: A Typology of Female Sanctity in the Early Sixteenth Century." In *Women and Religion in Medieval and Renaissance Italy*, ed. Daniel Bornstein and Roberto Rusconi, 219–303. Chicago: University of Chicago Press, 1996.

Zoepf, Ludwig. *Die Mystikerin Margaretha Ebner (ca. 1291–1351).* Leipzig: B. G. Teubner, 1914.

INDEX